Violence in Colombia 1990-2000

Waging War and Negotiating Peace

POLITICAL MAP OF COLOMBIA

Violence in Colombia 1990-2000

Waging War and Negotiating Peace

Edited by
Charles Bergquist,
Ricardo Peñaranda, and
Gonzalo Sánchez G.

A Scholarly Resources Inc. Imprint
Wilmington, Delaware

First published 2001
Printed and bound in the United States of America

Scholarly Resources Inc.
104 Greenhill Avenue
Wilmington, DE 19805-1897
www.scholarly.com

Library of Congress Cataloging-in-Publication Data

Violence in Colombia, 1990–2000 : waging war and negotiating peace / edited by Charles Bergquist, Ricardo Peñaranda, and Gonzalo Sánchez G.
p. cm. — (Latin American silhouettes)
Includes bibliographical references (p.) and index.
ISBN 0-8420-2869-2 (alk. paper) — ISBN 0-8420-2870-6 (paper : alk. paper)
1. Violence—Colombia—History—20th century. 2. Colombia—Social conditions—1970– 3. War and society—Colombia—History—20th century. I. Bergquist, Charles W. II. Peñaranda, Ricardo. III. Sánchez G., Gonzalo. IV. Series.

HN310.Z9 V588 2001
303.6'09861—dc21 00-063559Rev.

∞ The paper used in this publication meets the minimum requirements of the American National Standard for permanence of paper for printed library materials, Z39.48, 1984.

Contents

Preface

The goal of this book is to provide English readers with a deeper understanding of the political crisis facing Colombia today. *Violence in Colombia, 1990–2000: Waging War and Negotiating Peace* is a sequel to a volume we published with Scholarly Resources in 1992.* Even at that time, the crisis affecting Colombia was of considerable and growing concern to the international community, and to policymakers and citizens of the United States in particular. Yet, we believed, most U.S. citizens knew little about Colombia, and most of what they did know was "drug-related." The book we published in 1992 did not deny the importance of the drug trade, which by the 1980s was affecting virtually every aspect of Colombian life, but it argued that the problems facing Colombia, including the oldest and largest guerrilla insurgency in the Americas, had much deeper historical roots. We also believed that it was important that English-language readers have access to some of the most significant studies of the Colombian conflict written by Colombians themselves. In light of these concerns, eight of the fourteen chapters of the 1992 volume were historical in nature, and all but four were written by Colombian scholars.

Unfortunately, that book's prognosis—that without major economic and social reforms the violence in Colombia would worsen—has now become reality. During the 1990s, despite efforts at political reform and periods of negotiation between the government and guerrilla groups, the crisis confronting the nation, now complicated by the rise of powerful paramilitary groups, grew ever more severe. Levels of violence reached unprecedented proportions, corroding all aspects of social life and threatening the integrity of the nation itself. If the crisis still had its roots in history, it seemed to have taken on a life of its own, feeding on itself, enveloping society in a vicious circle of violence with no end in sight. Drugs, to be sure, played an increasing role, and despite, or because of, efforts by the U.S. and Colombian governments to curb the drug trade, exports of narcotics from Colombia continued to expand. Still, the drug trade, by itself, could not explain the

*Charles Bergquist, Ricardo Peñaranda, and Gonzalo Sánchez, *Violence in Colombia: The Contemporary Crisis in Historical Perspective* (Wilmington, DE: Scholarly Resources, 1992).

crisis. If it could, why had other Latin American drug-producing and -trafficking nations not experienced a similar fate?

Hoping to contribute what we could to the understanding and possible solution of this ongoing crisis, we first considered simply updating the earlier volume, but the more we thought about it, putting together an entirely new book seemed a better course of action. A second volume could build on the historical analysis and contemporary studies of the first and devote itself exclusively to the 1990s. If that decade witnessed ever greater and interconnected forms of violence and a strengthening of both the leftist insurgency and the paramilitary right, it was also bounded by important efforts at negotiating peace. The 1990s began with peace negotiations between the government and some of the guerrilla groups that led to their demobilization and to the important political reforms codified in the Constitution of 1991. The decade ended with another serious attempt at negotiating peace, a historic understanding between the government and the largest and most powerful of the guerrilla groups to put a range of social and economic reforms on the negotiating table.

This new volume analyzes the escalating violence of the 1990s and the dynamics of waging war and negotiating peace during the decade. The organization of the book is straightforward. The introduction (Chapter 1) provides an overview of the decade as a whole and presents the themes explored in detail in the subsequent chapters. They compare the very different outcomes of attempts at revolution in Colombia and Bolivia (Chapter 2), explore the origins and outcome of the Constitution of 1991 (Chapter 3), assess the impact of drug trafficking on the Colombian economy (Chapter 4), review the question of human rights in Colombia (Chapter 5), examine the development of the paramilitary right (Chapter 6), probe the gendered meanings of Colombian violence and the fate of displaced people (Chapter 7), survey the impact of the violence on Colombian labor and social movements (Chapter 8), and review the literature on Colombian violence published since 1990 (Chapter 9; a comprehensive review of the literature published before that date was included in the earlier volume). The concluding essay (Chapter 10) provides a historical perspective on the current peace negotiations and introduces the Documents section that follows the essays in the book. The Appendix on homicide rates in Colombia and the Glossary complete the volume.

Except for Chapters 7 and 10 the essays were written by Colombian scholars. Four of the contributors to the book are historians, one is a philosopher, and the others are social scientists. As in the first volume, we have tried to make this material, written initially for a Colombian audience, accessible to non-Colombians. The Glossary defines Colombian terms and abbreviations, and the Chronology presents the sequence of important events of the decade. The Documents section allows readers to get a feel for the views of many of the parties involved in the crisis facing the nation and to judge for themselves the meaning of what they say. Introductions to the chapters in the book and to the documents place each in a wider context and alert readers to important analytical themes.

Translating all this material into English has involved considerable time and effort. Fortunately, as with the first volume, Scholarly Resources advanced funds for a significant portion of the translation work. A first draft of the translation of the essays in the book was done by Kimberly Hildebrand, a graduate student in Latin American history at the University of Washington. Charles Bergquist revised this draft and selected and translated the primary documents in the book. Material for the Chronology was collected by Angélica Nieto, a graduate student at the Institute for Political and International Studies at the National University of Colombia in Bogotá. Funding for her work was secured from the same institution by Ricardo Peñaranda. The three editors of the book collaborated on the Chronology. Charles Bergquist put together the Glossary and wrote the introductions to the chapters and documents. Andres Villaveces, a graduate student in the School of Public Health of the University of Washington, constructed the map.

The editors would like to thank all those who contributed to this volume, most especially the authors of the essays. Earlier versions of some of these essays were previously published in Spanish (Chapters 2, 4, 5, 6, and 7); we thank the authors for revising them for this volume and thank their respective original publishers for permission to include them here. The other essays (Chapters 1, 3, 8, 9, 10) are published here for the first time. We also would like to thank Richard Hopper, general manager, and Linda Pote Musumeci, senior editor, at Scholarly Resources, and Judy Ewell and Bill Beezley, the editors of this series, for their support and suggestions for improving the book.

This volume is dedicated to the victims of the violence in Colombia. Rural people and the poor have borne the brunt of the violence as noncombatants and as combatants in the struggle. Outside areas of combat, unionists, human rights workers, and political activists laboring for a more democratic and peaceful Colombia have been primary targets of violence. Finally, we wish to acknowledge the scholars, some of them colleagues and friends, murdered in their efforts to understand and surmount the violent crisis facing Colombia.

The Editors

Chronology

This chronology lists important political events for the decade covered by this book, 1990 to 2000. Those unfamiliar with the broader sweep of Colombian history may wish to consult our earlier publication, *Violence in Colombia: The Contemporary Crisis in Historical Perspective* (Wilmington, DE, 1992), which contains a chronology of important events from the time of the War for Independence (1810–1824) until 1990. Events chronicled there emphasize the historical roots of the violence that has enveloped the nation during the second half of the twentieth century. These include the formation, around 1850, of the Liberal and Conservative parties that still dominate Colombian politics today, the War of the Thousand Days (1899–1902), the largest of Latin America's nineteenth-century civil wars, the period of coffee-paced economic growth and political stability (1900–1930), and the era of Liberal reform during the 1930s and early 1940s.

The events described in that earlier chronology become directly related to the contemporary violence in Colombia following the assassination of popular Liberal leader Jorge Eliécer Gaitán on April 9, 1948. In the aftermath of Gaitán's death, the complex phenomenon known as "the Violence" (written with a capital "V") enveloped the nation. A mix of traditional party hatreds, Conservative government repression, and popular aspirations for economic and social betterment, the Violence claimed the lives of perhaps 200,000 Colombians in the following decade. The Violence was curtailed after 1958 under a political arrangement known as the National Front (1958–1974), during which the Liberal and Conservative parties shared power and alternated the presidency. The 1960s spawned Marxist-inspired guerrilla groups, two of which, the FARC and the ELN (these and other abbreviations and terms are explained in the Glossary), threaten the Colombian State today. In subsequent decades, powerful right-wing paramilitary groups, some with close ties to rural elites, drug traffickers, and the military, have emerged to challenge the guerrilla groups, increasing the levels of terror in the countryside and violence in the nation as a whole.

Meanwhile, during practically the whole of the twentieth century, the Colombian economy, which stagnated during much of the nineteenth century, experienced sustained growth and substantial diversification. Paced initially by coffee exports, and by midcentury by significant industrialization, since the 1970s the economy has been increasingly influenced (and distorted) by the illegal drug trade in marijuana, cocaine, and heroin. By the 1980s, Colombia was also exporting significant amounts of bananas, flowers, and petroleum. The main market for virtually all Colombian exports has been and continues to be the United States.

The earlier chronology ends in 1990, with the election of Liberal President César Gaviria. Gaviria's election followed a bloody campaign that witnessed the assassination of three presidential candidates representing reformist Liberal forces and the left. In the same year, Colombian voters approved the calling of a Constituent Assembly to consider constitutional reform as a means of quelling the escalating violence that seemed to threaten the existence of the nation itself.

The present chronology picks up the story at this point, and emphasizes important political events of the decade that runs from January 1990 to January 2000. English readers wishing to update this chronology can consult, among other sources, the indices of the *New York Times* and the *Los Angeles Times*. Spanish readers will want to review the periodic chronologies published by the Centro de Investigación y Educación Popular (CINEP) in Bogotá and the Instituto de Estudios Políticos y Relaciones Exteriores (IEPRE) of the National University of Colombia in Bogotá. These chronologies appear in the CINEP publication *Cien Días* and the IEPRE journal *Síntesis*. Spanish terms and acronyms used in the chronology are defined in the Glossary at the end of the book.

March 1990

Bernardo Jaramillo, presidential candidate of the leftist party Unión Patriótica, is assassinated at the airport in Bogotá. Violent protests break out in Bogotá's southern working-class neighborhoods, with many demonstrators accusing the government of complicity in the crime. At that point approximately three thousand members of the UP had been killed since the party's formation in 1985.

April 1990

Carlos Pizarro León-Gómez, presidential candidate of the M-19, is murdered aboard an airliner bound for Barranquilla from Bogotá. Pizarro is the third presidential candidate killed in a campaign. The first was Luis Carlos Galán, the candidate of the Liberal party, assassinated in August 1989.

May 1990

Car bombs explode in Bogotá shopping malls, killing nineteen people and wounding scores of others. The terror apparently is part of a campaign against extradition orchestrated by the leader of the Medellín drug cartel, Pablo Escobar.

César Gaviria Trujillo, the Liberal party candidate, is elected president of Colombia. He assumes office August 7.

August 1990

Beginning of term of Liberal President César Gaviria (1994–1998). Inheritor of wide popular support for the slain reformist Liberal presidential candidate Luis Carlos Galán, Gaviria's government manages to bring to fruition efforts begun during the previous administration to demobilize several armed guerrilla groups, including the M-19, the EPL, Quintín Lame, and the PRT (a small offshoot of the ELN). Successful demobilization of these groups is related to the calling of the Constituent Assembly, which writes a new, substantially more democratic, constitution for the country in 1991. Although the Constitution of 1991 prohibits extradition of those accused of drug trafficking, the Gaviria administration manages at great cost to break up the Medellín drug cartel. Meanwhile, critics charge, the administration fails to stop the growth of right-wing paramilitary groups. Other critics lament the administration's pursuit of neo-liberal economic policies designed to foster economic growth through free trade and the privatization of many government entities.

December 1990

M-19 wins the largest number of delegates to the Constituent Assembly.

President Gaviria launches an offensive against headquarters of guerrilla groups remaining in arms.

February–July 1991

Constituent Assembly writes new constitution.

July 1991

The Constitution of 1991, which replaces the Constitution of 1886, is promulgated July 4. It provides the legal basis for a more decentralized, pluralistic, democratic Colombia, and prohibits the extradition of native-born Colombians.

October 1991

Low voter turnout marks congressional elections in which the Liberal party wins a narrow majority.

May 1992

President Gaviria launches a military operation against the stronghold of the FARC high command in La Uribe, Meta.

July 1992

Twenty thousand unionized banana workers strike in Urabá in support of other farmworkers demanding roads, credit, medical clinics, and schools from the central government.

September 1992

Pablo Escobar, head of the Medellín drug cartel, escapes from his luxurious "high-security" prison in Envigado, Antioquia, sending the Gaviria administration, which had negotiated the terms of his surrender, into crisis.

October 1992

Marking the 500th anniversary of the European "discovery" of America, indigenous groups and allied organizations (including guerrilla groups) take to the streets in various Colombian departments demanding social justice.

The United States, Canada, and Mexico sign the North American Free Trade Agreement (NAFTA), creating expectations and pressures that will spur the neo-liberal opening of the Colombian economy.

November 1992

The Colombian Department of Justice orders the capture of Gilberto Rodríguez, head of the Cali drug cartel.

"Letter of the Intellectuals." Writers (including Nobel laureate Gabriel García Márquez), journalists, and academics address a public letter to the guerrillas urging them to abandon the armed struggle and pursue needed reforms through peaceful means.

December 1992

U.S.-based Americas Watch reports that 40 percent of Colombian political assassinations are attributable to government agents, 30 percent to paramilitary groups, 27.5 percent to the guerrillas, and 2.5 percent to the drug mafia.

The Colombian Congress passes an antikidnapping law that establishes sentences of twenty-five to sixty years. (There is no death penalty in Colombia.)

January–April 1993

The fugitive head of the Medellín drug cartel, Pablo Escobar, declares war on the government. Car bombs kill hundreds in Bogotá, Medellín, and other cities.

February 1993

President Gaviria announces a major increase in military personnel.

The Colombian National Committee of Victims of the Guerrillas denounces the Bogotá government and the guerrillas before the Organization of American States, a sign of the growing internationalization of the conflict.

March 1993

Production begins at the Cusiana oil field in the department of Casanare 100 miles east of Bogotá. Cusiana, with reserves initially estimated at 1.5 billion barrels, is touted as the largest oil find in the Americas since Prudhoe Bay in Alaska in 1969. Colombia's oil pipelines, long a target of guerrilla attacks, will be increasingly threatened in subsequent years.

The World Bank lends U.S.$250 million to the Colombian Agrarian Bank, an institution charged with making loans to farmers. During the 1990s the bank becomes a primary target of the guerrillas in their attacks on Colombian towns.

April 1993

Colombian newspapers reveal that, as part of the antidrug effort, U.S. personnel are building a military base in Araracuara, Vichada.

May 1993

The president of the Oil Workers Union (USO) is detained and accused of subversion.

November 1993

At a meeting of the Inter-American Press Society in Buenos Aires, a representative of the newspaper *El Tiempo* testifies that ten Colombian journalists have been murdered in the course of 1993.

Ex-guerrillas once associated with the EPL accuse the FARC of killing hundreds of banana workers in Urabá during 1993. For their part, the FARC and the UP attribute the deaths of their own partisans in the region to paramilitary groups now supported by ex-EPL guerrillas.

December 1993

Pablo Escobar is killed in Medellín at the hands of an elite government antinarcotics force. Meanwhile, negotiations proceed between government officials and lawyers representing leaders of the Cali cartel over terms of surrender.

January 1994

The Bogotá government announces the arrival of 120 U.S. military specialists in antinarcotics operations at a Colombian army base in the department of Valle, part of an exchange agreed upon between the two governments in October 1993.

Some twenty armed men, presumed members of the Fifth Front of the FARC, kill thirty-three and wound seventeen at a party in a working-class neighborhood in Apartadó, capital of the department of Chocó.

February 1994

Despite the violence, foreign investment in Colombia continues to grow rapidly—a response, in part, to neo-liberal economic reform. A *New York Times* article (February 10, 1994) notes that foreign investment in the country has doubled since 1990, reaching U.S.$475 million, and predicts that it will more than double again in the coming year.

According to a report of the banana workers' union Sintrainagro, since September 1993 more than three thousand members of the union have fled Urabá out of fear of assassination, reducing the union's membership from eleven thousand to eight thousand.

June 1994

Liberal party candidate Ernesto Samper is narrowly elected president of Colombia for the period 1994–1998. Within days, the defeated candidate, Andrés Pastrana, denounces the infusion of drug money into Samper's campaign.

August 1994

Beginning of presidential term of Ernesto Samper (1994–1998). The question of drug money contributions to his campaign will bedevil Samper's entire administration, sapping its internal initiatives and seriously compromising its foreign policy, especially its relations with the United States. During Samper's tenure in office, the leftist guerrilla insurgency and rightist paramilitary groups will both grow in power and combativeness, the production and export of narcotic drugs will expand dramatically, the national debt will more than double, and government spending will increase from 20 percent to 33 percent of the Gross Domestic Product.

Manuel Cepeda, a member of the Communist party and the only senator representing the UP party, is assassinated in Bogotá.

November 1994

The so-called United Self-Defense Groups of Córdoba and Urabá demand tripartite negotiations among the government, the guerrillas, and paramilitary groups such as theirs.

Thousands of small farmers in Guaviare and Putumayo protest aerial spraying of coca crops. Protests continue in different forms until an agreement is reached with the government in early January 1995 that provides for more public services and support for crop substitution.

January 1995

Following a campaign led by human rights groups and an independent investigation begun in September 1994, the government admits official involvement or toleration of the disappearance, torture, and assassination of 107 people in Trujillo, Valle, between 1988 and 1990 and agrees to punish the police and military personnel responsible.

April 1995

The Colombian Episcopal Conference denounces the guerrillas and government security forces as principally responsible for the forced displacement of some 240,000 people in the country between 1985 and 1994.

June 1995

On June 9 the supposed leader of the Cali cartel, Gilberto Rodríguez Orejuela, is captured by police, and in subsequent weeks several other high-ranking members of the group give themselves up or are captured by government authorities. On June 10 a huge bomb explodes in a park in Medellín, killing 28 and wounding 217.

The army denounces the assassination by the FARC of two U.S. missionaries kidnapped by the guerrilla group the previous January.

August 1995

William Jaimes Torres, president of the National Peasant Association (ANUC), is murdered in the union's offices in Bogotá.

The army accuses the FARC of killing nineteen more banana workers and "disappearing" four more allegedly sympathetic to right-wing groups in Urabá, bringing the total of workers killed in the region during August to fifty-two. In September the FARC is accused of killing an additional twenty-six workers in the region and is denounced by the Colombian government for human rights violations before the UN and the OAS. The alleged killings by the FARC continue; another massacre of banana workers occurs in February 1996.

November 1995

The long-time Conservative party leader Alvaro Gómez is murdered in Bogotá. The son of former President Laureano Gómez, and a former presidential candidate himself, Alvaro Gómez was one of the triumvirate that coordinated the deliberations of the Constituent Assembly in 1991. Later, government security agencies will be implicated in his assassination.

December 1995

The Constitutional Court rules as constitutional a 1989 government decree holding that military officers are obligated to disobey orders that illegally violate human rights.

January 1996

The mayor of Miraflores, in the department of Guaviare, is assassinated, the first in a long list of mayors murdered in subsequent months.

March 1996

Colombia is decertified by the U.S. State Department for providing insufficient support for the war against drugs, its government characterized as corrupt and heavily influenced by drug traffickers. The following year, Colombia is decertified again, compounding U.S. pressure on the Samper administration.

President Samper announces an effort to negotiate with paramilitaries to achieve their demobilization, although authors of gross violations of human rights would not be pardoned. Later in the month a "faceless" judge sentences ten members of a paramilitary group to thirteen years in prison for the murder of eighteen people in the town of Chigorodó in August 1995.

April 1996

On April 2, Juan Carlos Gaviria, brother of ex-president César Gaviria, is kidnapped by the group "Jorge Eliécer Gaitán"; seventy-one days later he is freed following negotiations that guarantee his captors passage to Cuba.

The UN decides to establish an office of the High Commission for Human Rights in Colombia.

June 1996

Following a long, controversial investigation, President Samper is absolved by a vote of the Colombian House of Representatives of charges of personal and criminal responsibility for the infiltration of drug money into his 1994 electoral campaign.

July 1996

Some fifteen thousand farmers and members of thirteen indigenous communities mount demonstrations in Miraflores and nearby towns in the department of Guaviare against government repression and efforts to eradicate crops. Protests spread in late July and August to the department of Putumayo, where eventually about thirty thousand protesters win concessions from the government before returning to their farms. The confrontation, supported by elements of the guerrillas, leaves seven dead, seventy-two wounded. During the confrontation there were seventeen attacks on the trans-Andean oil pipeline and an estimated loss of more than ten thousand barrels of oil into the region's rivers.

August 1996

On August 29, in a major defeat for the government, the FARC takes the military base in Las Delicias, Putumayo; fifty-four government soldiers die, seventeen are wounded, and sixty are taken captive by the guerrillas.

November 1996

In a new form of retaliation against the guerrillas, paramilitary groups begin kidnapping the relatives of guerrilla leaders.

February 1997

On February 23 the mayor of La Plata, in the department of Huila, is assassinated, presumably by the FARC, the first of many attacks on mayors and electoral officials during this year of local elections. The attacks are not new; during 1996 at least ten mayors were murdered, fifty-one threatened with death, and nine kidnapped by guerrilla forces. During 1997, intimidation of government officials in areas where guerrilla influence is strong becomes a common guerrilla strategy and results in death or renunciation for hundreds of candidates for posts in municipal government. Nevertheless, in elections held October 26, 9.5 million Colombians go to the polls. They back by an overwhelming majority the government's call for a Citizens' Mandate for Peace.

A huge strike by public employees wins wage concessions from the government and an agreement to set up a panel to study privatization plans.

April 1997

Self-Defense groups of Córdoba and Urabá and those of the Magdalena Medio and the Llanos Orientales unite to form a national organization, the AUC (Autodefensas Unidas de Colombia).

May 1997

President Samper orders the removal of military forces in the lower and middle Caguán River Basin, in the department of Caquetá, for thirty-two days in exchange for the liberation of soldiers held by the guerrillas. This act prefigures later territorial concessions by the government to the guerrillas that form the basis for wide-ranging peace negotiations in 1999.

July 1997

A large but undetermined number of people are murdered in the course of six days in Mapiripán, Meta, by a group of men presumed to be paramilitaries.

December 1997

The Jesuit-affiliated research, education, and human rights-monitoring organization CINEP (Centro de Investigación y Educación Popular) denounces the massacre of twenty-six people, presumably by paramilitaries, in the small town of Los Pisingos, on the border between the departments of Antioquia and Chocó. A short time later, the army asks the government to investigate CINEP researchers who denounced another massacre, also in December 1997, of an estimated forty people in Urabá. (Earlier, on May 19, 1997, two CINEP investigators and a parent of one of them were killed by unknown assailants in their apartment in Bogotá.)

March 1998

On March 3 the FARC inflicts another big defeat on government forces in the Caguán region, leaving fifty-eight soldiers dead, twenty-six captured, and twenty-nine unaccounted for.

April 1998

The ELN announces that its leader, defrocked priest Manuel Pérez, died of natural causes on February 14.

A UN human rights commission gives its approval to the Rural Associations for Vigilance and Security (CONVIVIR). These organizations had previously been declared legal by the Constitutional Court. The CONVIVIR had long been denounced by human rights organizations for vigilantism and ties to paramilitary groups.

The U.S. Defense Intelligence Agency warns that the Colombian army could lose the war against the guerrillas in five years.

Labor lawyer and human rights activist Eduardo Umaña Luna is murdered by three assassins in Bogotá.

May 1998

The *Washington Post* reports that the U.S. government is considering a possible investigation of members of the intelligence brigade of the Colombian army for involvement in actions against human rights activists. Later, in July 1998, the brigade is dismantled by the army.

Ex-Minister of Defense General Fernando Landazábal is killed by an assassin in Bogotá. He was an adviser to right-wing presidential hopeful General Harold Bedoya.

On May 16 a paramilitary group enters a northeastern neighborhood in the petroleum port of Barrancabermeja in Santander killing twelve people and reportedly kidnapping another twenty-five. Several days later, on June 4, twenty-six people being held by the paramilitaries are assassinated and incinerated. A general strike is called in the port to protest the massacre.

June 1998

Victor G. Ricardo, a member of the campaign staff of presidential candidate Andrés Pastrana, meets with the two top leaders of the FARC ("Tirofijo" and "El Mono Jojoy") to discuss the possibility and terms of future peace negotiations.

In a letter to the presidential candidates, the paramilitary organization Autodefensas Unidas de Colombia (AUC) expresses its unwillingness to sit at the same negotiating table with the guerrillas and sets conditions for a separate dialogue with the government.

On June 21 the second round of the presidential election is held, with victory going to the Conservative candidate, Andrés Pastrana, with

6,086,507 votes. Horacio Serpa, the Liberal candidate, minister of government during the Samper administration, gets 5,620,719 votes. The guerrillas had made no secret of their preference for Pastrana, publicly proclaiming him most likely to engage in serious peace negotiations. Pastrana, untainted by the Samper drug-money scandal, was also clearly, albeit less publicly, the preference of U.S. officials.

July 1998

A surprise meeting is held July 9 between President-elect Pastrana with the commander of the FARC, Manuel Marulanda Vélez. They discuss the withdrawal of the military from five *municipios* and exchange views on the nature of future peace talks.

On July 15, after three days of meetings in the German city of Mainz, delegates representing Colombian *gremios*, unions, and the Catholic Church and representatives of the ELN announce an agreement to humanize the war. The ELN will cease kidnapping children, women, and the elderly and suspend bombing of oil pipelines if a national petroleum summit is held.

August 1998

Before taking office, President-elect Pastrana meets with U.S. President Bill Clinton in the White House to discuss improving bilateral relations between the two countries.

The administration of Andrés Pastrana begins August 7, to run until August 2002. In the first months, Pastrana reestablishes good relations with the United States and fulfills his primary campaign promise to begin serious negotiations with guerrilla groups. By 1999, however, he is facing an economic crisis of serious proportions and is being severely criticized by the right for making undue concessions to the FARC to get the peace process moving. Success in the negotiations depends in large part on the continued backing and intentions of the United States and on the attitude of the guerrillas. It is not clear if either is truly committed to a negotiated settlement based on the significant, but far from fundamental, reforms that the government seems willing to offer.

September 1998

The terms of the projected withdrawal of government military forces from five *municipios* as a precondition for peace negotiations with the FARC are heatedly discussed by all concerned. The government grants political recognition to the FARC (and in October to the ELN) as the basis for peace talks. Discussions ensue between the government and the FARC over prisoner exchange.

October 1998

The ELN bombing of a central oil pipeline destroys the hamlet of Machuca in Segovia, Antioquia, killing fifty-six (later the toll would be fixed at seventy) and wounding many. In November the ELN admits responsibility.

November 1998

The FARC attacks Mitú, capital of the department of Vaupés, for three days. Government forces reestablish control at great cost, their own casualties estimated at 150 soldiers and police. This is the first time a guerrilla group attacks a departmental capital.

December 1998

Secret meetings take place between the FARC and the U.S. government in Costa Rica. Discussions reportedly focus on the elimination of illicit crops and on the terms of the peace dialogue in the zone cleared of Colombian security forces.

January 1999

Manuel Marulanda Vélez, head of the FARC, fails to appear at a meeting with President Pastrana: a setback for proposed peace talks.

A powerful earthquake strikes the heart of the Colombian coffee zone. The government response is termed inept by critics from both right and left.

March 1999

Three U.S. citizens trying to support Uwa Indians in northeastern Colombia in their resistance to oil drilling are murdered. The FARC will later admit that one of its commands is responsible.

April 1999

All 2,500 members of the Embera-Katio Indian tribe in the department of Córdoba seek political asylum in Spain, claiming that they face extinction at the hands of warring leftist guerrillas and right-wing paramilitary forces in their ancestral homeland.

May 1999

The government and the FARC announce an agreement to start peace talks. They will take place in the Switzerland-sized area around San

Vicente del Caguán, the stronghold of the FARC, from which all government security forces have now been withdrawn. Victor G. Ricardo, chief negotiator for the government, says the safe haven, also known as the Military Exclusionary Zone (see map), will remain under FARC control indefinitely.

The ELN kidnaps approximately 140 churchgoers in Cali. Although many women and children are released in subsequent days, about 60 people remain in captivity at the end of May.

June 1999

President Pastrana signs a bill extending the life and scope of "faceless justice" procedures. Much criticized by human rights groups, these procedures allow judges, prosecutors, and witnesses to remain anonymous when dealing with cases involving drugs and subversion.

Recently released figures reveal that the Colombian economy contracted by 5 percent in the first quarter of 1999, following a 3 percent decline in the last quarter of 1998. Meanwhile, the head of the New York Stock Exchange meets with the FARC guerrilla leaders to extol the virtues of free markets.

July 1999

The FARC attacks several towns on the doorstep of Bogotá; according to the government, there are heavy losses on both sides.

General Barry McCaffrey, U.S. drug czar, arrives for talks in Bogotá. He has called for a billion-dollar infusion in emergency U.S. aid to battle the drug trade; he claims that the trade enriches guerrilla groups.

August 1999

Colombia's credit rating is lowered to below investment grade by Moody's Investors Service, making Colombian borrowing much more costly.

A *sicario* (hired assassin) on a motorcycle guns down popular television personality and humorist Jaime Garzón. Working for peace, he had helped organize guerrilla news conferences.

September 1999

Labor unions and social movements, backed by guerrilla groups, mount an "indefinite" general strike to protest President Pastrana's austerity measures. The strike is called off by the leadership two days later after more than seventy people reportedly die in armed clashes with security forces.

Jesús Bejarano, an economic historian and long-time advocate of peace negotiations, is gunned down outside his classroom at the National University in Bogotá.

President Pastrana addresses the United Nations on the opening day of the General Assembly. He seeks U.S.$3.5 billion in foreign assistance to promote peace, prosperity, and a strengthening of the State.

October 1999

On October 24 formal peace talks between the government and the FARC begin as millions of Colombians march for peace.

December 1999

President Pastrana announces Plan Colombia, an ambitious strategy to resolve the crisis facing the country. The plan calls for large-scale international aid to help stimulate the economy, confront the drug trade, strengthen the State and armed forces, and promote human rights and the peace process.

Significant events on the military front include: The government inaugurates a new rapid-deployment force to fight the guerrillas. The guerrillas overrun a naval base near the Panama border killing twenty-three. The army reports killing more than sixty rebels heading for the Military Exclusionary Zone in southern Colombia. The FARC accedes to government calls for a holiday cease-fire. And the government holds talks with the ELN within Colombia following months of discussions abroad.

January 2000

President Clinton responds to the Colombian government's call for support by announcing a $1.3 billion, two-year emergency aid package, the bulk of it to be spent on support for the Colombian military in the "war on drugs." Colombian, European, and U.S. critics claim that this action is a major step toward U.S. involvement in a conflict reminiscent of the Vietnam War and denounce the human rights record of the Colombian military. They argue that aid to Colombia should focus on protecting human rights and helping poor and displaced persons, and that the U.S. "war on drugs" is best fought through treatment at home.

Chapter 1

Introduction
Problems of Violence, Prospects for Peace

Gonzalo Sánchez G.

In this introductory chapter, Gonzalo Sánchez assesses how the phenomenon of the violence has changed during the decade of the 1990s. He shows how complex and intractable the violence has become, how it is now an international problem, not simply a national one, and how, despite all the obstacles, it might be overcome. He pays special attention to the psychological and cultural implications of the violence. The chapter introduces, and traces the connections among, each of the subjects explored in detail in the other chapters of this volume.

Gonzalo Sánchez is a historian at the Institute of Political Studies and International Relations at the National University of Colombia in Bogotá. He is the author of numerous works on Colombian violence, including *Guerra y política en la sociedad colombiana* (Bogotá, 1991), and, with Donny Meertens, *Bandoleros, gamonales y campesinos* (Bogotá, 1984; English edition, forthcoming, University of Texas Press). He was head of the presidential commission that wrote *Colombia: Violencia y democracia* (Bogotá, 1987), a part of which was reproduced as Chapter 12 of *Violence in Colombia* (1992). In March 2000 he was awarded the Martin Diskin Memorial Lectureship by the Latin American Studies Association. The award recognizes his outstanding scholarship in the field of violence studies in Colombia and his commitment to finding a peaceful solution to the country's problems. He was a signatory of the "Letter of the Intellectuals" that called on the guerrillas to give up the armed struggle in 1992 and wrote a reply to the guerrillas' response to that letter (see Documents section, Part 2).

The lives of most Colombians born after the Second World War and, in particular, after the massive insurrection following the assassination of the popular leader Jorge Eliécer Gaitán on April 9, 1948, have been spent under the sign of violence. Although this is quite often perceived as simple repetition of previous experiences, it is, in fact, a violence that has progressively invaded all spheres of public and private life. Consequently, it is reasonable to suggest that violence has become the reference point for Colombian politics, society, and economy during the second half of the twentieth century. Indeed, during the current era of globalization, violence has had even more disturbing effects than it did during the classic era of the Violence of the late 1940s and 1950s.

In the last two decades Colombia has experienced an unresolved tension between, at the least, two opposing dynamics. On the one hand, there are impulses toward the relegitimation and strengthening of the State under the ethos of participation, citizenship, and ethnic and cultural pluralism delineated in the 1991 Constitution. On the other hand, there are the growing predominance of the logic of the war, the escalating protagonism of private armed actors, the fragmentation and delegitimation of State institutions, and the struggle surrounding civil society. In fact, at times civil society has been seen as a target of bellicose actions and at others as territory to be conquered. In either view, the objective of the various armed actors is to convert civil society into a tactical resource or strategic element for their own objectives.[1] In this context, even democratizing processes such as political decentralization have been utilized by the insurgents to augment their own resources and to exercise control over political and administrative decisions in many towns and regions.

The growing intensity of the armed conflict has also provoked serious repercussions at the international level: along Colombia's borders with neighboring states, in the illegal drug market, in the channeling of economic aid by multilateral organizations, in the warnings of governments and nongovernment organizations (NGOs) of the violations of international humanitarian law, and in the ecological damage resulting both from the expansion of illegal cultivation of coca leaves and heroin poppies and from the methods used under international pressure to destroy these crops. It follows that Colombia has increasingly gained world attention and that the elements of this sudden, and negative, internationalization have fostered a complex pendular movement regarding the not necessarily dichotomous options of international intervention or mediation. From different perspectives, international intervention is demanded in such areas as the creation of conditions of mutual trust for peace negotiations, the construction of a common agenda for such negotiations, and the verification of compliance with the agreed-upon compromises. In Colombia we are thus far away from the current situation of El Salvador and Guatemala, which is now one of reconstruction.

For this reason the position or course of action one takes, both within Colombia and outside it, depends in large part on one's diagnosis of the dynamics of actors, scenarios, and conditions for the application of international systems for regulating war. This essay aims to clarify the ingredients of violence in Colombia by advancing our understanding of the interrelationships among its many facets, and by outlining some guidelines for fostering a negotiated solution to the conflict.

The Peculiarity of the Colombian Case: Multiplicity, Interdependence, and Hierarchy of Violence

At least since the 1980s the distinctive feature of Colombian politics is the multiplicity of violence. Colombian violence has been multiple in terms of its origins, objectives, geography, modi operandi, and strategies. And in all the violence, questions of pragmatism and immediate gain would seem to be winning at the expense of ideological commitment. Organized crime, guerrilla struggle, dirty war, and diffuse social violence—differentiated forms of violence but quite often intertwined—can be part of a single situation.

This multiplicity is obviously overdetermined by the underground economy and by the criminal and commercial networks of drug trafficking, at both the national and international levels. The international networks are principally American (Cosa Nostra) and Italian (the Sicilian and Neapolitan mafias), and constitute a kind of globalization of markets and illegal organizations, each with its own structures, hierarchies, division of labor, sociocultural norms, and specific articulations to local powers.[2] Domination of the market, recourse to violence, and a tendency toward fragmentation, three features so characteristic of the present age, unite here with particular intensity.

At the internal level the explosion of violence is extremely diversified in its regional and historical expressions. For example, violence can be associated with the *struggle for land*, a struggle in which the guerrillas frequently operate as protectors of certain sectors of the peasantry against landlords, local political leaders, and the army and the police. Meanwhile, other sectors of the peasantry seek refuge in zones controlled by paramilitaries. In this way, a fragmentation of the peasantry is produced but one that is difficult to relate exclusively to the relative wealth, access to land, or conditions of labor of the people involved. This struggle has also resulted in massive migration to, and colonization of, frontier areas, in a gigantic agricultural contra-reform orchestrated by the drug traffickers, and in a new social, geographical, and political configuration of the country. One could even speak of the foundation of a new country without a State.

Thus, historically we have two principal processes of colonization in twentieth-century Colombia. On the one hand, the Antioqueño coffee colonization of the first half of the century, a great transforming and integrative force that created the basis for a middle peasantry, consolidated the links with the international market, and made possible the early industrialization of the country. And, on the other hand, we have the colonization of the contemporary era, which is permeated by guerrilla activity and drug cultivation and plays in many respects a destabilizing role. The political options for the peasantry are today very limited. They are trapped between traditional patronage networks and armed insurgence.[3]

Violence can also be associated in its origins with territorial disputes between the armed actors and *labor conditions*, that is to say, wages and working conditions. An example is the agro-industrial banana zone of Urabá along the Panama border. There the principal protagonists of the labor disputes are, on the one hand, great landowners organized in the Sociedad de Agricultores de Colombia and the big banana producers organized in the Asociación de Bananeros, and, on the other, the agricultural unions Sintrabanano and Sintagro, often at odds politically with one another and frequently shot through with guerrilla pressure. The Urabá banana zone was socially constructed as a region by way of multiple processes of colonization and served for decades as the base of operations of the United Fruit Company; today it is also of crucial importance in the marketing of drugs and the contraband arms trade. The same applies to the agro-industrial areas of the Magdalena Medio. In both areas, Urabá and Magdalena Medio, trade unions of different affiliations have been forced since the 1980s to take sides in the war of contending factions: that of guerrillas against guerrillas, and that of guerrillas against paramilitary groups and the army. The pressures and the violent actions of some contenders force out administrators of the great industrial enterprises, while those of other contenders inflict punishment on the workers of certain political affiliations. The result is an unending chain of vengeance in the struggle for control over territory and organized social actors. This has catastrophic consequences, especially for workers who are victims not only of organized capital, but also of the hyperpoliticization of regional life. Social actors are displaced by political actors in pursuit of the expansive projects of the armed actors.[4]

Violence can also be associated with *tributary extraction* in strategic mining centers. An example is the emerald zone in the west of the department of Boyacá. There the great bosses have developed a power typical of the mafia, one that not only privatizes the use of violence (and negotiating capacity) but that also acts above and beyond the traditional networks of control, social mediation, and patronage of political parties.[5] The following centers are also a scene for this kind of violence: the unprotected (and poorly studied) gold mines in Antioquia, the coal mines in César and La Guajira in the northeast of the country, and, above all, the petroleum zones in Santander,

Arauca, and Casanare on the Venezuelan border. A good part of these oil fields are located in areas of recent agricultural settlement and they have been converted into one of the largest sources of financing for the Ejército de Liberación Nacional (ELN). Over time and at great cost to society, these zones have become strategic points of confrontation among the State, the mining companies, and the guerrillas. In many cases, these actors work out their earnings, losses, and demonstrations of force at the expense not of one another but of third parties. It is even suspected that petroleum multinationals speculate on Colombian insecurity, that is, insecurity has been converted into a beneficial factor, giving way to what Nazih Richani defines as a system of autoperpetuation of violence.[6] War in Colombia, under the terms now developing, requires considerable financial resources that in practice translate into a triple tribute (to the guerrillas, the paramilitary forces, and the State), all of which results in an increasingly unsustainable hemorrhage of the productive sector.

As the examples illustrate, these are generally processes which, contrary to a supposed automatic correlation between violence and poverty, show that violence has been concentrated in zones of great dynamism and economic expansion: the coffee zones during the 1950s Violence and the relatively prosperous zones of agricultural colonization and development today. More than in the regions of limited social mobility, the violence is predominately nourished in the zones of greatest mobility, those to which new capital, migrants, and forms of authority flow. There are those who allege that it is the very velocity of the economic and social changes of many regions (such as the petroleum regions of Arauca, Casanare, and Putumayo and the banana zone of Urabá) that underlies the problem. Such change is evidently out of step with institutional transformations, and that could explain the greater incidence of criminality in some zones of the country. More than their overall poverty, it is the internal imbalance of these regions, the corrosive coexistence of prosperity and poverty, and the sense of injustice which results, that may function as a detonator for violence.[7] In addition, in the particular case of guerrilla strategy, especially in the initial phase, beyond the role of objective conditions there were strategic considerations. These included decisions about the functionality of certain territories and sectors of the national economy. Guerrilla groups sought zones of refuge and areas ripe for expansion and for gathering resources. They often found themselves in competition for power and legitimation with paramilitaries, drug traffickers, self-defense groups, and the State.[8]

Another factor that cannot be omitted in deciphering contemporary Colombian violence is that of a new work ethic, so distinct from what are known as the Protestant or the Catholic work ethic, which now holds sway in social life and in the dynamics of the war. This is effectively an ethic driven by the law of employing the least effort and the shortest time possible to acquire wealth and win the war—no matter the method or price.

In addition to all this, there is the most direct form of political violence, political assassination. We must remember that an entire party, the Patriotic Union, a Communist-Socialist coalition that emerged from the first peace agreements in 1985, was decimated between 1989 and 1992. What is more, the assassination of the charismatic presidential candidate from the Liberal opposition, Luis Carlos Galán, and of many guerrilla leaders who had entered into the political arena (Carlos Toledo Plata, Carlos Pizarro León-Gómez, Bernardo Jaramillo Ossa, Oscar William Calvo) severely compromises the sense of trust vital to any negotiated settlement of the conflict. The military occupation of La Uribe, sanctuary of the central command of the FARC in the department of Meta, during the administration of President César Gaviria Trujillo, wounded the honor of the guerrillas and destroyed any possibility of linking the guerrilla movement to the discussions concerning the new Constitution.

Multidimensional violence for the control of resources, territories, social forces, and power is additionally becoming the biggest threat to Indian and Afro-Colombian populations. In particular, it constitutes a threat to the *survival of communal identity* in departments such as Chocó and Cauca, where ethnic communities have been guardians of ecological niches since time immemorial. In this sense, in many zones scattered throughout our national geography, Colombian violence is playing a role similar to that of the war in Guatemalan Mayan territories, or that of the Sendero Luminoso (Shining Path) in the Ayacucho region of Peru; it is a machine that demolishes ethnic and community identities.[9] What a painful experience this is for a nation like Colombia! From time to time (as in the Constitution of 1991), it discovers the "other" through pacts and laws, but more regularly it has been discovering itself (its borders, its aborigines, its African-American communities) through the paths of violence.

Up to this point, some of the most visible expressions of the recent violence in Colombia have been characterized. We now turn to the new geographical regions in which it is present. In effect, the violence of today is rooted not only in the marginal areas of recent settlement but has also returned to the traditional regions of the coffee-export economy, once the principal axis of the national economy but now in decline. In these regions, Colombian guerrillas—wealthy groups, in contrast, say, to the Guatemalan Army of the Poor—at times pay agricultural workers better wages than average farmers can afford. This also occurred during the 1996 rural strike and general mobilization of agricultural settlers in the department of Caquetá in the south of the country.[10]

Violence has also ceased being an exclusively rural phenomenon in the last ten years and has adopted multiple *urban* faces. Given its magnitude and complexity, this phenomenon deserves special attention. In the first place, we have the impact of narcoterrorism and hired killers (*sicarios*), a kind of "death industry" in cities such as Medellín and Cali. Narcoterrorism and the activities of *sicarios* continue today in spite of the physical liquidation of Gonzalo Rodríguez Gacha and the imprisonment of prominent drug kingpins.[11]

The second notable expression of the urban violence is the implantation of "popular militias" in poor neighborhoods of big cities (Ciudad Bolívar in Bogotá, Distrito de Aguablanca in Cali, northeastern parts of Medellín), and even in medium-sized cities such as Barrancabermeja. Frequently, although not necessarily, linked to the guerrillas, they initially operate (with the complacency of the inhabitants) to eliminate the gangs that plague such neighborhoods.

A third modality of urban violence is "social cleansing," operations that frequently include participation by police or ex-police agents against beggars, prostitutes, and street delinquents in Cali, Medellín, Pereira, or Barranquilla, to cite only the locations of the most notable instances of this neo-Nazi activity.[12] There is no lack of places in which these "social cleansings" are carried out under the euphemism of "popular justice" on the part of groups or militias that proclaim themselves revolutionaries.

We are not dealing here only with changes in the spatiality of the violence and the trespassing of certain symbolic frontiers, such as those of universities and churches, sacred places of thought and religious practice, the first shaken by assassinations, the second by collective kidnapping or hostage-taking, as happened at Cali's Iglesia de la María. (For their part, Protestants in territories dominated by the guerrillas are suffering harassment and repression reminiscent of the worst police excesses during the Violence of the 1950s.) We are also concerned with the transformation in actors' identities and with the emergence of new actors, whose characteristics oblige one to take note of cultural aspects of the violence. Consider once more the young contract *sicarios* who frequently kill on demand. They are initiated in semisatanic rituals and socialized in crime (in gangs, guerrilla militias, drug networks, "justice" groups against common delinquency). They establish spatial boundaries ("territories of fear") in which they exercise their jurisdiction.[13] Initially bound by primary ties of kinship and neighborhood identity, from an early age these young people suffer from the absence of a paternal figure in their lives (a figure they often equate with the law or authority) and exhibit a prolonged dependence on the maternal figure, which, particularly in Medellín, is interchangeable with or complementary to the Virgin Mary. It would seem that both feminine figures are mythologized as expressions of tolerance and comprehension, and these young people even invoke the help of both to achieve greater success in their criminal activities.

Perhaps it is reasonable for some observers to see in these forms of violence expressions of a traumatic and inconclusive transition from a religious-Catholic to a civil-lay ethic, one which gives meaning to a new political order. These are young people who have been stranded without a future and who live life as it comes, anxiously enjoying the moment: Death is their only certainty. But even as they transgress all societal norms, they demand inflexible fulfillment of those of their own organizations. For example, they practice an exalted, almost sacred, honoring of one's word once given, and mete out unmitigated punishment for treason. In terms of numbers, there is nothing like this culture in any other country of the Western Hemisphere. In Medellín between 1985 and 1990, it is estimated that at least 122 gangs operated, not all of them located in the poorest neighborhoods. The relationships among these gangs are very complicated. They frequently cooperate with one another; sometimes they are rivals, sometimes a mixture of the two. On occasion there is a peculiar division of the market, with certain bands having exclusive domain over certain types of crime.[14] The overall effect of this proliferation has been the saturation of available territories and an ambiance of general mistrust.

Material privation is not the only motivation of young people enrolling in these gangs. More important are cultural relations that have to do with family, gender, religion, school, and community ties. Through armed intimidation, gang members aspire to patterns of consumption that others have acquired through inheritance, corruption, or speculation. These young people do not present themselves as an alternative to the society of consumption; rather, they seek sudden incorporation into it through chance shortcuts and violence.

Young women have also participated in all these forms of illegality and rebellion. The gangs often constitute spaces for adolescent women who have been mistreated or abandoned in their early childhood and who are in search of recognition and seek to mend broken affective ties. For those young women who enlist, especially in the case of "militias," the gang can be not only a place of altruism and redemptive dreams but also a place for social decomposition and "lumpenization." In a single day and at the cost of the life of an unfortunate, such young people attempt to resolve the privations that have accumulated for years. Joining the "militias" can be a way to sever social ties and cancel forms of submission that have been perpetuated in daily life, but, and even without intending it, the gang can also be a place for self-destruction.[15]

Such new forms of irregular sociability are affecting the ways people construct memory and comprehend time. The guerrillas boast of marching to rhythms much longer than governments do—in biblical time, they say. Other violent actors move in the opposite direction, for example, the *sicarios*. "The *sicario* has absorbed the ephemeral sense of time particular to our epoch. Life is an instant. Neither the past nor the future exists. *Sicarios* take consumer society to an extreme: they convert life, their own lives and those of their victims, into objects of economic transactions, into disposable objects. The *sicario* transforms death into a daily occurrence. To kill and to die is normal."[16] This is the desacrilization of death, the banalization of life. On precisely these inverted visions of life and death rest two startling recent novels, *La Virgen de los sicarios* by Fernando Vallejo and *Rosario Tijeras* by Jorge Franco Ramos. In these novels, life appears insignificant and senseless: Fatality dominates. Death, in contrast, is not a passage to another life as in traditional Christianity, but is itself a healing, even gratifying, force. Death can be imagined as a desirable good: one that permits flight from a useless life that is replete with privations and injustices. There is in the young *sicarios* a perverse fascination with death, the game of death: to bear it, execute it, and tell about it.

With violence an everyday affair for Colombians, the time of the living has become the time of the dead. Personal and political calendars have filled up with crosses. But in contrast to what happened in the countries in the Southern Cone such as Argentina, where past violence, long officially denied, was recognized, dramatized, and exorcised in a great national process of exposure and self-criticism,[17] in Colombia, on the contrary, violence and massacres tend to be routinized and incessantly displaced to a kind of frontier between memory and nonmemory. Fear, pain, trauma, and memory are some of the many themes that Colombian scholars have urgently begun to investigate.

Even so, for years the country has confronted a surprising paradox. Since 1980, in a sea of violence and tribulation, Colombia has been the Latin American country with the highest average rate of annual economic growth (3.7 percent). This was a reassuring statistic for businessmen, who assumed a certain autonomy between economics and politics, but this comfortable assumption dramatically disappeared beginning in 1998. Since then, with the economy in crisis, analysts began to think more about the negative impacts of the violence, such as those caused by cattle rustling, the destruction of individual homes and public buildings in towns and cities, the sabotage of highways, the burning of vehicles and goods, the risk of collective kidnappings and robberies on the major roads, the weight of resources destined for security, the decline in investments and tourism, and the disruption of productive activities. Analysts have even begun to analyze crime in terms of economic theory.[18]

The first general conclusion could be, then, that in a Latin American or larger context, what is remarkable in Colombia is the extraordinary diversity of violences. This diversity, accompanied by aberrant indices of impunity, favors the reproduction and expansion of crime and, more recently, the growing instability of the social and political order. Such a situation, however, does not necessarily feed into a revolutionary process in classic terms, as one can judge by the political platforms of the different armed actors.

This was largely the general picture presented ten years ago by a group of intellectuals commissioned by the president of Colombia to report on the violence.[19] Although the commision's report was relatively well accepted in governmental and academic circles, and the idea of multiple and interrelated violence gained general acceptance, three major objections were also raised. First, that the report ran against a holistic view of the violence and, more than that, reinforced a fragmented vision of the phenomenon. Second, that in the effort to underline the variety of violence, a system of violence, its authors unwittingly contributed to minimizing the political dimensions of the phenomenon. And third, that this study of violence has had a negative impact on the official policies of peace because it overemphasized the weight of the "objective causes" of the violence, thus creating, in fact, a discourse that legitimized political insurgency.[20] We examine some of these points below.

A Methodological and Strategic Premise: Negotiable and Nonnegotiable Forms of Violence

Other parts of the study mentioned above caused less controversy at the time, but have been increasingly debated since. These include the crucial distinction between political and nonpolitical violence and, even more significantly, the distinction between negotiable and nonnegotiable violence. The latter is a concept that was very much celebrated by Peruvian and Central American students of contemporary conflict. The idea was to establish a clear line of demarcation, for academic and political purposes, between guerrilla-state confrontation and other expressions of violence related to public safety—that is, the security, not of the State, but of citizens as such—and to social behavior.

As far as *negotiable* violence is concerned, Colombia has a long tradition, and even a particular routine, in the way this type of violence is handled. This tradition is revealed in the armistices of nineteenth-century civil wars; two-party coalitions, such as the National Front after the period of the Violence; and the armistices with former guerrillas in the 1990s. It applies even to the 1991 Constitution, inasmuch as it is a pact between the government and an important sector of the guerrilla movement, the popular-nationalist M-19, and the Quintín Lame, a movement named for the most prestigious Indian leader of twentieth-century Colombia.

With regard to *nonnegotiable* violence, the criteria of the 1987 commission appointed by the government were to highlight new expressions of violence that had been ignored by state agencies and social scientists. It is important to point out, however, that the frontiers between negotiable and nonnegotiable are also shifting. A few years ago, before pressure from the United States on the issue increased, drug trafficking was considered negotiable, while the criminality associated with urban militias, then regarded as nonnegotiable, was nevertheless partially solved through negotiations. Many Medellín gangs became political organizations of sorts and were treated as such by city and departmental authorities with the approval of the central government. In reality, one of the peculiarities of contemporary Colombian society is the fluidity between the voluntary and coercive, the legal and the illegal, the institutional and the para-institutional, the revolutionary and the criminal. There is not only a blurring of these dichotomies but a growing political complexity in dealing with them as well.

In any case, the increase in criminality is forcefully reflected in homicide figures. Colombia had, at the turn of the decade (1989–1992), a rate of intentional homicides of around 77.5 per 100,000 inhabitants (the highest rate was 86 in 1991). Significantly, the most affected by these extraordinarily high mortality rates are young males between fifteen and twenty-four years old. Considering the impact in terms of gender, we note that in 1994 males between twenty and twenty-four years of age reached a rate of 42.5 per 100,000 inhabitants, while the rate for females was only 9.3. In terms of regional distribution, it is worth emphasizing that the highest rates are found in the departments of Antioquia, Caldas, and Valle, that is, in the great poles of economic development of the country. Together with the capital city, Bogotá, whose rate is that of the national average, in the mid-1990s these departments accounted for close to 70 percent of the total homicides in the country.[21] By 1985 homicide had become the principal cause of death in Medellín, with a rate of 100.8 violent deaths per 100,000 inhabitants, by far the highest rate in the country at that time. And, although at the end of the 1990s the rate of homicides in the country as a whole was decreasing (72 in 1995 and 56 in 1998), it is still, in comparative terms, and excluding countries at war, among the highest in the world today. In comparative terms, in 1995 the homicide rate per 100,000 inhabitants was: France, 4.6; United States, 8.0; Peru, 11.5; Mexico, 20.0; Brazil, 24.6; Colombia, 72.0.[22]

During the last five years the composition of criminality in Colombia has probably changed. For instance, there would seem to be fewer homicides and more kidnappings. But as Alvaro Camacho and Alvaro Guzmán have indicated, Colombian criminality was almost three times higher in 1995 than that of Brazil, the second-ranking nation in South America in terms of homicide rates. And in absolute numbers, during the same year, there were three times more homicides in Colombia than in the entire Republic of China.

If we consider the annual average of intentional homicides in Colombia between 1986 and 1995, which was about 24,000, and make the projection for that decade, the total number is equivalent to that estimated for the bloody decade of the Violence (1948–1957), a total which only a few years ago we would have thought unduplicatable. (See Table.) Today, violence is the greatest public health problem in Colombia, and it consumes 26 percent of the costs of the health system, which starkly contrasts with 3.3 percent for Latin America and 1.5 percent for the rest of the world.[23]

What is more worrisome is the simultaneous growth of criminality and impunity. The phenomenon of impunity is not new, but the dimensions of it are. Since World War II, in effect, the Colombian judicial system has annually increased its inefficiency. This is true not only in terms of the volume of undecided cases, but it has also lacked criteria to give priority to investigations of the most socially serious crimes, those against life itself. Since 1990, almost half of judicial processes have ended in impunity, thrown out of court on the basis of a simple technical ruling. On the other hand, the parallel (and interrelated?) growth of homicides and organized crime in recent decades has reduced to the minimum the penal risks of delinquents. Only 6 percent of the homicides committed are brought to trial and those that are penalized are but 4 percent of the total. (And these figures are based on reported crimes; the total number of homicides is surely higher.) This situation constitutes a true collapse of the judicial system. There is even an inverse relation between the most serious forms of criminality and judicial action: "The more homicides, the fewer detained assassins."[24] On top of all these indicators of the collapse of the penal system, one must add the crisis of the country's jails where disorder, corruption, and internal violence are the norm. Prisons in Colombia are not centers for rehabilitation but veritable "Universities of Evil." Thus, violence is also a function of the law, of justice, and of authority.

Homicide Figures in Colombia, 1982–1998

Year	*Total Homicides*	*Political Homicides and Extrajudicial Executions*
1982	10,580	525
1983	9,721	524
1984	10,694	542
1985	12,899	630
1986	15,672	1,387
1987	17,419	1,651
1988	21,100	2,738
1989	23,312	1,978
1990	24,267	2,007
1991	28,140	1,828
1992	28,224	2,178
1993	28,026	2,190
1994	26,807	1,668
1995	25,398	1,031
1996	26,642	NA
1997	23,379	NA
1998	23,096	NA

Sources: Comisión Colombiana de Juristas, *Colombia, derechos humanos y derecho humanitario* (Bogotá, 1996); Policía Nacional, *Criminalidad* (Bogotá, 1998); Saúl Franco, *El Quinto: No matar* (Bogotá, 1999).

As a result of multiple violence, daily life in Colombia has been deeply transformed. *Forms of sociability* (such as parties, evening meals in restaurants) have been greatly reduced, *recreational activities* for children in the streets and parks have been limited (due to the threat of kidnapping), *forms of dress* in the streets have become very austere (women, for example, cannot wear jewelry or carry valuables). Homes are becoming real prisons surrounded by iron fences and metal bars. There has been a growth in the construction of closed communities, which can be considered a type of spatial apartheid, with impassable barriers for "undesirables."[25] In neighborhoods in many cities, the streets, especially for young people, "have been sown with death";[26] they are zones of socialization for criminals. In Colombian cities, walking on the street or hailing taxis at night are high-risk activities. In a word, all collective practices have been affected in one way or another by the various forms of violence.

As a consequence of these trends, the already fragile public sphere has shrunk and, in a way, has become a world of fear and force. In contrast, the private sphere is cherished and considered the world of refuge and safety.[27] In Yi-fu Tuan's expression, the streets have become "landscapes of fear"[28]—fear of terrorists, fear of thieves, fear of neighbors, fear of security guards, fear of beggars, and even fear of the victims of violence *stretched out in the streets*. This state of affairs called forth an explosion of private guards who watch over residences, public buildings, and banking institutions, and, in extreme cases, it has brought forth community self-defense groups. The city has become a world of inhabitants living incommunicado.

Not only has fear become a collective experience, so too has the pain expressed upon the departure of loved ones, which we call mourning. How many burials of relatives, neighbors, school friends, colleagues or fellow political party members, caused by the violence, has each Colombian attended in the last ten years? And how many times in the intimate experience of these overwhelming episodes have we passed from the pain of the funeral march to rage, and then impotence?

Given the scope of this collective experience of violence, it is not possible to expect that peace will be an immediate result of the negotiation process. This situation is, as a matter of fact, so complex that even if we could negotiate institutional reconstruction with the guerrillas tomorrow, the reconstruction of the State and the social fabric could take decades. It is a long road from the situation we have today, a kind of *social Hobbesianism*, to a situation of "generalized reciprocity" in which everybody can take for granted that all others are following the same rules. It will not be easy to make this transition precisely because violence has destroyed civic traditions that now must be reinvented. In this sense, ours is more than a political crisis or a crisis of the State. It is a *crisis of a society*. Colombian society has to be reconstructed in terms of the values, solidarities, and modes of conduct that precede all political order. The combined effects of violence and drug trafficking have transformed Colombian society: its structures of commercialization; the foundations of accumulation (where illegality substitutes for socially accepted earnings); cultural values; links between money, justice, and politics; the way one relates to life and death. It is a society that beyond the prospect of formulating a project of unity or national order is involved in a perpetual process of "negotiating disorder," of making it, in lieu of eliminating it, at least bearable.[29] Of course, this type of society, in order to survive, must also develop strategies and unpublicized forms of cultural resistance, but this theme is beyond the scope of this essay.

The point is that the situation presented in the diagnosis by the "violentoligists" ten years ago—a diagnosis presented to English readers in 1992 in *Violence in Colombia*—has worsened and taken a different path. Political violence, instead of being a marginal form of violence among others, must now be recognized as the context in which the reproduction of all other forms of violence occurs. Or, to phrase it differently, "*Organized violence has become the context for nonorganized violence.*"[30] Political violence not only facilitates the expansion of other forms of violence, but also is affected and fundamentally contaminated by them.

Let us now survey some indicators of this worsening situation. First, the military equation. If ten years ago the guerrillas were located mainly in peripheral regions, the regions of recent colonization, this is no longer the case. Today, guerrillas are not only present in nearly 93 percent of the *municipios* (counties) of recent settlement, but also in at least half of the *municipios* of the entire country.[31] Even though often these figures do not distinguish between a permanent or occasional guerrilla presence, they are in any case indicative of the dimensions of the phenomenon, the level of penetration of the guerrillas into the pores of society, a level never seen in previous epochs. The data thus support the warnings of those who, from the most inflexible positions, maintained that the truce and the negotiations of the mid-1980s were one more example of the old Communist tactic of the "combination of all forms of struggle" to obtain military advantage, as is to some extent natural in the initial phases of any negotiation. In any case, with the liquidation of the Unión Patriótica and hundreds of subsequent political assassinations, the left's tactic of having simultaneously an open electoral political front and another clandestine (armed) one was proven bankrupt. Consequently, the transition from war to politics in future negotiations will have to follow uncharted paths.

According to estimates published in 1995, which reveal a tendency that has continued to date, the guerrillas expanded from 7,673 persons and 80 fronts in 1991 to 10,483 persons and 105 fronts in 1994. In many regions, "the guerrillas are something like a semi-clandestine, semi-public form of local government."[32] This growth has continued at an almost exponential rate until today, elevating the levels of kidnapping, extortion, participation in the drug trade, and the appropriation of public resources that financially sustain such an expanding irregular army. It has been possible to establish that between 1991 and 1994 the earnings of the FARC and the ELN, due to the methods listed above, grew 87 percent, and still it is not clear wherein lies the level of social tolerance for these practices.[33] The payment of more or less permanent tribute to the armed actors by wealthy sectors and the multinational corporations has become a form of negotiated cohabitation with the violence, a process that tends to reproduce itself and that can even work against State efforts to eliminate it. Its operative capacity has permitted even the exercise of what has been called an "armed superintendency"[34] over local and regional officials and budgets.

Henry Kissinger has illustrated the asymmetry in the dynamic of the armed contenders, stating that "the guerrillas win if they do not lose; the conventional army loses if it does not win."[35] With the figures listed above, it is easy to imagine the triumphant air of the Colombian guerrillas and the army's feeling of failure, demoralization, and deception. According to one of the most respected retired generals, Valencia Tovar, who led the military operations in which the revolutionary priest Camilo Torres was killed in 1966, the Colombian establishment began to lose this war thirty years ago, for two main reasons. First, a military reason: the army's failure to understand the nature of the emerging guerrilla movements of the 1960s, associating them with banditry, or in any case viewing them as a result of the traditional political rivalries between Liberals and Conservatives of the past. Second, a political reason: the failure of State policies that were unable to accomplish all the necessary tasks of economic and social reconstruction in the regions most affected by the Violence of the 1950s, paving the way for the revival of armed struggle.[36] This is to say, the failure to resolve the old Violence placed us, almost without our knowing, in the present violence. And only now, after the Cold War, is it possible for the military, but also for the elite in general, to begin to inquire into the internal causes of that violence.

A second sign of current political deterioration is *internal displacement.* The numbers of the displaced persons (and the numbers of refugees in neighboring countries, mainly Venezuela) are becoming overwhelming. Displaced persons now amount to more than 1.5 million. This means that one in every forty Colombians is fleeing his/her own region because of violence. In 1998 alone, the number of newly displaced people was 308,000. The Urabá region, the south of the department of Bolívar, and the Magdalena Medio, areas of confrontation between guerrillas and paramilitary groups, are the ones most affected by the forced displacement of people. Along with their lands and resources, the displaced lose many other cultural referents as well. Only now is this beginning to be spoken of in the international press, in spite of the fact that figures for Colombia are exceeded only by the more elevated numbers for Sudan, Afghanistan, and Angola.

A third sign is what might be called *political involution*, a disturbing result of the economic, military, and geographical expansion of the guerrillas in this decade. Political involution is a consequence, among other things, of functional and tactical alliances between the guerrillas and the drug traffickers in some areas, alliances that yield great economic advantages, certainly, but also involve great ethical costs. It is also clearly connected with the widespread use of practices associated more with common crime than with political goals. I am thinking in particular of kidnapping for economic reasons, which has expanded dramatically, especially after the collapse of the socialist bloc, that long-time provisioner of resources and arms to Marxist-inspired guerrillas in the rest of the world, including Colombia.

Colombia has the largest number of kidnappings in the world today (50 percent of the entire world total) and more than one-third of these are carried out by the guerrillas. The total number of kidnappings more than doubled between 1995 and 1998: in 1995 there were 1,158 kidnappings; in 1996, 1,608; in 1997, 1,986; and in 1998, 2,609.[37] This without counting, of course, the low incidence of reporting, estimated to be 20 percent, because often relatives of victims prefer to negotiate out of the public eye. In light of these figures it can be said that Colombia is today a besieged society. A past representative of the cattlemen's association has indicated that "to be kidnapped in Colombia is not a risk, it is a great possibility."[38] Between 1987 and 1998, the total number of kidnappings was 15,181. Kidnapping and extortion have become, according to a recent study, the basis of what one might call "an insurgent taxation system," a method to transfer resources principally, but not exclusively, from the agrarian sector to armed groups. That study warns that the toll suffered by the agrarian sector from kidnapping and extortion from robbery, from the killing of cattle, and from the burning and destruction of farm buildings and equipment is contributing greatly to the growing costs of the war in Colombia. The relationship between kidnapping, money, and politics is extremely complex.[39] In his book *Noticia de un secuestro* (News of a kidnapping), Gabriel García Márquez shows how the retention of a number of important personalities in Colombian politics by Pablo Escobar and the *extraditables* activated all the networks of power and solidarity among the elites. Such actions could also operate as a mechanism of effective pressure to induce changes in the legal and judicial system of the country, including the formulation of specific clauses of the new national constitution promulgated in 1991.[40] Many of the guerrilla kidnappings are also oriented toward modifying decisions of the executive and legislative branches and the public powers in general, to press for the liberation of political prisoners, and to impose a specific course on negotiations.

Analysis of the phenomenon of kidnapping cannot be limited to its political and economic dimensions, especially the "ransom," which is what usually interests the abductors. The means cannot be divorced from the political end proclaimed by the abductors. Kidnapping involves many aspects of a human rights drama, which often begins with the risks of the operation itself, in which victims are torn from their natural, professional, and family environments. For this reason, from the first moments until the last, for the relatives and negotiators the rituals of "proof of survival" become essential, and these are, at the same time, proof of the identity of the captors. The hopes of the kidnapped person and his/her relatives swing between execution and voluntary liberation, escape and armed rescue. The suddenness of the act of kidnapping and the uncertainty concerning the identity of the abductors (are they common delinquents, drug traffickers, or guerrillas?) create great initial confusion and anguish for the victim and his/her family. Gradually, they discover that there is a certain sequence of events, certain rules, and stages in the modus operandi of the kidnapping, even during standstills in the negotiation process. If the guerrilla is the abductor, the very act of publicly acknowledging the kidnapping has advantages: It obliges those responsible minimally to behave as political actors. All told, it is also important to determine which specific group is responsible, because some have a reputation of more barbaric treatment of victims than others, even though this consideration often loses importance when common delinquents sometimes "sell" their victims to the insurgents, and anonymity permits the guerrillas to avoid the political responsibilities of the operation. Kidnapping is thus a totally unheroic attribute of the guerrillas.

The victims' Calvary continues as they are transported in vehicles, eyes blindfolded, or forced to walk for days to an unidentifiable site, a nowhere whose environs should not be recognizable. There, they must submit to an additional torment, that of solitude. There, victims are under the physical and mental control of their executioners, with whom, in the majority of cases, communication will be limited to insults and interrogations concerning their wealth and property. All this transpires under the perpetual threat of violence and death, and, additionally, in the case of women, the threat of rape. The dignity of men and women captives alike is violated daily when they are forced to bathe and relieve themselves under the vigilance of guards or while tied to a rope. For some, one of the most perpetual anxieties is that of perishing in captivity without anyone's knowledge, "without a tomb for anyone to visit."[41] Kidnapping thus submits victims to a process of becoming a "thing"—simple, negotiable "merchandise." Victims are surrounded by an organizational structure that, like those of the torturers of dictatorships, has specialists in applying physical and psychological pressure, in extracting information, and in apportioning just the right amount of torture so as to conserve the monetary "utility" of victims while securing the eventual cooperation or submission of their families. Victims experience extreme solitude waiting for a transaction on which their liberty and lives depend, and are surrounded by controls that prevent emotional contact or shows of sympathy with their captors. Sometimes, in order to confuse their victims, captors eliminate ways to register the passage of time, of the hours, days, and months. Such intent to plunder the memory obsesses the prisoners as well. Kidnapping is thus the symbol par excellence of the guerrilla paradox: proclaiming itself the champion of an emancipating project against alienation, at the same time the guerrilla reduces the bodies of its victims to debased capitalist merchandise.

It is understandable that a traumatic experience of such dimensions exacerbates the religious sentiments of both kidnap victims and their families. The families often resort to mediums, astrologists, and spiritualists. Religiosity offers the only security imaginable, since in fact it is mistrust (of food, of news, and of people) that governs relations among the kidnappers and between the kidnappers and their victims.

The victims' families often experience guilt over the kidnapping and relinquish many daily pleasures in order not to offend the captive. A psychologist who has professionally attended to many kidnapping victims notes that the families

> live through a devastating experience. In a certain sense they too are kidnapped. They cannot leave the house because they wait for a call; they are afraid that they are being watched, or that they will be taken in exchange for the victim; and they feel that their personal integrity is threatened. The tension is so strong that the whole family enters into a state of crisis. Each member reacts to the situation in his or her own way. For this reason previous conflicts within the family multiply and become more intense and affect family union.[42]

When the victim is freed, either through negotiation or by the action of the authorities, the memory of captivity generally is suppressed. For victims the arduous work of reconstructing family, affections, and confidence now begins. With reason, the aberrant practice of kidnapping has been defined as a "suspended death."[43] For the captors the experience ends with justifications and the often contentious division of the booty.

Colombia is the only country in the world where there is an NGO that specializes in the struggle against kidnapping (País Libre). There have been massive demonstrations against kidnapping in the last five years, and repeated calls for the imposition of the death penalty to cope with it. The kidnapping and subsequent assassination by the FARC of three North American environmentalists at the beginning of 1999 muddied the relations of insurgent groups with the NGOs of Europe and the United States and weakened the elements of the U.S. government most clearly interested in supporting the peace process. More important, the growth of kidnapping has been one of the main reasons for the expansion of paramilitary groups, to whom potential or real victims preventively or punitively resort. Today such groups are experiencing growing social support and the cooperation of local communities, just as was the case with the Guatemalan "civic patrols" and the Peruvian Rondas Campesinas.

Another sign of the involution-degradation of the conflict is circularity among the various violent actors. Examples include those guerrillas or ex-guerrillas who become paramilitaries. In the ranks of Carlos Castaño's Self-Defense groups there are not only numerous ex-combatants of the EPL and ELN, but also, and even more serious, deserters who were officers in the regular army. Insurgent groups, to give another example, offer military training in their camps to gangs of juvenile delinquents in Medellín under the auspices of peace agreements signed during the administration of President Betancur.[44] In addition, drug traffickers and criminal organizations lend their services to insurgent groups. There are identity changes to cover, or attribute to others, operations (especially kidnapping) that generate public repudiation. Furthermore, as has been detected in Medellín,[45] there exist blurry and complex borders between urban militias, the multifaceted juvenile gangs, and groups of *sicarios* associated with drug trafficking. If, of the guerrillas of the 1950s it is possible to say they were moving in the direction of becoming real guerrillas, that is, social revolutionaries, of those today, one would have to say, in spite of the numerous guerrilla codes,[46] they are moving, in many respects, toward degradation or involution.[47]

A New Model of Counterinsurgency: The Privatization of the War

The Colombian Self-Defense groups held their first regional conference in 1994. Three years later, in June 1997, they celebrated their first national conference, and following the same patterns as the guerrillas, they established a full military and political strategy to defeat subversive forces. The Self-Defense groups have their own military commands, a radio station, a regular newspaper, uniforms, emblems, and a model to apply, "Puerto Boyacá." That was the first region from which the guerrillas were completely expelled in the late 1980s. The Self-Defense groups have achieved almost the same result in Urabá. In this bloody war against the guerrillas, the Self-

Defense groups were responsible for thirty-two of the fifty-five massacres that took place between October 1995 and September 1996; thirteen, in contrast, were attributed to the guerrillas. Authorship in the other ten cases was in doubt or unspecified.

The Self-Defense groups have multiple historical roots. These include the private armies that played an important role in the nineteenth-century civil wars, the various forms of private police that landowners used to counteract agrarian conflict at the beginning of this century, and, more clearly, the counterguerrilla groups of the two-party confrontation of the 1950s. But, strictly speaking, in their current configuration, the Self-Defense groups are a typical product of the well-known "national security" doctrine that spread all over Latin America during the 1970s and the 1980s as part of a worldwide strategy against Communism. In Colombia, the Self-Defense groups received initial support from associations of cattle ranchers and from the drug traffickers, who were the newest and some of the largest landowners in the country. With time and the collapse of Communism, the dynamic of the Self-Defense groups, as with the guerrillas, became less an ideological project and more a pragmatic one involving struggles for territory and resources. Most of their military operations today are retaliations against kidnapping, extortion, and cattle rustling.

As with the Violence of the 1950s, family vengeance is a central component in the initial phase of the Self-Defense groups. Following the assassination of his father by the FARC, the current chief of the Self-Defense groups, Carlos Castaño, set out at the beginning of the 1980s, along with various relatives, to retaliate in northeastern Antioquia. Theirs was "a private project to restore public order."[48] It could be said, evoking the terminology that circulated in Central America some years ago, that the Self-Defense groups are the contras of the Colombian guerrillas.

Applying the principle of "an eye for an eye, a tooth for a tooth," the Self-Defense groups kidnapped a certain number of relatives of the high guerrilla commanders in 1996 and forced others to go into exile. They did so, they said, so that the guerrillas could experience for themselves the horrendous and inhuman practice of kidnapping. Some of their captives were subsequently released to an international committee (composed of representatives of the International Red Cross, the Dutch NGO Pax Christi, and the Catholic Church). In freeing their captives, the Self-Defense groups stressed their respect for international humanitarian law, emphasizing, through this very gesture, their difference from the guerrillas.[49]

In some regions, in spite of the rejection of the citizenry and the warnings of the international human rights organizations, Self-Defense groups received a kind of legalization hidden under the rubric CONVIVIR (Cooperativas para la Vigilancia y la Seguridad Privada, created by Decree 356 of 1994). The CONVIVIR functionally resemble the Peruvian Rondas Campesinas, which contributed to the dismantling of the Sendero Luminoso (Shining Path), and the Guatemalan "civil patrols," which sowed terror in the past decade.[50] The Colombian Self-Defense groups boast of being the only effective contra-insurgent force, a clear allusion to the inefficiency or lack of resolve of the government armed forces. At the present time they are in transition from being simple death squads to becoming vehicles for the intensification of counterinsurgency—"the organized citizenry in arms," to borrow their own words.

The Self-Defense groups are gaining as political protagonists. They claim to be the real alternative to the Colombian guerrillas. They are assuming the traditional antisubversive role of the army. The army, as a consequence, is operating as a simple rear guard for this new politico-military force. This trend is clearly reflected in statistics on the different perpetrators of human rights violations. (The total of violations committed by State agents and paramilitary groups together has remained roughly the same. See Table below.)

Human Rights Violations: Percentage of Total Violations Attributed to Different Armed Actors, 1993–1996

Year	*State Agents*	*Paramilitary Groups*	*Total*	*Guerrilla Groups*
1993	54.26	17.91	72.17	27.48
1994	32.76	35.33	68.09	31.91
1995	15.68	46.03	61.71	38.29
1996	10.52	62.69	73.21	26.79

Source: Comisión Colombiana de Juristas, *Colombia, derechos humanos y derecho humanitario* (Bogotá, 1996), 7.

From the military point of view, the Self-Defense groups maintain that, unlike the army, which fights a conventional war against the guerrillas, theirs is an irregular war, since according to their manuals of military history, "There are no antecedents in history in which a regular army has defeated an irregular army. An irregular army is only deterred by an army of the same characteristics."[51]

As one can imagine, the impact of this new kind of confrontation on the civil population is overwhelming. It is estimated that in 1998 there were 194 massacres (collective assassinations of more than three people): 103 attributable to the guerrillas and 91 to Self-Defense groups.[52] Another indicator is *internal displacement*. Between 1985 and 1996, there were approximately 1 million displaced persons, the highest percentage of them (45 percent) from Antioquia, which is the department with the greatest number of massacres, followed by César (10 percent), Córdoba (8 percent), Santander (7 percent), Sucre (5 percent), and Caquetá (5 percent). The rhythm of growth is even more worrisome. In 1995 there were 89,510 newly displaced persons; in 1996 that number rose to 181,010, with 33 percent of those displacements attributable to the paramilitaries and 29 percent to the guerrillas; and in 1998 the number rose to 308,000, the most critical case being the petroleum city of Barrancabermeja. As noted previously, these figures indicate that today one in every forty Colombians has fled his/her region because of violence.[53] Displaced persons include peasants, union or political militants, human rights activists, indigenous and African-American minorities, and many others. Of these persons, 55 percent are under eighteen years old. They will provide the seed for future violence.

As one peasant told a human rights official, the dilemma is, "If we stay, they kill us; and if we go, they burn our farms." The gravity of the situation is such that a presidential council to deal with displaced persons has recently been created. The formation of this council is significant, but it is necessary to point out that, as in the case of rehabilitated guerrillas, government support can be interpreted by the inhabitants of receiving communities as unacceptable privileges for the displaced, and hence that support becomes a vehicle that creates new tensions and conflicts.[54]

There are also new political and military developments in these Self-Defense groups that are changing the nature of the war in Colombia. In political terms, the Self-Defense groups are showing much concern for their public image. Texts from their Third National Summit emphasize that the obstacles to the operative capacity of the armed forces created by human rights organizations had placed Self-Defense groups in "the vanguard of the struggle."[55] In the first issue of their journal *Colombia Libre*, in contrast, they gave precise instructions to their followers about the different aspects of international humanitarian law that could be applied to Colombia.[56] This stance cannot be taken very seriously from actors who continue committing massacres, contrary to their new discourse. Yet, in October 1997, they expelled from their national organization one of their southeastern regional fronts (in the deparment of Meta) because of its responsibility for the massacre of a judicial commission. And during the municipal and provincial elections that same month, they asked their rank and file to vote "yes" for the "Mandato Ciudadano por la Paz, la Vida y la Libertad" (Citizens' Mandate for Peace, Life, and Freedom). That plebiscite contained specific points related to international humanitarian law (an end to kidnapping and to the participation of civilians and children in the war) and a clear statement in favor of a peaceful resolution of the armed conflict. Self-Defense groups control common crime in their own zones, give long-term credit to some peasants, and, in some areas, are implementing their own agrarian reform.

In military terms, the Self-Defense groups' expansion is quite impressive. In a recent interview, their commander in chief, Carlos Castaño, noted that they have twenty fronts, each one ranging from one hundred to one hundred fifty men. Their immediate aim, he said, is to gain control from the guerrillas of the southern departments of Guaviare, Caquetá, and Putumayo. These departments supply the key source of income for the guerrillas: coca, which is grown mostly by small farmers with no realistic alternative for income. The strategic importance of these regions becomes evident if we take into consideration the fact that the drug trade, or exactions imposed on it, represent the primary source, roughly 50 percent, of the income of the FARC (the second most important source is kidnapping). At 20 percent, drugs represents the third most important source of income for the ELN (the first being extortion from oil companies, the second, kidnapping).[57] (These data show, incidentally, the growing diversification of the guerrillas' financial resources.)

At present, part of this strategic territory, five *municipios* of the southern departments of Caquetá and Meta (La Macarena, Mesetas, San Vicente del Caguán, La Uribe, and Vista Hermosa, with a total area of 41,000 square kilometers and a very low density of population, approximately 100,000 inhabitants in all), are a "cleared zone." "Cleared" means the total withdrawal of government armed forces from that area, which has become the geographical locus of the peace negotiations between the government of President Andrés Pastrana and the FARC guerrillas commanded by the legendary "Tirofijo" (Sure-shot) Manuel Marulanda Vélez. Marulanda Vélez has been in the Colombian mountains since 1949, a fact which underscores the continuity between the old Violence of the 1950s and the violence of today.

For all these reasons, the Colombian Self-Defense groups represent the first counterinsurgency project with a national projection. They are today in a good position to obtain some form of political recognition, which would enable them to have a say in a future negotiating process along the lines of the principle, already accepted by former President Ernesto Samper, of "one single process, two negotiating tables." The struggle over what exactly this means, which has not been clearly defined by the current President, Andrés

Pastrana, could stall the peace process. This is because, just as the FARC demands as a condition of going forward unequivocal proof that the government is committed to dismantling the Self-Defense groups, the Self-Defense groups, in turn, demand as a condition for not sabotaging that process, that they be accorded the status of politico-military actors on a par with the guerrillas. The kidnapping, in May 1999, of the prestigious Liberal senator, Piedad Córdoba, by Carlos Castaño's Self-Defense groups was in protest to what they called "Liberal party guerrilla diplomacy." This occurred at a moment when the discontent of the military and other sectors over the decision to prolong the "cleared zone" was mounting. Many considered that decision a simple abandonment of sovereignty without concessions on the part of the guerrillas. It appeared that the government had lost the initiative in determining the central points of the agenda of negotiation. The headline of one of the major newspapers in the nation was "Peace Process Kidnapped."

Significantly enough, both guerrillas and Self-Defense groups explain their origins in almost identical terms: the incapacity of the State to fulfill specific economic, social, and cultural obligations in the case of the guerrillas, and, in the case of the paramilitaries, the State's inability to carry out the essential function of the modern nation, that of guaranteeing public security with reference to the life, property, and freedom of all citizens. Here we have in a nutshell the nature of the Colombian crisis: two opposing rivals, against an absent enemy, the State. The State is neither a social regulator, nor a guardian of order. The war has entered into an accelerated process of privatization with the consequent delegitimization of the State and of public institutions.

Partial Peace, Protracted War: The Changing Models of Negotiation

One of the most surprising features of the endemic violence in Colombia is that it has been accompanied by a permanent (indefinite) process of negotiation since the 1980s. After the first, inconclusive, negotiations that took place during the administration of President Belisario Betancur between 1982 and 1986, peace agreements have been signed with different groups: in 1990 with the M-19; in 1991 with the EPL (Ejército Popular de Liberación), the PRT (Partido Revolucionario de los Trabajadores), and Quintín Lame; and in 1994 with the CRS (Corriente de Renovación Socialista). This *model of negotiation*, of dealing with guerrilla groups one by one, yields a very peculiar image of Colombia because it can be presented simultaneously as an example of successful negotiation, as it was to some extent during the first year of Betancur's administration, or as a counter-example of a never-ending conflict.[58] *Doses of peace seem to equal programmed war.* Partial negotiations, the Colombian experience seems to indicate, do not arrest the magnitude of the overall conflict, but simply serve as space for the repositioning of the principal actors in the war.[59] Moreover, the demonstrable tendency or norm is that after every negotiation, new divisions and radicalizations are produced.

The government model has reasonable grounds: Negotiate first with those who want to negotiate, take into account the diverse nature of rebel groups, and so on. However, this pragmatic approach involves a major problem because the interests of peace and of war clash at every turn. The transition from armed conflict to civilian life and permanent peace requires, in effect, a mutually agreed upon definition of several security matters. These include the purging of undesirable elements from the army, as well as reconsideration of its budget and size, the incorporation of former combatants into the State's armed apparatus, and last but not least, the reconsideration of the role of the military in relation to politics. With all their many complexities, this has been the route in the peace agreements in El Salvador and Guatemala.

In Colombia, on the contrary, with its model of partial and unconnected negotiations, the necessary adjustments are much more unpredictable. If one accepts peace, one accepts State authority, in other words, the legitimate monopoly of force by the State. And if one becomes part of the State, of the existing system, one also becomes a military target for those who remain at war, sometimes one's own former fellow-guerrillas. And this is exactly what has happened. One of the groups incorporated into political life, Paz y Libertad, formerly of the EPL, reported that, between 1991 and 1994, 274 of its comrades had been assassinated, most of them, not by the army or by paramilitary groups, but by the remaining guerrilla groups in their original strongholds, Córdoba and Urabá. If we add to this the fact that entities of the State often work at cross-purposes, some aiding the mediation process while others, simultaneously, playing a repressive role (even to the point of assassinating negotiators or intermediaries), we begin to understand the exposure and orphaned state of the parties involved in negotiated solutions. But even accepting the model of negotiation that was put into practice with these groups, one should not forget that, in the end, the State, as well as the community that receives the ex-guerrillas, has been profoundly affected by the war and for that reason reinsertion must be carefully prepared.

The logic of a fragmented peace is that the space left open by one of the actors is immediately taken over by another with an even more radical discourse, which appropriates the name of the group, its banners, insignia, programs, norms, symbols. Instead of being a process of cumulative peace, fragmented negotiation becomes a process of reproduced violence. Fragmented peace is continuous war. The only effective negotiation, it appears, is overall negotiation, negotiation that involves all groups simultaneously.

On the other hand, the transition from life as a combatant, with its rigidities and hierarchies, to life as a civilian, where one must consider and weigh decisions and actions, is very complex, not only in political terms but also in personal terms. While one is in a collective guerrilla community, according to a psychoanalytic study, "the engagement with history erase[s] family obligations and places individual concerns on a secondary plane." Now, with the return to individualist society, "for the ex-combatant it is almost unbearable to think that from now on his or her life will be dedicated to solving such banal problems as grocery shopping, or paying the rent, or school tuition."[60] Detachment from the guerrilla collective is accompanied by a fundamental change in daily referents that often makes past guerrilla experience look useless in the context of the new forms of political, social, and cultural organization in which ex-guerrillas find themselves. Even the image of being "rehabilitated" or "beneficiaries" of governmental programs transforms people into, as one of them would say, "victims of the peace," that is, into passive stigmatized subjects, instead of proponents of peace.[61] History repeated itself in the negotiations of the M-19, the EPL, and the other groups. Simple political reinsertion was privileged in these agreements; social reinsertion was relegated to a secondary place.

By taking into account a number of factors, it is possible to understand why so many former combatants miss their old guerrilla lifestyle and are nostalgic about the collective feeling of security, power, and belonging that they experienced in their underground activities. Many see their return to civilian life as a loss of identity, income, and prestige because not infrequently society resists full reincorporation of ex-guerrillas into professional, economic, and social life.[62] There is deliberate or unconscious marginalization of ex-guerrillas in the representative bodies such as Congress and municipal councils. Traditional regional *caciques* (political bosses) often oppose the fulfillment of government promises that guarantee political representation for ex-guerrillas irrespective of their electoral force. The authorities continually fear, whether justifiably or not, that demobilized people serve as a cover for still-active groups, obtain legal benefits (such as pardons) for former comrades, or win economic benefits (such as loans or subsidies) for them. They believe that political favors should be available only to those who have expressly declared their desire for "reinsertion." On top of all this there are the conceptual and operational limitations of the Peace Fund.

The worst that can happen to a peace process is that its participants perceive it as a simple confiscation of arms, a repudiation of their ideals, or as having more disadvantages than advantages. In that case, the peace process is perceived by ex-insurgents as a failure instead of being viewed as an opportunity for shaping new forms of social, cultural, and political relations, an opportunity to transform old ideals. A quick review of what has been happening in the way of productive projects, land distribution, housing, and secondary and university education for the former cadres and militants reveals that these programs fall far short of the need for such aid. The obvious temptation for former guerrillas is to take up arms again or, worse yet, to follow the path of common delinquency.

All of this invites thought on the ambivalences of the reintegration of ex-combatants as individuals. In one sense reintegration, by definition, integrates; but in another, it simply disperses and uproots. Reintegrated persons suffer a real ideological dismembering through their treatment by the State, since it treats ex-combatants separately as individual political and social actors.

Serious negotiations, as Malcolm Deas has observed,[63] must take into account material issues, such as the resources, organization, experience, arms, and zones of influence of the guerrillas, as well as the symbolic capital they have accumulated through having totally opposed the status quo for decades. That capital derives from their having been the potential avengers of abuses and arbitrariness and the originators or promoters of significant institutional changes. I think what is needed is a balance between the social debt of society to the guerrillas and the historical debt of the guerrillas to society.[64] It is possible to indicate in a general way what such a balance might entail, but its basic terms must arise from the negotiating process itself.

Looking back on the most recent peace processes, it is clear that the ex-guerrillas have left an important mark, codified in the Constitution of 1991, that included the gestation of new rights, the structuring of a new institution aimed at fostering greater democracy and participation, and the recognition of new political-cultural identities.[65] However, from another point of view, those processes have not led to very encouraging outcomes. The M-19, after having played a decisive role as the third force in the Constitutional Assembly of 1991 and after having won considerable congressional representation, was co-opted in practice and made politically invisible. Following a traumatic reinsertion that did not permit it to cut its own political figure, the EPL followed a path of disintegration and denaturalization; many of its contingents were then incorporated into paramilitary forces. The CRS, a minor force in Congress, has practically been made invisible.

To pass from being a contestatory force to one that is a cocreator of public policy is a shift that requires maturation and preparation. Moreover, it is a shift that requires, in addition to the efforts of newly reinserted citizens, the commitment of society and the State to give the process a sense of collective construction.

Thus has arisen the demand for change in the model for negotiations. In effect, in the last ten years there has been a change from a model of individual reincorporation of ex-guerrillas (as happened as well in the Violence of the 1950s and 1960s) to the rehabilitation of "zones of violence" and the reintegration of whole political or ethnic communities. The latter was the approach during the Barco (1986–1990) and the Gaviria administrations (1990–1994). Finally, we have today's proposal, the definition of a new social-political pact, not just for the insurgent forces, but also for society as a whole. The long process of negotiations, with its ups and downs, has led in the last two decades to the demystification of the guerrillas. But it has also led to a growing devaluation of the discourse of peace. This leads us to raise a final and crucial question: How to make peace desirable?

Repoliticization, "Denarcoticization," and Depolarization: The Key Questions Today

Before supplying elements of the answer to this question, one must insist on the necessity of continual efforts at repoliticization of the conflict, not only on the part of civil society, but also on the part of the government itself. One must not forget that in Colombia, time marches against the interests of an overall settlement. The previously noted contradiction between the military and territorial expansion of the guerrillas and their loss of political space in some zones, the decline of ideological commitment among many guerrilla groups, and the growing evidence of banditry and "lumpenization" among others are all disturbing signs. It would not be useful to the guerrillas, or to the country, to suddenly have, instead of ten thousand guerrillas, twenty thousand bandits in addition to drug traffickers, paramilitaries, and common delinquents. One or two thousand bandits constituted a sufficiently large trauma for the still-rural Colombia of the early 1970s, a fact we should not forget when examining the course of current events in the largely urban Colombia of today.[66]

Outside their own zones of control (as was also the case in the violence of the past), the Colombian guerrillas increasingly resort to practices that contradict their discourse. This is most evident in their terrorist operations and in the massacres carried out against the social bases of their presumed or real adversaries. In contrast, inside their own zones (in a kind of spatial rationalization of the exercise of violence, which may obey a purely defensive logic and be implemented through openly autocratic means), the guerrillas have codes that impose severe limits on common delinquency. Such delinquency, of course, threatens their goal of completely monopolizing the use of force.[67] Once their initial penetration of peasant communities is complete, the police are dislodged, and the population is subordinated to their designs, the next phase is that of political consolidation. Political consolidation involves the control of local power and eventually of municipal resources. This is a process that one analyst, parodying the institutional processes of political decentralization, has termed "armed decentralization."[68] Breaking down hostility, forging consensus, and achieving collaboration appear to be the three phases of this relationship. One author has described it as a transition from a predatory to a parasitic and then to a symbiotic relationship.[69]

The question of how to make peace desirable is one of the principal issues today because of the fact that today's guerrilla groups are not the rural poor that they might well have been in the 1960s. (The costs of war and the profitability of peace are two of the newest terms incorporated into the Colombian political lexicon.) If the core of the negotiations in the past has been political (new constitutions included), the core of the future negotiations must be social. The scope of the concessions that would have to be made, given the power and the territorial coverage of the guerrillas today, are still unpredictable. There are, however, some obvious issues. These include conditions for the expropriation of lands held by drug traffickers and the alternative ways such lands might be redistributed or made productive; the questions of social investment in the new oil-producing areas and new terms of negotiation with oil multinationals; and the issue of certain forms of territorial autonomy. All these issues require more tangible reforms than the abstract principles of a new national constitution. Moreover, as proposed in 1993 by the FARC in their "Platform for Reconciliation and Reconstruction," there needs to be a social, not military, handling of the production, consumption, and commercialization of drugs. We need a drug policy that aims at avoiding illicit crops not through repression and terror, nor through the ecological catastrophe of aerial fumigation and eradication, as the U.S. authorities obstinately insist on. We need a drug policy based on the formulation and financing of programs of alternative development for the coca and poppy cultivators in the regions involved. We need to make a clear distinction between the affairs and interests of the drug traffickers and the social background of the peasant production zones. With or without the insurgency, for the small farmers of these regions the cultivation of the primary material for drugs is a necessity. This is true particularly in the regions of recent settlement such as Meta in the southeast, and in Guaviare, Caquetá, and Putumayo in the Colombian Amazon. Given the decisive presence of the insurgency in these zones, the guerrillas could become, for the international community and especially for the United States, the true guarantors of a lasting solution to the cultivation of mind-altering drugs.[70]

All this suggests a growing interaction of all topics related to drug traffickers with those related to guerrillas. This is what has been called the "narcoticization" of the peace process and of the relations of Colombia with the United States. In effect, with the centrality of the drug theme, which acts as a substitute for the ideological enemy that collapsed with the Berlin Wall, the Colombian conflict has advanced to the upper level of U.S. preoccupations. The key issue in the dilemma facing Washington is whether to pressure for negotiation or create legitimacy for some type of intervention. What will be the U.S. strategy?

The guiding principles of the present Colombian government in peace negotiations are the following:

1) *Recognition of the political character of the guerrillas.* This means to accept, first, that in spite of their many condemned actions, the guerrillas are not simple bandits, terrorists, or narcoguerrillas, that they are instead rebels with an ideology, resources, and specific aims that are contrary to the existing order. In other words, at least in theoretical terms and in contrast to the mafias, they accumulate resources and power with a collective pretext. Second, this recognition implies the acceptance of the impossibility of a military victory and, therefore, the need for a *negotiated settlement.* President Pastrana provided the most persuasive recognition of the political character of the guerrillas, first as a presidential candidate and later as acting president, when twice he personally met with the foremost leader of the FARC in the Colombian mountains.

Such changes are not always based on principles; they express the changing relations between the rebel forces and the State. Between 1990 and 1992, after the fall of the Berlin Wall and the end of the Cold War, official expectations were that the guerrillas would experience reduced capacity in the years to come. Nevertheless, the degree of financial autonomy that the guerrillas reached with respect to external sources of support and the tremendous threat that international drug policies based on eradication represented for large parts of the Colombian peasantry provided the guerrillas with new and unexpected bases of social support and political legitimacy. (This occurred despite the general deterioration of political legitimacy noted in other parts of this essay.) The model for negotiation with these guerrillas could not be that of individual reinsertion and atomization. There now appears to be a clear consensus on this point. Models of social and political development and territorial power will be key elements in negotiations from now on.

2) *Application of international humanitarian law.* This means recognition of the practical matter that even if the conflict is insoluble, it has to be "civilized," submitted to the minimal historical rules of war. This includes many matters we have referred to in this essay, such as kidnapping, forced disappearances, treatment of prisoners, recruitment of children, and protection of women caught up in the crossfire, prohibition of any use of antipersonnel mines, and so on. This is perhaps, after drugs, the aspect in which a greater and growing international vigilance over the Colombian political process is observable. It is a question that hinges on the necessity of military reform so that repressive action is once again contained within the boundaries of national and international legislation.

Although we are talking about norms that are continually violated, they nevertheless operate like an ethical horizon for the war and as universal precepts whose acceptance or rejection helps define the level of international legitimacy and the nature of other international dimensions of the conflict. Levels of human rights abuses help determine whether we are talking about *international mediation or humanitarian intervention*, whether we are dealing with international pressures or with multinational military intervention.

3) *Negotiation amid war.* This principle was accepted as an appropriate assumption in the agenda, and it has led to an emphasis on certain rituals that can be seen as generating signs of confidence in the solidity of the negotiations. For society, what would be most desirable is a truce, the suspension of armed operations, while the parties make progress at the negotiating table. Yet the notion of negotiating while the war goes on is simply the realistic acceptance of the dynamics between war and politics (war as a continuation of politics, politics as a continuation of war by other means), as defined by Clausewitz during the Napoleonic Wars.

4) *Participation of civil society.* This is probably the element that is most important for Colombia today. In contrast to its passivity toward the previous processes of negotiation, today civil society is very active in the peace

process. It generates proposals, tries to mediate, seeks to create a favorable climate for negotiation, and constitutes a force able to sustain eventual agreements. Examples of this new attitude can be found in the Church, which sees the struggle as a way to restore lost ties with its social bases; among industrialists—and private businesspeople in general—who are increasingly being forced to recognize that sooner or later they will have to negotiate fundamental aspects of the economic model; and among the trade unionists, members of the new social movements, and the NGOs who will have to demonstrate to the armed actors the worth of political action to depolarize the conflict. The immediate future depends very much on the degree of autonomy that civil society can preserve in the face of the armed factions. In any case, it is recognized that the content and itinerary of the negotiations, now that so many democratic demands have been placed on the table, is not an exclusive affair of the political and guerrilla elite. The huge marches against kidnapping around the country, which have unified social extremes at the local, regional, and national levels, are a clear indication of the eruption or rebirth of public opinion, blocked for many years by narcoterrorism,[71] and of the awakening of a civil society that wishes to play a central role in the drama of war and peace in Colombia. The Network of Initiatives for Peace, the National Commission for the Reconciliation, and the Citizens' Mandate for Peace, among other organizations, are part of this large cast of actors who hope to play their own roles in the negotiations.

Great expectations reign today in Colombia and in its neighboring countries concerning the direction of U.S. policies with respect to the situation of the nation in coming years. In fact, the United States is increasingly involving itself, and in multiple forms, in the Colombian conflict. Colombia is today the third largest recipient of U.S. military aid, after Israel and Egypt. For many Colombians, events such as the recent crash of a U.S. spy plane during an antinarcotics mission over rebel-held territory prove that Washington is already deeply implicated in our internal war.

Depending on the international developments we have analyzed and the type of international pressures exerted on Colombia, it would seem that the conflict will take one of the two following roads: either there will be further polarization between guerrillas and Self-Defense groups, or there will be a growing mediating role for civic and international organizations, which Juan Gabriel Tokatlián has called a "citizens' diplomacy" for peace.[72] In any case, it seems clear that the present situation is untenable in the long run.

But, and this is the main conclusion that should be drawn from what I have presented here, Colombia's central problem today cannot be reduced to peace, understood as a simple end to hostilities. The basic problem, as many studies have noted,[73] is that of democracy, which goes far beyond the guerrilla-State agenda. In addition to the themes already outlined, we would have to consider others that aim at a reconfiguration of the relations of power, a basic reorientation of public investment, an agrarian reform that satisfies the long-delayed needs of peasants, a widening of political space, new relationships between geographical peripheries and the central government. In sum, it will be necessary to think of ways to construct a national agreement that permits a redefinition of the country as a new *consensual political community*. Given these conditions, Colombia is perhaps the Latin American country with the greatest responsibilities as it enters the twenty-first century. The outcome concerns not only Colombia, but the international community as well.

Notes

1. María Teresa Uribe's essays are pertinent to this theme. See especially "Antioquia: Entre la guerra y la paz," *Estudios Políticos* 10 (January–June 1997): 126–37.

2. Ciro Krauthausen, *Padrinos y mercaderes. Crimen organizado en Italia y Colombia* (Bogotá, 1998).

3. María Teresa Uribe, "La reinserción en Urabá, un proceso inconcluso," in Cecilia Isaza, ed., *Los caminos entre la guerra y la paz: La reinserción* (Bogotá, 1993), 29–37.

4. See, among others, William Ramírez Tobón, *Urabá: Los inciertos confines de una crisis* (Bogotá, 1997).

5. Maria Teresa Uribe, *Limpiar la tierra: Guerra y poder entre los esmeralderos* (Bogotá, 1992).

6. Nazih Richani, "The Political Economy of Violence: The War-System in Colombia," *Journal of Interamerican Studies and World Affairs* 39, no. 2 (Summer 1997): 37–81.

7. These relations are questioned or are treated differently in Fernando Gaitán Daza's essay in Malcolm Deas and Fernando Gaitán, *Dos ensayos especulativos sobre la violencia en Colombia* (Bogotá, 1995).

8. Camilo Echandía, "Expansión territorial de las guerrillas colombianas: Geografía, economía, violencia," in Malcolm Deas and María Victoria Llorente, comps., *Reconocer la guerra para construir la paz* (Bogotá, 1999), 101, and passim. See also Jesús Antonio Bejarano, Camilo Echandía, Rodolfo Escobedo, and Enrique León Queruz, *Colombia: Inseguridad, violencia y desempeño económico en las áreas rurales* (Bogotá, 1997), 135–36.

9. Yvon Lebot, *La guerra en tierras mayas: Comunidad, violencia y modernidad en Guatemala, 1970–1992* (Mexico City, 1995); Carlos Iván Degregori et al., *Las rondas campesinas y la derrota de Sendero Luminoso* (Lima, 1996).

10. This guerrilla expansion is not only indifferent to rising rates of common crime outside its own territories, but the guerrillas do not even try to differentiate themselves from it, so long as it is functional to guerrilla growth. What is more, frequently the guerrillas subordinate common crime to their own strategies, incurring an ethical and political cost that will only be appreciated with time. Guerrillas with a vision of the future should now be

thinking of the problems of reconstruction, the problems of violence after the conflict is over, and assimilating the lessons of El Salvador and Guatemala where one of the most typical and preoccupying characteristics of the postwar situation is the alarming growth of common criminality, which has blocked the implementation of the peace accords and may even destabilize the peace process.

11. Alonso Salazar J., *No nacimos pa' semilla* (Bogotá, 1990). See also Carlos Miguel Ortiz Sarmiento, "El sicariato en Medellín: Entre la violencia política y el crimen organizado," *Análisis Político* 14 (September–December 1991): 60–73; and Arturo Alape, *Ciudad Bolívar: La hoguera de las ilusiones* (Bogotá, 1995).

12. Luisa Stannow, "Social Cleansing in Colombia" (Master's thesis, Simon Fraser University, British Columbia, Canada, 1996). A systematic purge of police organizations was initiated only in the mid-1990s: Between 1995 and 1997, 5,044 police of all ranks (353 officials, 517 subofficials, 647 of other nonspecified levels, and 3,527 agents) had been separated from the institution for various reasons. This translated into a notable change in public perception of the police. See María Victoria Llorente, "Perfil de la policía colombiana," in Deas and Llorente, *Reconocer la guerra para construir la paz,* 393. This same study observes (548) that in the last decade an average of 329 police officers have died in the line of duty each year, which places them among the principal victims of violence.

13. I am extrapolating here from the title of the interesting book by Soledad Niño Torres, César Rozo Montejo, and Leonardo A. Vega U. concerning the cultural production of fear, *Territorios del miedo en Santafé de Bogotá: Imaginarios de los ciudadanos* (Bogotá, 1998).

14. Alonso Salazar J. and Ana María Jaramillo, *Medellín: Las subculturas del narcotráfico* (Bogotá, 1992), 89. See also Ana María Jaramillo Arbeláez, Ramiro J. Ceballos Melguizo, and María Inés Villa Martínez, *En la encrucijada: Conflicto y cultura política en el Medellín de los noventas* (Medellín, 1998), 70.

15. Alonso Salazar J., *Mujeres de fuego* (Medellín, 1993).

16. Alonso Salazar J., *No nacimos pa' semilla,* 200.

17. Julie Taylor, "Aides' Memoirs and Collective Amnesia in the Wake of the Argentine Terror," in Michael Ryan, ed., *The Body Politic* (Boulder, CO, 1993), 192–203.

18. Mauricio Reina, "La mano invisible: Narcotráfico, economía y crisis," in Francisco Leal, ed., *Tras las huellas de la crisis política* (Bogotá, 1996), 153–79. See also Chapter 3 herein and the study by Jesús Antonio Bejarano et al., *Colombia: Inseguridad, violencia y desempeño económico.*

19. Comisión de Estudios sobre la Violencia, *Colombia: Violencia y democracia* (Bogotá, 1987; 4th ed., 1995). The author was the coordinator of this commission, comprised of nine academics and a retired army general. Part of that report is reproduced as Chapter 12 of *Violence in Colombia* (Wilmington, DE, 1992).

20. The most sophisticated work in this last perspective and a true manifesto against impunity is that of Mauricio Rubio, *Crímen e impunidad: Precisiones sobre la violencia* (Bogotá, 1999). For a severe criticism of that work, see Francisco Gutiérrez, "Imprecisiones sobre la Violencia," *Revista de Ciencias Sociales* 3 (1999): 133–36.

21. For these and other figures, see Saúl Franco, *El Quinto: No matar: Contextos explicativos de la violencia en Colombia* (Bogotá, 1999), 82, and passim. See also the Appendix to this volume. In certain moments and regions the figures are truly alarming. For example, according to Franco's study, in Antioquia in 1994, a rate of 1,044 homicides per 100,000 inhabitants was registered for men twenty to twenty-four years old, that is to say, one of every one hundred male Antioqueños within this age range was assassinated. Upon comparing the

total of deaths in the country with the total of homicides, Franco concludes that "more than half of adolescent men who died in 1994 in the country were victims of homicides" (93).

22. For Medellín, see Alvaro Camacho and Alvaro Guzmán, "La violencia urbana en Colombia: Teorías, modalidades, perspectivas," in Alvaro Camacho et al., *Nuevas visiones sobre la violencia en Colombia* (Bogotá, 1997). See also Alonso Salazar J. and Ana María Jaramillo, *Medellín*, 80.

23. Mauricio Rubio, *Crímen e impunidad*, 175.

24. Saúl Franco, *El Quinto*, 11. See also Mauricio Rubio, *Crímen e impunidad.*

25. The expression is from Diego Pérez Guzmán and Marco Raúl Mejía, *De calles, parches, galladas y escuelas* (Bogotá, 1996), 171.

26. Alonso Salazar J., *No nacimos pa' semilla*, 180.

27. Alvaro Camacho Guizado and Alvaro Guzmán Varney, "La violencia urbana en Colombia: Teorías, modalidades y perspectivas." Paper presented in the seminar "Violencia, terrorismo y secuestro," organized by the program La Casa, Universidad de los Andes, Bogotá, March 20–21, 1996.

28. Yi-fu Tuan, *Landscapes of Fear* (New York, 1979).

29. I take this formula from María Teresa Uribe and use it out of context. See "La negociación de los conflictos en las viejas y nuevas sociabilidades," in Bonaventura de Sousa Santos et al., eds., *Conflicto y contexto: Resolución alternativa de conflictos y contexto social* (Bogotá, 1977), 168.

30. Daniel Pecaut, "Presente, pasado y futuro de la Violencia," *Análisis Político* 30 (January–April 1997): 3.

31. Data developed by Camilo Echandía and reproduced in *El Tiempo*, July 9, 1995.

32. Herbert Braun, *Our Guerrillas, Our Sidewalks: A Journey into the Violence of Colombia* (Niwot, CO, 1994), 24.

33. Jesús Antonio Bejarano et al., *Colombia: Inseguridad*, 35.

34. Ricardo Vargas Meza, *Drogas, máscaras y juegos: Narcotráfico y conflicto armado en Colombia* (Bogotá, 1999), 47.

35. Henry A. Kissinger, "The Vietnam Negotiations," *Foreign Affairs* 47, no. 2 (January 1969): 214, cited in I. William Zartman, ed., *Elusive Peace: Negotiating an End to Civil Wars* (Washington, DC, 1995), 9.

36. *El Tiempo*, September 13, 1996.

37. National Police, Republic of Colombia, *Criminalidad 1998* 41 (Bogotá, 1999): 55.

38. Sandra Afanador Cuevas et al., eds., *Rostros del secuestro* (Bogotá, 1994), 19. In this text it is claimed that someone is kidnapped every five hours in Colombia.

39. See, for example, Mark Turner, "Kidnapping and Politics," *International Journal of the Sociology of Law* 26, no. 2 (June 1998): 145–60. Colombian law identifies three modalities of kidnapping: political, extortive, and terrorist.

40. Gabriel García Márquez, *Noticia de un secuestro* (Bogotá, 1996). The English translation was published in 1997.

41. See the multiauthored book, *Rostros del secuestro*, 98.

42. Ibid., 316. This account is by the psychologist Cecilia Gerlein.

43. Emilio Meluk, *El secuestro: Una muerte suspendida: Su impacto psicológico* (Bogotá, 1998).

44. Alonso Salazar J., *No nacimos pa' semilla*, 86–87.

45. Ana María Jaramillo, "Criminalidad y violencias en Medellín, 1948–1990," in Jorge Orlando Melo, ed., *Historia de Medellín*, 2 vols. (Medellín, 1995), 1:556.

46. The historian Mario Aguilera is currently engaged in an innovative study of "insurgent justice."

47. This is one of the central theses of my book *Guerra y política en la sociedad colombiana* (Bogotá, 1991). In part this was the trajectory of the Philippine rebels, the Huks, who barricaded themselves in the mountains after World War II and were confronted by the government with a mix of authoritarianism first, and agrarian reform next at the end of the 1950s. Later they entered into a process of involution that by the mid-1970s had definitively placed them outside the political spectrum, to be replaced by modern guerrillas. The partial success of the Philippine government had some echo in Colombia in the so-called plans of rehabilitation at the beginning of the National Front, the bipartisan accord that marked a formal end to the Violence.

48. William Ramírez Tobón, *Urabá*, 139.

49. *El Tiempo*, March 29, 1997. One recalls that, under the Argentine dictatorship and the "Dirty War" of 1976–1983, kidnapping-disappearance-torture (in their double dimensions as punitive and as judicial-investigative instruments) were the characteristic traits of operations by police organizations and the paramilitary groups.

50. In October of 1997, and on the eve of a decision of the Constitutional Court concerning the juridical status of CONVIVIR, it was estimated that there was a total of 414 such associations with an approximate membership of 3,531 (*El Tiempo*, October 29, 1997). The journalist and political scientist Hernando Gómez Buendía has defined with precision the dilemmas of these organizations: "The associations of rural vigilance are useless if they respect the Constitution, and if they are useful they violate it. . . . The CONVIVIR exist only because the State is not capable of controlling armed groups; but their legality depends on the State's ability to control them as an armed group" (*El Tiempo*, September 9, 1997). The ruling of the Constitutional Court that supported their legality by the narrow margin of 5 to 4 reflects the uncertainties concerning their legality and the ambivalence and division of Colombian society in general over them (see *El Tiempo*, November 7 and 8, 1997).

51. *El Tiempo*, September 28, 1997.

52. Vicepresidencia de la República de Colombia, Observatorio de los Derechos Humanos en Colombia, *Boletín* 1 (June 1999): 6.

53. *El Tiempo*, March 14, 1997, according to data published by the Consultoría para los Derechos Humanos y el Desplazamiento (CODHES) and the United Nations Children's Fund (UNICEF).

54. *El Tiempo*, July 27, 1997.

55. "III Cumbre Nacional Movimiento Autodefensas Unidas de Colombia" (mimeographed pamphlet, no date or place).

56. *Colombia Libre* (Autodefensas Unidas de Colombia, AUC) 1 (July 1997): 12–14. In clear contrast to the most shocking guerrilla practices, the other themes of great prominence in the first number of this publication of the Self-Defense groups were: "The Crime of Kidnapping," by the AUC Commission of Public Affairs; "We Accuse: Violation of Human Rights," by the AUC Commission for Human Rights, which includes instructions concerning the treatment of the civil population and condemns the inhumane use of children in war; and "Let's Be Green: Preservation of the Environment," by the AUC Commission of Environmental Affairs, which includes a plan to fight dynamite attacks on petroleum pipelines and refineries and the cutting of forests in national parks.

57. Consejería Presidencial de Seguridad y Defensa Nacional, cited in Richani, "The Political Economy of Violence," 46.

58. A useful presentation of the Colombian case within the framework of conflict-resolution theory is that of Jonathan Hartlyn, "Civil Violence and Conflict Resolution: The Case of Colombia," in Roy Licklider, ed., *Stop the Killing: How Civil Wars End* (New York, 1993), 37–61.

59. Comisión de Superación de la Violencia, *Pacificar la paz* (Bogotá, 1991). This commission was coordinated by Alejandro Reyes Posada.

60. Observation by the psychoanalyst Javier Jaramillo Giraldo, in his Prologue to the interesting book by María Clemencia Castro and Carmen Lucía Díaz, *Guerrilla, reinserción y lazo social* (Bogotá, 1997), iii.

61. Ildefonso Henao, "Reconstrucción del imaginario de proyecto de vida en la reincorporación social del guerrillero: El poder de lo simbólico," in *Guerrilla, reinserción y lazo social*, 110.

62. The following appears in a recent edition of the magazine *Alternativa*: "The reaction of Colombians [to the accords] has been contradictory. In spite of applauding the peace processes, ample sectors of the population criticize the government on the grounds that millions of Colombians are in equal or worse condition than the ex-combatants but nevertheless receive no help or attention by the State." What is more, according to Tomás Concha (the General Coordinator of the Rehabilitation Program), "they ask me, how many years does one have to be a guerrilla or what does one have to do to get access to what they have?"

63. Malcolm Deas and Fernando Gaitán Daza, *Dos ensayos especulativos*, 73, and passim.

64. See my Prologue to the second edition of Alvaro Villarraga S. and Nelson Plazas N., *Para reconstruir los sueños. Una historia del EPL* (Bogotá, 1995). The book presents the memoirs of two ex-combatants.

65. María Emma Wills, "Las políticas gubernamentales frente al proceso de paz: Entre el peso del pasado y un futuro incierto," in Elizabeth Ungar, ed., *Gobernabilidad en Colombia* (Bogotá, 1993).

66. For a broader version of this theme see Gonzalo Sánchez and Donny Meertens, *Bandoleros, gamonales y campesinos* (Bogotá, 1993).

67. The FARC has turned to terrorism, especially in Urabá and Córdoba, zones where the paramilitaries have systematically been expelling them, and, more recently, they have been using terrorism in other regions of the north and south of the country. Political analysts such as Alfredo Rangel have highlighted the tendency of the Colombian guerrillas to utilize methods typical of the ETA (Euskadi Ta Askatasuna), as well as those of Pablo Escobar during the epoch of narcoterrorism. See, for example, *El Tiempo*, March 2 and 23, 1997.

68. Alfredo Rangel Suárez, "Las FARC-EP: Una mirada actual," in Deas and Llorente, *Reconstruir la guerra*, 43.

69. R. T. Naylor, "The Insurgent Economy: Black Market Operations of Guerrilla Organizations," cited in Rangel Suárez, "Las FARC-EP," 44.

70. Ricardo Vargas Meza, *Drogas, máscaras y juegos*, 49.

71. Daniel Pecaut, "Estrategias de paz en un contexto de diversidad de actores y factores de violencia," in Francisco Leal Buitrago, ed., *Los laberintos de la guerra: Utopías e incertidumbres sobre la paz* (Bogotá, 1999), 203.

72. *El Tiempo*, September 13, 1999.

73. A recent example of this type of study is the essay by Marco Palacios, "Agenda para la democracia y negociación con las guerrillas," in Leal Buitrago, ed., *Los laberintos de la guerra*, 59–107.

Chapter 2

Violence, Power, and Collective Action
A Comparison between Bolivia and Colombia

Rodrigo Uprimny Yepes

One of the limitations of studies of the violence in Colombia—a limitation common to country-specific studies in general, be they of Colombia, the United States, or any other country—is that they rarely place their subject in comparative context. Comparison can have the virtue of demonstrating that what we take for granted in interpreting one country's history is in fact problematic. In the essay that follows, Rodrigo Uprimny shows how comparison can help us to clarify the causes of the violence that has characterized Colombian history since the mid-twentieth century. By comparing the histories of Colombia and its Andean neighbor Bolivia, Uprimny argues that the violence in Colombia cannot be explained as a simple function of poverty, social fragmentation, or the drug trade. Instead, he contends, Colombia's violence seems to be a result of several other factors, central among them the inability of working people to develop powerful collective organizations able to transfer social demands into the political arena. That inability, in turn, helps to explain the enduring power of Colombia's two traditional parties, a feature of the nation's politics emphasized in virtually all the chapters in this book.

Rodrigo Uprimny is a lawyer and professor in the Faculty of Law at the National University of Colombia in Bogotá. He has published several studies on human rights, violence, and the judicial system in Colombia, including *La dialéctica de los derechos humanos en Colombia* (Bogotá, 1991); and "Narcotráfico, violencia y derechos humanos en Colombia," in Ricardo Vargas, comp., *Droga, poder y región* (Bogotá, 1995).

Let us pretend we are putting the following test question to a European student who has not read about Colombian violence: Which country is likely to be more violent, Bolivia or Colombia? Let us suppose we also give our imaginary student the following background information. Bolivia is significantly poorer than Colombia, so much so that Colombia is arguably

An earlier version of this essay appeared as "Violencia, poder y acción colectiva: Una comparación entre Bolivia y Colombia," in Alejo Vargas Velásquez et al., *Constitución, gobernabilidad y poder en Colombia* (Bogotá: Universidad Nacional de Colombia, 1996), 213–17. Reprinted by permission of Universidad Nacional de Colombia.

thirty years ahead of Bolivian social development.[1] Bolivia not only has more sharply defined ethnic divisions, but also exhibits a greater tendency toward military and dictatorial governments. Bolivia has had an average of one coup every ten months, while Colombia has only experienced five institutional ruptures in 170 years.[2] In addition, in the 1980s, Bolivia suffered an economic crisis and severe economic readjustment, while the same processes were far less drastic in Colombia.[3] Finally, Colombia is more economically developed and enjoys a stronger industrial base, while the Bolivian economy is essentially extractive. Even though Colombians receive, in absolute terms, more drug-trafficking dollars, the relative wealth of the drug economy is much greater in Bolivia than in Colombia.[4]

With this data, our imaginary European student would probably respond that the more violent country is Bolivia. It is poorer, has suffered a great economic crisis, and has been very unstable politically. Now, let us suppose that our student had read a detective novel. It follows that our student would recognize that the character who appears suspicious is innocent, while the guilty party, at first blush, is always above suspicion. Ergo, our student would respond that Colombia is more violent. In light of past experience and an analysis of recent happenings, we are left with the following question: Why is there a relatively low intensity of violence in Bolivia compared to Colombia?[5]

It would be absurd to attempt in these few lines to give a systematic response. I will limit myself to the presentation of a line of reasoning that I think will have interesting analytical consequences. The key to the differences in violence for the two countries is the weight of collective action. I can synthesize my argument in the following way: While in unstable and very militarized Bolivia, social and political collective action has been successful, in stable, democratic, civilian Colombia, collective social and political action has been much less successful. In Bolivia there appears to exist, since the 1930s, and particularly since the 1952 Revolution, a deep popular perception that instead of initiating violent individual action, it is more fruitful to fight through social and political collective action. In Colombia the political culture leans the opposite way. The failure of social movements, and the depoliticization that accompanied the National Front governments of the period from 1958 to 1974, tend to give greater weight to violent, and generally individual, forms of action. In effect, in Colombia, violence with political content is quantitatively less important than nonpolitical violence, which is commonly, and improperly, denoted as common delinquency. The reasons for these differences are discussed below.

The Strength of Bolivian and the Weakness of Colombian Popular Movements

Social movements—especially a peasant movement with strong indigenous roots and the miners' movement—have played a central and decisive role in the configuration of Bolivian politics since the 1930s. The tin miners' movement has had such great and permanent political influence that some authors have spoken of a veritable double power.[6] The tradition of peasant struggles—in defense of communities and reservations created by the colony but destroyed by the republic—started with the Tupac Katari uprising in 1781. In 1898–99, Pablo "Willca" Zárate's movement covered the highlands and demanded the restitution of all reservations and the creation of a peasant government. Peasant unions were organized in 1936, stimulated by the nationalist reaction to the Chaco War, and from the early 1940s were linked to revolutionary groups. The peasant and miners' movements were in permanent contact by the start of the 1950s, and their shared action permitted the transformation of a simple coup into a social and political revolution in 1952.

In Colombia, popular movements have been very weak. Historians and social scientists have tried to explain this phenomenon, invoking particular historical reasons,[7] the capacity of the bipartisan political system to co-opt popular movements and the opposition,[8] or the structural debility of the peasant movement due to the particularities of the coffee economy.[9] I cannot go into this issue further here, but it is obvious that export structures are fundamental to understanding the relative strength of social movements in Colombia and Bolivia.

The Influence of Social Conflict on the Colombian and Bolivian States

In Colombia, in particular since the epoch of the Violence[10] and the National Front, the political regime has been relatively impervious to social conflicts. This has historical roots. In Colombia the precariousness of the modern bourgeois State did not result in instability, owing to the existence of very efficient decentralized forms of domination based on patronage (or clientelism) and other patrimonial mechanisms. The role of the two-party political system in controlling the subaltern classes was central, even though it impeded the formation of a modern State capable of mediating social conflicts.

This institutional stability was also based on flexible agreements among dominant sectors. In Colombia, due to the particularities of the coffee economy, which permitted great flexibility in agreements between industrial, banking, exporting, and land-owning sectors, sharp conflicts did not exist between the agricultural export and industrial sectors as they did, for example, in Argentina. In the departments of Antioquia and Caldas, the coffee exporters' commercial monopoly was largely based on the control of coffee processing.[11] This created a common interest among agrarian, commercial, and industrial sectors, often united in the same families. For instance, the Echavarría family, founders of the textile companies of Coltejer and Fabricato, was also linked to coffee exportation and the importation of other goods. Indeed, in 1923, some twenty years after having founded these companies, the textile import house of Alejandro Echavarría and Sons still existed.[12] The very founding of these textile factories demonstrates the homogeneity of the dominant classes. In 1908, Alejandro Echavarría, a coffee merchant, decided to import four power looms, which he put to work along with twelve workers in the patio of his coffee-processing plant. That was how Coltejer was born.[13]

The Colombian bourgeoisie, in contrast to other dominant classes in Latin America, does not seem to have needed the state's aid to organize itself. It then tried to separate the defense of its interests from the sectarian party conflict of the political system. Hence, partisan politics was not the mechanism through which the dominant classes expressed their interests and made them count in the political arena. Those ends were achieved, especially after the failure of the modernizing project of the Revolution in March, through the organization of semiprivate economic interest groups known as *gremios*.

We thus have three elements that come together to explain Colombian institutional stability and the precarious makeup of the nation-state: effective but relatively decentralized mechanisms to contain popular demands through the two-party system; great social homogeneity of the dominant classes in spite of their partisan political divisions; and mechanisms of aggregating the interests of the dominant economic agents in which the State—as an independent and autonomous power—plays a minimal role. This allows for the existence of a precarious State—albeit directly influenced and controlled by private ruling-class interests—that nevertheless remains politically stable as long as the understandings among the dominant sectors and the loyalty of the subaltern classes are maintained. In addition, this explains the absence of sudden political changes in Colombian society, since social conflicts are not expressed directly in politics or in partisan struggles. The great cost of this, however, is the profound separation of the political and the social: The political does not appear as an arena for mediation of social conflicts, which are then left to chance.

In contrast, in Bolivia, in spite of, and perhaps because of, changes in political regimes and the alternation of dictatorships of different kinds, revolutions, and civil governments, the political system has managed to reflect the social dynamic more adequately. Bolivian governments pay attention to rumors in the streets and to the strategies of popular movements because they know that their fortune depends on them. There have been Bolivian governments that have only lasted a few days due to worker opposition. For instance, on July 21, 1978, General Hugo Banzer resigned as president and General Juan Pereda Asbún was proclaimed his successor. The following day, the miners' movement began a strike that, despite strong government repression, brought about the fall of Pereda Asbún. In November of that same year, a new coup brought to power a moderate junta that promised to hold new elections. In contrast, collective popular action has never achieved a change of government or national policy in Colombia. The closest brush with popular action was the fall of Gustavo Rojas Pinilla in 1957, but that was conditioned more by a strike of business people.

This is not to say that Bolivia has not had repressive and antipopular regimes that hoped to disable collective action. There have been many. For example, Juan Lechín, the historic leader of the Bolivian miners, has been in prison many times and has had to go into exile on various occasions.[14] And between 1972 and 1976, Banzer actively repressed the mining and peasant movements. Another military president, García Meza, a politician of the extreme right linked to drug trafficking, was responsible for the assassination of numerous political and union leaders. But even those two military governments had to be sensitive to popular action. Banzer, in spite of his antiunion and antipopular action, constantly had to win over and deal with the Central Obrera Boliviana (COB) and the peasant movement. According to some analysts, that is what permitted him to stay in power. The fall of García Meza was also conditioned by the pressure of the powerful COB.

In contrast, for all its civility and surprising and even boring institutional stability,[15] Colombian democracy has been based on what Alexander Wilde called "conversations between gentlemen," in other words, a democracy very close to an aristocracy. In comparison, militarized Bolivia seems to be a regime strongly conditioned by social dynamics, a kind of regime of crowds. In Colombia, the 1928 killing of banana workers did not result in the fall of even one cabinet official, state governor, or military commander. During the government of Miguel Abadía Méndez, the police and military dealt with social conflict under the leadership of Minister of War Ignacio Rengifo, who in 1927, by accepting that post, was placed in the line of presidential succession. In December of 1928, the Santa Marta banana zone was militarized, and under the command of General Cortés Vargas hundreds of striking workers were massacred. In spite of this massacre, there was no change in national policy or political leaders. Rengifo not only remained minister, but was also viewed as interim leader: "He was the strongman of the government; more: he was the strongman of the regime, of the system, indeed, of society as a whole."[16] General Cortés Vargas was named commander in Bogotá.[17] Conversely, the 1942 killing of miners in Bolivia's most important mining center, Catavi, provoked the fall of President Enrique Peñaranda and the establishment of a moderate reformist military regime headed by General Gualberto Villaroel. It was supported by the middle-class reformists and miners of the Movimiento Nacional Revolucionario (MNR) under the leadership of Víctor Paz Estenssoro. The peasant unionists eventually supported this government. In sum, in Colombia ignoring popular demands can garner political prestige, while Bolivian governments can hardly survive without some support from the subaltern classes.

Stable, Violent Colombia; Unstable, Pacific Bolivia

Under these conditions, political crises in Colombia need not be directly expressed as brusque shifts in political regimes. They are instead expressed through semiprivate forms of violence, as evidenced in the 1950s and also currently. Crises in Colombia tend to generate cycles of violence instead of mutations in the political regime. Given its political function, Colombian violence could play a role similar to that of changes in the political dynamic in other countries.

This is an interesting hypothesis, since it avoids hypothesizing violence as a constant in Colombian history. The clientelism of the country, combined with the precarious construction of the nation-state, explains not so much the unleashing of cycles of violence, but rather the fact that political crises assume forms of semiprivate violence and certain repression rather than developing into overarching and coherent strategies to win political power. Some authors, such as Alain Touraine, have proposed that many military dictatorships in Latin America develop as mechanisms of repression against populism unleashed in previous periods.[18] In fact, recent studies show that repression of gaitanismo and of the urban popular movement played an essential role in the Violence.[19] It is as if a similar phenomenon—

the disarticulation of the populist movement and the breaking down of urban organizations of the subaltern classes—changes into different forms in the different Latin American countries. In Colombia we see semiprivate violence within a certain continuity of the State and the political regime. In other Latin American countries we see State repression accompanied by the comings and goings of radically different political regimes.

The Heroic Myth of the 1952 Revolution and the Negative Myth of the Violence

All of the preceding factors combine to structure two different processes that are the basis of what could be called the founding myths of Bolivia and Colombia in the last decades: the Bolivian Revolution of 1952 and the Colombian Violence of the 1950s. In July 1946 a coup deposed the moderate reformist General Villaroel. The following military governments of Enrique Herzog and Mamerto Urriolagoita strongly repressed the opposition (various leaders of the MNR had to go into exile). Social reform programs were frozen, and the military government aligned itself with the tin magnates and multinational corporations. In late 1951 elections took place in which an opposition candidate, Paz Estenssoro of the MNR, won, but the military government did not recognize the results. General Urriolagoita resigned in favor of a council of three generals and eight colonels who declared the election null and void. This provoked a truly popular insurrection supported by certain sectors of the armed forces, and especially the police. The MNR triumphed after more than a week of armed conflict and the presence of the miners in the streets of La Paz armed with sticks of dynamite. Even though there was not a massive rising of peasants during this week of struggle, acting independently of the miners, the peasant movement on its own had already evicted the landlords of the Cochabamba region during the preceding months. A virtual worker-peasant government was then formed, so that, as Touraine says, Bolivia is in Latin America "the country in which the working class has been closer than in any other country to directing a class-based revolution."[20]

The new president, Paz Estenssoro, then nationalized the mines and turned over their operation to a government institution, the Mining Corporation of Bolivia. An agrarian reform of great breadth was also promulgated. Six and one-half million hetacres were rapidly distributed to some 170,000 families. In this way, at the beginning of the 1960s, according to Augusto Céspedes, "Agrarian reform liquidated, without exception, all the great estates. The reform recognized the rights of the old property owners over medium-sized properties and mechanized haciendas, but the rest was distributed between those who actually worked the land."[21] The electoral rules were also modified. The right to vote, previously sharply limited by economic and cultural restrictions, was greatly extended. "In this way 95 percent of the [adult] population had access to the polls as opposed to 10 percent before 1952."[22] Finally, in order to contest the power of the army, the MNR formed popular militias and armed the peasants and especially the miners. This demonstrates the validity of the idea of Bolivian miners' exercising "dual power."

Even so, the evolution of the Bolivian Revolution and of the alliance among workers, peasants, the military, and the government is not a rosy story. After a few years, at the beginning of the 1960s, Bolivian peasant unionism divided into political factions and distanced itself from the miners' movement to such a point that Paz Estenssoro's successor, Siles Suazo, utilized it to limit miners' power. Later, peasant unionism supported the military coup of General Barrientos in 1964,[23] who would then combat the Che Guevara-led guerrillas. Nevertheless, with all these ambiguities, one can say that the 1952 Revolution is the founding myth of contemporary Bolivia. This revolution is the clearest expression of the power of collective action in Bolivia.

In contrast, as we know, in Colombia there is quite a different history. Our recent evolution is marked by the events of the Violence, which, as Daniel Pecaut rightly emphasizes, also operate as a founding myth, albeit a negative one. The Violence is a period that all Colombians accept as having had a determining role in subsequent history, but in which no one wants to recognize himself.[24] Since this period, we Colombians have been trying to escape violence, but we have ended up perpetuating it. More than anything else, the Violence symbolizes in many ways the failure of collective action in Colombia. For it resulted in several failures: the failure of popular urban movements, shattered by conservative repression; the failure of gaitanismo and of populism as alternative forms of political power; the failure of a peasant movement that for the most part has to limit itself to developing resistance movements, and when it does manage to mount a powerful insurgent movement—the guerrillas of the eastern plains during the early Violence—it is thwarted by the clever maneuverings of the Liberal party; the failure, in sum, of politics as the collective construction of a democratic order and a modern state.

If we compare the recent founding myths of these two countries, I think we have very interesting keys to understanding them. Modern Colombia starts with the negative myth of the Violence, a myth that results in the depoliticization of Colombian life, in the distrust of politics (which itself is a symptom of violence), in the precariousness of collective action. Bolivia starts with the 1952 Revolution, the closest approximation of a triumphant worker-peasant movement in Latin America. The weakness of Colombian civil society at the grass-roots level contrasts with the relative strength of popular action in Bolivia. In this contrast we find an interesting way to contemplate the differing impact of violence on these two countries. In Colombia, by trying so hard to escape violence, especially violent action by popular forces, we have ended by condemning ourselves to it. In Bolivia, fed by the image of the popular triumph of the 1952 Revolution, and prepared to make use of popular protest openly and even arm popular movements, Bolivians have managed to avoid the recurrence of violence.

Even so, it is useful to point out that this schematic comparison obviously exaggerates the differences between Colombia and Bolivia and that it can lead to an idealization of Bolivia's political history, a subject I am not expert in. I am well aware that Bolivia is not a model of national integration, that it is not a just society, nor a democratic State. The divisions are strong, the inequalities extraordinary, and tensions that could result in intense violence exist. In particular, the following question remains: Why has such an apparently strong popular movement not managed to improve the Bolivian people's conditions of life? Nevertheless, I think that Bolivia is an example of how the precariousness of a State does not necessarily result in violence, when a developed social fabric exists and there are consolidated social actors. This has important consequences and practical lessons for reflection about the violence of our country.

Conclusion: Violence, Power, and Civil Society—Theoretical Elements for Practical Action

This comparison between Colombia and Bolivia has led me to emphasize the precariousness of collective action as an explanation of the persistence of violence in Colombia. By emphasizing the weakness of popular forces in Colombian civil society as a factor in the violence, I do not wish to posit a new monocausal interpretation radically opposed to current analysis. Today, there exists a consensus among Colombian scholars that the problem of the violence in our country is very complicated, and for that reason simple explanations will not do. Few scholars today would try to attribute violence to only one factor. For example, we know that violence does not depend only on socioeconomic conditions, such as poverty or economic growth; or on political factors, such as the doctrine of national security of the armed forces, or the supposed infiltration of international Communism, or the narrowness of the political regime. The persistence of drug trafficking is also not a satisfactory explanation. Even those who insist on the importance of cultural factors to explain Colombian violence recognize that, although cultural elements help energize violence and give it a certain form, they do not by themselves constitute a sufficient explanation. Perhaps the only explanatory concept that generates a degree of consensus among some investigators is the relative weakness or precariousness of the Colombian State. But even this consensus is equivocal. As I have tried to show elsewhere,[25] it is a kind of false consensus, given that there are diverse notions of what constitutes the precariousness of the State. For some, State "precariousness" is synonymous with the need for better police and military controls capable of reining in a society prone to violence. For others, this precariousness refers to the insufficiencies of democracy and the state of law in Colombia. The theoretical and practical consequences of one thesis or another are profoundly different.

For all these reasons, I do not think that the weakness of popular forces and collective action is the determining factor in Colombian violence. Nor do I believe that the idea of the precariousness of the State should be replaced with the concept of the precariousness of civil society. In this essay, I have simply tried to maintain the importance of this dimension of analysis. Of course, this is not an original idea; it has been vigorously highlighted by other authors such as Luis Alberto Restrepo[26] and the Commission to Surmount the Violence.[27]

This analysis of the relationship between the weakness of collective action and the intensity of violence in Colombia can be linked to a more general concept, based on the distinction between power and violence proposed by Hannah Arendt. According to her, we should not equate power with domination and violence. Power is the capacity to act collectively; violence, in contrast, is the individual utilization of instruments of violence against others. Violence, according to Arendt, can be the tool of one or of many; power is always collective. In effect, "Power corresponds to the human aptitude not only to act, but also to act with collective purpose. Power is never the property of an individual. It always belongs to the group and is sustained while the group stays united."[28]

Using this distinction, it is possible to formulate the difference between the Bolivian and Colombian cases with greater precision. The lesser violence in Bolivia derives from the greater power of social actors, especially popular actors who have managed to create a culture of collective action. In contrast, the greater violence in Colombia derives from the precariousness of popular and social power due to the difficulty that we Colombians have in consolidating collective action. In turn, the increase in Colombian violence tends to heighten the fragmentation of social actors; what then results is a vicious circle in which the absence of citizens' power begets more violence and vice versa. From this we deduce that giving power to social groups and to citizens can contribute to de-activating violence.

This conclusion is obvious, but not for that reason unimportant. It coincides with the basic sense of some of the recommendations of the Commission to Surmount the Violence. The commission emphasized that the "first role" of the State should be "the promotion of civil society." In the present conditions, "prior to political solutions that foster participation in the State, it is necessary to construct a social fabric from the basic solidarities of the movements and organizations of civil society."[29] Obviously, this is easier said than done, but I think having a basic clarity concerning these matters is an important element of action.

Growing citizen and community power should also contribute to overcoming the disjunction between civil society and the State, between the social dynamic and politics, which has caused so much damage in Colombia. In effect, if one compares Colombian history with that of other Latin American countries, two uniquely Colombian characteristics leap into view: institutional stability and violence. These traits appear to derive in part from the same source: Colombian politics does not adequately function as a mechanism of the representation of social interests and conflict mediation. Society then drifts, and private and violent forms of conflict resolution come to the fore, since communities of people in Colombia have been unable for so long to act in concert.

Strong communities, capable of collectively mobilizing people, could make the State more amenable to their demands. Naturally, the results of these types of processes are neither immediate nor spectacular; they are the result of slow democratic transformations of the social fabric. What is important about these reflections is that they show that it is possible to confront Colombian violence through democratic participation.

Notes

1. While in 1990 Colombia had a human development index of 0.757 and occupied 61st place among 160 countries, Bolivia's index was 0.416 and it occupied 110th place. The per capita share of Gross National Product (GNP) in Colombia in 1988 was U.S.$1,180, while in Bolivia it was $570. In Colombia, life expectancy was 68.8 years, illiteracy was 15.3 percent, and average years of schooling was 5.2, while in Bolivia those indices were 54.5, 27.5, and 4. Perhaps the most illustrative indicator of levels of social development is infant

mortality. In Colombia, the number of children 5 years old or younger who died per 1,000 live births was 157 in 1960 and 50 in 1989, while in Bolivia the number changed from 282 to 165 during the same period. These data are taken from *Desarrollo humano: Informe 1991* (Bogotá, 1991), Tables 3 and 4.

2. Dating from the military insurrection that deposed General García Meza and that permitted the transition to a more or less stable constitutional regime, without counting failed coup attempts, Bolivia had 190 coups between 1825 and 1981. That is 190 coups in 156 years of independence or one coup every 10 months. In this same period, Colombia had two military coups, that of General Melo in the mid-1800s and that of Rojas Pinilla in 1954; a putsch, that of Marroquín against Sanclemente at the turn of the nineteenth century; and two coups d'état, that of Simón Bolívar in 1828 and of Ospina Pérez in 1949. That is five institutional ruptures in 170 years or one every 34 years.

3. Between 1980 and 1985 the GDP in Bolivia fell by 20 percent, per capita consumption diminished by 30 percent, family earnings fell 28 percent, unemployment doubled, exports fell by 25 percent between 1984 and 1986, and inflation reached 24,000 percent in 1985. Data are taken from: Committee on Government Operations, *United States Anti-Narcotics Activities in the Andean Region*, 38th report (Washington, DC, 1990), 67. In contrast, in Colombia, in spite of the crisis between 1980 and 1986, the GDP grew at an average annual rate of 3 percent, exports at 5.4 percent, and inflation was maintained at approximately 25 percent. *Economía Colombiana* 230 (June–July 1990): 53 and 65.

4. According to some estimates, in Bolivia the coca economy and the drug dollars that enter the country represent almost 25 percent of the GDP, and the coca economy employs 20 percent of the economically active population. In Colombia—even in the highest estimates—those earnings have not reached 10 percent of the GDP.

5. Unfortunately, I could not obtain reliable data concerning violence in Bolivia. I consulted the United Nations demographic yearbooks—perhaps the best source for comparative studies on mortality—from 1960 to 1988, but Bolivia appeared only once, owing to the unreliability of statistical information in Bolivia. Even so, the low level of homicidal violence in Bolivia can be confirmed in two ways. Direct consultation with various Bolivian academics revealed that homicidal violence is not a major problem. In addition, the only public United Nations data record 497 homicides and deaths resulting from military operations in 1966. This is equivalent to a rate of 11 per 100,000 inhabitants. This rate is not only low in comparison with Colombia at any point during the last forty years, but 1966 was also the exceptional year in terms of Bolivian violence and armed conflict. In 1966, General Barrientos, who was then in power, began operations against the Bolivian guerrillas, an offensive that ended in the death of Che Guevara the following year. This information leads me to believe that homicide rates for other years would be much lower.

6. According to Touraine, "Bolivia represents the country in which one social class, or its nucleus, the tin miners, played a central political role to such a degree that R. Zavaleta speaks of 'double power.' " Alain Touraine, *La parole et le sang* (Paris, 1998), 169.

7. Some historians emphasize the parochialism of Colombian politics: the absence of large-scale European immigration in the republican era (as opposed to countries such as Venezuela, Chile, or Argentina), which allegedly prevented Colombia from assimilating socialist and revolutionary thinking. Others find the cause in the fact that in Colombia, unlike almost all other Latin American countries, Liberals lost out in the late nineteenth century with the triumph of Rafael Núñez and the Regeneration. The result was Colombia's entry into the world economy via coffee under the direction of a conservative political regime.

This permitted the Liberals—revitalized through opposition—to co-opt the popular movements, while in other countries alternative movements were founded to contest the policies of the liberal regimes in power.

8. See especially the history of unionism by Daniel Pecaut, *Política y sindicalismo en Colombia*, 2d ed. (Bogotá, 1982).

9. See the work of Charles Bergquist, *Labor in Latin America: Comparative Essays on Chile, Argentina, Venezuela, and Colombia* (Stanford, 1986). In my doctoral thesis concerning State accumulation and legitimacy in Colombia, I followed a similar line. The weakness of Colombian popular movements derives from the fact that the export crop is produced by peasant owners who, after gaining lands, are not disposed to participate in popular struggles. In contrast to countries such as Venezuela, Bolivia, or Chile, this means that other popular sectors—even if they are strong—are unable to affect the central or coffee sector of the Colombian economy. This considerably weakened Colombian popular struggles. If Colombia had been an oil country, history would have been different; imagine all of Colombia like the oil town of Barrancabermeja.

10. When I speak of Violence with a capital letter, I am referring to the period of the 1950s. Use of the lower case denotes diverse violent phenomena.

11. Mariano Arango, *Café e industria, 1850–1930* (Bogotá, 1981), 214, and passim.

12. Ibid., 220.

13. Salomón Kalmanovitz, *Economía y nación*, 3rd ed. (Bogotá, 1988), 240, and passim.

14. Any Colombian union leader would note that at least they did not assassinate him.

15. In effect, one can contrast the monotony of Colombian bipartisanism with the changing political history of almost all the Latin American countries, possibly excepting Mexico. One anecdotal example will illustrate. The Larousse historical atlas includes an outline of Latin America's political evolution between 1930 and 1987, which assigns a different color to each type of political regime. Although almost all the countries are a mosaic of color, the Colombian area is almost monochromatic. With the exception of the Rojas regime, the rest are defined as bipartisan regimes with little popular participation. Nueva Enciclopedia Larousse, *Atlas histórico* (Barcelona, 1988), 317.

16. Mario Latorre Rueda, "1930–1934, Olaya Herrera: Un nuevo régimen," in Alvaro Tirado Mejía, ed., *Nueva historia de Colombia*, 6 vols. (Bogotá, 1989), 1:272.

17. Six months later, in June 1929, during a kind of aristocratic street protest, a student named Gonzalo Bravo Pérez died in Bogotá. He was a personal friend of President Abadía. The following day, the elite met in the Gun Club and decided to speak with President Abadía. As result of this meeting, the whole cabinet fell; the next day the president designated new ministers, a new governor, and a new police commander (Latorre Rueda, "1930–1934," 274). This shows exactly what kind of pressures Colombian politics are susceptible to. While the willful massacre of banana workers does not move the government, the death of an elite student makes the cabinet fall. Make no mistake, the death of a student through police abuse is serious and, in a democracy respectful of citizen rights, it should result in sanctions against those responsible, as happened here. What I wish to emphasize is the contrast between government reaction to this death and its response to an infinitely more serious occurrence a short time before in which hundreds of workers were deliberately massacred.

18. Touraine, *La parole et le sang*, 377, and passim.

19. Medófilo Medina, "Las bases urbanas de la violencia en Colombia," in *Historia Crítica* 1 (January–July 1989): 20, and passim. Gonzalo Sánchez, "Violencia, guerrillas y estructuras agrarias," in Tiradó Mejía, ed., *Nueva historia de Colombia*, 2:127, and passim.

20. Touraine, *La parole et le sang,* 170.

21. Augusto Céspedes, *Bolivia* (Washington, DC, 1962), 21.

22. Ibid., 21.

23. Those elements could explain why the Guevarist attempt to make Bolivia the nucleus of armed struggle in Latin America failed. The military government of Barrientos was not only supported by the United States but also received the support of the peasant unions.

24. Daniel Pecaut, *Crónica de dos décadas de vida política* (Bogotá, 1988), Introduction.

25. See "Violencia, poder y acción colectiva: Una comparación entre la dictatorial Bolivia y la civilista en Colombia," in Alejo Vargas Velásquez et al., *Constitutión, gobernabilidad y poder* (Bogotá, 1996), 213–17.

26. See Luis Alberto Restrepo, "El protagonismo político de los movimientos sociales," *Revista Foro* 2 (February 1987).

27. See Comisión de Superación de la Violencia, *Pacificar la paz: Lo que no se ha negociado en los acuerdos de paz* (Bogotá, 1992), esp. 274, and following pages.

28. Hannah Arendt, "Sobre la Violencia," in *Crisis de la República* (Madrid, 1973).

29. Comisión de Superación de la Violencia, *Pacificar la paz,* 279.

Chapter 3

The Constitution of 1991

An Institutional Evaluation Seven Years Later

Ana María Bejarano

In December 1990, in a climate of crisis following a bloody electoral campaign that witnessed the assassination of three presidential candidates, Colombian voters approved the idea of calling a Constituent Assembly to write a new constitution for the nation. The Assembly produced a document that sought, in the words of its preamble, "to strengthen the unity of the Nation, and ensure its people life, community [*convivencia*], work, justice, equality, knowledge, liberty, and peace within a democratic and participatory juridical framework that guarantees a politically, economically, and socially just order." Clearly, the lofty goals of the new Constitution have not been realized in the years since its promulgation. The State today is less in control of the nation than it was at the start of the 1990s, and the achievement of a peaceful, democratic, and just national order seems even more remote today than when the Constitution of 1991 was put into force.

Still, as Ana María Bejarano argues in this measured assessment written in 1998, it would be a grave mistake to dismiss the Constitution of 1991 as a meaningless exercise in utopian politics. This is true first, because it expressed the aspirations of many Colombians and addressed the widespread dissatisfaction among them with a political system dominated by the two traditional parties and viewed by many as hopelessly unrepresentative, corrupt, and clientelistic, and second, because aspects of the Constitution, particularly the articles dealing with fiscal and administrative decentralization, political representation for ethnic and religious minorities, and citizen control over the State, have had significant (and often unexpected) consequences for Colombian political life. (A sampling of these articles is included in the Documents section of this book.)

Bejarano stresses the weakness of the Colombian State as a primary cause of the failure of the Constitution to realize its framers' expectations. She also shows how the absence from the Constituent Assembly of representatives of the largest guerrilla groups, the paramilitaries, and the military restricted the reforms and compromised their implementation. For example, the Constitution studiously avoids the question of major economic or agrarian reform and does not address military issues.

This essay was first presented at a conference, "Hacia el Rediseño del Estado," organized by the National Department of Planning and the Ministry of Finance and Public Credit, Bogotá, April 27–29, 1998.

Finally, and perhaps most important, the failure of the Constitution to realize its democratic and participatory potential obeys a feature of Colombian politics addressed again and again in the essays in this book and in the 1992 volume, *Violence in Colombia*: the continuing electoral weakness of third parties. That has allowed the two traditional parties to continue to dominate the political scene, especially Congress, which is charged with implementing the reforms called for in the Constitution.

Ana María Bejarano received her Ph.D. in political science from Columbia University in 2000. She teaches in the Department of Political Science and is director of the Centro de Investigaciones Sociojurídicas at the Universidad de los Andes in Bogotá.

> It is clear that institutions and constitutions cannot perform miracles. But it would be difficult to have good governments without good governmental instruments. So why then do we give so little attention to the way political structures do or do not function and how they can be improved?
>
> —Giovanni Sartori[1]

There exists a marked contrast between the sober and temperate way that foreign observers appraise the content and significance of the Colombian Constitution of 1991, and the impassioned judgment that we Colombians pass on it just seven years after its composition. For foreigners, there are no constitutional miracles, only processes of slow institutional evolution that can take years or even decades. Remember, for example, the most famous and long-lasting of written constitutions, that of the United States. It took several years before it was ratified by all the states in the union and still, seventy years after its ratification, the states of the South had the audacity to conspire with the intention of overthrowing it and replacing it with a distinct political system. We Colombians, on the other hand, tear out our hair when we see that after less than seven years of operation, the Constitution of 1991 has not fulfilled all our expectations and has not provided a solution to all the problems that we intended to solve with it. So, in an act of collective exasperation, we are ready to modify it, amend it, even exchange it for another, resorting to a new constituent assembly in search of a constitutional miracle that has been so elusive in the century and one-half since Independence.

It is always healthy to keep in mind other examples of constitutional evolution—including our own with respect to the Constitution of 1886—in order to understand that the institutionalization of the principles, norms, and procedures contained in a constitution takes time, requires a certain ripening, and, above all, does not depend only on the written text but also on the way in which this text is fleshed out through the concrete action of its interpreters and executors, public officials as well as citizens. As one student of the U.S. Constitution notes, "The Constitution of 1787 functioned, in the end, because a sufficient number of the relevant actors worked within its parameters during a sufficient amount of time to establish, in the expectations of all, that there was no sense in not working within its parameters."[2]

Putting the constitutional debate in its place implies, first of all, reducing the unrealistic level of expectations we held for the Constitution of 1991 in the euphoric phase of its approval and recognizing it for what it really is: a "navigational chart" that signals the way, a map with a destination, a blueprint for a project under construction—that of a more pluralistic and just society, a more democratic political order, and a State that serves as the institutional framework for advancing toward both.

A call for sobriety in the discussion of the Constitution does not imply that we cross our arms and sit for years until it produces the hoped-for results of its own accord. It is also not a call to renounce criticism of the Constitution's holes, limitations, failures, and errors in design. Very much to the contrary: Only balanced criticism, free from the excesses of unfounded optimism and paralyzing pessimism, can lead to an adequate appreciation of the true potential of the Constitution for restructuring our society and regulating and modifying the way politics is practiced in Colombia.

I begin with a kind of inventory of the problems detected in the constitutional process itself and then concentrate on those areas of the Constitution where it is possible to identify problems in design that merit modifications and adjustments. Given that one of the great changes introduced by the Constituent Assembly was to make more flexible the procedures for constitutional reform[3]—whose previous rigidity largely led to the impasse of the late 1980s—there is no reason to believe that the required adjustments merit the premature convening of a new constituent assembly, nor the creation of a new political charter. Once again cautioning against the belief in constitutional miracles, I attempt to disentangle the mass of complaints against the Constitution of 1991 and offer a measured and clear evaluation of its evolution and impact during the last seven years.

Virtues and Defects of the Constituent Assembly

Certain observers attribute some of the problems of the Constitution of 1991 to the political process that led to convening a constituent assembly, to the actors involved, or to the conditions under which the creation of the new Constitution developed. This emphasis on the constitutional process makes sense if we understand that it can help to explain the origin of some of the most important features of the final document. Here we follow the recommendations of "historical institutionalism,"[4] which posit that studies of institutional arrangements based on the concept of constitutional engineering are insufficient. It is true that, once created, political institutions in general, and constitutions in particular, mold the preferences of actors in such a manner that certain results are more probable than others. Even so, in order to understand why a certain institutional arrangement is chosen and not another, it is necessary to trace its historical origin and, in this case, to return to the constitutional process itself. That process is best understood as a series of negotiations among diverse actors with varied interests and different capacities for political leverage.[5]

Some have judged the convening of the 1990 Constituent National Assembly as a "coup of public sentiment"[6] against the enemies of constitutional reform in Colombia, in particular the members of the traditional political class. The first aspect of note with respect to the constitutional process of 1991 is the extremely unusual procedure used for putting it in motion.[7] The process was led by the president-elect, César Gaviria, who was backed by an ample but poorly organized body of opinion that included a small and sporadic but highly mobilized student movement, and two political trends different from traditional bipartisanism, the nascent Democratic Alliance M-19 and the Movement of National Salvation.[8] The traditional parties and the political class that represented them in Congress not only were at the margin of this convulsive process, but were also seen as the ones responsible for the institutional stagnation that had resulted in the crisis. This antipolitical spirit was reflected, throughout the deliberations of the Assembly, in the warm reception accorded "participatory" discourse. Directed against the principle of representation, it called for the replacement of supposedly defective representative institutions by a panacea called "participatory democracy."[9] What is more, in the middle of the sessions of the Constituent Assembly, a decision was made to revoke the mandate of the congresspeople put in office the previous year (in the 1990 election). That decision ratified the extent of the opposition of the majority of the constituents to the traditional political class.

This brief synthesis of the constitutional process reveals several problems. First, there are the doubts raised by the constitutional and legal procedures used to affect constitutional reform. Even if one admits that the process openly violated existing constitutional norms, the argument can be made in its favor that it was the only political solution available to surmount the impasse in which the country found itself after the critical juncture of 1989–1990. The shadows of irregularity that fell over the process seemed to dissipate, however, when the Supreme Court, which was charged with reviewing the constitutionality of the decree that convened the Assembly, took the surprising step of declaring the meeting constitutional, thus opening the doors to a wide-ranging reform of the Constitution.[10]

More serious than the doubts concerning the constitutionality of the procedure is the fact that the whole process was realized not only behind the back of, but also *against*, the traditional political class. Immersed in a kind of Latin American or perhaps universal zeitgeist, which defames the political class and rejects politics as a corrupt and contemptible activity, we Colombians wanted to conduct our reform of the rules of the political game *without* the politicians. Even though this attitude is understandable, given the visibly corrupt, antireformist, and self-serving conduct of Colombian politicians during the past decades, the costs that we have had to pay for this exclusion have not been few.

The first cost of isolating the politicians from the constitutional debate was the very high level of abstention (74 percent) that characterized the election of the delegates to the Constituent Assembly. Some viewed this level of abstention positively, arguing that the 26 percent who did vote revealed the existence of a "clean" uncontaminated body of opinion, which was not tied to or mobilized by the clientelist machines of the parties. Nevertheless, those elected to the Assembly represented only one-fourth of the population eligible to vote in Colombia. That is a very slim margin of representation, which may partially explain the difficulties encountered later with disseminating the Constitution, winning acceptance of it, and executing it.

Another of the costs of the "antipolitical" bias of the constitutional process has been congressional implementation. Postconstituent congresses (elected in 1991, 1994, and 1998) have been increasingly dominated by the same political class that the Constituent Assembly attempted to displace with the revocation of the 1991 mandate.[11] The politicians have taken their revenge by recovering their control of Congress, blocking the implementation of the Constitution of 1991, or regulating it in a spirit openly contrary to that which was intended. Since 1991, political competition in Colombia has been viewed as "progressive politicians versus traditional politicians," the first understood as being proponents of the Constitution of 1991, the second as their enemies, carriers of the worst vices of the Colombian political class. In such a polarized environment, it is difficult to coordinate within

Congress itself the necessary actions for the legal instrumentation of the Constitution.

Of course, it is not true that the traditional parties were totally absent from the constitutional process. The Liberal party had a high proportion of delegates (twenty-four), but the percentage of the total vote that these represented (33.3 percent), coupled with the traditional fragmentation of the party itself, signified a decline of its relative power in the Assembly.[12] The traditional Conservative party, renamed the Social Conservative party, managed to win only 7 percent of the vote, electing five delegates to the Assembly. Additionally, two lists of independent conservatives won 5.5 percent of the total vote, managing to elect four members to the Assembly, which revealed once again the tremendous fragmentation of the traditional parties.

As a result of these internal divisions within the traditional parties, political, ethnic, and religious minorities had unprecedented access to the Constituent Assembly. The Movement of National Salvation managed to elect eleven representatives (having garnered 15.3 percent of the total vote), which appeared to confirm the creation of an independent rightist movement confronting the traditional parties. The greatest surprise, however, came from the Democratic Alliance M-19. Formed only a few months earlier, that coalition won 26.4 percent of the vote (nineteen delegates), which up to that time was an unimaginable figure for a third party in Colombia, especially one calling itself leftist. The traditional left (the Communist party and the Unión Patriótica) maintained its historically low levels of electoral support (2.7 percent of the total vote) and elected two delegates to the Assembly. The second big surprise was the access of ethnic and religious minorities to the Assembly. The indigenous movement obtained 2.7 percent of the vote, winning two seats (plus another with voice but no vote, as a consequence of the reincorporation of the indigenous guerrilla group Quintín Lame). The Christian Union, comprised of groups of non-Catholic Christians, also managed to elect two representatives to the Assembly, having won 2.7 percent of the total vote. Finally, the guerrilla groups that were concluding a negotiation and reincorporation process with the Gaviria administration (the Popular Liberation Army [EPL] and the Revolutionary Workers' Party [PRT]) gained three places in the Assembly (two for the EPL and one for the PRT) with voice but no vote.

The composition of the National Constituent Assembly signified a historic change in political representation in Colombia. For the first time, the traditional parties were not able to monopolize the decisions concerning the future of Colombian politics. The historic bipartisan coalition did not operate in this Assembly. For the first time, also, leftist movements and some social minorities usually excluded from the national debate had access to a decision-making entity of vital importance. The Assembly turned out to be a body made up of a multitude of minorities where no force, no matter how numerous it looked, managed to impose a unilateral and exclusionary political project.[13] The fact that no political force managed to gain absolute control over the Assembly caused movements and parties, which up to then had considered themselves irreconcilable enemies, regularly to effect transactions, alliances, and coalitions.

The widening of the spectrum of representation and the dynamic of negotiations and alliances can be considered favorable results of the constitutional process. But the fragmentation of political forces also resulted in the writing of a text of excessive length and internal heterogeneity that some have judged a "patchwork," a text with articles that are sometimes unconnected and other times clearly contradictory. More serious than this, the fragmentation, weakness, and volatility of the many forces that participated in the fashioning of the Constitution limited the ability of these forces to implement it once it was signed. Many of these forces, such as the Democratic Alliance M-19 and the Movement of National Salvation, disappeared from the political scene shortly thereafter. One observer has reasonably commented that the Constitution of 1991 does not have "mourners." That is to say, it lacks the backing of political forces, which, going beyond the formal process of putting the Constitution into effect, actually incorporate it into real political life, converting the written text into a living, functioning guide for the practices of politicians, public officials, and citizens.

Given the internal composition of the National Constituent Assembly, we should not be surprised at the fact that its final product has not been a great "peace pact," "armistice," or "social pact" among Colombians. In addition to the fragmentation of political forces operating within the Assembly, we must not forget that many of the forces involved in the conflict during the 1980s, such as the Revolutionary Armed Forces of Colombia (FARC), the National Liberation Army (ELN), and the paramilitary groups, did not take part in the Assembly. On the other hand, it is true that the penetration by drug traffickers of several political groups, and the traffickers' capacity for armed intimidation, influenced the decision to make extradition unconstitutional. Even so, representatives of the organized drug-trafficking groups, in spite of their tremendous importance as actors in the national political drama, were compelled to remain outside the agreement because of their illegal status. Military personnel, both active and retired, were also kept outside, and the Assembly avoided any substantial modification of their role in Colombian politics.

In the absence of a previous armistice between armed actors, it is too optimistic to call the Constitution of 1991 a "peace pact" among Colombians. It is preferable to accept it for what it is: a *political pact* among some parties and movements tending to promote a way out of the crisis in which Colombian politics found itself at the beginning of the 1990s. Marco Palacios believes that the greatest difference between the new constitution and the ones that preceded it resides in the fact that although the earlier constitutions were the result of civil wars and victors imposing their will on the vanquished, the Constitution of 1991 is better seen as the result of improvisation, of the necessity for a very unorthodox and unstable coalition to deal with the circumstances of the moment.[14] Perhaps the weak consolidation of the new constitution simply reflects the dispersion of political actors and the current fluidity of Colombian politics, where it is far from clear who are or eventually will be the victors and the vanquished. Perhaps in this lack of clarity lie the greatest virtues of the Constitution of 1991—but also its greatest weaknesses.

Evaluation of the Constitution as an Institutional Arrangement: How Effective and Efficient Is It?

Not all of the limitations of the Constitution can be explained on the basis of its genesis, the actors involved, and the context in which the constitutional process developed. It is also necessary to look critically at the institutional arrangements that resulted from the Constituent Assembly and to evaluate their subsequent effectiveness and efficiency.[15] What has been their capacity or incapacity to produce the desired results and to what extent has their real impact generated unanticipated consequences?[16]

Toward this end, it is important to differentiate the original purpose of a given constitutional norm (where what is important are the desired effects) from the real unfolding or implementation of it (where we not only should observe its desired effects, but also its unanticipated and sometimes undesired effects). Such an evaluation should take into account, in addition, the possibility that some of the unanticipated effects can be positive in the sense of reinforcing a dynamic of efficacious institutionalization; others, on the contrary, can be negative in the sense of reinforcing a dynamic of perverse institutionalization.[17] Additionally, as Jon Elster notes,[18] a functional approach to institutions (with emphasis on their real effects and not on their aims) can alert us to why certain institutions are maintained, although they may have been originally designed with different aims.

No one can demand of the drafters of a constitution a prospective, predictive, almost prophetic vision. In fact, one of the limitations of constitutional engineering is the inability to foresee all the consequences (anticipated or unanticipated, positive and negative) of the introduction of institutions designed to regulate human conduct. Nevertheless, I think that, beyond good intentions, one can expect from them a minimum of consideration for the consequences of their actions.

Of course, the analysis offered here is retrospective and hence able to evaluate what the real effects of certain constitutional provisions have been. It should be borne in mind, however, that, given the scope and complexity of the Constitution, a detailed evaluation of every aspect of the document is beyond the scope of this essay. For that reason, I have decided simply to highlight some of the themes that appear worthy of deeper analysis, either because of the success of results or because, at first sight, they show a great discrepancy between desired aims and effects. The latter may be the areas where adjustments in the institutional design may be warranted.

Relative Successes

Most analysts agree that the Constitution of 1991 is a relative success in terms of the changes made in the role and power of the judiciary.[19] Even though the creation of certain institutions, such as the Public Prosecutor's Office (Fiscalía) and the Superior Council of the Judiciary, have been questioned, two other new institutions, the *acción de tutela* (which gives citizens recourse to the courts when they believe public officials have violated, or failed to protect, their constitutional rights) and the Constitutional Court, have been well received by judicial analysts.[20] In particular, they recognize that the mechanism of *tutela* (Article 86) has the capacity to protect the fundamental rights of citizens specified in Title II of the Constitution.[21] In addition to playing a similar role, the Constitutional Court rules on the constitutionality of actions taken by the legislative and executive branches, making for a more balanced relationship among the powers.

The reforms of the Constitution of 1991 were minimal in the economic sphere.[22] Among them are norms that guarantee the independence of the Central Bank. The text reads that the charter of the Bank of the Republic "will be organized as a public corporation, with administrative, patrimonial, and technical autonomy and governed by its own legal procedures."[23] Similarly, its functions are clearly defined (among them are the issuing of legal tender, and monetary, exchange, and credit regulation), as are the limits of the authority of the Directive Council and the manner of electing its chair. More than an innovation, the chapter on the Central Bank ratifies a long tradition in the management of the Colombian economy, thanks to which certain economic policymaking entities are protected against partisan and political pressures.[24] Since this norm "constitutionalizes" a very deep-seated practice in the country, it is possible that its success is rooted in the coincidence between dictum and reality.

The Constitution of 1991 contributed in various ways to broaden the process of decentralization in progress in Colombia since the middle of the 1980s. It made territorial entities uniform throughout the country (eliminating intendencies and commissaries) and established the popular election of governors and mayors (the popular election of mayors had already been sanctioned by a law passed by Congress in 1986). It also established three different mechanisms for the transfer of national revenue to departments and *municipios*. In addition to general transfers, there is a special mechanism for transfers of funds for education and public health and another that allows departments and *municipios* to share in the profits and compensations derived from the exploitation of nonrenewable natural resources (such as oil). The Constitution established that the transfers of national revenue to *municipios* should increase annually (until they reach 22 percent of national income by 2002).

In fiscal matters, Chapter 4 of Title XII, entitled "Distribution of Resources and Taxing Authority," is perhaps the most radical change from the previous Constitution. Although this new distribution of resources strengthens the model of decentralization, it has been criticized on various counts: first, for its negative effect on the finances of the central government; second, because the redistribution of resources did not specify which expenditure responsibilities belonged to the nation and which to the *municipios*; and third, because some have argued that greater availability of funds in some localities has led to excessive and inefficient expenditures.[25] Despite these results, there is no doubt that decentralization constitutes one of the most important and relatively most successful areas of the reform of the Colombian State.

Relative Failures and Mixed Results

The complete dismantling of the political restrictions inherited from the National Front constitutes one of the most significant achievements of the new Constitution. The institutions that inhibited open competition among diverse political forces and that guaranteed the monopoly of the two traditional parties were removed; new institutions aimed at promoting citizen participation in elections and in decision-making processes were created, especially at the local level. Finally, new mechanisms of control and accountability over public power were introduced. What have been the results of these reforms of the political regime?

Let us begin with the new mechanisms for political representation. At the level of national representation, the creation of new electoral districts for the Senate and the House aimed to widen the space of representation, permitting access of new political and social actors previously excluded from the political arena. Nevertheless, its results have not necessarily been the expected ones.[26] In the first place, senators are now elected on a national, not regional, basis, a reform which should have favored the representation of minorities and new political movements, while undermining the local and regional control historically exercised by bosses of the two traditional parties. The effects of this institutional innovation have been mixed: Although there has been a relative opening for the representation of ethnic, religious, and political minorities, the elections held since 1991 have still ratified the predominance of the traditional parties and their political machines in Congress, including the Senate. In his investigation of the political consequences of the reform that established the national election of senators, Felipe Botero has shown that it was insufficient. The reform pointed in the right direction, but traditional politicians were able to accommodate themselves rapidly to the new situation. The reform did not include sufficient incentives or sanctions to oblige them to drastically modify their way of conducting politics based on what are called their "fiefdoms."[27]

In the second place, the creation of the special districts for the Senate and the House as new political spaces for guaranteeing the representation of minorities should be noted. In the Senate, a "special national district" was created to elect an additional two senators to represent indigenous communities.[28] In the House of Representatives, in spite of the fact that regional electoral districts were maintained, the Constitution left the door open for Congress to create a "special district to ensure the participation . . . of ethnic groups, political minorities, and Colombians who are foreign residents."[29] The Assembly anticipated, in addition, through transitory Article 12, mechanisms to facilitate access to representative bodies by the guerrilla movements in the process of negotiation with the government. Even though the presence of indigenous peoples in the Senate constitutes an undeniable improvement, the other districts either have not been implemented (as in the cases of political minorities or residents abroad), were never utilized (as in the case of reincorporated guerrilla groups), or failed (as in the case of black communities). In all these instances, the reforms fell victim to the political battle between diverse factions bent on controlling the new districts.

With regard to Congress, the new Constitution aimed to strengthen it to make it more representative. The Constituent Assembly was concerned with correcting the disequilibrium between the power of the executive and the legislative branches. Without eliminating the presidentialism characteristic of the Colombian political regime, it sought to enhance the decision-making and control capabilities of Congress. In this sense, the norms that limit the legislative role of the executive when it assumes extraordinary power, the prohibition on the executive's issuing codes, and the granting to Congress of the capacity to modify decrees issued by the government are all notable. The new charter affirms as the exclusive right of Congress the creation of statutory and organic laws, which are the basis for implementing the norms of the new constitution, and it prohibits promulgation of such laws by the president acting under extraordinary powers.[30] In addition, Congress recovered certain budgetary powers,[31] as well as powers to intervene in decisions made by the executive during periods of national emergency.[32] But the greatest innovation in the political control that Congress can exercise over the executive is contained in the power to censure cabinet ministers.[33] Nevertheless, this power has yet to be used. In spite of all these reforms, the inability of Congress to control the executive continues. That inability rests today more than ever on the enormous fragmentation and atomization of the parties in Congress.

The series of measures designed to return Congress to a central role in political life was part of the attempt by the framers of the Constitution to make political representation more effective. It would not be worthwhile to widen and expand channels of congressional representation unless Congress became truly deliberative and able to legislate autonomously and control the executive. But the crisis of Congress could not be solved only on the basis of these modifications. To "cleanse" the image of a Congress in decline, it was necessary in addition to institute strict mechanisms of control to curb the most disturbing vices of the institution: corruption and clientelism.

As a symbolic act that was intended to erase in one fell swoop old practices and create a completely new legislative power, the Constituent Assembly decided to close Congress, revoke the mandate of the congresspeople elected in 1990, and convoke new elections at the end of 1991. At the same time, certain restrictions were created with the long-term objective of modifying congressional behavior, but their effects have been only partial until now. First, substitutes for candidates in popular elections for public bodies were eliminated, so that congresspeople lost an instrument to "make electoral compromises, elude responsibilities, and share the rewards resulting from occupying a seat in Congress."[34] But congresspeople then came up with the idea of replacing the substitute with a temporary replacement, the second person on the party electoral list, which had even more perverse effects than those of the original system. "Parliamentary auxiliaries," a symbol par excellence of clientelism practiced through the privatization of State resources, were also eliminated, but new slush funds have been created, resulting in the same effects. A new system for determining incompatibilities and conflicts of interests has also been introduced,[35] the application of which has led to the loss of investiture of various congresspeople, not for political but judicial reasons.

With these and other measures, such as separating the holding of presidential elections from the other elections,[36] the Constituent Assembly aimed at undermining the corrupt practices of the traditional political class and untangling the clientelist networks that extended from the local to the national levels. To date, experience shows that constitutional reform did not manage to solve the most problematic aspects of political representation. It appears that the incentives and sanctions contained in these institutional innovations have not been sufficient to produce a substantial change in the opportunistic behavior of the Colombian political class. That is, at least in part, because, as noted above, the innovations were designed behind the backs of and against the politicians who were their targets. We should also note that measures such as the creation of a true "civil service," the best antidote against clientelization of the State, were not incorporated into the constitutional reform.

With regard to political parties, the new Constitution not only eliminated restrictions that granted the traditional parties a monopoly on representation, but also specifically recognized the right of all citizens to "construct parties, movements, and political groups without limitation, to freely form part of these groups, and spread their ideas and programs."[37] Although the balance of the resources continues to tilt strongly in favor of the traditional parties, the introduction of State financing of political campaigns and equal access to the communications media owned by the State for all legally registered parties and movements[38] demonstrate an intent to democratize the means of acquiring power.

But the impact of these reforms on party organizations and the party system has been contradictory, inefficient, and ineffective. The traditional parties not only have resisted the change, but they have also rapidly accommodated themselves to the new institutional situation without modernizing, democratizing, or strengthening themselves. On the contrary, in this process of accommodation, they have intensified their historical tendencies toward pragmatism, fragmentation, and clientelism. The changes, above all those affecting the electoral system, have in fact accentuated the most problematic traits of the parties and the party system in Colombia rather than transforming them.[39]

Finally, it is necessary to note the resounding failure of the creation and consolidation of a political opposition in Colombia. This has occurred despite constitutional recognition of the legitimacy of political opposition and the inclusion of a series of rights that should guarantee its operation.[40] Worse than errors in institutional design, this situation is the result of one of the most serious problems confronting the implementation of the Constitution of 1991: the lack of a State able to back up and invigorate the norms and rights contained within that document.

We turn now to the subject of the new mechanisms of political participation sanctioned by the Constitution of 1991. It is important to emphasize that one of the greatest advances of the Constitution is the amplification of forms of political participation beyond the realm of the purely electoral. Apart from according the right to elect and be elected through the vote, that is to say, the right of choosing representatives, the Constitution broadens the rights of the citizens to participate in the "creation, exercise, and control of political power" (Article 40). In addition to the vote, the possibility of constructing parties, movements, and groups with political ends, and the right to take on public functions and posts, the Constitution creates an ample range of new mechanisms of participation for citizens. These include the plebiscite, the referendum, popular consultation, the town meeting, the legislative initiative, and the recall of elected officials (Articles 103, 104, 105, and 106).

The novelty here is not only the widening of the repertory of opportunities for participating, but also the fact that a good share of them constitute mechanisms of direct or semidirect participation of the citizens in the decision-making process. The legislative initiative puts citizens on an equal footing with the government and the members of public bodies in initiating the process of creation of norms, be they laws, legislative acts, ordinances, agreements, or resolutions. The town meeting gives citizens the capacity to debate questions of local concern with the local authorities. The recall returns to electors the ability to control the public actions of their elected officials. Finally, the popular council, the plebiscite, and the referendum constitute mechanisms of direct participation by civil society in the making of government decisions.

The utilization of these measures, nevertheless, has been minimal during these years. In this instance, the limitations were imposed by Statutory Law 134 of 1994. This law introduced a series of prerequisites and conditions for the activation of all the mechanisms of citizen participation that substantially complicate their use.[41] The way the new mechanisms for citizen participation were regulated reduced the incentives for collective action; the thresholds require for participation are set too high and presuppose a previously mobilized and organized society. That, as is obvious to any observer, does not exist in Colombia.

Finally, there is the question of the institutionalization of citizen control over the State.[42] Democratization is not exhausted in the widening of the participation or in the perfecting of the mechanisms of better representation. It is also necessary to create and strengthen the mechanisms of control over the State apparatus. That way, representation is not converted into a simple delegation of authority but involves responsibilities. Accordingly, the Constitution strengthened the internal (horizontal) mechanisms of control of the State through assigning new and more precise functions to the offices of the Solicitor General (Procuraduría) and the Comptroller (Controloría), the creation of the figure of the Defender of the People, and the transitory creation of the controversial post of the Overseer of the Treasury (Veedor del Tesoro). The Constitution also emphasizes the autonomy of the National Electoral Council and amplifies and energizes its functions. Even so, for these agencies of control, as well as for the high courts, it looks as if the new Constitution has opened the door to excessive meddling by the parties, the political classes, and Congress in the election of people to fill these posts. This possibility would be a serious defect, because the autonomy and independence of these organizations from party controversies as well as from the Executive are crucial for the successful functioning of the State and the effectiveness of democratic liberties.

The Constitution introduced a series of mechanisms of control "from the ground up," which contributes to the effective public and societal control over the State. The idea was that representatives should act on the premise that those they represent are capable of following their actions and evaluating them and of introducing new elements and modifying others. Article 133 established that "elected officials are politically responsible to society and their electors for completing the functions of their investiture," creating a hitherto missing link of responsibility between the elected and the electors. This link is made effective through new mechanisms of control such as the programmatic vote[43] and the recall. This last measure was only approved for governors and mayors, which left popularly elected bodies beyond citizen control.[44] Regarding the exercise of the administrative functions and their necessary oversight, Article 270 obliges the legislative branch to organize forms and systems of citizen participation that permit vigilance over public affairs at different administrative levels.

To date, these mechanisms of citizen control have only been announced. Their real efficacy depends on their implementation by Congress and on the capacity of civil society to appropriate and act on them. This requires, of course, that organizations of civil society overcome the dispersed and episodic nature of their actions and become permanent agents of control over the actions of the State. Once again, the creation of constitutional mechanisms is a necessary but not sufficient condition for the democratization of the State. The strengthening and autonomy of civil society is also required.

To sum up this section, we can say that the Constitution of 1991 represented a serious effort at democratization of the regime and the Colombian State. It widened and restructured the channels of citizen access to the process of State decision making and, above all, created mechanisms that permitted permanent control and oversight by society over the State, the sine qua non of democracy. The promulgation of the Constitution buried once and for all the argument, made by many, that stigmatized the political regime for its "restricted" or "limited" character. In this way, the work of the National Constituent Assembly resulted in the solution of at least one dimension of the political crisis: that which demanded democratization of the political regime. Nevertheless, following this restatement of the rules of the political game, deeper and perhaps more difficult problems came to light: the profound weakness of civil society and the extremely limited capacity of the State to make the constitutional reforms effective.

The Distance between the Text and Reality

No constitution can be purely descriptive. All constitutions imply a tension and a difficult compromise between what is and what should be, between the point of departure and the social utopia that is proposed and visualized in the constitutional text. In the Colombian Constitution of 1991, it appears that the distance between the written constitution and the real constitution, between the text and the reality that it intended to regulate, proved too great.

In 1991, as in the famous Rionegro Constitutional Convention of 1863, the Colombian delegates committed the error of inventing a constitution "for angels."[45] Knowing that we Colombians are far from being angels, the delegates would have done better to consider a constitution for human beings of flesh and blood whose ambitions and interests must be domesticated by adequately designed institutions. Kenneth Shepsle attributes the success of the U.S. Constitution of 1787 in part to the realistic sense and pragmatism of its creators: "By making a constitution for a new nation, [James] Madison took it for granted that men were not angels, but ambitious and egotistical. Through the institutional design, he aimed to put one ambition in competition against another."[46]

This does not mean that we have to create a new text that is the measure of our vices and defects and forget the possibility of designing through constitutional utopianism a better future. Nothing prevents us from dreaming of traveling to the Far East, but what makes a great difference is knowing, before embarking on such a voyage, if we are in the waters bordering the northern Pacific, or navigating in the Caribbean. What I am trying to say is that although there is nothing wrong in dreaming of a different country, it may be fatal to calculate the point of departure erroneously. We should not fool ourselves about this. Colombia enters into the twenty-first century in a deplorable situation on many fronts: fragmentation and violence in civil society, precariousness in the State apparatus, a crisis of political representation, economic decline, and international vulnerability. These are the central conditions that frame the present crisis. The disenchantment of Colombians—comprehensible if one looks at the nature of the crisis—offers a measure of the enormous distance that separates the point of original departure from the utopian destination outlined in the Constitution of 1991. Taking into account these conditions, it was naive to think that the society that we invented in the Constitution of 1991 could come into being from one day to the next.

Then, the second error of the delegates was to start from a simplistic diagnosis of our problems. If all our problems supposedly originated in the narrowness of the political regime, all that was needed was to topple the institutional restrictions that constricted politics, and we would magically arrive in a "wonderland." I do not think that this diagnosis was completely erroneous, but it was, at the least, incomplete. It was not enough to reform the Constitution, eliminating the rigidities of the regime, making it more flexible, more ample, more "democratic." It was necessary to recognize that behind a weak and incomplete Colombian democracy lurked a precarious State unable to back up and enforce basic democratic institutions, freedoms, and rights. These institutions and rights form the framework in which civil society develops. Behind a weak and incomplete Colombian democracy there lurked as well a weak, fragmented, and, in some sense, "Hobbesian" civil society marked by multiple conflicts among powerful armed actors—with the guerrillas, the paramilitaries, and the private drug traffickers' armies figuring most prominently.

It is worth remembering that citizenship, participation, and representation do not only depend on "the effectiveness of a complex web of legal relationships" but also on "state organizations willing and able to make rights affirmed in pertinent laws effective."[47] In good measure the Constitution of 1991 has not produced the results we all hoped it would because there does not exist in Colombia a State capable of supporting and enforcing constitutional norms. The efforts to democratize the State were not simultaneously accompanied by parallel efforts to strengthen it. For example, the Constituent Assembly did not touch two vital points of the State that are in dire need of reform: the armed forces (an issue ignored except for minor reforms in the way the police operate) and the administrative-bureaucratic apparatus. The way the civil service operates has not been modified and, as a result, corruption, clientelism, and all manner of particularistic practices that contradict the democratic character of the reforms are perpetuated.

In part as a result of these omissions in the charter, but also as a result of the historical development of the Colombian State, serious problems remain in spite of the constitutional changes. The State continues to demonstrate that it is incapable of providing basic public goods: defense, security, and justice. For this reason, peace continues to be an elusive proposition, and the armed actors who often violate the fundamental rights of Colombians, especially the right to life, continue to exist. This incapacity is also dramatically expressed in the justice system, in its inability to resolve the conflicts present in Colombian society. The levels of impunity for criminal acts (calculated at 97 percent) only add to the downward spiral of violence that reinforces the precariousness of the State. This problem is not derived directly from the design of the Constitution itself. No constitutional design, no matter how good it is, can substitute or compensate for the precariousness of the State. It is for this reason that the solution of the crisis is not to be found only in the democratization of the State apparatus and regime; it also depends on the strengthening of a precarious and weak State that is incapable of carrying out its most basic functions. Therefore, the strengthening of the political capacity of the State constitutes the sine qua non for the construction of the democratic regime outlined in the Constitution of 1991.

The majority of constitutions exist with the primordial aim of limiting and controlling the power of the State.[48] In Colombia we demand much more from a constitution: It should simultaneously revive and strengthen the State, recreate and empower civil society, and finally regulate its relationships in a democratic manner. Is this too much to ask for? We thus come full circle and return to the initial theme of this essay, the excessive expectations that we Colombians attach to the potential of a new political charter.

Notes

1. In his *Ingeniería constitucional comparada: Una investigación de estructuras, incentivos y resultados* (Mexico City, 1994), 8.

2. Russell Hardin, "Why a Constitution?" in Bernard Grofman and Donald Wittman, eds., *The Federalist Papers and the New Institutionalism* (New York, 1989), 117–18. [Translator's note: This and the other English-language quotations cited in this essay have been retranslated into English from the Spanish in the text.]

3. See Title XIII, "De la Reforma de la Constitución," which addresses not only the possibility that the citizens present Congress with their initiatives for reform but also the possibility of convoking referendums to approve constitutional reforms. These options are in addition to the now-traditional reform via Congress, and the extraordinary recourse of convoking a constituent assembly.

4. "Historical institutionalism" has been identified as one of the four representative themes of the new institutionalism. See Peter Hall and Rosemary Taylor, "Political Science and the Four New Institutionalisms," unpublished paper (Harvard University, 1994). The best-known work in this field is undoubtedly Sven Teinmo, Kathleen Thelen, and Frank Longstreth, eds., *Structuring Politics: Historical Institutionalism in Comparative Analysis* (Cambridge, MA, 1992).

5. See Gabriel Negretto, "Constitution-Making as Bargaining: The Reform of Presidentialism in the Argentinean Constitution of 1994," unpublished paper (Columbia University, 1997). It would be desirable to construct a model of the constitutional process as a "bargaining process" using the tools offered by game theory. Limitations of time and space prevent me from attempting this exercise here.

6. Marco Palacios, "La gobernabilidad en Colombia: Aspectos históricos," *Análisis Político* 29 (September–December 1996): 16.

7. For a discussion of the various phases of the convulsive process of convoking the National Assembly, see John Dugas, "La Constitución política de 1991: ¿Un pacto político viable?" in John Dugas, comp., *La Constitución política de 1991: ¿Un pacto político viable?* (Bogotá, 1993), 15–44.

8. The Democratic Alliance M-19 appeared in March of 1990 after the reincorporation of the M-19 guerrilla movement to civilian life; it was an alliance that included various other leftist groups. The Movement of National Salvation, in spite of its leadership by Alvaro Gómez, a recognized Conservative party figure, represented an attempt to unite sectors of the right from both of the traditional parties into an independent political movement.

9. This is not the place to outline a critique of the theory and practice of participatory democracy. Suffice it to say that this discourse reflects one of the errors of the delegates in assessing the Colombian situation: In Colombia a representative democracy has never existed. It was enough to aspire to institute and perfect the mechanisms of a true representative democracy. But the delegates resolved to replace it with a "supposed" participatory democracy whose conceptual definition was never well specified. The idea was left floating in the air that participatory democracy was somehow better.

10. The Court's ruling came on October 9, 1990.

11. Some authors, such as Elisabeth Ungar, attribute the reconquest of Congress by the traditional politicians to the fact that the delegates themselves disqualified themselves from participating in the elections of the first postconstitutional Congress in 1991. See her essay, "La reforma del Congreso: ¿Realidad o utopía?" in Dugas, *La Constitución de 1991*, 162–90. I think that this explanation is unsatisfactory, because even though the delegates disqualified themselves as individuals, the movements to which they belonged were able to participate. If the Democratic Alliance M-19, the Movement of National Salvation, the indigenous peoples, the Christians, or other political forces did not manage to maintain their representation in the following congresses, this is due to their own weakness as political parties and movements, and not only to the revenge of the politicians facilitated by the "hara-kiri" of the delegates.

12. Given that the Assembly was composed of seventy-two delegates, the vote by absolute majority required a minimum of thirty-seven votes.

13. This opinion is shared by the analysis of an outside observer of the process (John Dugas) as well as by the Presidential Counsel for Constitutional Development (Manuel José Cepeda), both of whom were at the side of the president during the Assembly debates. See John Dugas, "El desarrollo de la Asamblea Nacional Constituyente," in Dugas, *La Constitución de 1991*, 45–76; and Manuel José Cepeda, *La Constituyente por dentro: Mitos y realidades* (Bogotá, 1993).

14. See Palacios, "La Gobernabilidad en Colombia." According to Gabriel Negretto, in contrast, the fact that in Argentina the two principal parties reached an agreement in 1994 made it possible to effect a constitutional reform that, for the first time in that country, is not seen as a mere imposition of one faction on the rest of society, and this fact is considered one of its strengths. See Negretto, "Constitution-Making."

15. Following Juan Linz, the "effectiveness" of a political system is understood as "the capacity to implement the policies formulated with the desired results," and should be differentiated from "efficacy," understood as the capacity to make decisions or formulate adequate policies. See Juan Linz, "Crisis, Breakdown and Reequilibration," in Juan Linz and Alfred Stepan, eds., *The Breakdown of Democratic Regimes* (Baltimore: Johns Hopkins University Press, 1978), 20–22.

16. Every one of the institutional innovations incorporated into the constitutional text is susceptible to analysis by way of the construction of a model that indicates, following game theory, the hypothetical behavior of the actors after the introduction of this or that institution (law or procedure). We can also determine the desired effects of each. Based on these models, we could evaluate the effectiveness and efficiency of each institution in contrast to its real impact.

17. For the definition of "virtuous or perverse institutionalization," see Ana María Bejarano, "Perverse Democratization: Pacts, Institutions and Problematic Consolidations in Colombia and Venezuela" (Ph.D. diss., Columbia University, 2000), especially chap. 4. Here it is enough to clarify that the terms "virtuous" and "perverse" are not used in the moral sense, but in the sense of their contribution to a dynamic of democratic consolidation. "Virtuous" are those processes, cycles, or patterns of institutionalization that contribute to democratic consolidation; "perverse" are those that obstruct, distort, or impede it.

18. See Jon Elster, "Ulysses Revisited: Precommitment and Constitutionalism," unpublished paper (Columbia University, 1996).

19. See Title VIII of the Constitution, "De la Rama Judicial"; and Jaime Giraldo Angel, "La reforma constitucional de la justicia," in Dugas, *La Constitución de 1991*, 97–133.

20. See Eduardo Cifuentes M., "Derechos fundamentales e interpretación constitucional," *Revista Foro* 21 (September 1993); and Hernando Valencia Villa, "Los derechos humanos en la Constitución del 91," in Dugas, *La Constitución de 1991*, 208–25.

21. This is paradoxical in a country where the State is incapable of protecting the lives of its citizens, the primordial human right.

22. See Title XII of the Constitution and the analysis of Caroline Hartzell, "Las reformas económicas en la Constitución de 1991," in Dugas, *La Constitución de 1991*, 77–96.

23. Title XII, Chapter 6, Articles 371–373, "De la Banca Central."

24. This long tradition appears to have started after the monetary and fiscal disaster during the War of the Thousand Days (1899–1902). It was subsequently ratified by the institutional arrangement of the National Front (1958–1974).

25. See Daniel Castellanos and Gelkha Buitrago, "Gasto redistributivo, transferencias a las regiones y democracia," unpublished paper (Facultad de Economía and Centro de Estudios del Desarrollo, Universidad de los Andes, 1997).

26. Article 171.

27. See Felipe Botero Jaramillo, "¿Porqué las viejas formas del ejercicio de la política no murieron? Un análisis del sistema electoral." Final research report presented to COLCIENCIAS, Bogotá, 1999.

28. Article 171.

29. Article 176. Law 70 of 1993 defined the special electoral district for black communities who had the right to two seats in the Senate after 1994. But the district was called into question during the legislative period of 1994–1998, and in the congressional elections of 1998 the black communities lost the opportunity to elect their two representatives to the Senate.

30. Article 150.

31. Articles 345–354.

32. Articles 212–215.

33. Article 135.

34. Article 261. The quotation is from Elizabeth Ungar, "La reforma al Congreso," 183.

35. Articles 179–187.

36. Article 262.

37. Articles 40, numbers 3 and 170.

38. Articles 109 and 111. See also Law 30 of 1994.

39. See Eduardo Pizarro, "La crisis de los partidos y los partidos en la crisis," in Francisco Leal, ed., *Tras las huellas de la crisis política* (Bogotá, 1996).

40. Article 112.

41. The details of Law 134 are amply examined in Pilar Gaitán and Ana María Bejarano, "Posibilidades y límites de la participación política en Colombia." Unpublished paper presented to the Consejería Presidencial para la Modernización del Estado, Bogotá, June 1994.

42. This section takes up parts of the author's "Recuperar el Estado para fortalecer la democracia," *Análisis Político* 22 (May–August 1994): 68–69.

43. The programmatic vote requires candidates for mayorships and governorships to present voters with a program for government that they are obliged to fulfill if elected.

44. Article 184 leaves open the possibility that any citizen can solicit the divestiture of congresspeople from the Council of State, but the sanction only operates for judicial motives, closing off the possibility of purely political sanctions.

45. Legend has it that the French writer Victor Hugo, upon reading the Constitution of 1863, exclaimed that it was a constitution for angels.

46. Kenneth A. Shepsle, "The Political Economy of State Reform: Political to the Core." Paper presented at the conference "Hacia el Rediseño del Estado," Bogotá, April 27–29, 1998, p. 16.

47. Guillermo O'Donnell, "The State, Democratization and Some Conceptual Problems," in William Smith, Carlos Acuña, and Eduardo Gamarra, eds., *Latin American Political Economy in the Age of Neoliberal Reform: Theoretical and Comparative Perspectives for the 1990s* (New Brunswick, NJ, 1994), 159.

48. On this postulate, Sartori notes, "Constitutions are, first and foremost, government instruments that limit, restrict, and permit the control of the exercise of political power." See his *Ingeniería constitucional*, 213.

Chapter 4

Drug Trafficking and the National Economy

Mauricio Reina

The general perception of people outside Colombia is probably that the enormous income from the drug trade has been a tremendous boon for drug-trafficking Colombians and for the nation's economy as a whole. Although the former is undoubtedly true, the latter, as Mauricio Reina argues here, is problematic. Illicit income from drug trafficking, Reina shows, has had complex and surprisingly negative effects on the Colombian economy, the most destructive among them being its impact on exchange rates. Until the end of the 1990s, however, the Colombian economy continued to grow, continuing a twentieth-century trend that often distinguished the nation from most of its Latin American neighbors. (Colombia escaped the debt crisis of the 1980s, for example, which devastated the economies of Mexico and Brazil and other Latin American countries and led regional economists to speak of a "lost decade" in Latin American development.) But beginning in 1998, the economy began to falter, and by 1999 it was in full recession. Official unemployment reached 20 percent during 1999, the highest in the Americas, while preliminary statistics indicated a growth rate for that year of minus 5 or 6 percent.

The economic crisis was the result of several factors, including the neoliberal "opening" of the economy, in progress throughout the 1990s, which devastated broad sectors of Colombian industry and agriculture thus exposed to the competitive pressures of the world market. The cumulative and worsening effect of the violence, which took its toll on productive investment, both foreign and domestic, also seems to have played a major role, as Reina notes here. But it is the corrosive effects of the illicit drug trade, the focus of his analysis, that may have done the most to weaken the vitality of the Colombian economy over time. Coinciding with serious peace negotiations between the government and the guerrillas, the economic crisis seemed to complicate prospects for the major economic and social reforms. Who, many asked, would pay the bill?

Mauricio Reina is an economist at the Universidad de los Andes in Bogotá. He is also affiliated with the semiprivate economic think tank, Fedesarrollo, and is a frequent contributor to the Colombian weekly news magazine *Cambio*.

An earlier version of this essay appeared as "La mano invisible: Narcotráfico, economía y crisis," in Francisco Leal, ed., *Tras las huellas de la crisis política* (Bogotá: Tercer Mundo Editores, 1996), 153–79. It is published here by permission of Tercer Mundo Editores.

In Colombia it has become customary to say the economy is doing well, but the country is doing poorly. This expression, which apparently suggests a total independence between the economic sphere and the rest of national life, in reality reflects the complexities of the ties between the two. Drug trafficking is one of the national problems in which the nature and implications of those ties are not clear. The uncertainty is so great that drug trafficking has become, in equal measures, hero and villain in different discussions concerning the performance of the Colombian economy.

This essay reviews the limited existing literature on this theme. It attempts to understand the ties between drug trafficking and the Colombian economy that have developed during the crisis that is affecting the country, and especially to clarify the means of warding off the crisis. This work does not pretend to be original in its basic tenets, a good part of which come from the bibliographic sources consulted. Its goal is to link some interesting hypotheses in this great debate so that the crisis affecting the country may, at the same time, become an opportunity.

The first section presents a review of the most relevant calculations concerning the size of the Colombian drug-trafficking business. The second section evaluates some hypotheses about the impact of illegal resources on the Colombian economy. The third centers on a discussion of the options that the country currently confronts in overcoming the drug calamity and its harmful effects. Finally, the conclusion we have reached is presented.

The Extent of Drug Trafficking in Colombia

For many national and international observers, it is disconcerting that no reliable analyses of the impact of drug trafficking on the Colombian economy exist. It is not easy to understand how a country that bears the heavy cross of being internationally recognized as the biggest processor and vendor of cocaine does not keep track of the effect of the black-market economy on its principal economic indicators. For some, the uneasiness goes even further. They argue that perhaps drug trafficking is responsible for the fact that the Colombian economy has maintained sustained growth during the last decades in a region characterized by economic instability and crisis.

Putting questionable interpretations aside, it is true that the analysis of the impact of drug trafficking has been absent from the immense majority of studies about the Colombian economy. Although there are lesser reasons, this absence has, in my judgment, a fundamental explanation: Drug trafficking is an illegal activity, and for that reason there are no existing reliable statistics that reveal its extent or trends. In spite of this obvious limitation, a few economists have ventured to make approximate calculations of the size of the illegal economy in Colombia. A brief outline of the conclusions reached by those analysts follows.

Students of the problem have tried to respond to two fundamental questions. How much do Colombians involved in the drug trade earn? What part of these earnings enters the Colombian economy and what is its impact on it? These two questions, even if clearly linked, are distinct in their nature and in the methodology required to study them.

The Earnings of Drug Trafficking

To estimate the participation of Colombian economic agents in the drug-trafficking business, the analysts have, in general, used the following methodology. They have outlined the distinct phases of the cocaine cycle, from cultivation of the coca leaf to the sale of the drug in small quantities in the final market. They have estimated the added value in each of these phases. And they have calculated the participation of Colombians in each phase. Some of the analysts have also included similar calculations for marijuana—especially important for the end of the 1970s and the beginning of the 1980s—and poppies—of special relevance in the last five years. If this methodology is conceptually sound, the rough nature of the available information concerning quantities and prices and the level of Colombian participation in each phase of the process has resulted in a dramatic range of estimates.

The most complete statistical analyses have been developed by José Hernando Gómez (1988 and 1990), Salomón Kalmanovitz (1990), and Eduardo Sarmiento (1990). Unlike other researchers, these economists have tried to construct consistent series for an extensive period of time, centered on the 1980s. The three studies utilize the above-mentioned methodology and, as primary sources, use data from U.S. governmental agencies (with all their potential biases) to estimate production of the different illegal drugs.

The three analyses come out with quite different estimates of the magnitude of Colombian drug earnings. But they all concur that earnings were highest and most variable at the start of the 1980s (Thoumi, 1994). In effect, these studies signal that the earnings attributed to Colombia through illegal drugs—without including operations *inside* the United States—oscillate between U.S.$2 and $4 billion per year. This range does not deviate substantially from the results of another analysis that, with the same methodology, concentrated on studying the phenomenon for one single year (Nadelmann, 1986).

There are several things that are worth highlighting about these results. In the first place, even if the authors explicitly recognize the limitations of their analyses owing to the scarcity of information, the great variation observed in the calculations is still surprising. For example, while Kalmanovitz calculates for 1987 that the value of exports of processed cocaine from Colombia reached U.S.$5.2 billion, Gómez estimates that it was U.S.$1.4 billion, and Sarmiento proposes a range between U.S.$1.4 and $3.7 billion. The differences are largely explained by each author's estimate of the volume of cocaine exported, which, in turn, reflects the relative weight assigned to each phase of drug production in determining overall earnings.

On the other hand, it is remarkable that in spite of the great differences in the estimates, the calculations reveal a similar tendency. This fact, which could be read as proof of the strength of the results, can be explained largely because the three studies use, as already mentioned, the same primary sources, data from U.S. governmental agencies.

These statistical results have generated diverse positions among distinct economic analysts. For example, for Francisco Thoumi, "the events of recent years suggest that these figures could have been enormously underestimated, at least after 1994" (Thoumi, 1994:202). From his point of view, Javier Fernández (1994) considers that "the very fact that in the estimates of diverse authors there exist substantial differences confirms that the result depends too much on suppositions and guesses."

Entry into the Colombian Economy

The second question to which studies try to respond is: What part of the Colombian drug-trafficking earnings effectively enters the Colombian economy? The economic resources from drug trafficking can enter the Colombian economy through a variety of ways, some of which are registered in the balance of payments.

In the case of operations registered in the balance of payments, the laundering of illegal dollars can artificially "inflate" or "deflate" earnings in legal transactions overseas. In this category appear, for example: falsely reported exports or the overinvoicing of exports, underinvoicing of imports, false earnings through tourism, or false remittances from Colombian workers abroad. Among the transactions that do not appear in the balance of payments, contraband of different types of products occupies a principal place. And the so-called black dollars serve to finance Colombian capital flight abroad as well as to pay for the purchase of diverse goods and services by Colombians in the rest of the world.

All of these operations end up affecting the legal economy in some way (see section below). From a methodological point of view, the principal difference among them is that those that are registered in the balance of payments are more easily estimated, while the calculation of the others is hardly more than a guess. In effect, some analysts have used comparative means to evaluate the credibility of the statistics of the balance of payments. To that end they have utilized variables such as the physical volume of Colombian exports and imports and the commercial statistics of other countries that trade with Colombia. They have also analyzed historical patterns in statistical series that should not show abrupt changes through time. Comparing these numbers with the registered figures in the balance of payments, the analysts have tried to detect distortions that can reveal laundering of illicit monies.

The estimates of contraband and other types of unregistered trade present much greater difficulty. The variability of the available data is so great that the figures cannot support very trustworthy analysis. As an illustration, the estimates concerning contraband vary between U.S.$1.8 billion annually, as calculated by the Office of Taxes and National Customs in 1992, and U.S.$5.5 billion, as calculated by the National Comptroller in 1995.

Taking into account all these procedures, calculations of the entry of capital related to drug trafficking into the Colombian economy oscillate between U.S.$0.5 and $4 billion per year. Once again, the range of estimates is surprising, and it has led to distinct positions on the part of economic analysts. For example, Thoumi indicates that, even though the limitations of the available information on the influx of capital from illegal drugs into the Colombian economy cannot be exactly estimated, "it could have been [U.S.$]2 billion per year, a great quantity in comparison with the size of the private sector's investment in the country" (1994:208).

Fernández analyzes estimates by the Departamento Administrativo Nacional de Estadística (DANE) of the volume of Colombian cocaine exports—estimates that use the same methodology as the previously mentioned authors—and compares them to the behavior of the Gross Domestic Product and the evolution of the differential between the official exchange rate and that on the black market. He warns that the "changes in the coca business, which because of their abruptness and magnitude resemble a stampede of buffaloes, do not even leave the trace of a butterfly on the economic landscape." Additionally, he presents the hypothesis that drug-trafficking earnings behaved in an almost stable way in the 1980s, reaching some intermediate value along the range estimated by DANE: between U.S.$0.7 and $4.5 billion.

Where Do Drug Profits Go?

If there are doubts and disagreement concerning the total earnings derived from drug trafficking as well as about the flow of illegal capital into the Colombian economy, the uncertainty is even greater when the total of accumulated resources through the years is discussed, and the final destination of those resources is analyzed. One analytic option consists in adding, year by year, the supposed total amount that has entered the Colombian economy and calculating a certain percentage of investment of those resources in distinct areas of the economy. Kalmanovitz (1990), for example, estimates that if the drug traffickers had invested U.S.$2 billion per year since 1980, at the beginning of the 1990s they would have 30 percent of the wealth of all Colombians. Thoumi (1994) calculates that drug traffickers' accumulation during the 1980s resulted in a total of between U.S.$39 and $66 billion. Although the author recognizes the flawed nature of the calculations, he concludes that the total earning power of accumulated capital by the drug traffickers would be so great that it could yield as much or more profit as the business of drug trafficking itself.

Even so, these calculations concerning the wealth accumulated by the drug traffickers should be taken with a grain of salt. These figures suffer from the same limitations as the estimates of drug-trafficking earnings rehearsed previously, because they are only an elaboration of the same suspect data. The sensitivity of the results to the suppositions adopted and the precariousness of the basic available information on which the different calculations are made make one think that the great variability of the ranges that result is a danger signal about the trustworthiness of the whole exercise.

But if the aggregated data do not permit a fairly precise calculation of the total accumulated assets from drug trafficking, there exist certain sectional or regional analyses that can throw some light on the areas of the economy that are most affected by the phenomenon. According to an interview-based project developed by Mario Arango (1988), the Antioqueño drug traffickers have demonstrated a great preference for rural and urban real estate, including the purchase of great blocks of land. In contrast, none of those interviewed showed interest in the industrial sector. The largest purchases of land were in the Magdalena Medio, the Llanos Orientales, and in parts of Antioquia and Córdoba (Thoumi, 1994:206).

The resources of drug trafficking have also been oriented toward the construction industry. Hernando Gómez (1988) warns how the boom in construction at the end of the 1970s in Barranquilla coincides with the takeoff of exports of marijuana, while Medellín suffered a like phenomenon during the middle 1980s, coinciding with the consolidation of cocaine exports. In this context, the finding of Giraldo (1990) also stands out: Since the middle of the 1980s, the amount of construction approved in Medellín has grown notably more than the amount approved for financing. This fact would seem to reveal the appearance of great volumes of financing for construction that previously did not exist, which are complementing traditional means of financing.

A study centered on evaluating the regional effects of drug trafficking (Vargas, 1994) shows how, in a medium-sized city in the north of Valle del Cauca known for the great influence that drug trafficking has on it, extraordinary urban growth has occurred since 1989. The same study shows that earnings from the export of illegal drugs have gone into investments in the agricultural sector (fruit processors), the commercial sector (agricultural implements), and the service sector (auto repair shops and taxis).

In sum, with respect to the destination of the resources generated by drug trafficking that enter the Colombian economy, the few academic analyses that exist suggest the following general traits. First, a substantial part of the resources of the drug traffickers is devoted to the consumption of luxury goods or services. The luxury goods involved are almost exclusively imported, although most of the service activities have low added value. Second, in the field of investments properly identified, the drug entrepreneurs have a marked preference for the purchase of real estate, be it homes, apartments, or rural properties. Third, an important part of illegal resources is quietly channeled through the Colombian financing system. Fourth, there is evidence for the investment of illegal capital in the commercial sector, especially at the regional level. Fifth, the evidence for illegal investments in the industrial sector is scarce.

The Effects of Drug Trafficking on the Colombian Economy

The uncertainty concerning the extent and characteristics of drug trafficking has been fertile terrain for speculation of all kinds about the effects of the business on the Colombian economy. At the end of the 1980s, it was common to hear questionable arguments that drug trafficking was the principal reason Colombia had not suffered the rigors of the external debt crisis affecting the majority of the countries in Latin America during the previous decade. Some analysts went further, noting that much of the growth of the Colombian economy in recent years was due to the earnings of drug trafficking. Some international commentators even went so far as to refer to Colombia as a drug-trafficking economy.

However, the available evidence, while limited, appears to demonstrate that the reality is quite different. It is obvious that the business of drug trafficking has been a source of wealth for various Colombians and that from it diverse investments have been made at the national and even international level. But the nature of that wealth and those investments is ephemeral. Save for a few exceptions, the economic resources of the drug traffickers have been utilized in a nonproductive and inefficient manner, generating many more negative effects than positive ones. The following paragraphs seek to illustrate this hypothesis.

As has been previously argued, the estimates concerning the extent of the business of drug trafficking are not very trustworthy. Even so, the available evidence about the mechanisms through which illicit resources enter the Colombian economy, as well as the fragmentary information that exists about the possible final destination of such resources, does permit hypotheses about the kinds of economic effects the business has had.

The Exchange Market

As previously indicated, the operations through which illegal dollars enter the economy can be recorded or not in the balance of payments. Generally, the recorded operations in the balance of payments mean a greater offering of foreign exchange in the legal market than would have been available in the absence of drug trafficking. Unrecorded transactions have the same effect in the balance of payments because of buying and selling between the black market and the official foreign exchange market.

If this greater availability of foreign exchange was convenient when external resources were scarce in the region, its benefits were incidental. It is true that, during periods of extreme pressure on exchange rates, the extra foreign exchange generated by drug trafficking worked against drastic macroeconomic adjustments, at least in the short term. But, in the medium term, those same resources have generated a strong distortion in the price of the dollar, with the consequent negative effects on the assignment of productive resources.

In this sense, it is evident that the illicit drug business has had a negative impact on the rest of the economy by driving the exchange rate lower. A type of Dutch disease, which some analysts call the Andean disease, has resulted (O'Byrne and Reina, 1993). This phenomenon results in a loss of competitiveness of those sectors of the economy that produce goods for export or goods that substitute for imports, because of the tendency for the peso to be overvalued.

Monetary and Inflationary Effects

It is evident that the Bank of the Republic can, in part, avoid this tendency toward overvaluation by buying part of the extra foreign exchange. These purchases of dollars add to the international reserves of the country, in this way raising the monetary base and pressuring a greater quantity of money into circulation in the economy. If this is true, the presence of drug-trafficking resources nevertheless generates a real revaluation of the peso by way of a greater pressure on prices.

But the inflationary pressures of drug trafficking do not only result from growth in the monetary base. Generally, it is possible to argue that all resources of illegal origin that enter the Colombian economy signify a greater aggregated demand, which translates into a rise in the general level of prices, an increment in production, or both. Nevertheless, the effect depends on the final destination of such resources. For example, as previously mentioned, much drug-trafficker spending is on luxury goods that are generally imported. Similarly, some analysts affirm that a not inconsiderable part of the imports of inputs into manufacturing and capital goods during the 1980s—a period in which the rest of the region experienced the rigors of the exchange crisis caused by the external Latin American debt—were financed with hot money while businesspeople who benefited looked the other way.

In these cases, not only would any effect on domestic production and prices be avoided, but the exchange and monetary effects already noted would also be neutralized. A similar case can arise with the resources destined for land purchases if, as Thoumi argues (1994:254), those who sell their lands to the drug traffickers end up removing the money so gained from the country.

Since this process of land purchase seems to have been particularly intense in the Magdalena Medio, the Llanos Orientales, and in parts of Antioquia and Córdoba—even if there are no totally trustworthy data—the available evidence suggests that an immense proportion of the best lands in the country have landed in the hands of drug traffickers. This process has translated into a general displacement of agricultural activity, both because the lands in question are now devoted to pasturage or recreational farms, or because, if they are dedicated to productive activities, technological improvements are introduced that result in bankrupting the competition (Vargas, 1994:291). This phenomenon is accentuated because the rise in demand for land has increased land prices exorbitantly in the affected regions, so that often it is better business to sell than to continue to farm.

In these ways, the high cost of land generated by the drug traffickers' limitless demand has worsened the problems of poverty, unemployment, and productivity in the Colombian countryside. Worse still is that, as this process advances, the real possibility of agricultural reform becomes ever more remote. It is much more difficult to deprive drug kingpins of their lands—they have veritable armies at their service and great regional political influence—than it is a simple landholder.

But the counterproductive effects of drug money are not limited to the displacement of productive activity in the rural sector. Again, the available evidence suggests that drug traffickers have little interest in investing their money in the industrial sector. In addition, the sectors in which they spend most of their money (imports, luxuries, land for nonproductive uses) do not have much impact on other sectors of the economy. The overall result is limited economic growth (Thoumi, 1994:256).

The only exception to this rule is not insignificant, and needs to be weighed. The immense flows of illegal resources destined for construction have had, without doubt, a stimulating effect on productive sectors such as iron and cement as well as on the employment of unskilled labor. Moreover, it is possible that the unproductive bias of activities stimulated by drug-trafficking money may change over time. This is because some drug kingpins are sending their children to study abroad with the aim of efficiently and legally administering their fortunes in the future (Vargas, 1994:229).

Special attention to the effects on production of two of the mechanisms through which illegal dollars are laundered is warranted here: the underinvoicing of imports and openly tolerated contraband. Their effects on national production are devastating, at least in terms of products with clearly distorted prices that in no way reflect their costs of production. In their operations, drug traffickers do not mind losing money on underinvoicing an import or selling a contraband product below its real value, because their ultimate objective is to accomplish the "legalization" of ill-gotten foreign exchange. Moreover, the losses incurred by selling products below their real costs are insignificant when compared with the immense earnings of the drug-trafficking business.

Drug trafficking has also negatively affected the Colombian economy through its chilling effect on foreign investment. Potential investors are put off by the violence associated with the drug trade. Such violence, coupled with the violence engendered by the guerrillas, severely compromises the sense of security of foreign investors. Add to that all the negative repercussions of the drug trade for the national economy we have reviewed to this point, and it is clear that Colombia is at a competitive disadvantage when foreign firms decide where to invest their money.

In this respect, even though some analysts have claimed that no important correlation exists between the collateral effects of drug trafficking and foreign investment decisions, it is not easy to explain in any other way why Colombia has not enjoyed greater flows of foreign investment. For example, investment in Colombia has a very different record from that observed in Chile, which is surprising in that they are the two most prosperous and stable economies of Latin America in recent years. In fact, if the distorting sectors, such as mining and petroleum, are excluded, the amount of foreign investment attracted by Chile is more than three times that of Colombia.

In Synthesis

Contrary to what conventional wisdom has indicated for many years, drug trafficking has had a net negative effect on the Colombian economy. Even though illegal resources have nourished large individual fortunes and have even energized some regional economies in the process, their effect on the national economy has been much more negative than positive.

On the one hand, drug trafficking has generated pressures for an overvalued peso, which in the context of the neo-liberal "opening" of the economy has worked against exports and the sectors that produce goods that could be exported. On the other hand, even if drug trafficking has pumped more money into the economy, that money flows into minimally productive activities that have nearly nonexistent links to the rest of the economy. The only important exception to this tendency is the resources invested in the construction sector, which have generated a demand for basic materials and unskilled manual labor.

The abundance of resources generated by drug trafficking has resulted in great distortions in different markets, causing many legally established businesses to cease to be profitable. This phenomenon has been particularly notable in the agricultural sector, because the purchase of rural lands is a preferred way for drug traffickers to spend their money. The industrial sector has been seriously weakened by the illicit competition generated by undervaluing imports and money laundering through contraband.

In addition to these direct costs of drug trafficking, the scourge of drugs has wounded the national economy profoundly in an indirect way. Drug trafficking's enormous capacity to generate violence and corruption has undermined one of the most important bases for vigorous and sustained economic development in the context of the global economy: rules of play that guarantee stability in all aspects of national life.

The inherent costs of violence and insecurity, anxiety generated by the fragility of the political system, and even the uncertainty concerning rights to property and life have gradually translated into elements of comparative disadvantage for attracting productive capital. It is understandable that, with these discouraging factors, it is increasingly difficult to maintain foreign investment. This impediment to acquiring the most advanced technologies is slowly becoming too burdensome for the development of an open economy in the increasingly competitive world market.

Given all these negative effects, it is clear that removal of the drug-trafficking business would be the best thing that could happen to the Colombian economy. In the absence of illegal transactions, the potential for economic growth and development would increase on various fronts simultaneously. The flow of illegal foreign exchange would wane, thereby reducing the revaluative pressures on the peso. Through a single shock in the exchange market, a more favorable exchange rate for the productive sectors putting out tradable goods would be reached, one more in tune with the potential of our productive apparatus. The result would be greater production and employment.

Moreover, the artificial distortions in various markets would be minimized, which would not only validate productive legal activities, but also help to define realistically the areas of natural competitive advantage in the international arena. In this way the detrimental competition to national production, derived from underpricing and contraband, would be neutralized. Finally, and more generally, a favorable environment for the slow restoration of the foundations for development of the economy and the citizenry would be attained—that is, security, justice, and confidence in political institutions.

From Crisis to Opportunity

As indicated by various authors, the principal reason drug trafficking has been established in Colombia is the comparative advantage the country offers for the proliferation of this type of business: a minimum risk of failing in illicit activities. According to Sarmiento (1990:90), for example, "The more dynamic evolution of drug cultivation in Colombia is explained not by the productivity of coca leaf farming but by the relative ease of the transport and commercialization of coca, the capacity for bribery and intimidation, and, above all, the ways profits can be utilized."

Thoumi (1994:177) warns that the most important factor in the comparative advantage of the country in the drug business "has been the progressive delegitimation of the government," a process generated, in turn, by the high level of violence, a tradition of contraband trade, and the long-term existence of an illegal foreign exchange market. To these factors Thoumi adds the geography of the country, the traditional tendency of Colombians to search for quick profits, and the legal and illegal migration of Colombians to the United States.

Fernández (1995:40) echoes these views and outlines the case in terms of traditional crime theory in which a country has a comparative advantage in the development of an illegal activity when its circumstances maximize the probability of success in such endeavors. Fernández also brings into focus Sarmiento's hypothesis that illegality is key to the high level of value added to Colombian drug trafficking. "Given that the producers of other countries could not compete with the price at which Colombia could sell, the Colombians could charge a much higher price than that which covers their costs. Thanks to more effective repression in the rest of the world, Colombian drug traffickers could gain extraordinary profits" (1995:41).

Putting aside the differences in shading and development of these three arguments, the truth is that the high probability of success of illegal activities guarantees the existence of a double phenomenon: Colombia's comparative advantage in the development of drug trafficking and the possibility for extraordinary revenues. Following this reasoning, it is clear which plan of action must be followed in order to resolve the problem.

According to Fernández (1995:45), "Whatever reduces the probability of success for drug traffickers, and augments the costs of their operations, will substantially reduce net revenues." After reaching a certain critical level of hindrance, the business can cease to be profitable—even if cocaine prices are sky-high—and drug traffickers will move to other countries. Following this logic, Fernández concludes that "the essence of the strategy [is] to destroy the criminal organization capable of generating corruption, intimidation, and, naturally, the assassination of those who threaten the business." In this way, the comparative advantage of Colombia in the business and the origin of its immense profits would be minimized.

Opposing, at least apparently, the argument that it is necessary to repress drug trafficking in Colombia is one that claims that so long as a demand for drugs exists and the business is illegal, all official efforts will be futile. At this point it is useful to differentiate between the problem of drug trafficking in general and its existence in Colombia. It is true that while there is a demand for drugs (a demand that is very inelastic in response to the changing price of drugs) and the business is illegal, the possibility of obtaining great earnings through production and distribution of narcotics will exist. But, as others have noted, the fact that there is drug trafficking—with all of its devastating consequences—does not imply that it has to be located in Colombia. In other words, until the international community finds a way to solve a problem whose ethical, legal, and public health dimensions make dealing with it extremely difficult and complex, Colombia's best strategy is to fight to eliminate its own comparative advantage in the business.

Toward this end, the country should work at the very least on the following fundamental fronts: (1) it should fight against corruption in the political, judicial, and State security spheres; (2) it should increase the efficiency and effectiveness of justice, both in the processing and in the sentencing of delinquents; (3) it should work to eliminate the tolerance that certain social sectors have developed for drug-related activities; and (4) it should reduce the economic spaces where illegal profits can be put to use. Necessarily, a considerable degree of force must accompany these measures in order to neutralize the vast military capability recently developed by the drug traffickers.

The first three arenas are beyond the scope of this essay. As for the fourth, there are two problems—contraband and the financial sector—on which it is especially urgent to take rapid and effective measures. Doing so would constitute a first step toward beginning to close the economic spaces that drug trafficking occupies. Once effective controls have been established in these two problem areas, the neutralization of money laundering and, with it, a reduction in the comparative advantage of Colombia in the drug-trafficking business, will have begun.

As discussed above, the available estimates concerning contraband are scarce and the results are too variable to be trustworthy. These range from U.S.$1.59 billion to $5.5 billion annually during the early to mid-1990s. In spite of the questionable quality of those calculations, it is clear that any value in this range is truly scandalous: The total of merchandise illegally entering the country each year thereby would be between 12 percent and 42 percent of the value of legal imports.

Considering the magnitude of the problem, it is evident that government efforts have been totally insufficient and, perhaps, poorly conceived. The results speak for themselves. According to government statistics, operations against contraband in 1995 captured goods valued at only U.S.$50 million, which is between 1 percent and 3 percent of the estimated totals. It is possible that the government's actions are poorly targeted. The Samper government's Plan of Action against Contraband is almost totally focused on the control of so-called technical contraband that involves distorting or falsifying legal instruments such as import manifests. Meanwhile, actions against contraband in goods are practically nil. Although it is true that there are important problems of money laundering involving underpricing or changes in the customs classifications of some imports, they involve a small proportion of the rampant contraband problem.

More important, if this poorly focused strategy is continued, it will end up hurting legal importers of goods without affecting the contrabandists. For example, no one doubts the virtues of mechanisms such as reference prices for certain sectors vulnerable to underpricing, so that official agencies can monitor the prices at which the merchandise is imported. But other recently implemented controls, whose hypothetical objective is to control the quantities and the prices of imports from the country of origin, have been highly inoperable and, according to various entrepreneurs, are nothing but a hidden surcharge added to the price of imports.

In sum, according to the arguments of several private economic organizations, what should be done now is to close the contraband loophole without harming the importers who follow legal procedures. In order to reach this goal, what is needed is the commitment of the most honest elements of the armed forces to support actions of the customs authorities. From the point of view of a holistic strategy against drug trafficking, a decisive blow against contraband is as important as the destruction of cocaine-processing laboratories. Both attack sensitive links in the chain of illegal business and undermine Colombia's comparative advantage in drug trafficking.

Beyond the cooperation of the armed forces, there is a factor without which no effort in the fight against contraband can be effective: the commitment of the ruling class. The episodes in which powerful regional political figures have defended local marketplaces where contraband goods are openly sold are well known and neutralize the few official efforts to carry out inspections and confiscations. Various analysts have noted the profound limitations in the fight against contraband of a government led by a president such as Ernesto Samper, whose election campaign was financed in part by representatives of those commercial establishments.

It is useful to emphasize the importance of viewing and treating contraband as a crime, especially when it is linked in some way to money laundering. In this way, contraband operations would be investigated first by district attorneys who can use legal and more effective coercive mechanisms to confront this type of activity. This is the kind of change that must be accomplished in many spheres of national life. We must stop accommodating norms to the massive deterioration of values, and begin restoring values through adequate application of laws and efficient administration of justice.

Within the financial sector there is much to be done to close openings for money laundering. In principle, it looks as if existing norms are well directed, but their application has been very limited. In effect, Order 1872 of 1992 established that intermediary financiers and stockbrokers should report transactions that seemed suspicious, either because of the sums involved, their questionable origins, or because the clients in question are involved in an economic activity that implies sufficient financial solvency to support such operations.

In spite of the existence of this law, the administrative sanctions that have been imposed on the financial entities that do not cooperate have been minimal. The adoption of these sanctions—which can go as far as removal of the functionary involved—on the part of the Banking Superintendency has been practically nil, so much so that the law has been termed a dead letter by the Association of Bankers itself. It is also important to note that with the passage of Law 190 of 1995, the laundering of funds has been penalized, but until now there has not been a single person detained for this crime.

It is no accident that Colombia's General Accounting Office has on several occasions called attention to the excessive tolerance with which the financial system treats hot monies. Any progress in closing existing spaces for illicit resources in Colombia's financial system will be fundamental for displacing drug-trafficking activities from the country. An encouraging proof of the importance of keeping a closer vigil on financing operations is the fact that the "Proceso 8000" legislation—which constitutes a historic opportunity to undermine Colombia's comparative advantage in drug trafficking—was initiated and has largely succeeded thanks to its investigation of bank accounts and financial transactions.

If the fight against contraband and vigilance over financial operations are necessary short-term priorities, there are other parallel actions that should be taken in order to close the spaces occupied by illicit resources in our economy. One of the most important consists of a commercial blockade of the economic agents involved in money laundering. Toward this end, the Clinton administration, in September 1995, issued an executive order aimed at blocking the business dealings of almost four hundred Colombian enterprises in the United States, thereby attacking the Cali cartel's material base.

One should not underestimate the effect that this type of blockade can have at the national level, either through the application of specific standards or through a change in the attitude of the population. In this regard, examination of a particular case that clearly reveals the importance of people's tolerance of the expansion of illicit activity is useful. A recent study analyzes how in two medium-sized cities of the Valle del Cauca, drug trafficking has had very different fates. In Villa Pujante—a pseudonym for what is apparently Cartago—money derived from illegal activity has flowed to all sectors of the regional economy, thanks to the welcome reception that the population has extended to promoters of the business. In contrast, the economy of neighboring Villa Señorío—apparently Palmira—shows no signs of those resources because the elite of that city never accepted the drug traffickers' presence (Vargas, 1994:290, 311).

In any case, Colombia has a historic opportunity to remove drug trafficking and all of its negative consequences from national territory. The development of the Proceso 8000 legislation has opened the space to work on the four fundamental fronts to eliminate Colombia's comparative advantage. It promotes the fight against corruption, the enhancement of the efficacy and efficiency of justice, the elimination of tolerance of activities related to drug trafficking, and the reduction of economic spaces that permit the mobilization of drug-trafficking earnings.

No one can be so innocent as to think that decisions of this type will not have specific short-term costs. An example is recent data on unemployment in different cities around the country. The average for the seven principal metropolitan areas rose to 10.4 percent in March 1996, while the figure for Cali was more than 13.5 percent. Several analysts attribute this evident regional disequilibrium to the powerful blows that the Cali cartel has suffered in recent months. But difficulties related to a potential dismantling of the drug cartels will be few compared to the benefits, detailed in this essay, that the national economy will receive as a whole.

These medium- and long-range general benefits should be taken into account by all national actors as they confront the difficult task of beginning the process of cleansing the nation. Initiating this process will not be easy. The way in which drug trafficking has been inserted into the national economy suggests a complex dialectic that cannot be ignored in weighing the viability of the solutions. The country has been both victim and beneficiary of drug trafficking's illegal resources. While some sectors have gained from the vast earnings derived from the business, others have suffered the economic costs involved in attempting to advance legal productive activity in the middle of an economy distorted by the effects of illicit monies.

This situation suggests a profound dilemma. In spite of the fact that displacing drug trafficking from the country would bring evident benefits to the national economy, it is very difficult to reach a consensus among the relevant national actors concerning the advisability of this option. Many actors are, of course, interested in continuing to derive economic benefits from illicit resources. And even those actors willing to separate themselves from activities linked to the business are unlikely to admit publicly to their having been involved in these activities.

The profundity of this dilemma has been made evident throughout the crisis affecting the country. For example, it is useful to remember that the decision absolving President Samper of responsibility for the entry of drug-trafficking monies into his campaign was in the hands of congressional members who not only participated in that very process, but who also have been traditionally elected with the help of drug-trafficking resources. Another facet of the same dilemma was suggested by Ernesto Samper himself when, in response to requests by leading economic interest groups that he renounce the presidency, he argued that in Colombia drug-trafficking monies had entered all sectors of the economy. In this way, the present situation reveals itself as a real Pandora's box, full of the skeletons of compromised people who are not ready to assume responsibility and redeem themselves in public.

But the complexity of the dilemma cannot be an insuperable obstacle to taking advantage of the historic opportunity before the country. All processes of cleansing are complex and painful, and in this case it is evident that it is worth doing. The current crisis cannot end with a national agreement of forgiveness and forgetfulness. If it did, it would extend a blank check to drug trafficking and it would make Colombia the most secure refuge for delinquency in the world. The challenge of converting the crisis into opportunity is not easy, but it never has been in the history of humanity.

Conclusion

The effects of drug trafficking on the Colombian economy have been negative. It is undeniable that illegal resources have had some effects that, at first glance, can be considered positive. Drug-trafficking monies have helped energize some regional economies. They have also permitted the consolidation of monumental fortunes in the hands of a few individuals; these fortunes far outweigh the value of the disposable income of the most important economic groups of the country. And they have contributed to the widening of the range of goods available in the country, contributing in this way to flows of consumption and investment.

In spite of the benefits listed above, what looks positive at a microeconomic and sectoral level is negative in the aggregate. First, abundant illicit resources have generated pressure for revaluation of the peso, which has worked against exports and sectors that produce goods that replace imports. Second, the evidence shows that illicit resources are generally used for activities that are not very productive and, with the exception of construction, have almost no productive links to the rest of the economy. The abundance of illicit resources has generated great distortions in national markets, which have weakened the viability of legal businesses. Furthermore, the industrial sector has been affected by unfair competition generated by undercharging for imports and by contraband used to launder illegal dollars.

In addition to these direct economic effects, the calamity of the drug trade has generated a comparative disadvantage for the country in attracting foreign investment. The drug trade's immense power to generate violence and corruption has undermined the existence of solid guarantees in all areas of national life. This greater difficulty in attracting productive capital constitutes, without a doubt, an obstacle for the development of an open economy in an increasingly competitive world market.

Taking into account the costs and economic benefits of drug trafficking, it is clear that it would be best for the national economy to free itself from this calamity. Colombia now has a historic opportunity to displace drug trafficking and all its negative consequences from the national territory. The development of the Proceso 8000 has opened space to work for the elimination of Colombia's comparative advantage. This is not an easy task, since the country has been both victim and beneficiary of activities related to illegal drugs. It is a complex and painful challenge that I hope we dare to meet.

Bibliography

Arango, Mario, ed. 1998. *Impacto del narcotráfico en Antioquia*. Medellín.

Fernández, Javier. "La huella económica del narcotráfico." *Carta Financiera* 90 (February 1994): 67–73.

———. "Implicaciones económicas del desmonte del cartel de Cali." *Carta Financiera* 98 (October 1995): 37–51.

Giraldo, Fabio. "Narcotráfico y construcción." *Economía Colombiana* 226–27 (February–March 1990): 38–49.

Hernando Gómez, José. "La economía legal en Colombia: Tamaño, evolución e impacto económico." *Coyuntura Económica* 18:3 (September 1988): 93–114.

———. "El tamaño del narcotráfico y su impacto económico." *Economía Colombiana* 226–27 (February–March 1990): 8–17.

Kalmanovitz, Salomón. "La economía del narcotráfico en Colombia." *Economía Colombiana* 226–27 (February–March 1990): 18–28.

Nadelmann, Ethan. "Latinoamérica: Economía política del comercio de cocaína." *Texto y Contexto* 9 (1986): 27–49.

O'Byrne, Andrés, and Mauricio Reina. 1993. "Flujos de capital y diferencial de intereses en Colombia: ¿Cuál es la causalidad?" In Mauricio Cárdenas and Luis Jorge Garay, eds., *Macroeconomía de los flujos de capital en Colombia y América Latina*, 259–90. Bogotá.

Sarmiento, Eduardo. 1990. "Economía del narcotráfico." In Carlos G. Arrieta et al., *Narcotráfico en Colombia: Dimensiones políticas, económicas, jurídicas e internacionales*, 43–98. Bogotá.

Thoumi, Francisco. 1994. *Economía y política del narcotráfico*. Bogotá.

Vargas, Ricardo, comp. 1995. *Drogas, poder y región en Colombia*. Bogotá.

Chapter 5

The Equivocal Dimensions of Human Rights in Colombia

Luis Alberto Restrepo M.

In this hard-hitting critique of the way human rights are understood and defended in Colombia and elsewhere in the modern world, Luis Alberto Restrepo, a philosopher at the National University in Bogotá, spares almost no one. Elites and common folk, paramilitaries and the guerrillas, human rights activists and passive citizens, foreign and national observers, and the governments of Colombia and the Western powers—all come in for criticism. Restrepo argues particularly that human rights defense aimed primarily at government violators and their allies on the right, while ignoring the abuses of guerrilla insurgents, is misguided, dishonest, and counterproductive. He argues his case by following the development of the concept of basic human rights from the time of the French Revolution to modern times. (Readers can supplement Restrepo's discussion by referring to the material in Part 3 of the Documents section.)

Luis Alberto Restrepo is the founder and director of the journal *Síntesis: Anuario Social, Política y Económico*. His books include *Autores en conflicto por la paz: El proceso de paz durante el gobierno de Belisario Betancur, 1982–1986* (Bogotá, 1988) and *Colombia: Entre la inserción y el aislamiento* (Bogotá, 1997).

Before reflecting on human rights in Colombia, it is necessary to consider the country's current situation and the recent evolution of human rights. By human rights I mean the fundamental rights of all human beings: the right to life and physical integrity, to dignity and liberty. The first two elements are, in reality, equivalent to only one, that is, the right to physical life in its entirety; the second two pertain to the rights of all human beings in social relations. Fundamental rights are simply the recognition of physical and social existence that all members of a society reciprocally owe one another.

The first version of this essay was written in August 1991 at the request of the Fundación Viva la Ciudadanía and later published as "Los equivocos de los derechos humanos en Colombia," *Análisis Político* 16 (May–August 1992): 23–40. The present version was revised and updated in April 1999. It is published here by permission of Tercer Mundo Editores.

The Human Rights Situation in Colombia

The majority of the Colombian population has become accustomed to viewing human rights violations as endemic occurrences or as natural disasters, as normal as landslides or earthquakes. By way of excusing Colombians, this insensitivity stems in good measure from the impotence of citizens isolated by an all-powerful, generalized, and out-of-control violence. We should recognize, however, that, together with impotence, indifference has also taken its place in the face of everyday violation of others' rights. Between indifference and impotence there is a circular causation. We Colombians are indifferent to violence because of our incapacity to control it, and we are impotent because we remain collectively passive in the face of it.

It is not that Colombians are completely insensitive to violence. Many, perhaps the majority, experience feelings of revulsion, at least for certain crimes, and we express our shock in private conversations. In the case of certain assassinations of great personages, such as that of Luis Carlos Galán, we have even taken part in gigantic mobilizations of public opinion. But even in these instances, it is a matter of fleeting bursts of sentiment—of hurt, anger, and frustration—that rapidly die out, giving way once more to passivity and indifference. Who knows since when—perhaps since the beginning—Colombian society has been in the habit of accepting with a certain resignation the terrible crimes of humanity. If one keeps in mind that respect for human rights is the fundamental premise of all ethics and judicial order, one must necessarily conclude that this premise is extremely weak and fragile in the minds of the Colombian people.

Elites and Human Rights

Human rights have never been a central preoccupation of Colombia's ruling class—be they members of the economic, political, military, religious, or cultural elite—and different social positions or political ideologies have not made any essential difference in this matter. Insensitivity to the violation of the rights of "others" has been, and continues to be, common to businesspeople and union leaders, guerrillas and military personnel, journalists and writers, priests and lay people, political leaders who defend the status quo and those who struggle for radical change. Faced with this situation, we all tend to excuse ourselves, saying to ourselves that this is not so, that we are deeply concerned about the violence, and that we are ready to defend the right to life and liberty. But the truth is that, in the great majority of instances, we do not go beyond this declaration, or, at the most, are ready to defend our own rights, but not those of other Colombians.

If this happens among the elites, it is all the more likely that preoccupation for the defense of human rights has been absent from the great majority of people, who frequently have barely time and energy enough to survive. In all societies, the majority is always profoundly influenced by the mentality and behavior of elites. Accordingly, even though the immediate agents of human rights violations are frequently humble people, they do not bear the greatest responsibility. There is a diffuse complicity on the part of elites in human rights violations. In not a few instances, concrete intellectual authorship of violent acts emanates from powerful, enlightened, and influential sectors. These sectors, due to their principal role in society, should be considered the central focus of the ethical decomposition of the country. The problem of respect for fundamental human rights is, for this reason, first a problem of the elites. Any search for a solution should begin with this acknowledgment.

The Recent Deterioration of the Ethical Climate

The ethical climate appears to have deteriorated in the last twenty years. The physical elimination of people has produced in others a certain silent or conspicuous satisfaction. No longer are we talking only about complacency engendered by political passion or the simple sentiment of vengeance regarding the death of the "other" or "enemy." As an example, witness the "social cleansing" campaigns, which from time to time take place in the largest Colombian cities: assassinations of social outcasts, vagrants, delinquents, drug addicts and dealers. The crimes committed against these "undesirables" are merely noticed. They do not galvanize public opinion. What is more, not a few Colombians in all walks of life view the process with secret satisfaction or they applaud it with a lack of consciousness and a cynicism as criminal as the crime itself.

The media—which have become, for better or worse, the modern-day civics class—frequently adopt a double standard. They develop intense public opinion about kidnappings or the assassinations of certain "notable" Colombian personalities or of foreigners whose deaths have international repercussions,[1] while real massacres of humble people rarely get their attention for more than a day. The harm lies not in the first, but in the second.

A Culture of Indifference toward Violence

I am not one of those who claim there is a "culture of violence" in Colombia. I do not believe that, in the majority of Colombians, there exists a spontaneous and permanent inclination toward the exercise of force as a method for conflict resolution. Instead, I believe that we share a "culture of social indifference" toward violence—a culture that provides the vital soil in which violence takes root and prospers. We are inactive before the violence we witness, closed within a circle of our petty private interests. We do not have the capacity for stable and effective mobilization against crime, based on a clear sense of social solidarity, comparable to that of certain cultures in which the defense of human rights has become intimately linked to collective survival.

The Disintegration of National Consciousness

Without a doubt, the issues we are reviewing here reveal the lack of solidarity, the high level of fragmentation and atomization that characterizes the national consciousness. The majority of Colombians are not conscious of being part of a single people, called upon to share a common, inescapable destiny. Rather, in Colombia there have coexisted many parallel societies that, until recently, survived side by side, attempting not to come into contact with one another. Now, these societies, obliged to live in progressively smaller spaces, bump into each other without recognizing each other. More: There predominates in Colombians an extreme individualism. It is as though there lives on in Colombians the adventurous spirit of an inconclusive conquest in which each individual confronts society as if it were a menacing jungle. And in the struggle of all against all, the moral, legal, or physical annihilation of contenders is accepted as a recourse that is perhaps undesirable and tragic, but licit nonetheless, or, at least, inevitable. It is unfortunately necessary to conclude that, for most Colombians, human rights violations—extortion, torture, kidnapping, disappearance, and assassination—appear as normal means to resolve conflicts and achieve social balance. The respect for fundamental rights and their timely defense is not a central concern in Colombian culture.

"Human Rights" as a Political Banner

Three decades ago, human rights began to become an issue in Colombia. At that time, human rights organizations appeared in the country, groups in solidarity with political prisoners and families of the disappeared, linked to the so-called left or sympathetic toward it. During the Turbay Ayala government (1978–1982), these organizations exercised great influence. Despite military victories won by the armed forces against the guerrillas, the military's excesses—rightfully denounced by those organizations—inflicted on the government a serious political defeat. The Human Rights Convocations held in the country at that time managed to gather together very different currents of opinion and had national and international impact. The Colombian human rights organizations won the support of similar entities and different political forces at the international level.

A kind of parenthesis in the activity of human rights organizations was imposed during the climate of negotiation with the guerrillas created by the administration of Belisario Betancur (1982–1986). The attitude of the president, more attentive to the guerrilla problem and more open to dialogue than his predecessor, his efforts in the search for peace, and his occasional firmness with some high-ranking military personnel seemed to lessen the need for human rights activity. It was not as obvious as it was during the Turbay administration that human rights violations could be attributed to the government. Instead, their violation was attributed to the "paramilitaries," dark forces without a face or identity. And even though the participation of the military in political assassinations was rightly suspected, as was suggested by the attorney general of the time, there did not exist self-evident proofs to demonstrate it, either because witnesses refused to give testimony for fear of reprisals, or because it was thought—probably with reason—that military actions did not reflect the will of the government. As a result, denunciations of abuses lost political effectiveness in the struggle against the State.

After Betancur's failure in the negotiations with the guerrillas, the administration of Virgilio Barco (1986–1990) attempted, in turn, to appropriate the banner of human rights to defend the State. It created a Human Rights Advisory Council charged in principle with promoting respect for human rights in the armed forces and among the Colombian people. The main efforts of the council, however, were concentrated on excusing the government before national and international critics by explaining the systematic elimination of the political opposition as the sole responsibility of the drug traffickers. In this way, the evident participation of some drug traffickers in the systematic annihilation of the Unión Patriótica, a political movement launched by the FARC during the Betancur administration, was used by the government to hide the responsibility of the armed forces in the appalling genocide that was just beginning. It proved sadly necessary for three Supreme Court justices to be assassinated by a band of *sicarios* before the government reacted to the phenomena. But this did not change the fact that the government would continue regarding the liquidation of the Unión Patriótica with relative indifference.

The two succeeding administrations, that of César Gaviria (1990–1994) and Ernesto Samper (1994–1998), maintained the Human Rights Advisory Council, which had demonstrated its worth in the international political battle. They expanded the number of offices concerned with human rights and continued with the practice, instituted by Barco, of choosing people to head the council from the old nonviolent left. In this way, convinced democrats had to confront the growing barbarity while the bipartisan governments they served continued to manifest indifference toward it. During the Barco and Gaviria administrations, the council did not receive much presidential attention, and while it advanced its well-intentioned educational campaigns, the political assassinations continued. Both administrations avoided reforming the military penal code and continued attributing the numerous political crimes not to the politics of the armed forces, but to the isolated actions of individual agents.

Only in the 1990s did growing international pressure, which initially came from the European Union, the United Nations, and the Inter-American Commission of Human Rights, oblige Colombian governments to take action. President Gaviria could think of nothing better than to call the Colombian ambassadors in Europe together in Bogotá in order to get them to launch an intensive public relations campaign focused on his administration's preoccupation with human rights. In contrast, Samper could not elude international pressures and those of the United States any longer. The president was forced to accept the creation and presence of the office of a United Nations High Commissioner for Peace and Human Rights, to give greater attention to the Human Rights Advisory Council, and to recognize for the first time the responsibility of the State in some massacres. He was also forced to promote with greater zeal—even if with equally great negative results—reform of the military penal code. High government entities also began to call to order some military figures, while the courts excluded human rights violations from military jurisdictions. All told, however, the deepening political crisis of the Samper administration (on account of charges of ties to the drug barons), the open indisposition that this created at some high levels, and the worsening of the internal conflict with the guerrillas did not permit his government to promote a policy capable of confronting the growing savagery in an effective manner. Instead, in the face of internal and international pressures on the government and armed forces, the "dirty war" progressively passed into paramilitary hands. Vigilante groups multiplied exponentially and they joined forces in what were called self-defense organizations. The Autodefensas Unidas de Colombia (AUC) developed into a veritable second army.

In this way, while almost all the private human rights organizations raised their prestigious banners to wage a successful international political battle against the Colombian State, the different administrations tried, with the help of the Advisory Council and other similar organizations, to neutralize the political effect of said campaign. High military officials went even further. They took advantage of their recently gained knowledge of human rights to denounce the atrocities of the guerrillas before national and international public opinion.

It is not easy to determine the reasons for the ambiguous attitudes of the Colombian administrations toward the situation. Combined here are the traditional indifference of the elites concerning violation of fundamental rights (especially if the victims are humble or from the opposition), the fear and incapacity of the administrations to reín in the military on which they increasingly depend, and the urgencies and priorities imposed by the growing armed conflict with the guerrillas. Whatever the exact mix of reasons, the least that can be said is that in the competition between the petitions of private organizations and the proceedings of the State on human rights issues, the fundamental rights of Colombians have been converted into political banners in the service of the conflict. Rather than acting as a containing wall against the abuses of all armed groups, human rights has become a figurehead in a war the principal victim of which has been, and continues to be, the defenseless civil population.

It is worth noting here briefly that the present humanitarian and presumably civilizing preoccupation of the Western powers concerning the subject is also not without ambiguity and a certain cynicism. As is well known, torture and disappearance were systematically developed by France in the Vietnam and Algerian wars and were then adopted by the Pentagon for its use in Vietnam. Based on this experience, the U.S. Army trained a good part of Latin American military officialdom and, in particular, officers from Colombia. The good intentions of President Jimmy Carter in promoting human rights, following the overwhelming defeat of his country in Vietnam and in the face of the growing political bankruptcy of the Latin American military dictatorships, did not manage to completely eliminate the practices supposedly demanded by national security. What is more, during the 1980s President Ronald Reagan promoted, in various parts of the world, the development of the famous "freedom fighters," that is, paramilitary forces dedicated to fighting against Communism, whose illegal, and frequently barbarous, practices are well known. President Bill Clinton himself was obliged to seek pardon from the Guatemalan people for the participation of the CIA in the terrible human rights violations in that country during the war.

In regard to Colombia, we recall Lewis Tambs, the celebrated U.S. ambassador who, during the Betancur administration, tried to torpedo the peace process by coining the term "narcoguerrilla." This did not deter him from later concealing, in Costa Rica, a major U.S. drug trafficker, a close collaborator of Colonel Oliver North in supporting the Nicaraguan contras. As was discovered in "Contragate," this unholy policy was promoted from Washington by the ineffable North, who was then a member of the National Security Council under the direction of Admiral John Poindexter. It is a rather curious coincidence that it was precisely during the Tambs tenure that, with the generous support of some drug kingpins, the first Colombian paramilitary groups began to develop under the auspices of high-level Colombian military officials and with the participation of British and Israeli ex-military officials.

Thus, it is only at the end of the Cold War, with the disappearance of the Soviet and the Communist threat, with the pressures of private and human rights organizations on the Congress and government of the United States, and with the chorus of the "international community" (in this instance, composed of the European Union, the United Nations, and the Organization of American States), that Washington appears to have become a fervent standard-bearer for human rights in Colombia and in other parts of the world. But even now its policies in this area are selective and accommodationist, so that, for example, although it has not tolerated Cuban government abuses, it has accepted Chinese misconduct. It is no accident that numerous Colombian officials are upset with Washington and view it with resentment.

European Union countries, whose preoccupation with Colombian violence is highly esteemed, need also to remember their own imperial and colonialist pasts. We have already mentioned France, today the principal promoter of the presumed "right of humanitarian interference." But France is not the only exemplar, as the old European metropolitan powers well know. Fortunately, the enviable current position of the European Union—it has become a great economic power but is free, up to a point, of its own political responsibilities in the world—allows it to adopt humanitarian concerns that would have been unthinkable in the past.

May these brief reflections serve to remind Western powers that today's circumstances should not lull them into forgetting past practices. Their valuable humanitarian concerns can become unacceptable arrogance when they lead to the desire to remedy by force the ills that violence engenders, violence that derives from complex historical circumstances. The current escalation by NATO in Kosovo is guilty of just this kind of arrogant and mistaken humanitarianism. Let us hope that the Western powers do not some day also try to teach us Colombians respect for human rights by violating them in the name of humanity.

Added to the growing pressures by the "international community" on the Colombian State and its armed forces, there is the new demand, made by the guerrillas at the start of the administration of Andrés Pastrana, in August 1998, that the government put an end to the paramilitary forces as a condition for advancing peace negotiations. Some government actions, such as the elimination of the famous CONVIVIR self-defense associations, created by law during the Samper administration, are perhaps a step in this direction. But so long as the Colombian State sees itself ever more besieged by the guerrillas, no administration will be in the position of wanting or being able to confront paramilitary groups that have now become, as we have said, a veritable irregular army.

In spite of everything, at least since 1989, there has been a slow but substantial change of attitude in Colombia concerning human rights. Although not without difficulty and setbacks,[2] some sectors of society are beginning to consider the possibility of universal defense of the fundamental rights of all Colombians. In this regard, certain private entities played a pioneering role, although one not yet completely free of political bias. The same can be said of the efforts by some State functionaries, in particular, by the heads of the Human Rights Advisory Council. The current attempts in favor of reconciliation and peace, especially those that have developed since the Samper administration, are not unaffected by the painful collective discovery of the need for guaranteeing minimum rules as a condition for possibly living together.

Evaluating Human Rights Defense to Date

Based on the brief historical account sketched here, the defense of human rights in Colombia has been subordinated to specific political interests. At least until 1989, public and private human rights organizations had not even questioned whether it was necessary to defend the rights of all Colombians, without regard to political ideology. Private human rights groups limited their actions to the defense of the rights of leaders of popular and leftist organizations. Nor did government entities wholly assume that task, either. Under the pretext of human rights protection, they have first undertaken the defense of their own political interests. High-ranking military officials, for their part, launched a veritable public relations campaign in this direction. In such a way, the defense of human rights was absorbed, subordinated, and manipulated by political adversaries. The aspirations and legitimate rights of civil society were subsumed and annulled, once again, by factional rivalry.

Impact on Ethical and Judicial Consciousness

In thinking through the situation, one can ask if this type of human rights defense has contributed to the maturation of the Colombian ethical and juridical consciousness, or rather, on the contrary, if it has contributed to its deterioration. The mere formulation of the question may seem to many gravely unjust. It could be considered an insult to those Colombians—State officials and private citizens alike—who have risked and even sacrificed their lives in the valiant denunciation of human rights violations committed by the forces of the State. Even so, it is necessary to reflect deeply on the question.

For my part, I am not sure if the defense of human rights accomplished during the last thirty years has improved the ethical climate of the country and strengthened respect for the law among Colombians. On the contrary, I fear that its unilateral manipulation in pursuit of specific political projects has made it lose credibility in society as a whole. Instead of a bastion of the whole society against the unjust violence of those who claim to represent them, human rights have often become a new weapon in the hands of the contending factions, leaving the bulk of society utterly defenseless before the onslaught. Often human rights have been used as a weapon, and the majority of unarmed society has been left completely defenseless.

A Fundamental Reflection on Human Rights

The situation of human rights in Colombia and their defense invites us to reflect deeply on the origin of the doctrine of human rights and its original meaning. Societies can come to appreciate the urgent need for truly universal rights through two paths: by way of education and the formation of citizen consciousness, or through the rejection of potentially universal violence.

Is Education the Source of Human Rights?

The first path is the more desirable, but, unfortunately, it has not been the most common historically. It is part of the humanist illusions of eighteenth-century Europe, which did not always lead to the desired results. Civic education has a certain efficacy in relatively balanced and homogeneous societies in which there exist certain foundations for equity among citizens. Under such conditions the reiteration of the humanist ideal serves as a lubricant for a social machine that is already running. In contrast, in societies marked by acute long-term imbalances, as in Colombia, education for the respect of human rights can coexist—as do religious faith and democratic ideology—with the most terrible violence. It can even become a screen for the violence itself. A good example is the result of the education campaigns promoted by the Colombian Human Rights Advisory Council.

Rights via Terror

The other path to rights is war, violence, or generalized terror. This claim looks like a facile and irresponsible literary paradox. Nevertheless, terror and insecurity have been a permanent school of universal rights. This has been so in Colombia.

Here it is useful to adduce the reason for the change in the comprehension and defense of human rights in Colombia. The change was initiated, between 1989 and 1990, by the crisis of insecurity and terror resulting from the war between the State and "narcoterrorism" and was stimulated again during 1993 by the panic induced by Pablo Escobar and his cartel. Today the crisis is fed by diffuse street crime, the virulence of the armed conflict, and the danger of an open civil war. When, in the late 1980s, violence entered the cities and threatened all society, a consciousness began to awaken in Colombians—still fragile and reversible—of the necessity for creating certain guidelines for living together so that we would not all be destroyed. Through abhorrent means, drug trafficking and delinquency managed to do what no one had done before: make elites of all hues recognize their common destiny. Since then, a renewed comprehension of human rights has come into view, one that is less political and partisan and more universal and focused on society than what was common before. Paradoxically, then, terror has planted the seeds of a possible ethical and judicial rebirth (or perhaps birth?) of Colombian society. The end of narcoterrorism in the mid-1990s permitted a certain relaxation of this new consciousness and fostered a resurgence of voices invoking human rights in exclusive defense of their own interests. But the omnipresent violence and the escalation of armed conflict keep alive a certain instinct of collective survival.

The recognition of the violent origins of universal rights lies in the fundamentals of the anthropological observations and political ethics of Hobbes.[3] In nature, generalized insecurity rules. It is insecurity that induces humans to make a pact or collective contract with the sovereign to whom they concede the monopoly of violence in order to be protected from reciprocal threats, insecurity, and fear. The sovereign imposes law and rights on all. Locke,[4] Rousseau,[5] and Hegel,[6] among others, outline a similar idea. In some circumstances, only when terror has equalized all citizens in defenselessness, and has thereby eliminated the privileged position of certain sectors, is a condition created that we can call "negative original equity," over which it is possible to construct consciousness of the necessity for universal rights. Then, after the leveling of differences and privileges through terror, education can indeed effectively reaffirm the necessity for a reciprocal universal recognition among citizens.

This equalization through panic and insecurity is, in my estimation,[7] the taproot of what can still be called today "natural law." I do not mean to invoke an "instinct of sociability," in the classical way. Nor do I wish to appeal to something supposedly derived from the rational nature of human beings, even if it be neutral reason (neither selfish nor universal) as in Locke, or reason naturally oriented toward the universal good, as in Rousseau and Kant. Rather, I would say, in the spirit of Hobbes, that generalized fear of self-destruction obliges individuals to respect a minimal code of ethics. The universality of human "reason" and "natural law" are seated in this selfish calculus, focused on preserving one's own life, integrity, and liberty. The fear of death and slavery underlies the absolute value of life and liberty. Extreme situations, such as the one Colombia is going through today, of profound and extensive disregard for the life and liberty of others, oblige us to search for a stronger foundation for public life.

The Educational Limits of Terror

Unfortunately, not even the horrendous school of terror guarantees that lessons about morality and rights will be learned. There are populations with thick heads and weak memories. In Colombia, numerous armed agents persevere in the search for supposed solutions through force. And one cannot help asking if the violence has not yet been sufficient to induce us to search for mutual understanding and respect, even if only as a foundation for the inevitable conflicts that characterize all social life. We cannot discount even the extreme hypothesis that, for some peoples, no level of violence is enough to make them understand that they share a common destiny and that they should adhere to common rules. That does seem to be the situation today when one contemplates the tragic history of the Balkans. Sometimes one has the impression that, for some Colombians in certain regions, the intense and fleeting enjoyment of life and liberty as individuals is more valued than their conservation through collective means. Colombians of other regions, in contrast, appear prepared to dissolve into the whole, and not even individual existence appears to have for them an absolute value. If that is so, if the attraction of the fleeting passions or of indifference to individual existence weakens Colombians' "instinct of conservation," then there would not be much hope for founding a society on universal rights. Where the capacity for fear disappears, rights cannot consolidate.

Even so, we should assume the best: that Colombians are capable of learning the lessons of terror and that they are ready to practice respect for and defense of human rights. Building on that assumption, let us next reflect on the origins and meaning of the doctrine of human rights proper.

Human Rights in the French Revolution

The proclamation of the Rights of Man in the French Revolution is closely linked to the recognition of popular sovereignty. Through the proclamation of those rights, the French revolutionaries hoped, first, to "subvert" (a literal translation would be "turn inside out") the ancien régime. In effect, in the French absolutist State, the monarch received power directly from "on high," from God and the noble families. The power of the king was removed from all control of the citizenry. When things went to extremes, subjects had only revolutionary force as a recourse against the whims of the king. In contrast, the power of the new revolutionary State came from "below," from popular sovereignty. Popular will came to support, for the first time, the legitimacy of the State. In order to prevent the new State apparatus from falling into abuses similar to those of the ancien régime, the revolutionaries promulgated the Rights of Man as protection against State abuse. Against the power of the State, they counterposed this normative code, which permitted popular legitimization or condemnation of power. In that way, the French revolutionaries even forestalled all future violent revolutions. From that point on, revolutionary violence would only be justified if it confronted a dictatorial power that completely disregarded popular will, pretending instead to impose only its own through the use of State force.

The recognition of human rights by modern societies accords civil society enormous power over the State. It accords civil society, at the same time, the position of potential accuser, witness, and judge. Society can interdict the legitimacy of the government and, in extreme cases, of the State itself. Since popular legitimacy is the only modern source of State power, the government is obligated to modify its conduct or cede its place to new political forces. The State can be compelled to modify its constitutional foundations. In this way, the apparent unarmed fragility of rights gives society sovereign power against the overweening power of the State. Just as the people concede to the State the monopoly of force so that it can carry out the law, the proclamation of human rights authorizes civil society control over the ethical and political legitimacy of State force.

It is important to emphasize that the protagonists of the French Revolution promoted the doctrine of human rights as an ethical and political, rather than a judicial, fire wall against possible excesses of State power. For them, the doctrine of human rights codified the transformation of the "natural law" of the theorists of political modernization into a "social pact." As a result, fundamental rights are the essential ingredients of that social pact and, as such, constitute the moral foundations of political life. These rights are the ones that constitute the *polis*, or life in society. They are the marrow of what today in Colombia we call civil or citizen morality.

Only much later, in the twentieth century, did the fundamental political rights of humanity become transformed under the pressure of different movements and international organizations into norms of international law and even into articles in the constitutions of numerous democratic states. I should note in passing that this transformation of human rights into judicial principles was partly a result of the political battle of the Western powers against Moscow and its allies. And it is this version of human rights that has prevailed in current practice, appearing to be almost traditional and thereby obscuring the moral and political sense of the original proclamation.

Human Rights Today

It is in this traditional sense, that of defending the citizen against State abuses, that international human rights organizations based in Western industrialized countries, such as Amnesty International,[8] have traditionally understood their work. In doing so, they have proceeded in perfect accordance with the historical context in which they operate.

In effect, the current Western powers, be they European or North American, are in some sense comparable to France in the post-Revolutionary period. In these countries, the State exercises a real monopoly of force. There do not exist other armed organizations that dispute the State's ethical and political legitimacy and can threaten the basic rights of citizens. Understanding this state of affairs permits us to appreciate better the attitudes and points of view of the human rights organizations based in these Western nations. It also makes it possible to identify the differences between these nations and Colombia. The situation of these Western nations is not that of our country, nor that of many other nations.

We all know that in Colombia the State has never had a monopoly of force. We also know that, especially during the last forty years, various guerrilla organizations have been challenging State power through force of arms. Colombian society includes not one, but various armed actors who seek popular support and legitimization. Both the guerrillas and the State seek the backing of the citizenry in fundamental ethical and political terms that transcend legal jurisdictions or mere electoral endorsement. But if we rely on the narrow perspective of human rights of the French Revolution, society would find itself defenseless before the possible abuses of the new armed actors, the guerrilla organizations.

In spite of Colombia's special circumstances, private human rights organizations have defined the defense of human rights in a traditional and limited sense and completely ignored violations of citizens' rights by the armed opposition. In addition, they have added another restriction: They have left to one side official violations of the basic human rights of the average person, who is not a political activist. In short, they have restricted their efforts to the denunciation of official crimes inflicted on the political opposition. This endeavor is, without a doubt, worthwhile and useful, but, in countries such as Colombia that are affected by prolonged and violent power struggles, it is totally inadequate and insufficient for the protection of civil society. Furthermore, because it is limited in this way, it loses credibility.

Human Rights According to the Armed Rebels

Obviously, according to the armed rebels, they themselves never violate human rights. In defense of this position, they invoke various reasons. Let us examine the principal ones with care. Before we start, a presumption, not exactly a reason, comes into play. The insurgents consider themselves "representatives of the people," and, accordingly, for them it is unthinkable that they could be violating the people's rights. It is important to note that their use of the word "people" in this context has a completely different meaning from the way it was used during the Enlightenment and the French Revolution. For the French revolutionaries, "the people" was made up of the entire society, and the subject of human rights was the whole citizenry without distinction, considered both as individuals and as a collectivity. For today's revolutionaries, the "people" is only a social sector, the "popular classes." For them, perhaps, these supposed "classes" translate into Marx's proposition that the proletariat was the universal class, whose particular interests would encompass the interests of all others. In the name of the supposed universal nature of proletarian and popular interests, revolutionaries believe they are authorized to disregard the particular rights of the rest of society. For them, extortion, kidnapping, and assassination of "class enemies" do not constitute violations of human rights. Rather, these actions are part of an inevitable process of making human rights more universal. Of course, a mountain of sophisms is hidden in this simple reasoning. The conversations between leaders of the FARC, recently made public by military intelligence, in which they apparently decided to assassinate three U.S. environmentalists reveal even more barbaric and narrow thinking. According to them, the three U.S. citizens could be assassinated because "they are not part of our family."

In arrogantly assuming popular representation, the armed guerrilla organizations ignore and violate the principles and fundamentals of the way political power is legitimated in the modern era, that is, popular sovereignty. Like monarchs, they claim to personify the people without submitting to some mechanism of initial consultation and subsequent control. What they ask of the Colombian State, they do not practice themselves. They cite as an example of popular backing what is in fact the ambiguous solidarity of unarmed people who render support in the face of intimidating armed pressure. With this unusual system of representation, it is not strange that, in some regions, the same people who used to support the guerrillas now organize vigilante groups against them.

In addition, as previously noted, the reduction of all society (the "people" of the French Revolution) to one of its parts and the invocation of a pretended right of this portion to impose its particular interests as universal rights, destroys the possibility of all recognition and respect of human rights. If only the fundamental rights of one class are worthy of respect, these are not then "human" rights, but specific and unique "class" rights, be they "popular" or "proletarian." Using similar arguments, any other class could claim the right to consider its own interests universal, thus negating the essential rights of other classes. Based in such principles, revolutionaries could hardly invoke respect for human rights by a State of their own, except as a false, tactical dodge.

Supported by the opinion of not a few experts in the law, the armed rebels also cite the argument that only the State is obligated to respect human rights, since only the State can be held accountable to its own judicial norms, not those who ignore its legitimacy. To this generic argument, Marxist theorists and militants add, like Marx himself, that human rights, like all judicial norms, constitute a form of class, capitalist, and bourgeois domination that the dominated cannot be expected to comply with. If we were to accept Marx's argument, according to which human rights are merely a cunning class ideology, not only would the guerrillas be exempted from respecting them, but also the State. A mere ideological fiction cannot compel compliance by anyone, even if it be of his or her own creation. The only law in force in society would then be that of the war of all against all without ethical or political limits. Not only would the State have to accept that law, but also the guerrillas, and the whole of society.

Instead, we must posit that all modern States have as their first and fundamental obligation that of recognizing, respecting, and guaranteeing the rights of all citizens. The law formally requires it. A State that systematically violates its citizens' rights, or that is incapable of making rights generally respected, puts its judicial legitimacy in question. But the tie that binds the State to respect citizens' rights is not only formal and legal. Human rights do not arise only from mere written norms, as Marx appears to suppose. As we have noted above, they constitute the unwritten moral and political code that underlies all affirmative law in any modern society. The State is bound by an earlier and more powerful imperative than the written law: the obligation to win ethical legitimacy and the necessity of securing and constantly resecuring political legitimization as the foundation for judicial legality. Nothing damages the ethical legitimacy of a State more, nothing creates greater popular opposition, than the abuse of arms and the violation of citizens' rights.

Here, the State and the guerrillas face the same challenge. They are subject to the same fundamental rules: the respect and promotion of the rights of all citizens as an essential condition for the acquisition of their own ethical and political legitimacy. What is more, if the insurrection does not consider itself a mere blind agent of mechanical social contradictions, but rather aspires to some type of legitimacy, that legitimacy will come only from a credible promise to guarantee better than the State the full realization of human rights. Finally, the fight for greater economic equity and for greater democratic participation by the oppressed is nothing but a later stage of the fight for the human rights that are fundamental to life and liberty. For the guerrillas, as well as for the State, the respect for fundamental rights constitutes an absolute requirement.

This, then, is the new situation that could not be taken into account by the French revolutionaries once they had become the State, and which is not adequately understood by some national and international human rights organizations today, either. In countries such as Colombia, the State is not the only actor that must subject itself to judgment rendered by society on the basis of an ethical and political code comprised of the most elemental rights. The guerrillas are also subject to this code, even though they may wish it were not so.

A Necessary Reformulation of Human Rights

As we have seen, in order to recover the deepest original meaning of the doctrine of human rights, it is necessary to reach beyond its now-traditional formulation. Originally, human rights doctrine was intended to give unarmed society an ethical and political defense against the eventual arbitrariness of armed political actors who presumed to represent society. Before it became a legal norm, human rights doctrine constituted the political expression of unwritten "natural rights" on which the social pact was based. In France in 1789, the armed actor at which human rights doctrine was aimed was only the State. The same is true in the industrialized nations today. But in Colombia, as in many other nations of the world today, this is not the situation. The revolutionary guerrillas also rely on the ethical and political legitimization that only society can grant them, and winning that legitimation is precisely the precondition for achieving one day a new legal order.

In general terms, we must concede that all armed actors hoping to win social legitimacy are subject to the tribunal of civil society whose central principle is the respect for human rights. Only in this way can society conserve some control over the armed actors who hope to represent it. The trampling of citizens' lives, integrity, dignity, or liberty by the guerrillas makes them criminals in the eyes of the public, just as it does the State.

To say, as some do, that to attribute to the guerrillas the capacity to violate human rights would be to equate them with the State and, for that reason, recognize them as having the legal status of a belligerent, is, of course, an intelligent argument in international law. But it, in turn, depends on the recent reduction of the significance of human rights to narrow, judicial terrain, forgetting the original, fundamentally ethical and political, meaning of the concept.

The Universality of Law

A right, any right, must be universal or it does not exist at all. It must be applicable to all or it is applicable to none. This is true especially with regard to what we call "human rights." In the ancien régime, "rights" were, in reality, particular benefits named as such. Consequently, they were more privileges than true rights. The emancipation brought about by the French Revolution consisted precisely in the abolition of an order founded on privileges and the recognition of the universal validity of the law. All men and women should be recognized as holders of fundamental rights: the rights to life, integrity, dignity, and liberty—just like all other citizens. As a result, any privilege derived from ethnicity, social condition, political beliefs, or religious creed was abolished.

A similar reflection derives, as we have noted above, from the "human" extension of those rights. When we speak of "human" rights we allude to the respect that is due to all men and women without any distinction because of their status as human beings, irrespective of additional considerations. Here there is no room for the defense of the "rights of the left," "of the right," of the reds, greens, or blues.

There is no way to defend the human rights of some citizens while disregarding, at the same time, the identical rights of others, simply because the latter do not share the same political ideology. To do that would not be defending a right, but a particular privilege of a given group or faction. A partial defense of human rights would imply the unconscious restoration of an order of privileges like that of the ancien régime. What is wrongheaded about such an attitude, of course, is not the defense of the rights of citizens against the arbitrariness of the State, which is legitimate and absolutely necessary. What is wrong is that this defense is not also extended to all citizens, including people not linked to the political opposition, or, worse yet, that such defense is accompanied by a complacent silence concerning the abuses of other, equally arbitrary, armed political forces, such as the contemporary guerrilla movements.

Human Rights as the Ethical, Political, and Judicial Foundations of Society

The triad of life, liberty, and dignity is the ethical and political basis for human coexistence. It constitutes the nucleus of the "social contract" that lays the groundwork for civilized political society. It is the foundation of all ethical, political, and also, therefore, judicial order, and it is the basis for all other rights. For this reason, these primary rights have an absolute obligatory force and cannot be subordinated to the attainment of any other derived right.

In effect, rights to property, work, education, culture, political participation, and so on cannot be understood as anything other than derivative rights, following upon the fundamental rights to life and liberty. In fact, these derivative rights had their historical origins in the rights to life and liberty. While the French Revolution proclaimed the civil and political rights of citizens before the State, the later emergence of socialist revolutions fostered the recognition of the social rights of workers, and today, environmental and other rights have begun to gain recognition. One cannot violate these fundamental primary rights in the name of the others. The ethical and political decay of a society begins when life and liberty cease to be unconditional ends and begin to be converted into means to serve other aims, into currencies at the service of economic and political objectives, no matter how just.

Human Rights Organizations in Colombia

Taking into account the previous considerations, it becomes necessary to redefine the task of human rights organizations. It is the task of all such entities to publicly denounce abuses committed by all armed political actors, including the State and the guerrillas, against the civilian population or even against armed enemies not involved in combat. Theirs is the difficult task of denouncing not only the arbitrariness of the State against its political opponents but also the abuses inflicted by the State on all citizens regardless of their ideology. Furthermore, they must publicly disclose human rights violations committed by the guerrillas. This task requires these organizations to situate themselves above all ethnic, religious, social, and political divisions in order to defend exclusively the rights of civil society against the abuses of armed political actors. Human rights organizations are the voice of civil society in reclaiming the absolute primacy of natural law (however one understands it) as the foundation for legal legitimacy. The principles and rights they invoke are the basis of social coexistence and come before any partisan opposition.

This impartiality is difficult in a country such as Colombia, whose hard-fought national cohesion has been based (although it may seem to be a contradiction) on profound political and partisan antagonisms. But only such high-mindedness can guarantee the existence of a coherent and self-conscious civil society, one that sees itself as existing before the advent of partisan antagonisms. Only by making that distinction, which allows civil society to proclaim and defend the equality of essential human rights irrespective of differences and conflicts, can a true state of law be constructed.

Mass Communications and Human Rights

The force of civil society lies in the elusive concept of "public opinion," on which the legitimization of the State ultimately depends. For this reason, the fundamental ally of human rights organizations should be the mass media. Unfortunately, in many parts of the world the media cannot be said to fulfill this function. In fact, one can even say that human rights organizations have arisen in order to take the place of the media, which have steadily abandoned the field. Originally intended as a channel for free citizen expression against the eventual abuses of power (which, by the way, justified the uncompromising defense of the "freedom of the press"), the media have been transformed into fundamental instruments and sources of power—economic, if not always political.

In Colombia some elements of the press bravely and decisively echoed the denunciations of human rights organizations and forums during the Turbay Ayala administration (1978–1982). But later, perhaps disillusioned by the double standard that the actions of those organizations inspired, they closed their doors to denunciation. In the 1980s the media appeared to grasp only the seriousness of the outrages committed against well-known Colombians, disregarding the rights of a multitude of citizens. And in the 1990s they repeated the by-now-inescapable denunciations and pressures of international organizations and foreign governments, as well as reported on the inchoate processes begun by government judicial entities. But none of the mass media has unconditionally taken up the fight against the barbarity of Colombian human rights abuses as its own cause.

Whether we like it or not, the media are the modern school of citizenship. If they ignore the uncompromising defense of all citizens' rights, they sow indifference; or worse, they nurture, in public opinion and the consciousness of the citizenry, a ranking of privileges foreign to the state of law and to a culture of living together in harmony.

Human Rights, Common Delinquency, and the Guerrillas

Let us now address some indispensable complementary considerations. Obviously, what we say here with respect to the guerrillas cannot be applied to the armed, nonpolitical actors such as drug traffickers and gangs of common criminals. These actors also unquestionably violate the rights of citizens (and do so to an alarming degree), and clearly the full force of the law and the courts should fall upon them. But, in contrast to the State and the guerrillas, common delinquents do not aspire to social recognition or legitimization. The hopes of "narcoterrorists" cannot in any way be confused with those of the State and the guerrillas, who aspire for social acceptance through ethical or political legitimacy. The "narcoterrorists," it is true, hope for social acceptance, but they try to impose it by force and at any cost, while legitimacy only comes spontaneously from society.

Confronting the State is not enough to make the drug traffickers into political delinquents. All delinquents confront the State in some respect, and we cannot say, for that reason, that they all have a political quality. The nature of a crime is not determined by the condition of the chosen enemy, but by manifest intention and the acts associated with it. The narcoterrorist is not, in any way, a political delinquent.

It is more difficult, of course, to maintain the distinction between the guerrillas and common delinquency so that one can unequivocally identify the guerrilla as a political actor and not as a mere form of common organized crime. Here we would have to identify not only the political intention of the armed actors, but also the coherence of their acts with regard to this intention. The highly political nature of the guerrillas' acts should be aimed at winning society's approval or at least at militarily defeating the State, but in Colombia, this is not the way it happens.

For a long time, Colombian guerrillas have used the same methods as common criminals, such as extortion, kidnapping, and the killing, outside of combat, of defenseless civilians. Since 1998, they have even used the abominable practice of the *pesca milagrosa* (literally, miraculous fishing), in which they randomly kidnap civilians on the highways in order to extort ransoms. Not even young women, who have been held for months, have been exempt from this outrageous crime. One cannot see how these practices can be understood as part of the quest for political legitimacy or military triumph over the State. They are, simply put, a means of finance, a business. And to the extent that the guerrillas make a specialty of these practices, they cross the threshold of political organizations into a way of life based on the practice of common crime.

Even so, Colombian guerrillas cannot be denied completely a political label, at least for now, while they continue to publicly attest to political aims and repeatedly use this label to recruit new members and to call for legitimization. The Pastrana administration has courageously recognized this distinction, contrary to the practice adopted by high-ranking military officials of lumping the guerrillas together with drug traffickers and bandits.

When the methods of guerrilla actions are degraded, however, it becomes increasingly necessary to enter into juridical casuistry and efforts to distinguish between acts and intentions in order to rescue the political nature of the guerrillas. After all, Colombian guerrillas are still sensitive to the need for social recognition of their real or supposed altruistic aims. For that reason, denunciation of the guerrillas' human rights violations by socially recognized (because of their political impartiality) organizations should still make them feel some pressure. If the denunciations leave the guerrillas indifferent, it is a sign that, even without recognizing it, they have completely abandoned political terrain and have entered into common crime. With that, civil society is impotent, and the coercive, judicial power of the State is all that is left.

An Objection to the Doctrine: Legitimate Defense and "Self-Defense" Groups

Before continuing, it is useful to discuss a possible objection that, if true, would invalidate the whole doctrine of human rights and ruin any effort to defend it. According to this argument, human rights are not universally applicable since there are at least four exceptions: the right of a State to take away the liberty of a delinquent, the right of an individual to legitimate defense when assaulted, the right to wage war when one people is attacked by another, and the right of a people to rebel against a prolonged tyranny that seriously damages the common good. These last three conditions are only different expressions of the right of individuals or groups to legitimate defense against unjust aggressors. Now, neither the right of a State to suppress the liberty of a delinquent, nor the right to suppress the liberty, integrity, or even the life of an unjust aggressor can be considered exceptions to the universal obligation to respect fundamental human rights. On the contrary, they are resources that guarantee the most universal defense of human rights.

Defense against attack is legitimate when aggression is unjust, the defense is in proportion to the aggression, and it is not possible to call on a superior, legitimate form of coercion or judgment. When an individual aggressor puts the life, integrity, or liberty of a victim in danger, that aggressor becomes a potential threat to the whole society. The aggressor virtually violates the rights of all. By defending him- or herself, the victim protects his or her own rights and those of all others. It is the aggressor who, negating the rights of all others, alienates his or her own rights and accords the victim a momentary judicial power in absence of, or due to the impossibility of resorting to, legitimate forms of judgment. If this is not so, the victim does not have the right to respond to the attack in a manner similar to that of the aggressor. The victim is obliged to utilize the law and the force of the State. A similar logic applies when the aggressor is a tyrant or an enemy State. In this setting, there does not exist, by definition, superior judgment, and the victim—a people—is also obliged to assume its own defense.

In principle, it is understandable that those who are unjustly attacked by the guerrillas, or by other armed social actors, and see themselves as unprotected by the judicial and coercive power of the State, have recourse to "self-defense" groups for protection. If the official neglect is serious and long-lasting, the logic of vigilante groups proceeds and can lead to civil war. Verification of a situation of permanent official neglect is, without a doubt, an attenuating circumstance when determining the responsibility of those who turn to self-defense, and it could even be cause for a pardon.

What is in no case acceptable is that the State declare itself incapable of applying the law and turn to civil society to take on that responsibility. The moment it does so, it abdicates its sovereignty, declares the law nonexistent, and turns over the force of arms to private actors who are asked to restore the law. What follows is an unending chain of private retaliation or war between civil factions. For these reasons, it was totally unacceptable that the Colombian State officially legitimize the existence of private self-defense groups, as it did the CONVIVIR groups until recently. These groups were supposedly created for the sole purpose of transmitting information to the army, but, as was well known, they in fact served as armed protection for different personages and for different regions of the country and, in many cases, they exercised their own brand of justice.

The problem of vigilante groups in Colombia is particularly complex. As has happened in other parts of the world where internal conflicts exist, these groups developed within Colombia at the start of the 1980s, not from a shared political ideal, or even a political idea, but from the indisputable necessity of protecting lives and private property. Hence, initially we are not considering only one organization but a patchwork of groups obeying different leaders, having distinct interests, and adopting very different forms of action. These groups were subsequently promoted by local politicians, merchants, and especially landowners, among whom there were not a few drug traffickers. These groups thus lacked the altruistic aura that political ideals grant the guerrillas, ideals that elevate them to the status of potential interlocutors of the State.

With the passing of the years, and with the risk of seeing themselves eventually subordinated to the rigor of the law, the numerous self-defense groups came together, as we have seen, under the AUC. They then developed a certain amount of national coordination, constructed a political discourse, and, like the guerrillas, began to solicit formal negotiations with the State. Far from encouraging an adequate State response, this centralization and functional "after-the-fact" politicization complicates it even more. It is difficult for the State to recognize these groups as political actors, ignoring their past and entirely private roots.

Other elements further complicate the scene. These groups, situated on the margins of the law, or, better said, conniving with many of the law's presumed representatives, have also acted at the margins of all political ethics. From the beginning, their forms of action have been particularly bloodthirsty, and almost all their victims have come from the unarmed civil population, in many instances people completely unrelated to the conflict. Some groups, especially those most directly linked to drug trafficking, have not limited themselves to the defense of the life and property of their sponsors. They have also launched campaigns to conquer and appropriate territory, after exterminating and evicting defenseless peasants. In engaging in such acts, they have gone completely beyond being self-defense groups and become instead simple marauders and murderers.

But this picture is turned right side up once again if we recognize that the guerrillas, in their eagerness to accumulate economic resources, have also converted the unarmed civilian population into a target of barbarism. Their methods are neither more political nor more inhuman than those of the paramilitaries, as demonstrated by the *pescas milagrosas* or the assassination of the three North American environmentalists, to mention only these recent and well-known offenses. The guerrillas have also been appropriating all goods within their reach, from lands to bank accounts, with purely economic aims. If, in spite of their methods, we continue to accord guerrillas a political status based on their proclaimed revolutionary intentions and political discourse, it will not be easy to find arguments to deny the same status to the self-defense groups.

Human Rights and the Application of Justice

The problems placed before us by the questions of legitimate defense and by the self-defense groups bring us to a central theme: the relationship between the defense of human rights by civil society and the application of justice by the State. As we have noted, human rights are the only weapon that unarmed society has to defend itself from the abuses of armed political actors and especially the State itself. As a result, the State is wrong to take over this function, expropriating it from society. The Colombian State is not to be asked to assume the defense of human rights, but to apply the law impartially.

The adequate application of the law by the State is the essential precondition for the preservation of human rights in all societies. Without justice, or when State justice is partial or ineffective, the rights of all citizens are endangered. The absence or decay of judicial power inevitably unleashes uncontrollable mechanisms of "private justice," that is, of retaliation and vengeance. And for blind, vindictive passion, law does not exist. The result of the rupture of justice cannot be anything other than social dissolution, generalized violence, and disregard of all rights, as is the condition in Colombia today. Without justice, the proclamation of human rights, the creation of human rights organizations, and the denunciations of abuses these organizations formulate are all in vain. The civil bulwark of rights loses its State support. From the Colombian State, society expects not the defense of human rights but the impartial application of justice. This should be the State's maximum contribution to the preservation of the fundamental rights of all citizens.

The first demand that Colombian society makes of the State judicial apparatus is the application of the law to its own officials. A State that is indulgent with itself, a violator of the law, or an accomplice in crime, loses all credibility and respect. It lacks the authority to impart justice to its citizens. In this case, its pretended "justice" tends to become instead a form of violence and arbitrariness visited on its weakest citizens. The State ceases to be judge and transforms itself instead into archetype, model, and promoter of crime.

Judicial officials are obligated to be particularly vigilant over the armed functionaries of the State. In effect, the monopoly of force is the maximum right that a society cedes to the State. Because of its exclusive nature, it is almost a privilege. On this privilege of the State rests—or should rest—the guarantee of all rights. In the right to the possession and the exclusive use of arms lies, in practice, the sovereignty of the State. In a supreme act of confidence, society gives itself up unarmed to its own creation. This renunciation has no reason for being except under conditions in which the armed forces, strictly subordinated to the law, prevent and make unnecessary the development of private violence to preserve the fundamental human rights of the citizenry. The existence of State forces is justified, in other words, by the elimination of violence among its citizens, a condition that guarantees total respect for essential citizens' rights.

In no domain is the State so obliged to carry out the law as in the use of force, and in no other domain need society be so zealous in ensuring that it does so. If the State abuses its privilege, if it uses arms outside the dictates of law, or if it tolerates such use by its armed forces, it loses its raison d'être, destroys its sovereignty, and completely undermines its legitimacy; above all, it undermines the credibility of justice. By violating the law, the armed forces cease to be a guarantor of peace and become promoters and perpetrators of violence. Indeed, they become armed bands and are, by definition, extremely dangerous because they are not controlled by any other force. If the illegal actions of civil State functionaries stimulate and propagate this corruption of State power, the abuse of official force generalizes violence. This is exactly the grave situation in which Colombia finds itself today.

For the Colombian State to guarantee respect for human rights, it first must concentrate on demanding the strict fulfillment of the law by the armed forces, and when these forces abuse their privileges, it must apply the law with rigor. A State that exempts the armed forces from the judicial-penal norms that apply to the rest of its citizens is nothing more than an accomplice to abuse, a criminal State.

The Task of the State with Respect to Human Rights

Even though, as previously noted, the function of the State is not to defend human rights, it can, however, create entities that facilitate the reception and transmission of complaints expressed by society with reference to the armed forces as well as to any other armed political actor. If these entities are not simply democratic facades for an authoritarian State, they can greatly aid in the consolidation and preservation of a state of law. For this to happen, these entities should be open to all citizens, have access to relevant secret military and police information, and have the capacity to set the judicial machinery in motion, monitor judicial decisions, and keep the public up to date concerning the state of their efforts and investigations. But human rights defense should not rest on State organizations nor should civil society put its whole confidence in them. "Reasons of State" is a powerful doctrine, and in the event of conflicts between the State and its citizens it always prevails over the democratic will of its functionaries.

Some Practical Applications

In light of these reflections it is possible to offer some practical considerations concerning the situation in Colombia. On the one hand, it is urgent to remove from the actions of existing human rights organizations all political partiality or, if this cannot be done, it will be necessary to create new organizations. These organizations should be places in which Colombians can meet with each other, mutually examine and judge themselves, and collaborate with one another without regard to their social or political differences. They should be watchful not only of State forces but also of the guerrillas. Only in this way can human rights organizations acquire public credibility, the only avenue for gaining the power required for effective action.

On the other hand, the human rights organizations promoted by the State merit close examination. It is true that some official entities such as the Solicitor General's Office (Procuraduría) have, in the last decade, worked laudably to investigate and punish some military leaders implicated in crimes against citizens. But this should not be confused with human rights defense; rather, it is part of the necessary application of the law and justice by the State to its own functionaries. As such it should continue, and its mechanics should be strengthened.

Other entities, such as the Office of the Defender of the People (Defensoría del Pueblo), created by the 1991 Constitution, cannot supplant the function of private human rights organizations that are totally independent of the State. The duty of State organizations can only be that of receiving and transmitting the denunciations and complaints of private human rights organizations. To do otherwise would constitute the meddling of the State in the realm of civil society.

If the Colombian State truly has the political will to aid in the defense of essential citizens' rights, its first obligation is not that of multiplying the official human rights organizations, but of reinstating the application of law. To achieve this, it must dedicate resources to modernize and develop the judicial branch, and these resources should be proportionately greater than those currently aimed at strengthening the military apparatus.

Justice should first be applied, as noted above, to the State's own military and police forces. It is a grave political, and thus military, error to think that the state of war in which the country finds itself requires indulgence and tolerance of the excesses and crimes of the official armed forces. Nothing damages the legitimacy of the State faster than the abuse of force, and nothing impairs the morale of the armed forces more than the systematic violation of the law. To guarantee the rule of law, the State and military forces require, more than anything, strict submission to it. The strength of the State rests, before anything else, on its own legitimacy. Arms should be at the service of legitimacy, not the reverse.

For the same purpose, a careful determination of military legal privileges (the *fuero militar*) is required so that military penal jurisdiction covers only crimes and acts committed by armed forces members on active duty, and in such cases "due obedience" must not be invoked. During the 1990 Constitutional Convention, political compromises prevailed over the law with respect to this point. Crimes such as torture, kidnapping, disappearance, and assassination—acts that are fortunately recognized as crimes under the new Constitution—should be excluded from military jurisdiction.

In order to preserve the fundamental rights of its citizens, the Colombian State is obligated to fight seriously for the dismantling of all the self-defense and private justice groups that for a long time have been developing in the country, with the knowledge of civil authorities and under the auspices of the armed forces or with their tolerance and complicity. To begin with, civil power should spare no effort to cut existing ties between the armed forces and paramilitary organizations. This has become increasingly clear to the government. But beyond this, the government must stop the slow militarization of civil society, a process that has been silently advancing for more than thirty years. Toward that end, the numerous military colleges in which a martial education is imparted to the young need to be eliminated. The naming of civilian leaders as reserve military officers should also be suppressed, and the sale of arms to civilians and the expansion of permits that allow people to carry arms should be suspended. The whole process of social militarization, permitted by civil power, is nothing other than preparation for the spirit and practice of vigilantism. Private justice groups, which replace the law enforcement functions of the State, are the logical result of such policies. In these conditions it is hardly surprising that violence in Colombia has proliferated and the violation of human rights has become generalized.

The 1991 Constitution presents an ample bill of citizens' rights. In principle, one cannot deny the worth of this bill of rights, at least as a judicial seed for a new political culture. Nevertheless, this proliferation of citizens' rights also calls attention to the almost absolute silence of the Constitution concerning existing structures and norms that regulate the military forces. It is difficult to believe that the Colombian State can guarantee the health of all its children, the protection of its mothers, the sheltering of the persecuted, and so on, when it is incapable of protecting the liberty and life of an adult population frequently threatened by its own security and defense forces. One cannot shake the fear that these norms, which arose from the democratic enthusiasm of the 1990 Constitutional Convention, and which were promoted under the judicial institution of guardianship (*tutela*), have been converted into a smoke screen that covers the abyss of injustice in Colombia and the lack of official and private will to check barbarism and impunity.

Conclusion

For the exercise of power, all modern political actors—that is, those who do not claim to have received their power by inheritance or divine appointment—require some type of legitimization and recognition from society. Without it they could hardly aspire to represent society. This is the most obvious and direct consequence of modern popular sovereignty. Three levels of social recognition have been outlined above: the moral legitimacy that political actors possess by reason of their conformity to "natural law"; the political legitimacy derived from the public recognition of this greater or lesser conformity; and finally, the judicial legitimation or legality of their representation of society. The greater or lesser ethical legitimacy of political actors is the basis for their political legitimization and is, in turn, the foundation for legal recognition of the power that society accords a given actor.

The respect for fundamental rights constitutes the minimal ethical and political requirements that any society establishes for actors who aspire to represent publicly the collective will, given that fundamental rights are the essential ingredients of the "social contract." In effect, the fundamental aim of life in society is to better guarantee the life, integrity, and liberty of those who come together in that society. This requirement is thus not derived only from judicial norms established by a given code of absolute rights. It is the ethical norm that makes coexistence possible, and, for that reason, it underpins the political. It is in this sense, as a foundation for life in society, that fundamental human rights were reclaimed by the French revolutionaries.

It is true that, with the passing of time, these fundamental rights were transformed into explicit mandates of international law and that from there they have passed into the written law of many national constitutions. Although the purpose of this transformation—to reinforce the capacity of international organizations to pressure States and bind them to fulfillment of their own laws—was well-intentioned and has been useful, it resulted in impoverishing human rights doctrine by making only States accountable to it. In reality, human rights are the fundamental weapon of defense of an unarmed society against the armed actors who claim to represent it, be these State actors or otherwise. It is even possible to think that, to the extent that a society rids itself of indifference, vigorously reaffirms the operation of fundamental rights, and internalizes them in its daily actions, it contributes to the expulsion of all forms of violence within it, isolates the common delinquent, and thereby reduces the proliferation of crime.[9] In contrast, a population that is indifferent to the violation of others' rights can only move down the road of political dissolution, self-destruction, and the "war of all against all."

As long as pluralist, impartial, and credible human rights organizations do not exist, and as long as the major media do not appropriate the universal defense of human rights, educational campaigns on the subject run the risk of scratching only the surface of the body politic and can become the functional complement of the daily and flagrant violation of human rights. The same can happen to a constitution laden with rights or one with a network of institutions dedicated to their defense. This essay is not exempt from this same problem. Nothing can substitute for efficient, fair, and universal justice, demanded by a truly democratic press and by a conscious citizenry mobilized in its own defense. Until this stage is realized, no future will exist for Colombians, and the form of collective life based on what the Europeans of old called "reason" will be only a caricature made up of printed words within our borders.

Notes

1. As occurred after the assassination of three environmentalists from the United States by the FARC in March 1999.

2. For example, the creation of País Libre, a private organization against kidnapping, although certainly understandable, nevertheless appears to enlist itself in the logic of partial defense of the rights of only one of the bands and sectors in conflict.

3. According to Thomas Hobbes's *Leviathan*, all people are guided by "self-love" or egotism, which leads them, naturally, to the "war of all against all."

4. Contrary to Hobbes's idea, John Locke proposes that humans in "a state of nature" are neither good nor bad. But "natural law," which prescribes the preservation of life, property, and liberty, also permits humans to punish those who violate their rights. It is from this that insecurity newly arises and induces humans to establish a reciprocal contract. This contract is the foundation for universal law and rights.

5. For Jean-Jacques Rousseau, in contrast, humans are naturally good, guided by "love of self," which is different from Hobbes's "self-love" since it is capable of compassion before another's evil. Even so, as is shown by the author in his *Discourse on the Origins of Human Inequality*, this original goodness is transformed into egotism; the "I" and its properties are

developed. In this way, a generalized situation of insecurity comes about, which gives birth to the social contract and general law.

6. George Wilhelm Friedrich Hegel rejects the fiction of a natural state and a social contract. In turn, he presents modern civil society as the locus of the war of all against all, as the antithetical realm of particular and private interests, from whose autodestructive potential arises the necessity of law and rights.

7. The historical and theoretical foundations of this thesis are outlined in my article, "Etica para una sociedad en conflicto: ¿Etica civil o pacto social?" in *Etica y conflicto: Lecturas para una transición democrática* (Bogotá, 1995), 81–108; and also in "¿Es posible una ética civil?" in *Colombia, una casa para todos* (Bogotá, 1991), 87–120.

8. Recently, Amnesty International and other similar groups have modified this stance, moving in the more inclusive direction advocated in this essay.

9. Some colleagues would prefer a more social and less political version of human rights. I share their thesis up to the point indicated in the text. But I believe that the search for legitimacy is an indispensable element in causing violent actors to feel called to account by the denunciation of human rights violations. And I do not think it wise to reduce human rights, as has been done, to a set of laws that includes all delinquents or to those who abuse power. As I have argued throughout this essay, I think that the obligatory force of primary rights lies in the fact that they constitute the foundation for life in a civilized society (the [Greek] *polis*), before all partisan, religious, ethnic, or other divisions.

Chapter 6

From Private to Public Violence
The Paramilitaries

Fernando Cubides C.

How does one analyze a clandestine organization, especially when one is an academic whom that same organization assumes to have leftist sentiments hostile to it? Here Fernando Cubides takes on that challenge by deconstructing the pronouncements of the paramilitaries themselves. He infers quite a lot from these statements about the historical evolution of these groups, the attitude of Colombians (including academics) toward them, their internal organization, motives, and ideological commitments. He finds, for example, that in opposing the leftist guerrillas, the paramilitaries have paradoxically come to mimic them in important ways. He also shows how, in contrast to the guerrillas, their public political platform was constructed after they came into being and was meant to rationalize and justify acts that began as private vengeance. Unlike many analysts, however, Cubides takes the paramilitaries' earnest proclamations in defense of the Constitution of 1991 seriously. And he cautions that paramilitary power is a fact of life in Colombia that will only go away when the force that called them forth, the leftist guerrillas, is also eliminated from the political scene. Readers can consult a paramilitary proclamation with many of the characteristics analyzed by Cubides in Part 4 of the Documents section of this book.

Fernando Cubides is a member of the Sociology Department of the National University in Bogotá. Among his many publications are two coauthored books, *Colonización: Coca y guerrilla* (Bogotá, 1986; 3d ed., 1989); and *La Macarena: Reserva biológica, territorio de conflicto* (Bogotá, 1990). He has also written many articles on violence and the peace process.

This essay originally appeared as "De lo privado y de lo público en la violencia colombiana: Los paramilitares," in Jaime Arocha, Fernando Cubides, and Myriam Jimeno, eds., *Las violencias: Inclusión creciente* (Bogotá: Centro de Estudios Sociales, Universidad Nacional de Colombia, 1998), 66–91. It is published here by permission of the Centro de Estudios Sociales.

Justo es hablar así sea por una sola vez
De la noche de los asesinos la noche cómplice
Porque también ella entra en el orden de nuestros días
Y de nada valdría pretender renegar de sus poderes.
—Alvaro Mutis, *Siete Nocturnos*, 1986

The Transformations

More than ten years separate the day that an editorial in the principal Colombian newspaper incorrectly cited and poorly applied Konrad Lorenz to justify the self-defense groups forming in various parts of the country and the day that another editorial in the same newspaper condemned the paramilitaries and even found them contemptible.[1] Although during this same period newspaper editorials have lost relative importance (a universal tendency noted by various media specialists, among them Umberto Eco), the change in the editorial posture of a newspaper such as *El Tiempo* reveals quite well to us the transformations that have occurred among the paramilitary groups. With no other organizations practicing violence can one observe such a drastic about-face. When the paramilitaries began, and were totally ineffective in operational terms, they enjoyed the explicit support of respectable sectors of opinion and a level of social consensus in their favor that might even have permitted them to be socially constructive. Now, when they have obviously become operationally effective, they are explicitly condemned, and there is a growing consensus that they are socially destructive. This is not a flagrant case of generalized double standards, even though it may seem so. It is a paradox, the result of the sinuous course of contemporary happenings that are worth clarifying, at least to the extent that the evidence allows.

But perceptions have always lagged behind the real evolution of the paramilitary movement. Between the initial and later attitudes cited above, there has been a complex evolution, but little of it has been perceived owing to the amount of time and effort devoted to semantic disquisitions on the subject and normative definitions of it. In effect, while diverse testimonies and accessible documentation today place the emergence of the first groups in 1982, in 1990, when the National Strategy against Violence was formulated, paramilitary groups were still not identified by what made them unique among "organized violent actors." In the study that was to provide the intellectual justification for that strategy, condensed in the book *Colombia: Violencia y democracia* (Bogotá, 1987), the paramilitaries are referred to on various pages, and there is a specific recommendation aimed at deactivating them. Even so, the form of violence attributed to them in that work, and the context in which they are located, already implies an error in perspective, an underestimation of their limits. In the classification of actors and forms of violence that this study of ten investigators delineates, the paramilitaries are defined as:

> Private organizations that resort to the physical elimination of presumed auxiliaries of rebel groups and of individuals seen as subversive of the moral order; *[they] are especially significant in certain cities of the country and direct their activities against homosexuals, prostitutes, ex-convicts, drug dealers, and other citizens who are considered to be socially defective. They mostly operate through death squads.*[2]

Back then, these investigators did not have sufficient evidence to realize it, but in light of information obtained later, what was incubating for five years before this study had a different scope and theater of action from the ones specified in the report. Today it is clear that the paramilitaries cannot be equated so easily with death squads. That death squads have operated episodically, and in the ways outlined in the report, is clear. But it is even clearer today that the paramilitaries have an origin and characteristics different from the death squads and that in their activities lies a method and a strategy that have been crucial for their growth and for the consolidation of the enormous territorial power they have acquired.

If the authors of the 1987 report had had a better understanding of the paramilitaries' origins and of the economic rationality that called them into existence, if they had better understood their modus operandi (all elements of which were then taking shape, but which have only risen to the surface with time), they would have created a special category for paramilitaries in their analysis, recognizing their singularities and their special weight in the framework of Colombian violence. Only following the publication of historian Carlos Medina Gallego's *Autodefensas, paramilitares y narcotráfico en Colombia* (Bogotá, 1990), which focused on the Magdalena and is based on observations and documentation gathered in that region, did Colombian social investigation begin to identify and use empirical methods of investigation to study the paramilitaries. These investigations have dispersed the fog and ambiguities that surrounded the subject and used a mass of evidence to cut through the semantic discussions that predominated in previous analysis and that had benefited the paramilitaries by permitting them to camouflage themselves.

The same year saw the publication of another study, *La irrupción del paraestado* (Bogotá, 1990), compiled by Germán Palacio, containing different perspectives on paramilitarism. One of them, in particular, an article written by Rodrigo Uprimny, is especially useful. Uprimny's analytical and comparative propositions manage to capture the diverse shades and organizational differences, and the differing regional contexts, of the groups that were being lumped together under the generic official label of "private justice groups." Through his analysis Uprimny offers valuable evidence of the interactions being established among these groups, the "functional alliances" being forged thanks to the growing polarization of society and the consequent identification of common enemies.[3]

From Uprimny's analysis of the different groups identified up to that point, that is, paid assassins or *sicarios*, private armies, and army-formed self-defense groups protected until recently by the law (these are the groups referred to so vehemently and imprecisely by the 1987 *El Tiempo* editorial quoted previously), and the paramilitaries proper, one can deduce that even then an amalgam of dissimilar elements was forming. And even though those categories were not exclusive, a sharp eye could already see the predominance that the most politicized component would acquire. I refer to those whose raison d'être is the struggle against the guerrillas, who adopt the greater part of the guerrillas' methods and organizational techniques, and who slowly start giving form to a strategy of confronting the guerrilla forces. The term "paramilitaries" is generic and comprehensive and it best captures the essence of the amalgam forming in the most recent period. For that reason, following much hesitation, it has gained widespread acceptance, even though the very protagonists to whom it refers are not happy with it.

Following April 1989, when the law permitting the existence of the self-defense groups was abolished, the differences in the way investigators approached the problem were dissolved in practice. The distinction between the defensive or offensive character of organizations lost its meaning, and interest in the semantic question was displaced. This is indicated by the increasingly colloquial treatment of the phenomenon by the media, which encompassed it with its prefix, the "paras." For a time the statistics on the violence continued to separate acts of violence produced by self-defense groups and the paramilitaries. But the path was opened to a comprehensive category that corresponds to its character: irregular forces of the state, extra-legal organizations that have taken the law in their own hands and that, in their struggle against the guerrillas, replicate guerrilla methods step for step. Such groups take as their preferred targets the support networks, the sympathizers or auxiliaries of the guerrillas, in regions where the guerrillas have recently installed themselves, beginning with regions where the abruptness of guerrilla installation has produced a growing reaction.

Without claiming that it be axiomatic, based on the available evidence, one can say this much: Even if not all of the paramilitaries were originally self-defense groups, all the remaining self-defense groups turned into paramilitaries after 1989. After that point, the discussion about the defensive or offensive character and other subtleties that until that moment had differentiated private justice groups, and permitted statistical tallying differentiating them, becomes byzantine. It is not that such distinctions have totally disappeared, but they have been subsumed by the organizational form that yields higher dividends, and that ends by imposing itself.

After 1989 the occasional "functional alliances" among groups noted above become a means for co-optation by paramilitary groups. We can sufficiently document the efforts to incorporate the self-defense groups that did not dissolve with the 1989 abolition of Law 48 of 1968, the law that had facilitated the legal existence of armed private groups. There are reports and testimonials demonstrating how the Castaño brothers proposed to incorporate *sicario* groups and military personnel who had served Medellín's northeastern sector into a rudimentary urban apparatus that would carry out the same functions as the guerrillas (including logistics, intelligence, propaganda, and psychological warfare aimed at the urban population). Recent information demonstrates that the different juvenile *sicario* gangs of the northeastern quadrant, cannon fodder for the Medellín cartel, as well as a good part of the urban militias initially influenced by the guerrillas who later took advantage of a government rehabilitation program, have been the object of a systematic recruitment program by the urban apparatus of the "paras." Through this mechanism many have passed into the paramilitaries' ranks. But the most significant example of this capacity to co-opt members or absorb other organizational schemes is the CONVIVIR security groups, authorized as a controversial measure of the Minister of Defense. Following an initial boom and rapid growth, they were hotly contested because of the nature of their functions, and finally abolished in 1999. Even so, they did not completely disappear, but became semiclandestine, and, according to various sources and the declarations of some of their leaders, put themselves at the disposition of the paramilitaries.[4]

To end this discussion of the tendency of self-defense groups to transform themselves into paramilitaries (a process still incomplete), it is enough to note that today none of the current leaders of the "paras" claims for himself the paramilitary label. And the most important nucleus of the federation of regional groups, which at the present time conducts itself under the principle of national coordination, continues to use the self-defense label: Autodefensas Campesinas de Córdoba y Urabá (ACCU).

From Consolidation to Expansion: The Economic Logic

Perhaps there has not been sufficient emphasis on the fact that the accelerated growth of the paramilitary groups coincides with the period following the declaration of the illegality of self-defense and all private justice groups. In their origins, these groups benefited from legal ambiguity, but once they were freed of all legal protection, and consolidated themselves as clandestine movements, imitating the mobility of the guerrillas and taking advantage of their intimate knowledge of the terrain, they entered into a stage of rapid expansion.

Since the publication of the Colombian Security Office's "Paramilitary Dossier" in April 1989, the media intermittently fix their attention on the paramilitary groups' principal leaders, who, in turn, begin to publicize their actions, hoping to disassociate themselves from those who might alienate the support they already have. See, for example, the "Declaración de Caño Alegre" (*Boletín* 4 [June 12, 1989], Self-Defense Groups of the Magdalena Medio), in which they condemn a recent assassination attempt against a high government official and differentiate themselves from narcoterrorists. At the same time, they hope to represent themselves in legal politics through intermediaries. Interviews with paramilitary leaders (Henry Pérez, Ramón Isaza, Fidel and Carlos Castaño) become frequent, and they continually demand to be represented in any peace negotiations between the government and the guerrillas.

An economic logic underlies all of this. Without claiming unicausality, there is an impressive correlation between the growth of huge agricultural estates as a result of the investment of drug money and the growth of paramilitary groups, as Alejandro Reyes has noted in several articles. To paraphrase Reyes, in Colombia, the struggle for territorial dominion has replaced social conflicts over land.[5] Something analogous has happened with the paramilitaries. From being defenders of newly acquired and threatened agricultural property, they have become controllers of territory. Through that process they have learned that violence, in addition to accomplishing retaliatory objectives to satisfy private aims, is an efficient mechanism of social control.

Economic Rationality According to Income

The devaluation of human life that is evident in the impudence with which paramilitaries describe their actions against unarmed persons has as its counterpart the explicit description of the economic rationality that permits them to consolidate themselves, secure regional support, and create a social foundation for their bellicose acts: They present themselves as the restorers of the social order lost with the arrival of the guerrillas. Here it is extraordinary how the analyst's description of the economic mechanisms involved neatly coincides with that of the paramilitaries themselves.

"One-third of the 800,000 refugees," writes Alejandro Reyes, "lost their lands at the hands of paramilitary groups, who appropriated [them] as booty in the war in order to reconstruct a social base submissive to the great haciendas. Buying cheaply where there were guerrillas, bringing in private security, and appraising the property became an enormous business that combined economic power and private use of force, the two privileged resources available to the mafias and great landowners."[6]

The paramilitary leader Carlos Castaño describes the same process this way: "We had just given away sixteen thousand hectares in the Sinú. We bought [these lands] cheaply because the guerrillas were there. Look, it's like this: you buy when there are guerrillas, [the lands] aren't worth anything then because all the cattle ranchers have left and there we bought cheaply; we then eradicate the guerrillas and, when the zone is liberated, we give away the lands."[7] The last part of this testimony should certainly be taken with a grain of salt. Even so, the implicit rationality in the devaluation-revaluation of the lands is clear, leaving in question whether the gains from these transactions fund subsequent bellicose actions or if paramilitary leaders are only pursuing occasional political dividends. In any case, one of the peculiarities of the guerrilla fight is that until they have consolidated their influence and gained clear control of a territory, the whole region is insecure. During this situation of generalized insecurity, particularly in regions where the guerrillas' arrival is recent, the paramilitaries flourish as a capitalist insurance policy.

In a valuable regional monograph, part of a recent book edited by Jesús Bejarano and others, one of the central questions proposed by one investigator was how the guerrillas' presence affected the land market and what economic effects stem from the subsequent arrival of the paramilitaries. To answer it, the investigator undertook a survey of business people engaged in agriculture and spokespeople for economic interest groups in the most conflict-ridden parts of the department of César, the Magdalena Medio, and Urabá. Despite the possible distortions caused by the suspicions generated by the types of questions the investigators were asking in such polarized regions, the conclusions are consistent with the process outlined above. "[The paramilitaries] paradoxically constitute security factors in activities such as ranching and palm oil and banana production. Undoubtedly, their incursions have lessened the pressure of the guerrillas in zones such as Urabá, the Magdalena Medio in Santander, and the south of César. . . . Nevertheless, the cost in human lives is great and significant displacements of the population are produced."[8] In none of the regions did the investigator find that the land market had been perceptibly distorted, or that there were massive sales, even though all those interviewed, with one notable exception, referred invariably to the fall in the price of land as one of the effects of guerrilla presence. "The interviewees emphasize that in the department of Córdoba and in areas contiguous with La Dorada, Caldas, the price of lands had notably recuperated as a result of the control exercised by the paramilitaries."[9]

Although the authors of this study are careful to note that, taken as a whole, the effects of the presence of paramilitaries are negative for the regional economy and create a climate of uncertainty and risk, the responses they received concerning land are important for understanding the persistence of paramilitarism. If we believe, based on more recent evidence, that the paramilitaries had purely instrumental origins, that they were simple tools in the process of hacienda expansion, we must also accept the fact that the initial successes in the fight to displace the guerrillas have had unexpected longer-lasting effects. These operate in the paramilitaries' favor in the medium range, surpassing their initial goals and offering them unforeseen possibilities.

Testimonies abound concerning the routine charging of a tribute by the paramilitaries, which does not seem much different from the famous *vacuna*, or "immunization" of the guerrillas. With even more fragmentary data than that available on the finances of the guerrillas, the risk of falling into untenable speculations concerning the management of the proceeds is inevitable. Statements of paramilitary leaders are as elusive about funding by drug traffickers as about the forced nature of the tribute they collect in their territories. In any case, there is a trace of truthfulness in their answers: For tactical reasons, hoping not to alienate their support, they attempt to differentiate themselves from guerrillas by avoiding ruinous levels of tribute and assuming the function of guarantors of the right to lands. They try to maintain a precarious equilibrium, demanding "voluntary" payments, amplifying the tribute base, and making sure that the earnings are reinvested in lands. These seem to be the surest ways to conserve and increase their support and reap political dividends. They also use what happened in Puerto Boyacá as a constant example in their testimonials no matter what region they are operating in. There the FARC's kidnapping campaigns and indiscriminate exactions created widespread exasperation (the so-called telethon of the

Magdalena Medio) and allowed the first paramilitary groups to gain a firm foothold.

Economic Rationality According to Expenditures

What was leaked to the media as the "Paramilitary Dossier" of the Colombian Security Office and was claimed to contain nothing less than "the origins, development, and current structure of the paras"[10] demonstrates that for the Magdalena Medio, the paramilitaries had a rudimentary administrative apparatus, as well as ties to business and interest groups and local government offices. That model tends to be imitated, but along the way (looking again at the testimony of paramilitary leaders), the need for a separate urban apparatus came to be understood. It would be clandestine, have a certain level of professionalism among its members, and a certain division of labor to ensure efficiency in the collecting and expenditure of funds. We only have fragmentary data about all this, mere signs, and, as in the financing of guerrilla activity, any generalization would be speculative. This is, in other words, slippery terrain. Nevertheless, Castaño plainly admits that all his combatants "are also salaried, but in addition to money, they have a cause,"[11] and that statement implies organization and costs and the concomitant necessity to account for costs. In the fragmentary accounts that can be gleaned from the interviews, invariably the cost of a communications network that functions twenty-four hours per day is calculated.

Salaried combatants also have to be provided for, through increasingly complex lines of provision. In their weapons and uniforms, and in equipment, one observes standardization, and in terms of quality of arms they strive to be on a par with the guerrillas and the army. They try to hide differences with the guerrillas with respect to the level of the conviction of their members by emphasizing military training. This can be deduced from the way in which the different leaders all identify training as a costly permanent necessity, toward which they apply a portion of their earnings without cutting costs, including at times payments to foreign mercenaries as trainers. Practice has taught them that the best combatant is the best trained, a professional. If we believe the Castaño brothers, the early symptoms of decay among the self-defense groups of the Magdalena Medio were related to finances. At that time, these groups were under command of Ariel Otero, a former army officer, and there was relentless infighting between factions for control of the organization, to the point that they were about to disappear. These problems were apparently a result of a large volume of income subject to no control. The breakdown of the structure of command that resulted served as a lesson for the future.

Although the paramilitaries reject time and again the label of mercenary (in the case of the Castaño brothers with a vehemence and level of conviction that stem from having initiated their business as a personal vendetta), their behavior is basically that of a capitalist adventurer. In this they are comparable, in more than one way, to what the North American tradition terms "typical frontier entrepreneurs" who, in turn, were also principal promoters of private justice organizations.[12]

If the interviews with Henry Pérez, Ramón Isaza, and Fidel and Carlos Castaño have something in common, it is that, along with historical references to the process of homesteading in their native regions and the use of military jargon (terms such as "logistics" and "security cordons"), they often employ technical language from the world of cattle ranching. They make expert references to the occupation of cattlemen, and to the cycles and changes the cattle business has undergone in recent decades.[13] Converted by force of circumstance into a new type of businessman, they attempt to illustrate the benefits of the security they offer with data that show a better standard of living and greater chances of obtaining government aid and construction projects in the areas they control. They also claim that once they have consolidated dominion over a territory and have expelled the guerrillas, security grows because there is the tacit additional guarantee that there will be no more sweeps by the army.

Armed Actors in the Conflict

"Actors" is a term much used in a contemporary French school of sociology that has lately been in vogue among journalists. The term implies that in the organization or social movement to which it is applied it is possible to discern rational actions, that the strategies of a given group are conscious and in some way related to the group's particular interests. I cannot precisely determine when "actor" was first applied to the paramilitaries, but almost imperceptibly, by applying this term, the idea that paramilitary ends were purely selfish and private was transformed into something else. The term is not bound up with an immediate recognition of paramilitary political status, but it does tend in that direction.

At any rate, quite apart from the analytical merits of this theory, what is interesting is how the paramilitaries themselves have appropriated it and used it to give form to their goals and arguments. A detailed study of the journalistic treatment of the paramilitaries affords a glimpse of this process of permeation, of linguistic imitation, stimulated by the growing interest of the media in the paramilitaries' statements. Very rapidly the paramilitaries have begun speaking "the language of actors."[14] Comparison of the interviews conducted by Germán Castro Caycedo and María Cristina Caballero with Carlos Castaño, both done in the field but two years apart, will surely reveal the difference in language.

According to the theory of social action we are discussing, constitution as "actors" implies consciousness, elaboration of goals, and options available to reach them; that is to say, the theory emphasizes the supposition that the actors have a strategy. The voluntarism that this conception implies is certainly attractive to those who find themselves at war, because it is related to what is popularly considered "epic" or "heroic." On occasion, the term "actor" is actually used in its theatrical sense, as if it concerned representation on the scale of a whole society. The analytic disadvantage of the term is that it is easy to use in a one-sided way, abstracting it from the interests that first gave it meaning. One of the theorists specifically warns against simplification, noting that it could lead to attributing an excess of autonomy to the political with respect to the social system.[15]

What can be corroborated is that, beyond the paramilitaries' ideological rhetoric (to which we will refer in detail in the next section), their actions following 1989 indicate an intention to expand regional support, diversify and project themselves on a wider plane, and attune themselves to the sectors particularly affected by the armed conflict. Additionally, they try to disassociate themselves from the most brutal actions, even at the price of giving up evidence that serves to advance judicial processes against old friends. The paramilitaries deliberately cultivate a self-critical tone toward actions that have received the greatest international condemnation, not only because there are judicial processes against them, but also because they have begun to discover psychological warfare and have flashes of understanding concerning the importance of international opinion.

In another article, concerning questions of military strategy,[16] I have analyzed this component of paramilitary expansion. In social action theory, however, strategy is understood in its most general sense as the conjoining of tools for action necessary for the attainment of the goals of a particular organization or social movement. It is this broad meaning of strategy to which I refer.

Since the case of Puerto Boyacá in the Magadalena Medio, in spite of slow judicial processes and many obstacles, indications and evidence have accumulated concerning the participation of Colombian Army soldiers and officers in the formation of various paramilitary groups. Even if ultimately we could prove this military participation, including the existence of design at the highest levels of the military hierarchy, the questions concerning paramilitary consolidation, expansion, and the degree of support for their most general goals would still remain. Not even the most foresighted and Machiavellian plan would have been able to contemplate such rapid growth, expansion, and regional diversification. It is enough to note that all the analysts who investigated the paramilitaries when they first appeared were mistaken in their prognosis, as even a glance at the literature confirms.

One must then recast the problem. The growth and diversification following 1989, which is evident in the statistics, can only be explained if it is admitted that more support for the paramilitaries exists than is openly expressed. The paramilitaries' advisers, counselors in the shadows, must have been able to persuade them that the ground for such expansion was fertile. The half-hearted efforts on the part of those charged with pursuing them once they were made illegal—collusion, in other words—is part of the explanation, but it is not sufficient.

It is important to note in this respect that the capacity of the paramilitaries to co-opt former guerrillas and effect a "change of uniform" has been growing. One could argue that "Vladimir" (who has not denied that he was previously a commander of the Ninth Front of the FARC) and Marcelino Panesso (Rodríguez Gacha's right-hand man in the formation of various paramilitary groups) were deserters from the FARC or had surrendered after capture by the military. But in addition to these special cases, one must add Carlos Castaño's special advisers, the former guerrillas whom Castro Caycedo found in the area, and many others. There are so many such examples that it becomes evident that co-optation is a systematic undertaking developed by the paramilitary directorship, not only because the paramilitaries value the guerrillas' expertise, but because in the zones where it occurs there is a predisposition to it. Eloquent in this respect are the several reports published in November 1996, concerning the entry into the ranks of the ACCU of more than two hundred guerrillas of the EPL without a formal agreement. The number of old, rehabilitated EPL members in the region (who were the principal target of the Castaño organization until 1990), the limited probability of effecting an authentic rehabilitation, given the level of polarization, especially in Urabá and in the Valle del Sinú, together with the campaign directed against them by the FARC, which had hoped to occupy the vacuum left by the EPL, did not appear to give these people any alternative.

All these factors indicate that in a situation of generalized violence, and in particular for those regions that have experienced irregular war over a long time, the return to normalcy requires more than specific plans for social investment. It is no accident that such a situation works to discredit the soldier who still knows and applies the rules of battle and who has the capacity to distinguish between combatants and the defenseless.[17] When the Second Geneva Protocol was finally adopted in Colombia, there were those who, owing to a kind of judicial fetishism, thought it would remove the most important obstacle to ending the armed conflict. They soon discovered that all the parties invoked it, but none appeared to be persuaded that its norms were wholly applicable to the Colombian situation, thus requiring adaptation to the kind of conflict being fought there.

In their relationship to the judicial system and institutional politics, paramilitaries have learned the advantage of moving beyond the battlefield. As for their capacity to project themselves into legal politics, the following is instructive. Two years after the self-defense groups were declared illegal, several representatives served as intermediaries for paramilitary interests during the 1991 Constitutional Convention and argued in favor of negotiations with them. Since then the paramilitaries have not ceased to flirt with and approach members of Congress. If one wanted examples of their understanding of political forces and the level of their awareness and knowledge of congressional maneuverings, one need only examine the video presented to Congress in April 1997. (In the same session, videos were also presented that summarized the more predictable and doctrinaire positions of the ELN and FARC.) Or one could look at the ingenious role that officious spokespeople played during the discussion of the effect of the law on public order and in the naming of delegations, such as the Senate's Peace Commission,[18] that have visited territories under paramilitary control. This situation signals a recognition of the de facto power that paramilitaries illicitly exercise, even though official rhetoric persists in denying any possibility of negotiation with them and in treating them as common criminals. The most the government has offered them is "penal subrogation." Even so the tactical signals are revealing, and the recognition and respectability of being considered social actors (although armed) provides enough to sustain them. To put this in diplomatic jargon, given the opportunity to choose, the paramilitaries prefer de facto power to de jure power.

Their attitude toward the International Declaration of Human Rights has also been subject to gradual modification and demonstrates a perception of pressures and demands in a wider context. From a stance of denial and suspicion, they have been moving toward theoretical and very conditional acceptance of human rights doctrine. This is a kind of reshuffling of the deck that brings with it a generic admission that they have transgressed, but that it was inevitable since their enemies had already done it and theirs was the only possible response. Of course, they also demand reciprocity in adhering to human rights doctrine. This position is illustrated by the way they have permitted the International Red Cross to mediate in the negotiations over the kidnappings of relatives of guerrilla leaders and, more recently, in negotiations with the heads of an NGO dedicated to human rights in Medellín.

An Ideology of the Printed Page

"An ideology of the printed page . . . but not a real ideology." I borrow this phrase from the historian Marco Palacios because it adequately defines the artificial and cunning character of the communications and documents that can be attributed to the paramilitaries and their recently formed organization for national coordination. Here there is no difficulty in distinguishing between "canonical" and "apocryphal" texts as there was for the early guerrilla movements. The paramilitaries' channels for distributing information work well, and, like the present-day guerrillas, they cultivate access to the most technologically sophisticated ones. Nor is the analyst distressed by a documentary mass that obliges him to refine his criteria and selectivity. Documents with programmatic pretensions have been few and extremely repetitive. The three so-called national convocations of the movement have left a few other documents. In addition to what can be gleaned through interviews dealing with the current situation, since July 1997 the paramilitaries have published a bulletin of varied content (like the FARC's *Resistencia*, it has a crossword puzzle, an ecological page, and a pedagogical section concerning human rights). None of this resolves doubts concerning the authenticity of this documentation in a more substantial sense.

In what follows I try to detail my sense of the ideas contained in these documents and how they might be interpreted. The first document worthy of mention is the "Declaration of the First National Convention of Self-Defense Groups in Colombia," which at first glance appears to have been written in Cimitarra in December 1994. The first part of this text is replete with technical military details, especially concerning intelligence, with acronyms and information that is largely inaccessible to laypeople. An initial surprise for the reader searching for the ideological orientation of the movement is that of the fifty-seven pages, twenty-three are dedicated to diagnosing, in detail, intelligence problems of the armed forces and to attributing the inefficiency of the antiguerrilla struggle to these failings. The lack of counterintelligence, the excessively centralized nature of intelligence organisms, and their lack of ties to the different regions are illustrated with examples of recent operations. At times, given the abundance of acronyms, the significance of the sentences is undetectable for the layperson: "The Br-20 limits its efforts to the department of Cundinamarca and occasionally collaborates with other brigades and tactical units. Rarely does the Br-20 feed or capacitate the B-2 and S-2 and only occasionally does it share information." Then, after several pages dedicated to the role of the intelligence analyst and to the importance of intelligence networks (pp. 32–38), one reaches a cryptic conclusion, which to a nonspecialist appears to be a kind of professional justification. It reads as follows: "The section of analysis is managed by one or two people who are not able to cover their entire jurisdiction and can only manage to send a [summary?] to the brigade."

If we apply to this text the tools developed for the analysis of linguistic production, the results are surprising. (I refer here to tools such as those applied to the political texts of May 1968 in France—discourses, pamphlets, bulletins, graffiti, and the like.) Such tools distinguish between functional and lexical forms in order to reveal guiding ideas. (The analyst establishes coefficients of lexical redundancy and other similar indicators.) Using such methods one finds that, in what is supposed to be a declaration of principles, a justification of the singularity of a movement, the terms and concepts of greatest weight belong in fact to the vocabulary of the most specialized job in the practice of the war: intelligence.

Thus is revealed the contrived nature of the document. It is the work of an adviser (and not exactly an inspired adviser) carried out in order to fulfill a requirement. A few rhetorical formalities precede a technical diagnosis of the question of armed conflict. The violence appears to be justified as a pure reaction, not far from the law of the jungle. The document affirms that, in the face of the crimes of the guerrillas and the erosion of all vestiges of authority in the territories where they act, the paramilitaries can only react in kind. The target of the violence they apply is the one they judge the weakest link of the enemy: the enemy's hidden auxiliaries, its clandestine support network. They assume that a direct confrontation with the guerrillas is not very likely, although they allude to some combat. They make use of the classic proportion, saying that nine-tenths of guerrilla activity is hidden from view and this same proportion applies to their own apparatus. This is an argument that, sure enough, we find again in the interview of Carlos Castaño by Castro Caycedo: "In this war much of the civil population dies. Do you know why? Because two-thirds of the effective forces of the guerrillas do not have weapons and are acting as part of the civil population."[19]

The idea that the violence they employed is a reaction to that of those who preceded them is more developed in the final paragraphs, where it is disconnected from immediate interests and appears as part of the discussion of "strategic interactions." In this discussion, the paramilitaries reserve for themselves a role that is parallel and complementary to, but much more effective than, the legal defense of order. The historical marker they frequently mention, and which is found in various interviews, is the Betancur administration's politics of peace, to which they refer as if it were a unilateral surrender.

Richer in ideological content, historical references, and definitions of interests (but no less problematic with respect to authenticity, in the sense of matching the real plans and interests of the group and its leaders) is the document presented by the Self-Defense Groups of the Magdalena Medio at one of the various national conferences dealing with peace initiatives, in particular one held in May 1995. The carefully written document begins by stating the "territorial compass of the proposal." By doing so, even though with the evident propagandistic intention of magnifying their radius of influence and presuming to represent the "communities of thirteen *municipios*" (which are enumerated), the document offers an approximation of the real extent of territory where groups directed by Ramón Isaza act. In this document, the professional language of the adviser is, evidently, that of a lawyer. At least, that is what the knowledge of the rules of contracts, of the impenetrable terrain of the Colombian petroleum legislation, and a certain number of archaic phrases regarding property rights and their variations in the document permit us to suppose. The document goes back a century in order to characterize historically the area known as the Territorio Vásquez and identifies (using the same guidelines employed by the historian Carlos Medina Gallego in his book about the region, but varying the emphasis) the problems in defining the territorial limits between Boyacá and Santander. It also refers to the uncertainties concerning property rights as well as the abuses of the first petroleum companies that arrived in the region. These accounts are presented as the primordial source of the social conflict and the propensity to violence in the region, which, according to conventional wisdom, has been intermittent in the Magdalena Medio.

Corroborating this deduction that the principal author of the document is a lawyer are the detailed knowledge of the judicial proceedings brought against some members of the group and the effort to exonerate those charged by including dispositions and documentary "proofs." Furthermore, in this effort to disassociate the current organization from some of the most criminal and condemned actions attributed to another organization of the same name (such as the massacre of judicial functionaries in Rochela), the document includes data, a good quantity of juridical-style arguments, and a detailed enumeration of the "misunderstandings and excesses," "detours from principles, errors, and repeated mistakes" committed by Henry Pérez and Ariel Otero's organization. There is even a detailed chronological enumeration of massacres committed. The mystification in which the principal author was engaged is evidenced by the fact that, even at this point, 1995, he insisted on distinguishing self-defense groups from paramilitaries as if there had been no prior confusion, as if on no occasion had the group deviated from its purely defensive posture. This contrasts, of course, with the list of violent actions that was included, actions whose authorship is attributed to "the other" self-defense groups. This is a closing statement of a judicial defense that is made to order.

In this document, in their eagerness to pardon themselves, the paramilitaries omit any reference to the violence that they themselves have continued practicing. If its readers lack basic information, they might regard the group as a collective and humane association that only by pure accident shares its name with other violent groups. There are passages of a nationalist flavor (against "voracious monopolistic extraction by the gringo multinational" Texas Petroleum) and others that express working-class demands—all of them nothing but a sham, written for internal Colombian consumption.

The rest of the readily assessable ideological material (the reports of the first and third national conventions and the *Colombia Libre* bulletins published since July 1997) does not contain variations on the central ideas outlined above and only perfects the discourse. Considerable care is taken with diagrams and illustrations in the text, which are done with the evident aid of specialists in the field. As the paramilitaries have perfected the form of their written materials, they have also striven to make their publications and style of communication resemble those of the guerrilla organizations. They try to swell their own importance by presenting a very specialized division of labor: a "Commission of Political Affairs," a "Commission for Human Rights," a "Commission of Ecological Affairs," a "Commission for Work and Study." In a recent report, the work of those commissions is presented in sixteen uniform pages divided into eleven articles, with no stylistic variation among them. The only thing that can be inferred from this is that specialists are aiding them in their work and correcting their writing style. At least, they have eliminated the errors in syntax and spelling common in the first documents.

What could be their manifesto, the doctrinal nucleus of their ideas, ends up being not very convincing because it is easy to detect the model that it follows. I refer to the document entitled "United Self-Defense Groups of Colombia: The Political-Military Nature of the Movement." It is replete with the political jargon they use: "local political power," "political space," "absence of the State," "subordinate the military to politics" (a tribute to [Carl von] Clausewitz), "unconcealable sociological evidence" (a tribute to [Auguste] Comte), "negotiated political solution," and, of course, "armed political actors." The greater the eloquence, the less convincing the passages are, and that also applies to the final section, which is dedicated to the question of human rights. There, perhaps, the paragraph that has the greatest fidelity to the acts that they promote is the one in which they characterize irregular war, the difficulties it poses in distinguishing between active combatants, combatants, active sympathizers, and so on.

By targeting the most celebrated and well-known of the conveyers of social science findings to the public, Alfredo Molano, in a polemical letter containing veiled threats,[20] the paramilitaries made a big impact on society and simultaneously sent a message to the entire intellectual community, especially professional social scientists. They assumed that the majority of social science professionals have an ideological affinity with the left, which has compromised their objectivity. That lack of objectivity, as they put it in their most doctrinaire statement, impedes recognition of "irrefutable sociological evidence" (by which they mean the low level of support that the left has received). At the same time, they are also saying: We can speak your language; it has ceased to be a specialized terminology, a professional jargon only for the initiated. Their intimidating incursions into, and their communications directed at, public universities, which until a decade ago were a sanctuary for leftist ideologies, serve the same purpose.

What do such diverse ideological materials have in common? There is a great temptation to disdain them given their overriding deceitful content, and this disdain has prevailed among analysts. They see this material as ideological babbling and are suspicious of the mystification it produces. They see it as a cacophony of contradictory ideas that belie the acts of those who spread them (acts which, of course, the paramilitaries acknowledge). Perplexity on the part of those who try to make sense of all this has been the norm.

Nevertheless, I will risk some judgments concerning the content of these writings, judgments that are the result of a serious effort to make sense of the ideas in these documents. In the first place, one must point out that we are dealing with an ideology forged a posteriori, after actions have occurred, in order to justify them. This is in contrast to the leftist guerrillas, whose rise has an ideological foundation, the doctrinal preparation of the original nucleus of members, which is axiomatic and is personified in the party commissioner or ideologue. It is because of this a posteriori condition that the paramilitaries use a tone aimed at exonerating themselves and tend to follow the argumentative logic of the defense in a judicial proceeding.

The historian Eric Hobsbawm used the notion of the prepolitical with the aim of identifying a certain type of Colombian bandit who, at the end of the 1950s, resorts to violence in a personal vendetta and, once embarked on it, discovers its wider application. Something analogous can be observed in paramilitarism. Originally, the violent actions committed are in a private context, but the logic of the confrontation places them on a broader stage. The type of enemy against whom they fight envelops them in issues of territorial domination and the questions of disaffected populations. It then becomes indispensable for them to find a cause, make explicit their extra-individual motivations, and add a public end to their private goals. Pursuing efficacy in combat, they replicate the strategic orientation of the "combination of all the forms of struggle by the guerrillas" and imitate their underground network. They learn that they can reap dividends by maintaining ties to legal politics and thus hope to be included in eventual negotiations. In the meantime, they have discovered that an organization is a structure of power and that diversification within it yields multiple additional advantages.

It can look antithetical, or worse, like an empty paradox, but in these documents a defense of the current Constitution stands out. And to some extent the paramilitaries feel they participated in forming it. At times they use the most constitutionalist of languages, but, in my opinion, there is no pretence in their vehement defense of the legislated order; here they express their real interests. Theirs is an elemental attachment, instinctive, if you will. Their frequently mentioning the Constitution is not a fraud. It is not a ritual formula. They may be truly convinced of the Constitution's intrinsic validity. At the same time, they are also convinced that the internal conflict and the power that the guerrillas claim are the principal obstacles to enforcing the Constitution. If we reconstruct the acts that preceded and accompanied the convening of the 1991 Constituent Assembly, we can show that, as was claimed in the official rhetoric at the start of the draft constitution submitted by the government, there were expectations in many sectors that the process would result in a "peace treaty." The effectiveness of the military actions against what was considered the general quarters of the FARC the same day that the Constituent Assembly was installed convinced many that the Colombian State was simultaneously employing its two principal tools to move the guerrillas to the negotiating table.

If we examine the levels of participation in the election of the delegates to the Constituent Assembly, we see that they were high for the regions where the paramilitaries were active. Moreover, the "movement" that acted as their political arm, thanks to "functional alliances," among them some with ex-guerrillas, won unexpected representation. As restorers of the pre-established order, they continue considering the text of the Constitution of 1991 suitable and intrinsically valid, and they are immune to criticisms of the Constitution and reject proposals to reform it. Theirs is a literal attachment to the Constitution, one not explained by the fact that they have legal advisers, as one might assume. Although they admit that many of the rights and institutions mandated by the Constitution have not been put into force, the exclusive reason, according to them, lies in the failure of military action against the guerrillas and in the persistence and widening scope of guerrilla territorial power. Thus, at least as far as one can infer, for them, the 1991 Constitution is the most abstract expression possible of a lost order that must be recovered. Consequently, they have taken some ideas from the text of the Constitution and integrated them into their limited arsenal of watchwords.

The dialectics of the confrontation (to use that rather archaic phrase), the effort by the paramilitaries to assimilate and adapt to the transformations of the guerrillas, to replicate what are considered to be the guerrillas' proven methods, has led them, step by step, to undergo changes not unlike those experienced by the guerrillas themselves.[21] Perhaps there is no better example than the question of kidnapping, which has not been given enough attention. In its origins, the paramilitary movement managed to justify itself as an answer to the anger of various sectors at the guerrillas' systematic kidnapping campaign. But when, in turn, the paramilitaries kidnapped relatives of guerrilla leaders, they brought about, for the first time, direct negotiations with the guerrillas. As if to accentuate the reciprocity, they, like the guerrillas, continue using the euphemism "retentions" for the kidnappings they carry out. Today, in hindsight, there is no doubt that there were direct, but hidden, negotiations between the two forces, and the liberation of the hostages was a result of them, all of which reveals a certain recognition of enemy status between the guerrillas and the paramilitaries.

In my opinion, it is the very efficiency of a type of violence that, in the experience of the paramilitaries, has led them from private action into the public sphere. Anyone who goes over the main facts of the paramilitary phenomenon for the last fifteen years cannot but conclude that the paramilitaries intend to stay, and that their existence and eventual disappearance are a function of the fate of the guerrillas. The Samper administration's plea, after one of the massacres committed by the paramilitaries, requesting support to pursue them unto "hell" was received with the same incredulousness as his vowing to achieve the "total eradication of illicit crops in the next two years." Both were formulations for international consumption, made in the knowledge that the government had neither the resources, nor the support, nor the necessary internal conditions to make good on these threats.

To reiterate, as the poetic text of the epigraph has it, the paramilitaries have "become a part of the reality of our time and it is useless to deny their power." We do not say this in the fatalistic sense that we should submit ourselves to the paramilitaries' power, but in the realistic sense that it is not enough to deny, curse, or dismiss that power as unqualified. We must begin to recognize that power for what it is if we are to confront it. We must eradicate the conditions that have permitted the paramilitaries to acquire such power.

Notes

1. *El Tiempo*, July 30, 1987: "The book *El sentido de la agresión* by Konrad Larens [*sic*] shows us how the living being, rational or irrational, carries deep within it the instinct of territorial defense. No one can touch it. For that reason, animals and humans delineate their territory so that the enemy does not occupy it, and faced with transgression by an enemy, they defend it until the death. Banditry is reaching the zones of peasants, farmers, and landowners large and small; it invades those territories. What the army has done is provide these people with necessary arms to detain those abuses. To not do so would go against the most elemental rights of the individual, consecrated in the constitutions of all the world." Contrast this with *El Tiempo*, December 4, 1997: "Those seduced by the strength and implacable bursts of firepower of the paramilitary organizations, and indignant and hurt by the blind radicalization of subversive organizations, have been listening to a perverse siren call. They think that massacres by the paramilitary or self-defense groups are an appropriate way to stop the armed conflict in Colombia."

2. Comisión de Estudios sobre la Violencia, *Colombia: Violencia y democracia* (Bogotá, 1987), 20 (emphasis mine).

3. In another of the essays in ibid., the following flawed prognosis is formulated: "Until now [paramilitarism] has been effective in its objectives of neutralizing the guerrillas and the popular organizations. *But its future may depend on the international character that the Colombian conflict is acquiring and, for that reason, on the interference of the United States.* Although the rise of the paramilitaries depended on the cocaine lords and on the army that hid them, it is not certain that their functioning depends only on the drug kingpins" (101–2; emphasis mine). Perhaps the only positive dimension of U.S. involvement in the Colombian conflict has been precisely in its efforts against paramilitarism. Illustrative are the statements of Ambassador Miles Frechette and Subsecretary Barry McCaffrey in November 1997.

4. See "La tercera fuerza: Con recursos internacionales y del sector privado colombiano las CONVIVIR logran financiar su fortalecimiento en la ilegalidad," *Semana*, March 22, 1999.

5. See his “Conflicto armado y territorio en Colombia,” in *Colonización del bosque húmedo tropical* (Bogotá, 1989), 55.

6. Alejandro Reyes, in his column “El problema de la tierra y el dominio del territorio,” *El Espectador*, February 16, 1997.

7. Carlos Castaño in an interview with Germán Castro Caycedo, published in Castro Caycedo's *En secreto* (Bogotá, 1996), 201.

8. Jesús Antonio Bejarano, Camilo Echandía, Rodolfo Escobedo, and Enrique León Queruz, eds., *Colombia: Inseguridad, violencia y desempeño económico en las areas rurales* (Bogotá, 1997).

9. Ibid., 244.

10. *Semana*, April 11, 1989.

11. In his interview with Castro Caycedo, published in *En secreto*.

12. See National Commission on the Causes and Prevention of Violence, *The History of Violence in America* (New York, 1969). Note particularly the chapter on private justice groups. “They were the typical frontier entrepreneurs. Their enterprise in commerce and land was often speculative, and they frequently skated on economic thin ice” (p. 176).

13. See the interview of Henry Pérez in *Semana*, April 16, 1991; of Fidel Castaño in *Semana*, May 31, 1994; of Ramón Isaza, *Semana*, December 3, 1996; and the previously cited interview of Carlos Castaño in Castro Caycedo's *En secreto*. Fidel Castaño claims, “My business has always centered on ranching and art.” The economic notions of Carlos Castaño all come from ranching; the estimate of land distributed is always in relation to its carrying capacity, and the type of cattle bred. In addition, Castaño extensively cites (and it is the only document that supports his argument) a letter from the president of the Federation of the Cattle Ranchers of Córdoba, which defends him and his brother Fidel.

14. “One says one thing publicly and another inside the organization. While we are in a war all of us actors use a language different from the one we want. Especially the guerrillas. . . .” Carlos Castaño in his interview with María Cristina Caballero, *Cambio 16* (December 15, 1997): 24.

15. “A purely strategic conception of change leads to reducing society to the relationships between the actors and in particular to the relations of power, separated from all reference to a social system.” Alain Touraine, “Les acteurs historiques: Acteur ou système?” in *La voix et le regard* (Paris, 1978), 78.

16. Malcolm Deas and Maria Victoria Llorente, comps., “La estrategia de los paramilitares,” in *Reconocer la guerra para construir la paz* (Bogotá, 1999).

17. In a history of an aspect of the military question, the North American historian Russell W. Ramsey calls Colonel Gustavo Sierra Ochoa “one of the first Commandants whom the Vargas Battalion had, and he had the opportunity to realize that conventional tactics and armies cannot defeat guerrillas” (*Guerrilleros y soldados* [Bogotá, 1981], 196). Ramsey does not emphasize the fact that this pioneer got carried away by the logic of irregular war, committed all manner of excesses, and that for his opponents, the guerrillas of the *llanos*, he was a primary example of how the army had taken on a partisan role in the conflict, fighting a war without quarter. Of Colonel Sierra's books, *Diálogos militares* (Manizales, 1951) and *Las guerrillas de los Llanos Orientales* (Manizales, 1954), the second appears in the specialized literature as the first to adopt the notion of the “internal enemy.” For the way in which the guerrillas perceived these actions, see chaps. 14 (Part 1) and 1 and 8 (Part II) of Eduardo Franco Isaza, *Las guerrillas del llano* (Bogotá, 1986).

18. See "Senadores visitan a Carlos Castaño," *El Tiempo*, November 19, 1997. The article reveals that members of the Commission traveled to meet the paramilitaries. "In addition to Castaño, congressmen Julio César Guerra Tulena, coordinator of the Commission, and Carlos Espinosa Faccio-Lince attended the meeting." In any other latitude, a congressional visit at this level by men who in addition had been presidents of their respective congressional chambers, would be a show of political recognition. Here it took place in an almost surreptitious manner.

19. Castro Caycedo, *En secreto*, 177.

20. The letter and Molano's answer were published in *Cambio 16* (August 25, 1997).

21. The admiration of Castaño is expressed openly and forcefully in various passages in his interviews: "We cannot ignore the fact that they have spent thirty-one years at war and that they are the big shots of the war" (Castro Caycedo, *En secreto*, 190).

Chapter 7

Victims and Survivors of War in Colombia
Three Views of Gender Relations

Donny Meertens

In this pioneering study, Donny Meertens explores some of the ways gender relations have structured the violence in Colombia. She first looks at the meaning of political violence toward women during the "classic" Violence of the 1950s and 1960s and compares it to the situation today. She then analyzes how today's violence affects men and women differently. She shows that women are still less likely than men to be killed in the violence, but they are increasingly being displaced by it. Persons displaced by the violence, estimated at 1.5 million in Colombia by the end of the 1990s, face difficult challenges in putting their lives back together. Meertens finds that men and women bring different skills and expectations to that struggle and shows that they experience different kinds of successes and failures in their efforts to build a new life.

Donny Meertens is a Dutch anthropologist who has lived and worked in Colombia for more than twenty years and is affiliated with the Program on Gender Studies, Women, and Development at the National University of Colombia in Bogotá. She has published several articles on the victims of contemporary violence in Colombia and is coauthor, with Gonzalo Sánchez G., of *Bandoleros, gamonales y campesinos* (Bogotá, 1984, English edition forthcoming, University of Texas Press).

Gender is an analytical category that permits the examination of differences between men and women both as cultural constructs and also, simultaneously, as constituents of asymmetric social relationships.[1] Here I develop three aspects of gender evident in the current dynamics of war in Colombia and in the consequences of various decades of political violence. (I should note at the outset that some of the people studied and interviewed here are occasionally active participants in the armed conflict, but most are

An earlier version of this essay appeared as "Victimas y sobrevivientes de la guerra: Tres miradas de género," in Jaime Arocha, Fernando Cubides, and Myriam Jimeno, eds., *Las violencias: Inclusión creciente* (Bogotá: Centro de Estudios Sociales, Universidad Nacional de Colombia, 1998), 236–65. It is published here by permission of the Centro de Estudios Sociales.

simply members of the civil population who have lived through the violence.) The first aspect concerns the symbolic representations of masculinity and femininity present in political violence. In all acts of violence, cultural representations of the enemy and of the social relationships of the aggressor and victim are implicitly or explicitly expressed. Gender, as one of the basic structural principles of society, is always present in these relationships. But this "gendered violence" reveals itself in different ways and degrees of intensity depending on the historical moment and the type of violence in question. The second aspect concerns the differing presence and roles of men and women as victims of violence.[2] The third concerns the trajectories of men and women as war refugees, specifically those who flee from the violence of the countryside and settle in the cities. By examining the question of internal forced displacement, we engage an aspect of the most important sociopolitical and psychological problem of the last two decades of the twentieth century, a problem that by 1998 affected more than 20 billion people in forty countries.[3]

The First Aspect: Symbolic Representations of Gender in the Violence

Since the late 1980s, and for the second time in the twentieth century, political violence in Colombia is in the news every day. Rarely does the information supplied in the news go beyond a tally of deaths, the recording of some minimal characteristics of the victims, the expression of indignation for the severity of the act, and, possibly, a hypothesis concerning the presumed authors. We frequently find stories in the media, or human rights organizations' reports, that speak of assassinations or indiscriminate massacres against the civil population, whose victims include women, children, or the elderly.

It is worth asking ourselves if these acts are really indiscriminate. What constructions of femininity/masculinity have been present in these violent acts? It is almost impossible to obtain information concerning the subjectivities of the armed conflict that still dominates Colombian political and social life. But we can reflect on the historical problem of the representations of gender during the period of the Violence (of the 1950s and 1960s) to construct a hypothetical view of the current situation.

Many observers have noted the important symbolic dimensions of violent acts during the "classic" period of the Violence, when the Conservative government's armed forces initially razed lands populated by Liberal peasants, and peasant guerrillas affiliated with the Liberals attacked the Conservative population. Before continuing, it is important to outline one difference between this classic period of twentieth-century violence and the civil wars of the nineteenth century. The civil wars of the nineteenth century were predominately confrontations between men in arms that produced masculine victims.[4] During the Violence of this century, in contrast, a greater proportion of the civil population was attacked, and, for the first time, victims were systematically distributed between both sexes. One of the most frequent and horrifying acts involving the civil population was massacres of entire peasant families, including women and children, of the opposite political side. In these massacres, women were not simply accessory victims. Their violent deaths—and frequently their rape, torture, and mutilation as pregnant women—fulfilled a powerful symbolic role: "They killed them all, and carved them up, little by little; they cut them in small pieces and the pieces jumped. When the sun rose there were bodies everywhere. They took a little child from a pregnant woman and they put one of its limbs in her mouth. I cried a lot and I didn't know what to do."[5]

Two elements play a role in such acts: first, a certain instrumentality, fed by political or economic motives and by the functional terror produced by the dissected cadavers; second, a profound hate, fed by political affiliations deeply rooted in family traditions that were a constituent part of social identity: "The most common methods of torture were to tie the victims with their hands behind them and rape the women of the household in front of the men. . . . They practiced a cut on the uterus of pregnant women, by which they extracted the fetus and placed it on top of the mother's stomach."[6]

In the first and classic study of violence by Guzmán, Fals, and Umaña,[7] there are recurrent references to these practices and the verbal expressions that accompanied them. These are summed up in the phrase: "We must not leave even the seed" of the opposing party. The combatants viewed women exclusively in their status as mothers, that is, as actual or potential procreators of the hated enemy.

Rape was also a frequent practice and in it was expressed not only the wish for maximum masculine domination over the opposite sex, but also, as in many other wars, the desire to profoundly humiliate and express absolute hatred of the enemy and his collectivity. A peasant from the Quindío related, "The bandits threaten people telling them that they will do what they did in Córdoba, tying up the husbands and men of the house and in their presence raping the women and after that the *corte de franela*."[8] Rape could also fulfill the functions of terror and silencing. One young woman put it this way: "They said that they did all of this to us so that we would not talk. They thought we would never talk of something so shameful. They also did it to show just how much they were capable of."[9] But, in reality, these motives appear to be secondary in comparison to the symbolic function of domination of the enemy and the violation of what we may consider the most constitutive and intimate aspects of their identity. For this reason, when armed groups, driven by sexual appetites and the urgency to secure total domination, rape women outside this symbolic frame, that is, when they violate not the women of the enemy but those of their own zone or supporting community, they sign their own death sentence. In effect, this is what happened during the last phase of the Violence. This type of action constituted one of the factors that seriously reduced peasant support for bandits such as "Desquite" and "Sangrenegra," who operated at the end of the 1950s and beginning of the 1960s in northern Tolima. In sum, rape was not tolerated as a perverse individual act, but it was allowed as a systematic practice of war, applicable only to a specific population. By using gender as a tool for analysis, we can thus conclude that women were raped during the period of the Violence in order to torture their fathers or husbands and that women were killed not because of their role in the dance of death, since they were not protagonists, but, ironically, for being generators of life.

This aspect of the Violence left an impact on Colombian society beyond serving as a historical antecedent to current political conflicts. Its cruel penetration into the most intimate spheres of the peasant family generated a reproduction of violence in personal histories. Sons and daughters of the Violence changed violence into an inevitable evil, into a whole way of life. For this reason, references to the past frequently appear in the stories of the current violence, whether rural, urban, or domestic.[10] In these stories not only continuities and reproductions appear, but also differences, particularly in the symbolism of gender. For example, in frontier women's life stories from the jungle zones of Guaviare and of Caquetá, the expressions used for the different periods of violence they have lived through are differentiated.[11] During the 1980s, all these women suffered the consequences of confrontations between the army and guerrillas, bombings, persecutions, and displacement to the provincial capital of Florencia. The older women among them, generally natives of Tolima and Huila, regions strongly affected by the previous Violence of the 1950s, vividly remembered the earlier period of Violence as well. For them the Violence was a vital referent. It profoundly affected their childhood and it was the principal cause of their migration to the jungle frontier. For them, the word "violence" only referred to this period of the 1950s and 1960s, when it was all-encompassing, diffuse, omnipresent, and directed at women and children not only because it was "indiscriminant," but especially because of their gender. In contrast, the violent episodes of the 1980s had a different psychological connotation. Now the women spoke in other terms, using the word "war"—a war between two adversarial bands—in which the civil population had been embroiled. In this war, too, women were victims, as part of the civil population affected by the bombings, as widows, as victims of torture used to exact information concerning their relatives who were guerrillas or peasant activists. In the 1980s, however, women were not systematic victims because of their gender; they were not victims as mothers and representatives of the community's collective honor.

Today, even though maternity and feminine sexuality are hot issues in the daily execution of war, more conflict occurs over these issues in the internal organization of armed groups[12] than in the symbolic definition of the enemy or in violent practice toward "the other." Maternity does not appear to serve as a motive for extermination. Here we sense a change not only in the social representations of women, who are seen increasingly as social and political actors, but also in the cultural dimensions of war. In the current dynamics of internal war, where the conflict is becoming less and less ideological and political projects mix with the defense of economic interests and territory, even acts of retaliation and vengeance are dominated by a high level of instrumentality. In this dynamic, the cultural, political, and social identity of the enemy loses importance when confronted with other determining factors such as socioeconomic conditions, support for a given band, or simply momentary geographic location. The idea of enemy "extermination unto the seed" loses importance, giving way to an interest in frightening, subjecting, and dominating a population and its territory, or causing the displacement of people in order to appropriate their lands. In this context, attacking maternity for its generative powers, or to profoundly humiliate the sexual honor of a community, loses meaning as a practice of war.

Gender is manifested in other ways in the current violence. The female guerrilla combatant is symbolically double-sided. She draws admiration for her equality to men in the occupation of war and rejection for ceasing to represent all that is traditionally feminine. Another symbol is that of the female victim who represents the rights of a civil population that is not involved in armed conflict. Still, the dominant representation of femininity is difficult to reconcile with the horrors of war. For this reason, after "indiscriminate" massacres that involve women, the elderly, and children, authorship is rarely publicly recognized. Silence regarding unknown killers expresses a public resistance to defining women as a part of the armed conflict, equal to men. It is a kind of symbolic resistance to stripping them of their condition as defenseless beings, mothers, citizens, and generators of life and peace. Such representations of femininity are exactly those that appeal to public sensibility concerning the violation of international human rights. Confirmation of this symbolism can be found in the data of the Colombian Commission of Jurists, which we will analyze in the following section. They demonstrate that in the violent deaths of women, authorship is more often unknown than in the violent deaths of men. On the other hand, rape, the maximum exercise of power over "the other," may be present but unacknowledged in many belligerent acts. Reports of rape are scarce and dispersed, but range from southern Colombia to the Atlantic Coast and involve all armed actors.[13] It is evident that in the actual practices of war "gendered violence" constitutes an underground modality that is rarely publicly recognized.

The Second Aspect: The Direct Victims of Violence

During the 1980s various political processes came together to intensify the dynamic of violence in rural zones. There were increases in the strength of guerrilla forces, civic movements, drug trafficking, and paramilitary groups. As a result, after 1988 the number of deaths by homicide and assassination shot up, reaching an annual rate around 80 per 100,000 inhabitants in the 1990s.[14]

These statistics, which register violence by political protagonists, conceal dramatic social realities in which not only men but also women are increasingly involved. The percentage of women among victims of homicide[15] during the last decade has oscillated between 7 and 8 percent,[16] thereby appearing to indicate that men continue to be the preferred victims of violent actions. But seen from another angle, violent death has ceased to be a monopoly of men, given that it is now the second leading cause of mortality for women between 15 and 39 years old.[17] The figures are even more chilling when one considers older adolescents. In 1994, homicides of adolescent men (15–19 years old) represented 53 percent of the mortality of their age group, and homicides among adolescent women of the same age, where the increase was relatively more rapid, accounted for 19 percent of deaths,[18] almost one-third the rate of men. Undoubtedly, these figures indicate a growing participation of young women in violent acts, either as rural guerrillas or as members of popular militias or urban gangs.

With respect to political violence, the proportion of male versus female victims is less documented. Up to this point, I have found data differentiated by sex in the statistics of the Center for Popular Research and Education (CINEP) for 1989, 1991, and 1993, and in the Annual Report of the Colombian Commission of Jurists for 1996.[19] Both sources indicate that the percentage of victims of political assassinations who are female has oscillated between 8 and 11 percent, one or two points higher than their participation in homicides in general.[20] Other CINEP statistics indicate that the percentage of females among guerrilla deaths is higher, rising to 16 percent in 1989. These figures suggest that the participation by women in violence, as actors and victims, is higher when it has political motives.

In Table 1 we see the incidence of women as victims of different forms of violence during 1996. The great majority (77 percent) of female deaths were produced by political homicides and extrajudicial executions, while in the case of men, the highest proportions were for political homicides and deaths in combat. Apparently, growing female participation in the ranks of armed groups[21] has not meant equal incorporation into combat and high-risk actions, since women's deaths generally occurred out of this context.

Table 1. Violation of Human Rights and Sociopolitical Violence, 1996 (By Type of Action and Gender of Victims)

			Victims			%
Type	*Men*	*%*	*Women*	*%*	*Total*	*Women**
Political homicides and extrajudicial executions	1,219	43.8	142	77.2	1,361	10.4
Disappearances	140	5.1	12	6.5	152	7.9
Homicides against social marginals	289	10.4	25	13.6	314	8.0
Deaths in combat	1,132	40.7	5	2.7	1,137	0.4
Total	2,780	100.0	184	100.0	2,964	6.2

Source: Adapted from Comisión Colombiana de Juristas, *Colombia: Derechos humanos y derecho humanitario, 1996* (Bogotá, 1997), Tables 2 and 11, pp. 6 and 23.

*Percentage of women among the total of victims by type of action.

In Table 2, male and female victims are categorized according to the presumed authors of violent actions. Before analyzing the differences by sex, we should note important changes in the authorship of political assassinations in recent years. Assassinations attributed to the armed forces fell from 54 percent in 1993 to 11 percent in 1996. In contrast, those attributed to the paramilitaries rose from 18 percent to 63 percent in the same period. Similarly, in these three years, the number of violent acts by known authors rose noticeably from 28 percent to 66 percent. This was due in good part, according to the Colombian Commission of Jurists, to the "notable rise in acts attributed to paramilitary groups, in which knowledge of authorship can be part of a strategy to frighten the population."[22] Yet, in spite of the reduction in unknown authorship, unidentified cases are much more likely in deaths of females. In 42 percent of cases involving female victims, the author of the crime has not been identified—twice the rate in cases involving male victims. As previously noted, these figures include victims of massacres, in which women count as part of the "indiscriminately" assassinated civil population. As Franco notes, "In addition to the objective of physical and collective elimination of opponents, massacres have an educational objective, of warning others of imminent danger."[23] But even though the frightened population usually knows the authors and understands the "warning," the authors generally do not publicly assume responsibility for their actions when women or children figure among their victims in order to prevent damaging their image in larger society. Thus, as a result of their growing participation in this type of violence and their primary objective of breeding terror, the paramilitaries play a greater role as authors of actions involving female victims than they do in those involving male victims.

Table 2. Violation of Human Rights and Sociopolitical Violence, 1996 (By Gender of Victims According to Presumed Authors of Actions)

	*Victims of Violent Actions**					%
Presumed Authors	*Men*	*%*	*Women*	*%*	*Total*	*Women†*
Without identification	580	19.5	80	41.7	660	12.1
State forces	746	25.0	17	8.9	763	2.2
Paramilitaries	697	23.4	54	28.1	751	7.2
Guerrillas	757	25.4	33	17.2	790	4.2
Cases in process	201	6.7	8	4.2	209	3.8
Total	2,981	100.0	192	100.1‡	3,173	6.2

Source: Adapted from Comisión Colombiana de Juristas, *Colombia: Derechos humanos y derecho humanitario, 1996* (Bogotá, 1997), Table 2, p. 6.

*These include political homicides and extrajudicial executions, disappearances, homicides against social marginals, and deaths in combat.

†Percentage of women among the total of victims by category of presumed author.

‡Adds to more than 100 due to rounding.

In sum, according to the information gathered by the Colombian Commission of Jurists, "on average, every two days a woman dies as a consequence of sociopolitical violence."[24] According to the same source, almost nine men die every day for the same reason. These very unequal proportions continue to be the greatest difference in gender in political violence. But the numerical presentation of the victims by sex offers only limited possibilities for analysis of gender. In contrast, in another setting, that of displacement due to violence, we detect important differences between men and women in their status as indirect victims and also as survivors of armed conflict.

The Third Aspect: Male and Female Survivors of Forced Displacement[25]

The phenomenon of internal displacement due to violence was always present in the second half of the twentieth century, but it began to gain force in 1988 and 1989. In those years, as seen in the previous section, the figures on political assassinations and massacres rose dramatically. This was true especially in those zones where three factors come together: a past of peasant struggles followed by conflicts between the guerrillas and the army; the purchase of land by drug traffickers; and the arrival of paramilitaries to "cleanse" the region of guerrillas and their suspected auxiliaries. The first national investigation concerning the phenomenon of forced displacement, carried out by the Colombian Episcopal Conference, found approximately six hundred thousand refugees in 1994, split between the Atlantic coast (Urabá, Córdoba), the Magdalena Medio region in the center of the country, the eastern plains, and the frontier and coca-producing zones of the south.[26] In 1996 and 1997, new zones were incorporated into the dynamic of violence and its aftermath of massive population displacement. Two merit special attention because of their particular characteristics: the Chocó, on the Pacific coast, which witnessed a movement of refugees to Panama (until they were sent back by that country), and the department of Cundinamarca, where the paramilitaries have been flexing their muscles at the very doorstep of the capital. The latest estimates (1997)[27] reach a figure between 1 million and 1.5 million refugees out of a total Colombian population of 38 million.

According to preliminary figures of the Episcopal Conference, 58.2 percent of displaced persons are women (7 points higher than the percentage of women in the total Colombian population) and 24.6 percent of refugee households are headed by women. Based on my own experiences in the different regions of the country, I believe this last figure is an underestimation and that the figure recorded in a 1995 study by the Presidential Commission on Human Rights of 30.8 percent female-headed households is closer to reality.[28] In the most recent study of refugees in Bogotá, the percentage of female-headed households is 38. Of these women, 40 percent are widows who fled with their children after the violent death of their husbands, and 18 percent were abandoned by males after displacement to the city.[29]

Even though displacement is a national phenomenon, it is estimated that Bogotá is one of the greatest receivers of refugees who arrive directly or after intermediate steps. During 1996, the number of refugees arriving in the capital was close to 50,000. They were members of some 9,700 households, which results in a rate of arrival of 27 displaced households every day.[30] In the regions farthest from Bogotá, flows of refugees are directed toward medium-sized cities in proximity to the zones of expulsion. Such cities often are departmental capitals, large enough to guarantee a certain degree of anonymity for the displaced families. Examples are Medellín and Montería for refugees from Urabá and the Atlantic coast, Barrancabermeja for the Magdalena Medio, Villavicencio for the eastern plains, and Florencia for the southern region.

During the worst years of assassinations, massacres, disappearances, and bombings of peasant zones, entire communities were displaced. The most organized exoduses took place in the Magdalena Medio in the mid-1980s, when paramilitary groups expanded, and in Caquetá, at the beginning of the 1980s, with the arrival of M-19 guerrilla groups. In contrast, the massacres that were perpetrated on the Atlantic coast during the period from 1988 through 1990 resulted in the exodus of many families who individually sought refuge. In the Magdalena Medio and on the Atlantic coast, the most visible exodus followed a more selective period of violent acts and resulted in the gradual arrival of families who silently settled in with city acquaintances. In Barrancabermeja, the violence was internalized within the city, provoking displacement of families from neighborhood to neighborhood in a desperate race to escape threatened death.[31] In Villavicencio, the refugees have been characterized by the presence of a great number of widows of leaders of the Unión Popular, who were accused of being tied to the FARC guerrillas. These regional differences in displacement, expressed in different levels of organization and political consciousness, greatly influenced the role women played in the process. They largely determined the possibilities for peasant women to anticipate displacement, resist psychological trauma, and meet the challenges of survival and the construction of a new life.

Especially in the spontaneous and individual exoduses, one perceives the differing effects of violence on, and the process of displacement for, men and women. We can examine them around two important moments: the destruction of lives, property, and social ties; and survival and the reconstruction of life and social relations in the city. In the following analysis, I combine qualitative information drawn from life stories gathered through interviews in different regions of the country with a more quantitative look at national data concerning displaced families. The national data allow us to compare female-headed with male-headed households.

A mid-1990s national study of displaced persons reported that the male-headed households represent a little more than double the number headed by women: In a sample of 796 households, 551 (69 percent) were headed by men and 245 (31 percent) by women.[32] The largest number of displaced families are headed by people between thirty and forty years of age; one-third of these families are male-headed and one-third are female-headed. Otherwise, the ratio of two to one between male- and female-run households is maintained in all the age categories, with the exception of the one encompassing people less than twenty years old, where there are more female heads. This information points to the existence of an extremely vulnerable group of adolescent mothers displaced by violence.

At the moment of destruction and uprooting, there are differences between the motives that cause men and women household heads to flee. Men cite threats as the determining reason for displacement. In contrast, women state that assassination is the principal cause for flight. Thus is widowhood revealed as a primary motive for female heads of households. "They took my husband away to kill him and they gave me three hours to leave. . . . We went to the road without knowing where we were going to go. . . . I remember that at that moment it was dark, I couldn't see clearly, we had a lantern and I couldn't see clearly. . . . I asked God to show me a clear path to follow, where I could find people to help me. We had stopped for about five minutes, and when we opened our eyes, we saw a kind of pickup truck . . . there was a man, and I told him what happened, and he cried as he listened and then . . . he put us into the car."[33]

But the specific problems that refugee women face do not lie only in their widowhood. They are also related to the different life trajectories that men and women followed until the moment of violence. The majority of female peasant refugees had been raised within a rural culture where masculine and feminine spheres were rigidly separated. The feminine sphere centered almost exclusively on household duties, motherhood, agricultural activities close to the home (gardening and processing)—all, without doubt, under men's orders. The childhood and adolescence of all these women was characterized by social and geographical isolation. Usually, relations with the market, the money economy, public information, and formal institutions were exclusively or predominately the patrimony of men. Even contact with civic and community organizations or entities were foreign to these women. In other words, the limits of the "world," of contact with society, were set by the heads of the household—first, their fathers, and then their husbands.[34] Being uprooted from this world has meant the destruction of social identity to a much greater degree for women than for men, whose liberty of movement, access to information, and possession of free time were givens and who were used to functioning within a greater geographic, social, and political space.

Taking into account these gender roles, we can consider displaced women triple victims: first, of the trauma resulting from violence (assassination of the husband or other family members, the burning of their homes, rape); second, of the loss of their means of subsistence (house, belongings, crops, animals), which implies rupture with the familiar elements of their everyday domestic existence and with their world of primary relations; and third, of the social and emotional uprooting that they suffer upon reaching another unknown peasant or urban region. "Then after the assassination, when I was sleeping in a passageway here in the city, hunched down with my children, policemen came and asked me what I was doing, and I told them: I am waiting for it to rain enough so that I can go jump off a bridge along with my child; I was at a point that I didn't know what else to do, I felt like a ship without a harbor."[35] In other words, such destruction goes much further than its material effects: It is a loss of identity as an individual, a loss of identity as a citizen and political subject.[36] It involves a rupture in the social network at the level of the family and community that produces a sensation of being completely at a loss, "like a ship without a harbor."

In the interviews I conducted with female heads of household, the magnitude of the personal drama affecting them was striking, but so also was their fortitude in assuming responsibility for the survival of their children and the reconstruction of their lives and social ties. The obligation to find ways they and their children can survive does not allow these women time to give in to their emotions. Immediate survival becomes their only goal. "My eyes were swollen from crying. . . . Five days after reaching the city, the landlady told me: It is not good for you to cry because you will not get anything that way and you have to think about raising your children. Harden your heart and tomorrow bathe yourself well and go out, even though you don't know the way, and talk to people if you think they can help you, and if you have to beg, beg, and don't be embarrassed."[37] For these displaced women—widows, heads of families, severely affected by the deaths of their husbands, and with no more belongings than their children—it is their children who constitute virtually the only motive to survive and begin a new life in the city because "dying is not a possibility."

Other women become heads of households in the place of exile, since relationships between couples often break down because of tensions, fear, and the difficulties of surviving in the new environment. Relationships also founder because of the inversion of gender roles, and even because of mistrust and assignment of blame in cases in which the wife was not aware of her spouse's political activities. Even when the relationship between the couple does not break down, many displaced women end up being responsible for the emotional and economic survival of the family when the men distance themselves or seek solace in alcohol. The necessity for immediate survival frequently leads to prostitution as the only available resource, and this in the midst of a total unawareness and suppression of the woman's own sexuality.

Women generally use more informal channels than men and are more resourceful in finding mechanisms for survival. It is well known that women look for, above all, solidarity with women (family members, market women, teachers) more than with men in front of whom they show a certain amount of inhibition and modesty. However, it is important to note that these women never look for solidarity with other widows or refugees from the same place.[38] The rejection reveals the necessity of forgetting the trauma they have suffered, but it also indicates the fear and secrecy that surround the survivors of a massacre.

The greatest contrast between women and men is in the opportunities they have to insert themselves newly into the labor market in the city and thus assure the survival and reconstruction of their lives in a more permanent manner. In Table 3, differences in gender are pronounced in the type of occupations people have before and after displacement, and especially with regard to the tremendous surge in unemployment for men following displacement (when it is more than five times the rate than before) in comparison with the lower level of unemployment of women heads of household.

Most male refugees were previously employed in agriculture and livestock raising, and which are not very useful skills in the new urban environment. While 63.2 percent of men had previously worked in agriculture, only 12.5 percent did so afterward (as migrant workers, leaving their families in the city); in the case of women in agriculture the decline was from 18.4 percent to 3.6 percent. Consequently, unemployment and a feeling of uselessness were the lot of men in the city. But for the women, who before displacement, even if they worked in agriculture, dedicated a greater part of their time to domestic labors, forced migration did not mean such an abrupt change in labor routine. Finding employment as cooks, laundresses, or domestic servants after their displacement helped them insert themselves more easily, if uncertainly, into the urban market of paid (usually domestic) labor. Women's unemployment rose, but a little less than three times, and their rate of employment in paid domestic work rose from 4.1 percent to 20 percent.

Women's place as head of the household and as the one responsible for family survival is also reflected in the decline in the occupation of housewife ("home"). More than 50 percent of these rural women reported being housewives while in the countryside, but with their move to the cities that percentage declined to less than 27 percent. Finally, employment in some form of informal sales ("sidewalk vendor") rose for both sexes, but it rose higher for men than for women.

Table 3. Occupations of 796 Heads of Household (According to Sex, before and after Displacement)

	Men				*Women*			
	Before		*After*		*Before*		*After*	
Occupation	*No.*	*%*	*No.*	*%*	*No.*	*%*	*No.*	*%*
None	34	6.2	190	34.5	16	6.5	47	19.2
Salaried agricultural	126	22.9	52	9.4	13	5.3	4	1.6
Farmer	222	40.3	17	3.1	32	13.1	5	2.0
Educator	34	6.2	26	4.7	17	6.9	9	3.7
Merchant	37	6.7	62	11.3	9	3.7	17	6.9
Public functionary	3	0.5	3	0.5	7	2.9	6	2.3
Employee	63	11.4	92	16.7	11	4.5	12	4.9
Sidewalk vendor	11	2.0	88	16.0	6	2.4	24	9.8
Professional services	10	1.8	5	0.9	1	0.4	1	0.4
Home	4	0.7	4	0.7	123	50.2	66	26.9
Domestic service	0	0.0	2	0.4	10	4.1	49	20.0
Other	2	0.4	5	0.9	0	0.0	5	2.0
Undetermined	5	0.9	5	0.9	0	0.0	0	0.0
Total	551	100.0	551	100.0	245	100.0	245	99.7

Source: Based on figures from the Council for Human Rights and Displacement (CODHES), 1995. This table was first published in Donny Meertens and Nora Segura Escobar, "Uprooted Lives: Gender, Violence, and Displacement in Colombia," *Singapore Journal of Tropical Geography* 17 (1996): 165–78.

It does not prove easy for men to handle unemployment in the city and to accept women as principal breadwinners. In this sense, displacement can add to tensions between couples. The self-esteem of the men suffered a serious blow in the gendered reorganization of the division of labor. One of the men interviewed in Villavicencio put it this way: "One who is educated in the countryside knows how to get along . . . but when a country person arrives in the city . . . that is a terrible thing! There are families who have gone to pieces . . . after one or the other deviates from what is normal . . . there is a lot of license for the women. There are times when women make the decisions, and that is touchy because women abuse liberty more than men."[39]

On the other hand, there are great differences among women in their ability to confront the problems of displacement. There are differences between women who previously had participated in organizing activities in the peasant community and those who had always been marginalized; between women who participated in the organization of the exoduses and those who fled on their own with their children, burdened by sudden widowhood; between those who were leaders and those who rarely left their homes.[40]

Women are most affected in their daily struggle to survive by the image that society has of their families as subversives, responsible for their own disgrace. These images intensify the confusion concerning women's social identities, and, given the repetition of violence and the impunity of its authors, make it hard to decide on the best path to follow. Berta Lucía Castaño, a psychologist specializing in the assistance of victims of violence, comments, "As a result we find that displaced women suffer mental alterations with greater frequency than men, who often find other women to support them emotionally and economically."[41] Ignorance of the civic and political work that her husband or companion carried out leads many women to adopt negative and fearful attitudes regarding the possibilities for organization in their new environments: "I began living with him; we built a little house and they killed him in '92 in a massacre that happened there in front of the police headquarters, in a restaurant. There they committed a massacre, killing three. He worked in Usuarios Campesinos [ANUC, The National Peasant Association], but I don't know what position he had. I didn't participate in that work because he didn't want me to, he wanted me to stay here at home. . . . I almost never go to meetings with other women . . . because I have to confront life by myself."[42]

Nevertheless, in regions where the organizing experience of rural women has been more open, nongovernmental female groups have been organized, and these have become important sources of strategies of organization and mutual support among displaced women. Examples include organizations that run cooperative stores, restaurants, carpentry and shoe-making businesses, and community kitchens.

One of the great dilemmas of forced displacement is a view of the future that the refugees, the State, and the receiving community all define as transitory. But transition to where? Given the opposing options of return to the site of origin or permanence in the city of arrival, most refugees, especially women, clearly lean toward staying in the cities. The continuation of conflicts in the zones of expulsion often makes return an unrealistic option. Some resolve this dilemma by saying they wish to go back to the countryside, but to a different place. A few want to return to their original communities, but only if they will have access to land.[43]

Female heads of households opt to return in very small numbers. We must remember that assassinations constitute an important motive for women's expulsion, so that not only economic factors, but also concern for security play a role in their rejection of the idea of returning. The predominance of maternal responsibilities, which coincide with their children's more rapid adaptation to their new environment and their opportunities for schooling, also incline women toward staying in the cities.

Another very important factor in women's decisions to stay lies in their own experience in urban settings. In effect, in spite of the many difficulties and deprivations, and the accumulation of responsibilities, the possibility of participating in the urban labor market through domestic service gives women a guarantee for survival that men lack. Rapid insertion into the labor market, precarious as it is, opens new horizons for women that did not exist in the countryside. Direct contact with the cash economy and access to new social networks permit them to break out of their isolation and find themselves with and through other women. It allows them to expand their relationships with the external world and redefine their position in the family structure. For these reasons, a considerable number of refugees perceive urban activities such as small businesses and salaried work as priority strategies for income generation.

From Victims and Survivors to the Reconstruction of the Future

As we have seen, political violence and its social consequences have affected women and men in different ways. "Gendered violence" as a dimension of political violence has changed in content and intensity on a par with the increasing instrumentalism of war-related activities. The proportion of women among the direct victims of violence has remained constant since the worst years of the war (1988, 1989, and 1991), reflecting the growing participation of women in armed insurgent groups as much as the intention of aggressors to intimidate the civil population through assassinations of *all* its members.

Among the survivors of the war, female peasant refugees have been especially changed by a tragic paradox. They are the most affected in their social identity, the least prepared to carry out new activities, and the most traditionally isolated from organized civil and political life. Yet it is they who must ensure the physical survival of the family and the reconstruction of a social identity in an unknown and hostile setting. Men, in contrast, appear to be equipped with more social and psychological experience to confront the destructive effects of violence and the rupture of the social fabric in rural settings, owing precisely to their greater geographic and social mobility, and their knowledge of public spaces. But in the reconstruction phase, the opportunities for men and women appear to be inverted. The impact of displacement is, for men, concentrated in unemployment, a situation that cancels their role as economic provider. In contrast, women appear to be better equipped to continue the routines of domestic labor—in the service of others as well as in their own homes—in pursuit of family survival. In spite of the traumas, poverty, and obstacles to organization for displaced women, there are also new possibilities and spaces for personal development. In the timid projects of economic generation or community organization, through refugee or in human rights committees, the role of victim begins to meld with that of new citizen.

The dynamics of the war do not only imply chaos and trauma but also an inevitable reordering of the social fabric. In the process of social reconstruction, the alternatives of criminality and solidarity are always present. That process also opens up the possibility of new lives for women and men, which implies a transformation of traditional gender relations.

Notes

1. Joan Scott, *Gender and the Politics of History* (New York, 1988), 42–44.

2. This article is limited to analyzing the scarce, and not very precise, data concerning male and female victims. An analysis of the gender of the actors, that is, of women's participation in armed groups, deserves greater and more specialized study. A first step was presented in my article ,"Mujer y violencia política en los conflictos rurales," *Análisis Político* 24 (January–April 1995): 36–49.

3. Roberta Cohen and Francis Deng, *Masses in Flight: The Global Crisis of Internal Displacement* (Washington, DC, 1998). Only since 1992 has the problem of internal forced displacement gained international recognition with the naming of the Sudanese diplomat Francis Deng as United Nations representative on internally displaced persons.

4. Carlos Eduardo Jaramillo, *Los guerrilleros del novecientos* (Bogotá, 1991), 60–74.

5. Interview conducted by Donny Meertens and Susan Sánchez with a Tolima woman in Armenia (Quindío), June 15, 1994.

6. María Victoria Uribe, *Matar, rematar, contramatar: Las masacres de la violencia en el Tolima, 1948–1964* (Bogotá, 1990), 167 and 175.

7. Germán Guzmán Campos, Orlando Fals Borda, and Eduardo Umaña Luna, *La Violencia en Colombia* (8th ed., Bogotá, 1977), 1:340 and 344, 2:226–34.

8. This form of decapitation consists of cutting off the head and placing a limb in the opening of the neck.

9. Cited in Eric Hobsbawm, *Bandits* (2d rev. ed., New York, 1981), 135.

10. See, for example, the stories in Alonso Salazar's two books, *No nacimos pa' semilla: La cultura de las bandas juveniles de Medellín* (Medellín, 1990) and *Mujeres de fuego* (Medellín, 1993).

11. Interviews in Florencia and Belén de Andaquíes (Caquetá), May 1994.

12. Meertens, "Mujer y violencia política en los conflictos rurales." See also the interesting study about Salvadoran guerrillas by Norma Vásquez, Cristina Ibañez, and Clara Murguialday, *Mujeres-montaña: Vivencias de guerrilleras y colaboradors del FMLN* (Madrid, 1996).

13. The untrustworthiness of the information and the continuation of the armed conflict impede a systematic analysis that goes beyond denunciations.

14. See, among others, Malcolm Deas and Fernando Gaitán Daza, *Dos ensayos especulativos sobre la violencia en Colombia* (Bogotá, 1995); Comisión Colombiana de Juristas, *Colombia: Derechos humanos y derecho humanitario, 1996* (Bogotá, 1997); and Saúl Franco, *El Quinto: No matar* (Bogotá, 1999).

15. A general figure including homicides caused by political violence.

16. Franco, *El Quinto*, 88–89.

17. Consejería Presidencial para la Juventud, la Mujer y la Familia, *Informe* (Bogotá, 1993), 24.

18. Franco, *El Quinto*, 95.

19. Comisión Colombiana de Juristas, *Colombia*, 6 and 23.

20. The term "assassination" covers the categories of illegal execution (by State agents) and homicide for a political motive (by non-State agents).

21. This growing participation has been noted in various testimonies and can also be inferred from the information concerning rehabilitated guerrillas: Approximately one-fourth of the rehabilitated cadres from the M-19, the EPL, Quintín Lame, the Partido Revolucionario de los Trabajadores (PRT), and the Corriente de Renovación Socialista (CRS) between 1988 and 1994 were women. Unpublished data are from the archives of the Oficina Nacional de Rehabilitación.

22. Comisión Colombiana de Juristas, *Colombia*, 5 and 7.

23. Franco, *El Quinto*, 122.

24. Comisión Colombiana de Juristas, *Colombia*, 23.

25. A great part of this section has been taken from a previous publication coauthored with Nora Segura Escobar, "Las rutas del género en el desplazamiento forzoso," *Revista Javeriana* 128 (1997): 361–69. The same investigators are now concluding a study of male, female, and child refugees in the cities of Bogotá and Bucaramanga.

26. Conferencia Episcopal de Colombia, *Derechos humanos: Desplazados por violencia en Colombia* (Bogotá, 1995).

27. Consultoría para los Derechos Humanos y el Desplazamiento (CODHES), *Un país que huye: Desplazamiento y violencia en una nación fragmentada* (Bogotá, 1999), 462.

28. Conferencia Episcopal, *Derechos humanos*, 43. The underestimation can be related to the fears women have of registering as heads of households and single mothers. In rural zones, that condition is stigmatized by some Catholics. The data from the Episcopal Conference were gathered from parishes. Underestimation can also be the result of the fear of being registered as widows of subversives, which is also not desirable in the predominant climate of insecurity.

29. Jorge Rojas, "Desplazamiento forzado, conflicto social y derechos humanos," unpublished paper presented at the National University of Colombia, Bogotá, November 1997. The highest figure for female household heads, 49 percent, comes from a study of displaced families in Cali, Comisión Vida, Justicia y Paz y Arquidiócesis de Cali, *Desplazados en Cali* (Cali, 1997).

30. Arquidiócesis de Bogotá y CODHES, *Desplazados por la violencia y conflicto social en Bogotá* (Bogotá, 1997), 39.

31. Interview conducted by Donny Meertens with women of the Organización Femenina Popular.

32. The national survey was done by the Sistema de Información de Hogares Desplazados por la Violencia. It covers a period of fifteen months, from July 1994 to October 1995.

33. Interview conducted by Donny Meertens with a refugee in Montería, Córdoba, May 1994.

34. The only exceptions that we find are the women who had in one form or another reached a leadership position in their organization or community. Their life stories revealed different ways to escape peasant women's typical confinement in the home, through independent migration, colonization of land, or domestic service in the city.

35. Interview conducted by Donny Meertens with a female refugee in Montería, Córdoba, May 1994.

36. This condition is sometimes symbolized by the lack of identification documents that are frequently lost in the flight.

37. Interview conducted by Donny Meertens with a female survivor of a massacre, Córdoba, May 1994.

38. At least they do not spontaneously seek these kinds of relationships. This attitude is an obstacle to organization for entities that work with displaced women. To overcome these attitudes, considerable psychological effort is required.

39. Interview conducted by Donny Meertens with a male refugee in Villavicencio, December 1995.

40. Interviews conducted by Donny Meertens and Susana Sánchez with displaced women in Montería, Barrancabermeja, and Florencia, April–May 1994.

41. Berta Lucía Castaño, *Violencia sociopolítica en Colombia: Repercusión en las víctimas* (Bogotá, 1994), 62.

42. Interview conducted by Haidi Hernández with a female refugee in Barrancabermeja, June 1994.

43. Return was the preferred option according to the objectives of official policy. It sought to "attend in a holistic manner the population displaced by violence so that, in the framework of voluntary return or resettlement, they successfully integrate into society." Departamento Nacional de Planeación y Ministerio del Interior, *Programa nacional de atención integral a la población desplazada por la violencia*, Document 2804 (September 13, 1995).

Chapter 8

Social and Popular Movements in a Time of Cholera, 1977–1999

Miguel Angel Urrego

Taking his title from Gabriel García Márquez's novel, *Love in the Time of Cholera* (1988), Miguel Angel Urrego emphasizes the negative implications of the Colombian left's embrace of armed struggle for unions, popular organizations, and political parties contending for democratic reform. In effect, the primary victims of paramilitary violence have not been the guerrillas but peaceful unionists, members of legal leftist political parties such as the Unión Patriótica, and human rights activists, academics, and journalists critical of either the government, the guerrillas, the drug mafias, or the paramilitary groups themselves. Thousands of such people—leaders in the civil struggle for peaceful social change—have been murdered in Colombia in recent decades. In almost every instance, their killers go unpunished, and often it is uncertain which of the armed actors is responsible for their deaths.

Urrego also emphasizes the negative impact that neo-liberal politics—the lowering of tariff barriers and other impediments to free trade, the privatization of public services, and the reduction of State involvement in the economy and society generally—has had on unions and popular organizations. These policies, urged on the Colombian government by the United States and major international financial institutions, have widened the gap between rich and poor and created severe balance-of-trade problems for Colombia for the first time since the world depression of the 1930s. By 1999, these policies, coupled with levels of violence that finally seemed to frighten even the most risk-taking investors (including drug traffickers), had plunged the economy into full recession and, as noted by Mauricio Reina in Chapter 4, brought the official unemployment rate to an astounding 20 percent. Even so, Urrego shows, recent years have witnessed militant union actions and combative regional mobilizations in protest of government policies. How labor and popular groups can have an effective voice in peace negotiations, however, remains unclear.

Miguel Angel Urrego is a historian at the Universidad Central in Bogotá, where he heads the research group Modernidad e Identidad Nacional and edits the journal *Nómada*. His publications include *Motines: Levantamientos y protestas populares en la historia de Colombia* (Bogotá, 2000); and *Sexualidad, matrimonio y familia en Bogotá, 1880–1930* (Bogotá, 1997).

The stage on which Colombian social movements act has significantly changed in the past two decades. The 1970s were one of the most important periods of expansion for Colombian social and popular movements in the twentieth century. The climax of radical behavior was reached during the September 1977 civil strike, which revealed not only the strength, but also the vitality of popular organizations.

Starting at the end of the 1970s, a period of decline and debilitation in the social and popular movements began. This is explained by, among other reasons, the repression unleashed by the Julio César Turbay Ayala administration (1978–1982) against opposition political and union organizations, the polarization and fragmentation of the left, and the beginning of a new period of rapid growth of the guerrillas. In practice, the left's focus on armed struggle led to the weakening of popular organizing processes and the supremacy of military over political struggle.

During these decades the context in which social movements evolved also changed dramatically. The polarized world of the Cold War crumbled, Nicaraguan Sandinismo fell, and the Republicans took power in the United States. Internally, Colombia experienced a boom in drug trafficking that culminated in a war against the drug cartels, paramilitarism and internal conflict intensified, certain insurgent groups were reincorporated into lawful society, a neo-liberal economic model was implemented, and political reform led to the proclamation of a new constitution.

In the last few years, however, popular and social movements have experienced a growing power. This is a consequence in part of the negative social effects of the application of the neo-liberal economic model, the unification of national labor federations, certain positive experiences gained through struggle, and the beginning of a new peace process that permits greater autonomy for popular organizations. As a result, important protest actions, briefly reviewed below, have taken place.

The Labor Movement

Three trends have characterized the union movement during these past decades. First, the ups and downs of the union unity process; second, the supremacy of the theme of war and peace over the demands made by the working class; and third, the impossibility of pledging labor harmony in deals with the State and at the same time adequately responding to workers' pressures from below in protest against neo-liberal measures. In 1986 the union sectors, influenced by the guerrillas, the Communist party, and the labor faction led by Jorge Carrillo, formed the Confederación Unitaria de

Trabajadores (CUT). This was possible in the context of the support given the peace talks by the administration of Belisario Betancur (1982–1986). The diversity of groups that came together in the CUT, and the special national circumstances in which it was formed, help to explain the divisions that soon surfaced within the organization and the crisis that ensued a few years after its creation. Important unions were marginalized by the 1986 agreement, and in 1988 they initiated a series of unity processes that culminated in the formation of another national federation, the Confederación General de Trabajadores Democráticos de Colombia (CGTD).

The political initiatives of the left, especially during the Betancur administration, were tremendously influenced by the peace dialogues between the government and the guerrillas. Popular and union movement activities were eclipsed in deference to the reading of the situation by the armed left. Unions, with very few exceptions, abandoned their workplace demands in the hope of contributing to a negotiated peace between the government and the guerrillas. Those unions that did not follow this policy met with failure, as is shown by the abortive civic strikes attempted at the beginning of the 1980s.

The differences between the political interests of the sectors involved in the peace process and the interests of the workers were amplified during the discussions concerning the so-called Democratic Opening and an attempted general strike in 1985. For some, the peace process and the widening of democracy through institutional reforms had priority. For others, the peace negotiations meant, as actually happened, the abandonment of union struggles and submission to an unclear process of struggle for democracy. On various occasions, the union movement was forced to declare itself in opposition to the actions of the armed movement. This was especially true of the petroleum workers' union, the Unión Sindical Obrera (USO), which denounced, in particular, guerrilla bombings of oil pipelines.

The union movement has shifted erratically during the presidential administrations of the 1990s, especially during that of Ernesto Samper (1994–1998), which proposed social pacts with labor while implementing neo-liberal measures that inevitably weakened labor organizations. This helps explain the decline of labor conflict and the rise in popular movements at the beginning of the 1990s. Even so, the period of labor decline reversed again in the middle of the 1990s. Some strikes culminated in the temporary abandonment of neo-liberal privatization schemes and even led to the resignation of government ministers.

Perhaps what is most significant about current union protest has been the rejection of President Andrés Pastrana's 1998 National Plan for

Development. The central labor federations, supported by popular organizations, instituted a never-before-seen protest against a government economic plan. The principal cities of the country witnessed daily demonstrations against the plan and, even though it was ultimately approved by Congress, unions continued to raise the possibility of a civic strike and civil disobedience demonstrations. In rejecting Pastrana's plan, the union movement has proclaimed its autonomy and now is projecting itself as a new political interlocutor. In effect, unions have distanced themselves from the peace negotiations between the government and the guerrillas. The last congress of the CUT approved the formation of a social and political front under the auspices of the labor movement itself.

Peasant and Indigenous Movements

The most notable happenings for the peasant and Indian movements were the formation of national unions and the realization of important mobilizations. In 1982 the First National Indigenous Congress was held under the banner "For Unity, Land, and Culture." It resulted in the formation of the National Organization of Colombian Indigenous Peoples (ONIC). The existence of the ONIC permitted the naming of its director, Lorenzo Muelas, to the National Constitutional Assembly of 1991, and the obtaining of support for candidates representing indigenous peoples in congressional elections during the 1990s. As a consequence, indigenous peoples have acceded to congressional posts and to the Bogotá City Council. Even so, some indigenous groups momentarily succumbed to the ideology of armed struggle, and a sector of the communities in the department of Cauca created the armed movement Quintín Lame. Quintín Lame never engaged in important armed confrontations, however, and was quickly reintegrated into lawful society.

One of the organizations that most surprised the country was that of the coffee workers. Traditionally at the margin of social confrontations, this sector has been submerged in a profound crisis due to the impact of the opening up of the national economy under neo-liberal policies, the way the National Confederation of Coffee Growers has been handling the coffee economy, the damages caused by a coffee fungus, and the high interest rates on loans. Beginning in the mid-1980s, small producers came together to found the Unidad Cafetera Colombiana, which has organized various regional strikes that have enjoyed widespread support in the coffee-growing departments and even from the Church.

A second large peasant movement was that of the coca producers. Peasants of Putumayo and Caquetá departments directed pressure against policies imposed by the United States for the eradication of crops, especially chemical fumigation. The mobilizations were begun by a relatively small number of peasants, but in mid-1996 the coca growers managed to gather more than twenty-five thousand Caquetá producers in the suburbs of Florencia, the departmental capital. Following forty-seven days of marches, six deaths, and more than seventy wounded, the government compromised with the peasants, granting 14 billion pesos for regional health care, education, and public works and providing for payment for each hectare of coca eradicated.

A third type of protest was peasant strikes. Peasant mobilizations in diverse regions of the country converged on the capitals of the departments and medium-sized cities and blocked the principal roads. A characteristic of these mobilizations was that most of them culminated in agreements that included ample concessions on the part of the government. A good example is the strike carried out by the peasants and indigenous peoples in the department of Cauca at the end of 1999. The peasants took control of the Panamerican Highway and blocked the arteries to the capital of the department, Popayán, for almost a month. They ultimately obliged the government to negotiate and promise to make substantial investments in education, health, public works, and roads.

The war between paramilitaries and guerrillas, and between the guerrillas and the army, has generated two dynamics that principally affect peasants in the zones of conflict. The first is a high number of paramilitary massacres among the civil population. Between 1980 and 1992, for example, 1,032 massacres (homicides involving more than three victims) were committed. The second is the displacement of thousands of peasant families from their homes to different cities where many have taken over public buildings, appropriated lands, and demanded security measures that would allow them to return to their regions. The magnitude of the number of displaced persons presents serious political and social problems for the coming years.

Civic and Popular Movements

The civic and popular movements of the last decades were a result of the experience accumulated by different groups of the left in the 1970s, the growth of new regional forces, and the unavailability of basic services to the population. The civil strike was established as a new tactic of popular protest. It required a type of organization able to mobilize the participation of the most diverse social and political sectors and the identification of precise objectives, such as the improvement of certain public services.

The creation of civil and regional movements led to the formation of new national organizations. For example, the Coordinadora Nacional de Movimientos Cívicos (CNMC) came into being in 1983 and played an important role in civil strike projects for the remainder of the decade. An extraordinary occurrence was the successful participation of some regional movements and citizens' coalitions in the popular election of mayors. This development, although limited, revealed the existence of an important sector of opinion able to express its discontent with the traditional parties at the ballot boxes.

The Armed Movements and the Left

The number of organizations in arms against the State has declined during the last two decades. The decline reflected crises induced by changes in the international context, political and military errors committed by different insurgent groups, the peace processes, and the public's weariness with violence. All this facilitated the demobilization accords with the M-19, a faction of the ELN, and the majority of the EPL. Paradoxically, however, the armed movement was simultaneously experiencing an opposite process. The past two decades have witnessed the rapid growth of the ELN and especially of the FARC. This development not only resulted in an increase in their operations but also in an expansion of their political and military capacity in general.

Perhaps the insurgent group that has achieved the greatest advances, to the point that today the Pastrana administration grants it all manner of concessions, is the FARC. From the taking of towns and bombings, it graduated to the destruction of military installations of great strategic importance (Las Delicias, Pastacoy, Miraflores, and others). These actions involved large concentrations of troops, utilization of a high capacity of fire power, heavy army casualties, and the detention of a large number of government soldiers whom the FARC is using to pressure the current administration for a prisoner exchange.

The Colombian left has experienced a phenomenon similar to that of the armed movement. After a boom period in the early to mid-1970s, it experienced a decanting process in the 1980s that has culminated in the survival of only the groups that politically and ideologically were the strongest at the beginning. The crisis of the legal left is explained by several factors. One is the way military tactics were privileged over electoral ones during the 1980s. Another is the sectarianism that led insurgent groups to expel or assassinate leftist activists contesting for control over popular organizations. The growing intensity of the "dirty war" also played an important role; leftist political activists were left unprotected from hired killers and the repression exercised by the State. Finally, there was the fall of the USSR and of the Sandinista regime in Nicaragua, which for many called into question the whole model of guerrilla insurrection.

Conclusion

In the past two decades, Colombia has experienced the implementation of a neo-liberal economic model, a transformation of the traditional political class, a revitalization of the U.S. presence, a crisis of the left, the supremacy in popular and social movements of military over political strategies, and growing savagery in the confrontation between paramilitaries and the guerrillas. In other words, the social movement is situated between a hardening of the right, a debilitation of the left, and a strengthening of the armed movement, all of which have contributed to a situation of escalating violence. As a result, popular movements have been weakened. Their traditional systems of organization and mobilization have proved inadequate in the face of the cruelty of armed confrontation and the disbanding of the actors of previous decades.

The positive side for the social movements is that the application of neo-liberal measures has generated important processes of unity and of new forms of struggle. In fact, the strike movements of recent years, particularly the strikes by State workers and the mobilizations against the approval of the National Plan for Development, have advanced with the support of all the national labor federations.

The greatest challenge for the social and popular movements is that the current peace process aims at peace in exchange for a neo-liberal economic model. And because of the high degree of improvisation on the part of the government in the peace negotiations, and the growing and seemingly boundless agenda of the FARC, it is still not clear how the cost of peace will be managed. Nor is it clear how it will be possible to negotiate significant social and economic reforms in the context of the National Plan for Development now approved by Congress. Finally—and this is the least clear—it is difficult to see how social and popular movements will be able to participate effectively in the dialogue for peace and reform.

Suggested Readings

Arango, Luz Gabriel, comp. *Crisis sociopolítica colombiana: Un análisis no coyuntural de la coyuntura.* Bogotá, 1997.

Delgado, Alvaro. *Política y movimiento obrero, 1970–1983.* Bogotá, 1984.

Gallón, Gustavo, comp. *Entre movimientos y caudillos: 50 años de bipartidismo, izquierda y alternativas populares en Colombia.* Bogotá, 1989.

Laurent, Virginia. "Población y participación política en Colombia: Las elecciones de 1994." *Análisis Político* 31 (May–August 1997): 63–68.

Múnera Ruiz, Leopoldo. *Rupturas y continuidades: Poder y movimiento popular en Colombia, 1968–1988.* Bogotá, 1998.

Ríos, Norberto. "El sindicalismo colombiano hoy." *Revista de la Escuela Nacional Sindical* 25–26 (1992): 62–67.

Romero Medina, Amanda. *Magdalena Medio: Luchas sociales y violencia a los derechos humanos.* Bogotá, 1994.

Chapter 9

The War on Paper
A Balance Sheet on Works Published in the 1990s

Ricardo Peñaranda

This overview of the literature on violence published in Colombia during the 1990s complements Ricardo Peñaranda's earlier review of the historiography of the Violence, which appeared as the concluding chapter in *Violence in Colombia* (1992). In both of these essays he argues that in recent decades academic studies of violence have been closely tied to a political project: to banish violence by understanding it. In the contemporary period, this tendency has carried scholarship out of the narrow realm of the academy into the center of public debate on the current crisis. The quality of the scholarship dealing with the violence, as we hope the chapters in this book demonstrate, is one bright spot on the horizon of a nation being torn apart by a frightening and seemingly uncontrollable crisis.

Ricardo Peñaranda is a professor at the Institute of Political Studies and International Relations of the National University of Colombia. He coedited, with Gonzalo Sánchez, *Pasado y presente de la Violencia en Colombia* (Bogotá, 1986); and compiled, with Javier Guerrero, *De las armas a la política* (Bogotá, 1999).

During the 1990s, as the panorama of the violences in Colombia became more complex, the number of studies on the theme grew exponentially. A review of the bibliographic material yields more than seven hundred titles of articles and books published since 1990. No longer the sole province of academics, the topic has become the central axis of Colombian politics and today enters into discussions of everything from economic to cultural affairs.

Accepting the impossibility of an exhaustive analysis, this balance sheet tries only to signal the principal tendencies under which these studies have developed during the last decade. It arranges them into three large groupings: first, efforts at overall interpretations; second, studies concerning the so-called classic period of the Violence (1946–1965); and third, studies of the multiple violences of the 1980s and 1990s.

Before entering into detailed discussion of this work, let me offer four generalizations about this body of literature as a whole. First, we can say that during the past ten years there has been growing recognition of the fact that there is not one violence, but many, and study of the interrelations among them has clearly advanced. Second, there has been a notable effort to improve the quality of the available figures on acts of violence, which has also permitted more sophisticated interpretations. Third, there has been an emphasis on ways the limited power of the State (especially its inability to impart justice and its incapacity to correct structural imbalances and social inequities) has worked to strengthen violent actors. Fourth, the debate has transcended the academic sphere, not only in the sense that the most recent developments and investigations have been partially reflected in official strategies, but also in the sense that public debate is increasingly structured by these advances. In part, the war, with all its painful consequences, has been transferred to paper.

General Interpretations of the Violence

The possibility of carrying out studies that offer a panoramic vision of Colombian violence is increasingly unlikely because, in addition to the effects of a prolonged conflict on politics and society, the activities of the various armed actors overlap. Even so, some authors or groups of investigators have tried during the last decade to carry out comprehensive studies that, from a historical perspective, or centered on the multiple intersections of the violences of today, permit a general view of a very complex scene.

The most ambitious of those attempts is probably that of historian Marco Palacios in his book *Entre la legitimidad y la violencia: Colombia, 1875–1994* (Bogotá: Grupo Editorial Norma, 1995), an amply documented work that proposes a historical explanation for the misfortune of Colombian society. Reviewing a century and a half of history, Palacios argues that the country has been profoundly affected by what he calls unfinished processes of colonization. While the majority of the population, previously rural but urban today, invents and practices forms of social and economic organization outside legal formalities and institutional rituals, the elites appear more preoccupied with assuring themselves control of the State than with leading a process of national construction. These circumstances, set on a stage marked by the accelerated processes of modernization and exacerbated in recent years by the presence of illegal economies, ended by making impossible the construction of a legitimacy that went further than the rhetorical. This process opened an enormous space in which the violence operated as a regulator of individual or collective conflicts.

Also from a historical perspective is Gonzalo Sánchez's *Guerra y política en la sociedad colombiana* (Bogotá: El Ancora Editores, 1991), which is composed of a group of essays focusing on the effect of the Violence on the Colombian political system. Although most of these essays reflect on the political violence of the 1950s, they are undoubtedly concerned conceptually with the violences of today. And it is concerning the contemporary period that the principal questions that inspired this study become more urgent. How is it that the Colombian political system has survived four decades of violence? How has the war worked to transform political actors and convert itself into a mechanism for the relationships among them? How did the violence become as politically profitable as it is today in Colombian society? Sánchez's book is one of the works of synthesis that have most influenced the academic debate during the last few years. It continues a line of reasoning begun in earlier works by Sánchez and others (see, in particular, Comisíon de Estudios sobre la Violencia, *Colombia: Violencia y democracia* [Bogotá, 1987], and Daniel Pecaut, *Orden y violencia* [Bogotá, 1986]). All this work probes the complementary relationship between apparently opposed poles such as war and democracy. This relationship, although durable, is not in any sense stable, and it could be reaching its own limits, as is demonstrated by the degradation of the Colombian conflict during the last decade. That has translated, according to Sánchez, into the "militarization of politics and banditization of war," and could result in a breaking of all remaining constraints on violence.

A work that stands out because of its polemical character is one by Malcom Deas and Fernando Gaitán Daza, *Dos ensayos especulativos sobre la violencia en Colombia* (Bogotá: Departamento Nacional de Planeación, 1995). This book is made up of two texts of very different origin, the publication of which was promoted by the Departamento Nacional de Planeación at the end of President César Gaviria's term. Deas, known for his penetrating critique of the common assumption that there is a violent tradition in Colombian society, suggests interesting comparisons with other countries that have at one time experienced such sharp conflicts, such as Italy, Mexico, Ireland, and Peru. This commentary is especially interesting in light of the fact that the introduction of comparative elements to local analysis is commonly overlooked. Fernando Gaitán depends on a wide range of statistical resources to combine economic, demographic, and criminal variables through time in an attempt to offer an explanation for the dynamic of the violence.

The general conclusion of the two authors, based upon data that show the nonlinear behavior of criminality, is precisely that economic and demographic variables do not correlate well with violence, and that Colombian violence is not the product of a cumulative process.

Both authors, but Gaitán the more so, start from this hypothesis and propose to orient State resources in a more efficient manner in order to resolve the causes of violence. They focus especially on investment in the judicial and political systems in order to break the chain of impunity that has doubtlessly elevated the "profitability" of criminality. It is on this point that Deas and Gaitán coincide with the unquestionably well-intentioned idea of the technocrats of the Gaviria administration. They believed that, once the political and administrative reforms of the 1991 Constitution were implemented, it would be possible to think of an ending to the violence. "Dinosaurs" was the term they used to refer to guerrilla groups. They would no longer have a place in the "new Colombia" the Gaviria administration was constructing. This emphasis on institutional factors leads the authors to de-emphasize the relationship between modernization and conflict that their own figures suggest. It is the deepening of this relationship that has been harnessed for the strengthening of the different armed actors, to the detriment of State control during the past decade.

To conclude this balance sheet of holistic studies we should comment on the collection compiled by Malcom Deas and María Victoria Llorente, *Reconocer la guerra para construir la paz* (Bogotá: Ediciones Andes/Grupo Editorial Norma, 1999). The eleven essays included in their book are the result of a notable academic effort promoted by the study group Paz Pública of the Universidad de los Andes, whose proposition is to construct a laboratory of observation and analysis of themes related to national security. This text offers a detailed reading of the available figures concerning the recent evolution of the actors of the conflict: the guerrillas, the paramilitaries, and the army. At the same time, it analyzes the policies implemented by the institutions directly linked to public security: the army, the police, and the justice system. The use of up-to-date information and the emphasis on security policies, including the evolution of public expenditures, make this text a valuable instrument for analysis of the Colombian conflict today. This does not mean, however, that the authors' claim to offer an alternative focus to previous studies is valid. Where there *is* a change of focus is in the solutions the authors propose. In this area, a good many of the essays emphasize the urgency of redesigning the control apparatus of the State in order to make it more efficient. The effect is to de-emphasize the necessity of seeking a negotiated solution to the conflict and of strengthening State legitimacy, proposals that are emphasized in previous studies such as that of the 1987 Comisión de Estudios sobre la Violencia, cited above.

Studies on "the Violence"

The studies that focus on the Violence of the 1950s merit special mention, given the importance they have for the interpretation of our modern history. Producing significant new work on this period is challenging, however, given the volume of existing studies and the limitations of the sources. The texts considered here were produced by well-trained investigators, most of them historians, who have sifted through primary sources to produce works that have enriched our understanding of this important period. The first of those works, Javier Guerrero's *Los años del olvido: Boyacá y los orígenes de la Violencia* (Bogotá: IEPRI/Tercer Mundo, 1991), is a study of the "initial violence" at the beginning of the 1930s, at the start of the Liberal government that put an end to a half-century of political control by the Conservative party. Even though this violence was confined to the northeast region of the country, the experience was determinative for the conflicts that affected the whole country for years afterward. In Boyacá, Conservative ideology, actively supported by the Catholic Church, was able to mobilize a mostly rural population marked by poverty and backwardness. Supporting Conservative leadership and forcefully opposing the modernizing pretensions of the new Liberal government, these people forged a mentality of resistance and of attachment to traditional values that would later reappear in the activities of the infamous *chulavitas* during the widespread political violence of the 1950s.

Another work centered in the Andean region that illustrates contemporary Colombian conflicts is Elsy Marulanda's *Colonización y conflicto: Las lecciones del Sumapaz* (Bogotá: IEPRI/Tercer Mundo, 1991). This is the history of an important agricultural region, physically close to Bogotá, the economic and political center of the country, yet in reality quite distant, given its lack of roads and other means of communication. In the past, Sumapaz was the epicenter of a vigorous agrarian movement, a center of armed resistance, a bulwark of leftist political organization. All of this gave the region an impenetrable character that is maintained even today; it continues to be a territory where the FARC exercises ample influence. Marulanda reviews almost a century of the region's history, showing how periods of conflict are superimposed on one another and how their persistence creates conditions that feed future confrontations. The great theme of this work is the consolidation of an ideology of peasant resistance that is nurtured by unkept government promises and failed plans for agrarian reform. This is not just any failure, since the impossibility of advancing a process of agrarian reform is the greatest failure of the Colombian elites. They have not wanted, or have not been able, to overcome resistance to the democratization of rural property. Contrary to what has been happening in other parts of the continent, land concentration has increased extremely rapidly in Colombia in recent years, with the frightful result of more than a million people being displaced from the countryside to the cities.

Two more works complete this panorama of regional studies with important national implications: Reinaldo Barbosa's *Guadalupe y sus centauros: Memorias de la insurrección llanera* (Bogotá: CEREC, 1992), concerning the Liberal guerrillas of the Llanos Orientales; and Darío Betancourt and Marta García's *Matones y cuadrileros: Orígen y evolución de la Violencia en el occidente colombiano* (Bogotá: Tercer Mundo, 1991), about the Violence in the coffee zone of northern Valle. The first is a valuable addition to the reconstruction of the history of the guerrillas of the Llanos, a force made famous and somewhat mythologized by accounts of the time but relatively little examined in detail. Probably the most important part of this study is the emphasis on the qualitative change that took place among the leadership during the second part of the llanero insurrection (1952–53). Originally influenced by ranchers and Liberal politicians and obedient to the directives of their party, the leaders of the revolt entered into a stage of class-based politicization and growing autonomy that permitted them to carry out unified offensive actions that, given their magnitude, constituted a real threat to the Conservative regime.

The work of Betancourt and García concentrates on the Violence in the department of Valle del Cauca, one of the regions most affected by agro-industrial modernization during the decade of the 1950s. After analyzing the distinctive nature of the agricultural struggles in the region, the authors focus on a particular agent of violence—the *pájaro* (a hired killer), who had a great impact on the southwest of Colombia during this period. The *pájaro* practiced a mode of violence probably more sophisticated and perhaps more effective than similar phenomena observed in other regions; he is capable of assassination with surprising coldness and with no ethical or moral burden. What is remarkable is that his actions are secretly backed and justified by the local Conservative authorities, by the National Directorate of the Conservative Party, and by the Church itself. This support permitted *pájaros* to act with the greatest ease and completely out in the open, achieving, in this way, a double effect: that of terror produced by the crime itself and that of fear generated by the impunity that shelters the criminal. The study of this type of violence, which approximates what we today call para-State violence, permits the authors to propose suggestive continuities between this never completely disactivated model of violence and that implanted several decades later by the drug traffickers and the *sicariato.* Drug trafficking, of course, has evolved into a huge criminal business with close ties to the established economic and political order.

This balance sheet of recent publications on the Violence would not be complete without mentioning some studies that have ventured into little explored areas, such as the ritual character of violence and the relationship between political culture and violence. An outstanding work dealing with the first theme is María Victoria Uribe's *Matar, rematar y contramatar* (Bogotá: CINEP, 1991). The book focuses on massacres and the symbolic treatment of death and poses fascinating questions concerning the cultural background of the Violence. On the second theme, the texts of Darío Acevedo, *La mentalidad de las élites sobre la Violencia en Colombia, 1936–1949* (Bogotá: IEPRI/El Ancora Editores, 1995), and of Carlos Mario Perea, *Porque la sangre es espíritu* (Bogotá: IEPRI/Editorial Aguilar, 1996), treat, from different viewpoints and methodologies, the construction of Colombian political mentality, a subject whose importance had been signaled some years ago by authors such as Daniel Pecaut and Herbert Braun. Darío Acevedo studies the complex mechanisms by which partisan identities were reconstructed or fortified during the years that preceded the Violence. Analyzing the makeup of the principal media of political communication of the period, including newspaper editorials, speeches, sermons, and caricatures, he shows how, as in previous epochs, political identity is constructed, starting with an emphasis on one's difference from one's antagonist. During this period, difference is established along the axis of the international ideological debate: Communism, Fascism, and the Cold War. The work of Carlos Mario Perea also focuses on the mentality of the elites during this same period, but he approaches the problem with a different methodology. His attempt is more centered on analyzing the construction of the "symbolic capital" that justifies the destruction of the adversary. This symbolic resource, or "gesture of confrontation," as he defines it, translates into a "pact of verbal destruction of the adversary." This pact replaces political or ideological antagonism, which, in his opinion, is not as determinant as other authors have suggested.

The Violences of Today

Academic work on violence during the last decade is concerned with dramatic changes in the nature of the phenomenon itself. There has been a strengthening of the many armed actors, whose actions intertwine, confront one another, feed on each other, and even sometimes complement one another. The result is a sensation of total chaos. But this sensation hides the frightful reality that the war has generated its own mechanisms of "order." These particularly interest the actors in the conflicts, but they have a high cost both for the State, whose legitimacy progressively erodes, and for the civil population, which directly supports the weight of the conflict. We can classify these investigations in three groups in accordance with their major themes: those that center on the dynamic of the armed actors; those that analyze the many faces of the conflict from a territorial angle; and those that study the impact of the multiple violences of today on Colombian society.

The Armed Actors

From this group of studies, which are probably the most numerous, we can first emphasize those covering the insurgent groups and the peace processes of the early 1990s. First, the study by Eduardo Pizarro on the FARC, *Las FARC: De la autodefensa a la combinación de todas las formas de lucha* (Bogotá: IEPRI/Tercer Mundo, 1991), emphasizes the formative stage of this most influential of the Colombian guerrilla groups, and Pizarro argues that it influences every aspect of the FARC's activities today. The enduring influence of the group's formative years goes beyond the symbolic; it includes the FARC's political stance and organizational structure. This same author employs a more sociological vision of the groups of armed organizations in *Insurgencia sin revolución* (Bogotá: IEPRI/ Tercer Mundo, 1996). In this important work, Pizarro analyzes comparatively the evolution of the Colombian insurgent movement in the context of the development of guerrilla experiences in Latin America as a whole. His principal hypothesis is that in Colombia all the conditions for the consolidation of the guerrilla movement existed, yet political conditions in the country as a whole precluded triumph at the national level. The result was that the guerrillas managed to root themselves in some regions, thanks to their role as political and economic regulators, but there was an impasse in the insurgent project for the nation as a whole. The author defines this situation as a "negative tie" between the guerrillas and the State, a concept that has stimulated much debate.

William Ramírez's *Estado, violencia y democracia* (Bogotá: IEPRI/Tercer Mundo, 1990) is composed of five essays that systematically probe the guerrilla phenomenon and the effects of its prolonged action on the character of the State, the political regime, and Colombian democracy itself. With a view fixed more on the future of the armed conflict, Alfredo Rangel's *La guerra en el fin de siglo* (Bogotá: Tercer Mundo, 1998) puts the accent not so much on the emergence of the guerrilla groups, nor on the evolution of their conflictive relationship with the State, but on the idea that their continued growth, fed by enormous provincial resources from illegal economies, will permit the breaking of the apparent equilibrium that exists today between the two main armed camps. This is a text that has opened an important debate, given that in recent years there has been undoubted growth in the armed capacity of the guerrillas. But that growing strength, more than signaling a future revolutionary triumph—there are strong internal and external barriers impeding that outcome—could lead instead to an unimaginable degradation of the Colombian conflict.

The peace processes that came about at the beginning of the 1990s are the subject of various investigations. These studies analyze the conditions under which the "reinsertion" of former guerrillas took place and the accompanying political results. From this group of texts it is useful to highlight Mauricio García's *De la Uribe a Tlaxcala: Procesos de paz* (Bogotá: CINEP, 1992), probably the best documented of the studies on the development of the peace negotiations with the groups that put down their arms at the beginning of the decade: the M-19, the EPL, the PRT, and Quintín Lame. García also examines the frustrated dialogues with the ELN and the FARC, which were interrupted in 1991. The report, directed by Alejandro Reyes and published by the Comisión de Superación de la Violencia (Bogotá, 1992), is an important analysis supported by extensive fieldwork on the dramatic efforts of the demobilized groups to consolidate an elusive peace. They were threatened by different armed groups and widespread intolerance, which in the end compromised the success of this process. Jesús Antonio Bejarano's *Una agenda para la paz: Aproximaciones desde una teoría de la resolución de conflictos* (Bogotá: Tercer Mundo, 1995), is a celebrated work by a former presidential consultant on peace that evaluates the negotiation processes at the beginning of the 1990s through a comparative analysis of like processes carried out at the same time in El Salvador and Guatemala. This text attempts to go beyond numerous studies on the nature of conflict and open a space for reflection on its transcendence. Finally, the collection *De las armas a la política* (Bogotá: Tercer Mundo, 1999), compiled by Ricardo Peñaranda and Javier Guerrero, underscores the efforts at re-entry into peaceful political life by the M-19, the EPL, and Quentín Lame. In the end, despite the hopes that it initially awoke, this process resulted in painful frustration, a consequence of the limitations of the political system as much as it was of the weaknesses of the plans that guided the former organizations themselves in their transit to civil life.

Finally, a view from inside the insurgent groups that has great documentary value can be found in three texts. One is Alvaro Villarraga and Nelson Plazas's history of the EPL, *Para reconstruir los sueños: Una historia del EPL* (Bogotá: COLCULTURA/PROGRESAR/Fundación Cultura Democrática, 1994). Despite its strongly testimonial character, this book provides a bare-bones, amply documented history of the evolution of this armed group from its emergence in 1967 until its dissolution in 1991. A second is Dario Villamizar's work concerning the M-19, *Aquel 19 será* (Editorial Planeta, 1995). In spite of its epic tone, this book provides an important group of documents and indispensable testimonials as well as the basic history of the M-19. The third is Carlos Medina Gallego's *ELN: Una historia contadada dos veces, entrevista con "el cura" Pérez y Nicolás Bautista Gabino* (Bogotá: Rodríguez Quito Editores, 1996). This text brings together the visions of two of the ELN's greatest leaders and constitutes a valuable source for the analysis of the values, ideology, political conceptions, and organizational model of this armed group.

Studies of paramilitarism have notably increased during the last decade, even if their number does not keep up with the growing impact of this phenomenon. A perspective on these actors as part of a wider phenomenon, that of parainstitutionality, can be found in the collective study, *La irrupción del paraestado: Ensayos sobre la crisis colombiana* (Bogotá: ILSA/CEREC, 1990). This is an early text that formulates important hypotheses about the nexus between the "dirty war," drug trafficking, and the crisis of the Colombian political regime. A reading of paramilitarism as a regional expression of counterinsurgent violence closely linked to drug trafficking can be found in the work of Carlos Medina Gallego, *Autodefensas, paramilitares y narcotráfico en Colombia: Origen, desarrollo y consolidación: El caso de Puerto Boyacá* (Bogotá: Documentos Periodísticos, 1990). This is a study of the development of an important ranching enclave in the Magdalena Medio, which constituted at the end of the 1980s a laboratory for what is today the paramilitary project. One must also mention a more ambitious work from this same author, *La violencia parainstitucional, paramilitar y parapolicial en Colombia* (Bogotá: Rodríguez Quito Editores, 1994), which analyzes paramilitary violence and its diverse regional expressions in Córdoba, Magdalena Medio, and Urabá, among other places, as a broad political and military project. For Medina, the counterinsurgency struggle is linked to other expressions of dirty war such as disappearances and genocide. Finally, it is important to highlight the work of Adolfo Atheortúa on the action of paramilitary groups in the municipality of Trujillo in northern Valle, *El poder y la sangre: Las historias de Trujillo, Valle* (Cali: CINEP/Pontificia Universidad Javeriana, 1995). There, territorial expansion of drug trafficking was accompanied by the reinforcement of parainstitutional mechanisms of control that have had a lengthy presence in the region.

We come now to studies that cover drug trafficking, undoubtedly one of the most perturbing ills of the nation today. The impact of drug trafficking is of such magnitude that it has internationalized the Colombian conflict and permitted its escalation to levels never before imagined. Many studies concerning drug trafficking highlight its political, judicial, and economic impact on Colombian society; others emphasize its criminal nature. Among the first group, Ciro Krauthausen and Luis Fernando Sarmiento's *Cocaína & Co.: Un mercado ilegal por dentro* (Bogotá: IEPRI/Tercer Mundo, 1991), concerns the business rationality of drug trafficking, a rationality also present in the way traffickers manage the political dividends of the drug trade. The collection *Narcotráfico en Colombia* (Bogotá: Universidad de los Andes/ Tercer Mundo, 1990), prepared by an interdisciplinary team from the Universidad de los Andes, analyzes the phenomenon on three fronts: the economic, the political-criminal, and that of international relations. The work of Francisco Thoumi, *Economía política y narcotráfico* (Bogotá: Tercer Mundo, 1994), is probably the most detailed investigation yet published on the economic dimensions of drug trafficking. Of particular concern to Thoumi is the catalyzing effect of the huge volume of capital generated by the drug trade on the processes of social and moral disintegration now observable in Colombian society.

Studies of the drug trade that emphasize its impact as a criminal business and as a stimulus to the development of other forms of crime include Juan Tokatlian's *Drogas, dilemas y dogmas* (Bogotá: Universidad los Andes/ Tercer Mundo, 1995), which focuses on the macrocriminal dimension of drug trafficking and its impact on politics and national security. The collection *Drogas, poder y región en Colombia* (Bogotá: CINEP, 1995), compiled by Ricardo Vargas, is one of the few studies that approaches the relationship between violence and drug trafficking and its effect on the evolution of human rights. Francisco Thoumi et al., *Drogas ilícitas en Colombia* (Bogotá: ARIEL/PNUD/Dirección de Estupefacientes, 1997), is a collection of essays that, incorporating an up-to-date assessment of the economic dimensions of drug trafficking and the size of the land area devoted to the production of illicit crops, covers important ancillary themes as well. These include the impact of the territorial expansion of drug-trafficking properties, the costs of combating drug production and the violence that it generates, and the evolution of the criminal policy toward drug trafficking. Also covering the criminal dimension of drug trafficking is Darío Betancourt and Marta García's history of the drug mafia, *Contrabandistas, marimberos y mafiosos: Historia social de la mafia colombiana, 1965–1992* (Bogotá: Tercer Mundo, 1994), which among other things links drug trafficking with the diverse illegal economies that preceded it, such as the contraband trade and arms trafficking. Finally, a critical analysis of the war against drugs and its effects on human rights can be found in the 1991 Washington Office of Latin American Affairs report on the risks of the growing involvement of the U.S. government in the Colombian antinarcotics struggle. This report was published in Colombia as *WOLA, ¿Peligro inminente? Las FF.AA. de Estados Unidos y la guerra contra las drogas* (Bogotá: Tercer Mundo, 1994).

To complete this section on armed actors, there are important recent studies on the Colombian armed forces, an area in which notable advances have been made during the past decade. There is an evident contradiction between the growth of the Colombian State's security budget and the increase in the operative capacity of the guerrilla organizations, which have dealt the army serious reverses during recent years. This state of affairs has raised important questions concerning security policies, the autonomy of the armed forces, and their efficiency. An important contribution to this discussion is Francisco Leal Buitrago's book *El oficio de la guerra* (Bogotá: IEPRI/Tercer Mundo, 1994). It critically analyzes the evolution of Colombian security policies, from the application of the Doctrine of National Security in the 1970s to the attempt to design a new security strategy based on civilian control after the proclamation of the 1991 Constitution. A more historical treatment of the evolution of the armed forces, from the period of the Regeneration to the dawn of the National Front, is Adolfo Atheortúa and Humberto Vélez's *Estado y fuerzas armadas en Colombia, 1886–1953* (Bogotá: Pontificia Universidad Javeriana de Cali/Tercer Mundo, 1994), which focuses on the efforts at professionalization of the armed forces in opposition to various attempts to make them an instrument of partisan politics. Finally, there is the work of Andrés Dávila, *El juego del poder: Historia, armas y votos* (Bogotá: Universidad de los Andes/CEREC, 1988), an innovative look at the costs to the Colombian regime of the autonomy of the armed forces, an autonomy that leads them toward becoming an additional protagonist of the violence.

Violences and Their Territories

The interpretation of Colombian violence as a plural phenomenon has also led to reading these multiple violences in their relation to territory. In effect, not only are there various violent actors today, but their behavior is not uniform and depends in good measure on the territorial reality in which they act. If to this we add that, during the last thirty years, Colombia has been the scene of complex processes of regional development, linked to the emergence of new poles of economic growth and renewed currents of migration, it becomes understandable that much research is oriented toward regional studies of the violence.

One of the regions that has particularly attracted the attention of investigators has been Urabá, a large coastal territory that borders Panama. There, in the context of a vigorous process of new settlement, an important banana enclave developed. The struggle over control of the abundant economic resources generated by banana production has unleashed one of the most violent conflicts of the last two decades. Clara Inés García's *Urabá: Región, actores y conflicto, 1960–1990* (Bogotá: CEREC, 1996) focuses on the actors whom conflict involves: rural property owners, unions, guerrillas, and self-defense groups. Contention among these groups, made worse by the absence of State regulation, began in the form of worker-owner struggle over the distribution of banana industry profits. But the struggle degenerated as armed groups became involved as substitutes for the original actors. Another study of the conflict in Urabá is William Ramírez Tobón's *Urabá, los inciertos confines de una crisis* (Bogotá: Planeta, 1997). This is a historical work that primarily concentrates on the advance of private control of territory at the expense of State sovereignty, a process in which powerful individuals destroy an already fragile historical process of building community.

Other regions whose development has been accompanied by an increase in violence have also attracted the attention of investigators, among them the emerald zone of Boyacá, the Magdalena Medio, and the lower Cauca Valley. The emerald zone in the north of Boyacá is examined by María Victoria Uribe in *Limpiar la tierra: Guerra y poder entre los esmeralderos* (Bogotá: CINEP, 1992). This is one of the most extreme cases of private violence, where strong local power structures, fed by the enormous economic resources generated by the exploitation of the mines, supplant the precarious State presence and become regulating forces in their own right, providing services, dispensing justice, and even arranging their own peace accords. The case of the Magdalena Medio, one of the richest and most conflictive zones of the country, is analyzed by Alejo Vargas in his *Colonización y conflicto armado* (Bogotá: CINEP, 1992). Vargas seeks to relate the development of the region—a process linked to the struggles of oil workers in the1920s and a wave of agricultural settlement in the 1940s—to the consolidation of an important cell of Liberal resistance during the bipartisan violence of the 1950s and to the presence of the different armed actors during the last decades. These factors have converted the region into a virtual laboratory for study of the Colombian war. Finally, the case of the lower Cauca, a rich mining and cattle-ranching zone, is analyzed by Clara Inés García in her work *El bajo Cauca antioqueño* (Bogotá: CINEP, 1992). This region has been the theater for powerful social mobilizations, and there is a strong presence of drug-trafficking capital.

The theme of the city as a space for violence merits special comment. This topic awakened an understandable interest at the start of the decade due to the surge in urban criminality. An example is the study by Alvaro Guzmán and Alvaro Camacho, *Colombia: Ciudad y violencia* (Bogotá: Ediciones Foro Nacional, 1990), which registers the development of new forms of violence associated with the accelerated urban transformations of the last decades. The interest in urban violence is also present in short testimonials that vividly depict the new urban protagonists of the violence such as the *sicarios* and the juvenile gangs. A good example is Alonso Salazar's *No nacimos pa' semilla* (Bogotá: CINEP, 1992). All told, however, in spite of the interest that urban violence provokes, and strong polemics concerning the policies of citizen security, the theme has not yet experienced the development one would expect.

Violences and Their Impact

Just as there has been significant development of scholarship on the actors in the armed conflict and the factors involved in violence, there is also growing interest in the effects of violence on the social fabric and institutions. After all, many of the characteristics of contemporary Colombia developed in coexistence with multiple factors of violence, an environment that no one now considers as tangential or temporary. Most of the studies oriented in this direction do not propose a global explanation of the violences, but instead analyze how they operate and affect Colombian society and its institutions.

A primary work in this vein is the collection compiled by Jaime Arocha, Fernando Cubides, and Myriam Jimeno, *Las violencias: Inclusión creciente*

(Bogotá: Centro de Estudios Sociales/Universidad Nacional, 1998). This is a collection of eleven essays by a multidisciplinary group of investigators, most of them associated with the Centro de Estudios Sociales of the Universidad Nacional or the Programa Paz Pública of the Universidad de los Andes. In addition to analyzing the behavior of the perpetrators of the violence, the authors evaluate the effects of the long duration of the conflict and present the point of view of the victims, survivors, and other silent protagonists, such as women and children.

Also in this vein are those works that have contributed to a greater understanding of criminality and its effects. The vertiginous ascent of homicide in Colombia in the last two decades, when the homicide rate became one of the highest in the world, surpassing 80 per 100,000 inhabitants, generated numerous questions concerning criminal behavior, its regional expressions, and its relation to impunity and to the evolution of other illicit activities. These questions have inspired several recent studies, among which that of Mauricio Rubio, *Crimen e impunidad: Precisiones sobre la violencia* (Bogotá: Universidad de los Andes/Tercer Mundo, 1999), merits special attention. Rubio's work opened a debate concerning the quality of available criminal statistics and the conclusions of several previous studies, particularly with regard to levels of impunity and the degree of criminal behavior among the actors of the conflict, including the insurgents, the paramilitaries, and the armed forces. Another important work is Fernando Cubides, Ana Cecilia Olaya, and Carlos Miguel Ortiz, *La violencia y el municipio colombiano, 1980–1997* (Bogotá: Centro de Estudios Sociales/Universidad Nacional, 1998), which deals with municipal-level homicide during the past two decades. This is a microanalysis, involving multiple variables pertaining to actors or victims, which paints a picture of a "banalized" or recurrent violence associated with a struggle for territorial control. This struggle involves an unfinished process of land settlement and is driven by the emergence of legal or illegal economies, both of which have as a common denominator a State that has renounced its regulating role in favor of private initiatives. Equally important is Saúl Franco's *El Quinto: No matar: Contextos explicativos de la violencia en Colombia* (Bogotá: IEPRI/Tercer Mundo, 1999), which analyzes homicide during the past decades from the point of view of public health. Franco gathers and compares the available data and proposes a new interpretation that views criminality within the context of patterns of overall mortality. This approach yields the surprising conclusion that homicide is the principal cause of mortality in certain regions of the country and has a particularly devastating impact on specific sectors of the population, especially young people, among whom it is a true epidemic.

The relationship between war and the law has also prompted numerous reflections in the last decade. In effect, at the same time that Colombia is a country of wars, it is also a country of laws. Colombia possesses a juridical tradition for the treatment of internal conflicts that has been overwhelmed by barbarism and the deformations caused by repressive statutes. But for many, that tradition must be recovered and revitalized in light of international law, precisely as one of the alternatives for finding an exit to the conflict. This is the thrust of studies such as Hernando Valencia Villa's *La humanización de la guerra: Derecho international humanitario y conflicto armado en Colombia* (Bogotá: Universidad de los Andes/Tercer Mundo, 1991). Valencia presents an analysis of the changes in the normative horizon of the Colombian guerrilla war and raises the possibility of overcoming the degradation of the conflict and the stalemate in the negotiations by humanizing the war. Iván Orozco Abad's *Combatientes, rebeldes y terroristas* (Bogotá: Editorial Temis, 1992) focuses on the evolution of the law of Colombian warfare and the transformation of the figure of the political delinquent, while Valencia also covers the outlook for the application of international human rights law to the Colombian condition.

To conclude this balance sheet, I should note that the theme of the relationship between violence and development has been taken up emphatically in the last few years. This theme involves an important debate because, after several decades of coexistence between economic growth and violence, everything now indicates that this paradoxical situation has reached its limits. The growing economic crisis at the end of the 1990s comes at the same time that initiatives for attaining a stable peace have increased. The result is vigorous debate over the conditions under which peace could be attained. A good example of this kind of discussion can be found in the collection *La paz: Un desafío para el desarrollo* (Bogotá: Tercer Mundo, 1998), which synthesizes the work of a multidisciplinary commission supported by the Departamento Nacional de Planeación.* This text identifies the costs that Colombians pay in terms of economic and social development for the various kinds of violence. It also establishes an agenda of strategic themes such as justice, agrarian reform, and policies of national security, the discussion of which is essential for any current or future peace agenda.

*Many of the documents used by the commission were later published in Alvaro Camacho and Francisco Leal, comps., *Armar la paz es desarmar la guerra* (Bogotá: IEPRI/FESCOL/CEREC, 1999).

Chapter 10

Waging War and Negotiating Peace

The Contemporary Crisis in Historical Perspective

Charles Bergquist

In this concluding essay, Charles Bergquist draws on his earlier study of the country's greatest nineteenth-century civil war (*Coffee and Conflict in Colombia: Origins and Outcome of the War of the Thousand Days, 1886–1910* [Durham, NC, 1978 and 1986; Medellín, 1980; Bogotá, 1999]) and his comparative analysis of twentieth-century Colombia's labor and the left (*Labor in Latin America: Comparative Essays on Chile, Argentina, Venezuela, and Colombia* [Stanford, CA, 1986; Bogotá, 1988]) to compare the crisis facing Colombia at the end of the nineteenth century with that confronting the nation today. He focuses, in particular, on prospects for peace, contrasting the position of the Liberal insurgents who laid down their arms at the start of the twentieth century with that of the Marxist insurgents involved in peace negotiations today. The essay links some of the themes of this volume to the historical concerns that animated our earlier edited work, *Violence in Colombia* (1992), and summarizes elements of the essays and documents in this book by emphasizing the kinds of reforms that a successful contemporary peace process may entail. The final part of the essay speaks to the question of how people outside Colombia, particularly U.S. citizens, might contribute to the peaceful resolution of the crisis.

Charles Bergquist teaches Latin American and labor history at the University of Washington in Seattle. He has been a visiting professor at the National University in Bogotá. His most recent book is *Labor and the Course of American Democracy: U.S. History in Latin American Perspective* (London, 1996).

One way to conclude this study of the crisis developing in Colombia during the 1990s, and assess current prospects for peace, is to examine the analogous situation Colombians faced a century earlier. The comparison developed here of these two critical junctures in the nation's history is not primarily a prescriptive exercise, but an analytical one. Understanding what brought Colombia peace at the start of the twentieth century will not have any direct application to finding a satisfactory formula for peace at the start of the twenty-first. But the comparison does allow one to identify certain commonalities in the processes of waging war and negotiating peace in these two quite different yet interconnected historical periods. And focusing on these similarities and differences, I believe, affords a way to sort out the complexity of the contemporary crisis and weigh the political choices confronting Colombians today.*

I

In February 1901 in the midst of Colombia's (and Latin America's) greatest nineteenth-century civil war, the government of Conservative President José Manuel Marroquín promulgated a decree that suggests how severe that civil conflict had become. The war, later called the War of the Thousand Days, had begun in October 1899, and during its first months was fought in a "conventional" way. That is, the armies on both sides of the struggle were more or less disciplined troops under the leadership of members of the social and political elite, people such as the generals Manuel Casabianca y Próspero Pinzón on the side of the Conservative government and Gabriel Vargas Santos and Rafael Uribe Uribe on the side of the Liberal revolution. But after the Battle of Palonegro, in May 1900, in which government forces defeated the Liberal army, the struggle was transformed into something else. The Liberals began a guerrilla war, and the leadership of both sides fell more and more into the hands of people of less privileged social origins.

The decree in question, promulgated February 18, 1901, provided for summary military trials for guerrillas accused of any of a series of crimes. These ranged from traditional offenses such as assault, armed robbery, murder, and the counterfeiting of money to more bizarre transgressions that, although one must be careful to distinguish between the language of a decree and real conditions, nevertheless seem to suggest the growing savagery in the countryside. Among these crimes were castration and mutilation of limbs; the wounding or abuse of any Catholic priest, person within a Catholic Church, or woman, child, or defenseless person; kidnapping, rape, or grave robbing; and finally, damage to another's property that redounded to the personal benefit of the perpetrator. Sentences fixed in these summary military trials could not be appealed and were to be carried out immediately. The only exception was for sentences of capital punishment, which could be appealed to the respective military governor, who was allowed forty-eight

*Throughout the essay, I use upper case to refer to the members and platforms of Colombia's two traditional parties, the Liberals and the Conservatives. When the more general meaning of these terms is implied, the lower-case spelling is employed.

hours to rule on the case (Decree No. 112, February 18, 1901; an analogous juridical institution today, the special regional courts that critics call "faceless justice" are the subject of a noted lawyer's communication in Part 6 of the Documents section.)

To justify such extraordinary measures, the Conservative government and its supporters dramatized (and often exaggerated) the excesses of the Liberal revolutionaries. For example, the governor of Tolima denounced the "cowardly mutilations" he claimed Liberal rebels routinely inflicted on their victims, and Conservative newspapers often spoke of the "savage ferocity" of the revolutionaries' crimes. Exaggerations aside, we know from a variety of sources that robbery, assassination, and cruelty were common in the theaters of guerrilla activity by the second year of the war. And there is also evidence that, by that time, the Liberal guerrillas were acting on motives that went far beyond the liberal political goals of elite party leaders. In the sacking of a Conservative's hacienda in the region of Sumapaz in southeastern Cundinamarca, for example, according to the detailed report of a Conservative newspaper correspondent, the guerrillas took "livestock, barnyard fowl, clothing, kitchen utensils, tools, cacao, coffee, and hides" before burning the buildings. "Since several [of the guerrillas] were in debt to [the hacienda owner]," the correspondent added, "they were very careful to pry open the locks of trunks and tear up the account books and the documents that bound them in debt" (*El Colombiano*, January 22, 1901).

A year later, in February and March 1902, the Liberal guerrillas were threatening Bogotá itself, and the repressive tactics of the government, implemented by Minister of War Aristides Fernández, had reached extremes never before seen in Colombia. Fernández, the illegitimate son of a provincial Conservative, had ascended rapidly through the civil bureaucracy and the police hierarchy during the war. In February he had organized citizens' militias among supporters of the government (today we would call them paramilitaries) to defend the capital. In March, reacting to a proposal for a prisoner exchange made by a guerrilla group operating close to Bogotá, Fernández threatened not only to execute a Liberal officer for each of the government officials being held by the guerrillas, but also to take the life and property of a Liberal in government jails for every Conservative prisoner who lost his life while held by the Liberal insurgents. Fernández's threats were enthusiastically supported by Conservative extremists in the capital, among them students at the elite secondary school San Bartolomé, directed by the Jesuits.

In his campaign to discredit the Liberal revolution and justify his methods of defeating it, on March 14, 1902, Fernández ordered the exhibition, in the main plaza of Bogotá, of what he claimed were the mutilated remains of three victims of guerrilla *macheteros* operating in Cundinamarca. Two days later a huge rally was held in support of Fernández in the same plaza. There he proclaimed that the mission of the government was "that of God, civilization, and the aggrandizement of the Nation." In contrast, he declared, by attacking the Catholic Church, Liberals encouraged the spread of divisive ideas. Liberal propagation of the principle of "absolute leveling" had fostered unhealthy ambitions and encouraged a hatred of superiority, authority, and restrictions. From a political ideal, Liberalism had degenerated into an "endemic disease . . . that corrodes and poisons the social organism." By pursuing a war they had no chance of winning, Fernández went on, Liberals had changed the countryside from a place where the simple patriarchal values of honesty and hard work prevailed to a theater for rape and plunder. The habit of laziness and the yearning for a life of adventure, values inevitably associated with revolution, were spreading throughout the countryside with alarming rapidity. In order to remedy evils of this magnitude, Fernández concluded, palliatives would not do. What was needed was "inexorable repression." Although the Papal Nuncio and the Archbishop of Bogotá beseeched Fernández to withdraw his ultimatum, he refused. Fortunately, three days before his deadline, the Liberal guerrillas freed the Conservative officers (*El Colombiano*, March 18 and March 21, 1902; similar assumptions and language infuse the policy statements of paramilitary groups today, as illustrated in Chapter 6 and the material on paramilitaries in Part 4 of the Documents section).

II

I recount these episodes from the most serious Colombian civil conflict of the last century to highlight their parallels with the current situation. One of the most striking aspects of the War of the Thousand Days is the logic unleashed by its prolongation through guerrilla activity. That logic not only justified the growing abuse, by both sides, of what today we call human rights, but it also contributed to the seemingly inevitable failure of all efforts to end the war through a negotiated reform of the Conservative institutions that had driven the Liberals to revolt.

Throughout the War of the Thousand Days there were repeated efforts by groups of the political elite to achieve a negotiated peace. Usually, these groups proposed certain liberal economic and political reforms as a basis for a peace accord between the government and the revolutionaries. Among the proposed reforms, the most important in the economic sphere was the abolition of the paper money regime. Unbacked paper currency, independent of the international gold standard, was anathema not only to most members of the Liberal Party but to many Conservatives as well because it discouraged capitalist investment, especially the foreign investment on which economic liberals pinned their hopes for the growth and prosperity of the nation. In the political sphere the proposed reforms sought to guarantee the representation of minority parties in elected bodies and protect freedom of expression by prohibiting official censorship of the press. These liberal economic and political reforms animated the coup d'état of July 31, 1900, that brought Marroquín to the presidency. And when Marroquín's government fell under the influence of intransigent Conservatives led by Fernández, these same reformist ideas and the same goal of negotiated peace motivated those who backed the failed coup led by Pedro Nel Ospina in August 1901.

Nevertheless, every effort at reform failed as long as the armed struggle continued. Things only began to change (and, as we shall see, even then not immediately) after the principal revolutionary groups led by Uribe Uribe and Benjamín Herrera on the Caribbean coast and in Panama sued for peace with the government in October and November 1902. The guerrilla groups in the interior of the country, meanwhile, were induced to put down their arms not so much because of the military pressure exerted on them by Fernández (that was the public explanation given by the government), but rather thanks to pragmatic doses of money, a pardon, and promises of government protection (the monetary compensation was offered secretly).

The intransigent Conservative bloc headed by Fernández continued in power for a good while after the revolutionary forces had given up their arms. The government did not declare public order reestablished until June 1, 1903, in that way maintaining its legal capacity to govern by decree. In January of that year, still controlled by Fernández, it promulgated a severe law regulating the press that established punishments for, among many other things, attacks on the "dignity and prerogatives" of civil and ecclesiastical authorities and the legal tender of the nation. It was also a crime "to assume the name of and representation of the people; oppose the legitimate organization of property; incite some social classes against others" (Decree No. 84 of January 26, 1903).

At the beginning of February 1903, Fernández sent a circular to all department governors regarding the important upcoming March elections for departmental assemblies and the national Congress. Fernández reminded them that the government had pardoned the revolutionaries and maintained their political rights. But these magnanimous acts, he went on, "do not in any way exclude social justice, nor do they tend to stifle the sentiments of understandable indignation and universal vindictiveness." It is the body politic, he went on, the citizens themselves, "who should apply this elevated concept of justice, which is not found expressed in artificial formulas [but] resides in the national conscience and should express itself in an explosion of patriotism, denying the vote to those who . . . making use of violence . . . insulted the religious sentiments, heart, and soul of the Colombian people" (Circular No. 151, February 4, 1903). It came as no surprise that under these conditions the electoral returns gave an overwhelming victory to Conservative candidates. Only two Liberals were elected to Congress.

The history of the postwar period reveals how liberal ideas in general, and the specific economic and political reforms the Liberal party championed before the war, gradually won the day in subsequent years. Supported by moderates of both parties, these reforms were incorporated into national legislation and government practice first in the Congress of 1903, then during the five-year government of Rafael Reyes (known as the Quinquenio), and finally in the Constitutional Reform of 1910. These liberal reforms established the institutional foundation for impressive economic growth under bipartisan governments in subsequent decades and fostered the relative peace of Colombian society until almost mid-century.

One can summarize this whole postwar process by saying that once the Liberal insurgents put down their arms, they realized the reforms they had fought for. Losing the war, the Liberals won the peace. This, of course, is not to say that what happened a century ago would repeat itself in the present circumstances. Obviously, today's circumstances are radically different in many respects from those that obtained a century ago. One essential and ironic difference between the two eras is that during the War of the Thousand Days, the revolutionaries saw liberalism as the solution to the great problems faced by Colombia as a nation. Insurgents at the end of the twentieth century, in contrast, view liberalism as the principal cause of those problems.

I believe, however, that the political logic sketched here for the War of the Thousand Days has a certain validity today in spite of these differences. As long as the armed conflict continues, effective reform of national institutions will be difficult, the abuses of human rights by both sides will continue or worsen, and the political line of the government, and especially that of its right-wing supporters, instead of opening up to real reform, is likely to become more intransigent, authoritarian, and reactionary.

III

The key to peace in the War of the Thousand Days was the decision by the Liberal insurgents to lay down their arms. As is the situation today, the insurgents had not been defeated on the battlefield. It may be instructive, therefore, to examine the circumstances that led the Liberals to sue for peace in 1902 and compare them with those facing the leftist guerrillas today.

There were three main considerations in the Liberals' decision to end the War of the Thousand Days. For the Liberal generals in command of regular armies, in particular for Benjamín Herrera, the head of the largest and most important liberal force, which operated in Panama, the central consideration was a growing conviction that the war was unwinnable. Herrera came to understand that expanding the war in Panama would inevitably bring about the intervention of the United States on the Isthmus. Such intervention, he believed, would stymie the Liberal army's efforts to take the war to the mainland of Colombia and severely compromise Colombian interests in the ongoing negotiations between the two countries over the construction and administration of an interoceanic canal. The importance of this factor in the decision by Herrera and his people is underlined by the name of the treaty they negotiated with government representatives to end the war: the Treaty of Wisconsin, signed aboard the U.S. warship of that name.

For Rafael Uribe Uribe, whose small force surrendered on the Caribbean coast a month before Herrera's, another factor weighed more heavily. Uribe Uribe believed that if he were to continue the fight he would have to adopt guerrilla tactics. Like many members of the Colombian elite by this point in the war, Liberals and Conservatives alike, Uribe Uribe was frightened by growing evidence that the social control exercised by elites over the popular classes was threatened by the logic of prolonged guerrilla warfare.

These concerns can be seen in Uribe Uribe's private correspondence and were expressed publicly by another Liberal officer, Celso Román, in a letter published in June 1902 in the pacifist Liberal press in Bogotá. Román was a member of the Liberal elite who, after fighting a good part of the war, had been captured and imprisoned. In fact, he was one of the prisoners placed under threat of execution by Fernández in May 1902. In his letter, Román argued that, as the war progressed, the most noble and valiant soldiers ran the highest risk of being killed. In contrast, those who went to war to enrich themselves were usually cowards and consequently ran less risk of death. Honorable people of all political parties now wanted peace, he claimed;

only those who derived economic benefit or made their living off the war wanted to continue the fighting. Román concluded his letter with a phrase that encapsulated what he felt to be the disturbing tendencies at work during the last stages of the conflict. Appealing to the class interests of traditional leaders of all parties to bring the war to an end, he wrote: "It is advisable that the tempest cease in order that people and things return to occupy the position and level to which, given their background and their conduct, they are suited" (*El Nuevo Tiempo*, June 21, 1902).

The third consideration that influenced the decision by the Liberal revolutionaries to sue for peace has to do with what might be called the "popularity" of the war. This is a complex historical question, but it can be outlined here. Without doubt, elements of liberal ideology—especially the democratic dimensions of its political vision—resonated deeply with certain popular sectors in Colombia during the nineteenth century, artisans being the best documented case in point. But, as many studies of nineteenth-century liberalism have shown, the democratic political potential of liberal ideology was often undermined in practice, while many of the economic reforms of the Liberal party—free trade, in particular—often worked, not to favor the popular classes, but rather elements of the social elite. Moreover, several studies of the Colombian political system have come to the conclusion that, with the partial exception of religious issues, political conflict, especially in the countryside, is better understood as a struggle for personal favors and spoils rather than one of ideological differences between contenders. In any case, from the beginning, popular support for the Liberal revolution of 1899 was less than had been expected by its leaders. And it appears that what enthusiasm there was at the start of the conflict was eroding as the war dragged on and seemed more and more difficult to win.

These observations on the decision by revolutionary Liberal leaders to sue for peace can be summarized as three fears: the fear, as Colombians, of the consequences for the country of U.S. intervention; the fear, as members of the elite class, of losing social control; and the fear, as Liberals, that the revolution lacked sufficient popular support. Looking at the present situation in these terms, the balance sheet appears quite different. Of the three motives that induced the Liberal insurgents to sue for peace in 1902, the second is hardly viewed as a threat by the present-day guerrillas. Quite the contrary: their greatest hope is that the ruling class will lose its influence over the popular classes. Since, as discussed below, that has not happened despite four decades of concerted effort on the part of the Marxist-inspired insurgents, the real threat facing them is the inverse of that confronted by their Liberal counterparts at the end of the last century. Having failed to persuade or induce large numbers of Colombians to support the overthrow of the established social order, the insurgents must now moderate their ideological stance or face ever greater political isolation. In theory, this situation should favor an eventual peace accord based on significant reforms. What better way for the insurgents to demonstrate their ideological moderation and avoid political isolation?

The other two fears also have echoes in the present situation that merit serious reflection. It seems clear (see, in this regard, President Clinton's call for more aid for Colombia in Part 5 of the Documents section) that the United States will attempt to step up the various kinds of intervention it already employs in Colombia, especially should it appear that the government is losing the war. What is not so clear is who, in the long run, would benefit most from such intervention, the government or the insurgency? This question is closely tied to the third consideration—how popular is the insurrection, and how popular might it become? Stepped-up U.S. military aid and training may increase the military capacity of the Colombian government, but it also may work to revitalize the nationalist credentials of an insurgency that has lost most of the limited legitimacy it once enjoyed.

Just as with Liberal ideology and practice in the nineteenth century, it would be difficult to demonstrate widespread popular support for the ideology of the insurgent forces in Colombia today. Even at the start of the contemporary insurgency, the antiliberal, anticapitalist (or, to put it in positive terms, the pro-Marxist, prosocialist) ideological stance of the guerrilla forces had limited appeal for the vast majority of the people. Throughout the twentieth century, in fact, Colombia has had the weakest left of all the major Latin American countries.

In the minds of many leftists, scholars and activists alike, the weakness of the left is explained by the sagacity and repressive nature of the Colombian ruling class. (The statement by guerrilla leaders in Part 2 of the Documents section is a telling illustration of this point of view.) The political monopoly exercised by the two traditional parties, for example, is often attributed to the diabolical formula of the National Front. It eliminated the opportunity for third parties to win political power through electoral means, making armed struggle the only way to achieve a more just society. But the monopoly of the two parties was established a century before the National Front and continues long after it. And the influence of third parties, especially those on the left, has been minimal in Colombia during the entire twentieth century. While important leftist parties and powerful social revolutionary movements appeared in many Latin American countries during this century, in Colombia the two traditional parties, both of them procapitalist, have maintained their hegemony over politics.

The main reason for this, I believe, does not lie in the special skill or repressiveness of the political elite. Colombian political leaders have probably been no more capable and no more repressive than those of other countries. Rather, as I tried to show in *Labor in Latin America*, the reasons for the historical weakness of the left are to be found in the lived experience of the majority of Colombians. Throughout the twentieth century, Colombians experienced, under liberal economic and political institutions, a degree of economic growth and social mobility unmatched in most Latin American countries. In this history, the role of small producers—part reality and part myth—has been of central importance. The experience and influence of small coffee farmers, in particular, helps to explain both the economic dynamism and political conservatism of twentieth-century Colombian history.

The revolutionary insurgents of the 1960s in Colombia, like their middle-class intellectual supporters, tended to equate Colombian history with that of countries such as Cuba, whose economies revolved around industries owned by foreign capitalists and worked by proletarianized labor. If the Colombian economy had come to depend on banana or oil exports, the twentieth-century history of the nation in general, and the fate of leftist third parties in particular, might have been different. (Certainly the historical strength of labor and the left in the banana and oil enclaves, as suggested in Chapter 2 and Part 6 of the Documents section, would appear to support this argument.) But it was coffee, much of it produced by small owner-operators, that became the axis of the modern Colombian economy. And it is the economic, social, political, and cultural ramifications of coffee production, I believe, that largely explain the historical weakness of the Colombian left in the Latin American context.

This traditional weakness of the left—and its own misleading explanation for that weakness—has had grave implications for recent Colombian history and for the peace process today. Blaming extreme ruling-class repression for the weakness of leftist electoral politics has served as the pretext for resorting to violence and force to achieve political power. But just as most Colombians historically denied the left their electoral and ideological support, they have never come to support the left's contemporary armed insurgency. The insurgency grew strong militarily in peripheral areas where the State and mainstream institutions were weak. It has always had limited support in the core areas of the nation where the majority of Colombians live. Moreover, as discussed in greater detail below, the existence of armed insurgency has undermined the limited appeal and organizational strength that leftist labor unions and political parties once enjoyed in Colombia. Guerrilla insurgency has called forth an armed paramilitary right that not only targets the left but human rights and freedom of expression generally. Paramilitary organizations with significant popular support now even threaten the control by the left in peripheral areas long dominated by the guerrillas. Only large-scale intervention by the United States, it would appear, could strengthen popular support for the guerrillas at this stage of the conflict.

The leftist insurgents are thus faced with difficult choices as they enter into peace negotiations with the government today. Like the nineteenth-century Liberal insurgents before them, they must weigh the prospects for the nation and themselves if they continue the fighting. If they prolong or escalate the war, quite apart from the immense suffering continued warfare will inflict on the Colombian people, they will undoubtedly face ever greater levels of U.S. intervention in support of the government and greater paramilitary violence against them. It is possible, as noted above, that U.S. intervention may also confer greater legitimacy on a politics and an insurgency that have never enjoyed much support among the majority of Colombians. On the other hand, demobilization, even if tied to significant reforms, carries its own risks. Given the traditional weakness of the left, how likely is it that the reforms would be implemented and protected in the future? Questions like this one are not easy to answer. But comparison with the era following the War of the Thousand Days suggests some useful ways of thinking about them.

IV

Although the insurgent Liberal forces who laid down their arms in 1902 won no immediate reforms from the Conservative government, within a few short years Liberals saw all the major reforms they had fought for on the battlefield enacted into law and put into practice. What made this paradoxical outcome possible? Liberals won the peace in large part because, even before the war, and with growing intensity during and after it, a broad, moderate cross section of the Colombian political elite supported the reforms the Liberal revolutionaries advocated. The growing consensus on the need for reform was part of a widely shared perception, not only in Colombia but around the globe, that liberalism was the "wave of the future." By the end of the nineteenth century, the Nationalist Conservative regime that had come to power in Colombia during the crisis of Liberalism and the economy in the 1880s was an anomaly in world politics. Its illiberal economic policies, in particular, fought against the tide of orthodox liberal economics in the world. Liberals won the peace in Colombia, in other words, because liberal reformers believed, and convinced others, that they had history on their side.

Today, it would seem that the situation confronting the leftist insurgents is the inverse of that facing the Liberal revolutionaries a century ago. It is the insurgency, not the government, that appears to be swimming against the tide of world history. The socialist vision that inspired the Marxist insurgency in Colombia forty years ago is in total disarray following the collapse of the Soviet bloc. Neo-liberalism, not Marxism, appears as the order of the day. The Marxist insurgents in Colombia never succeeded in winning the support of a large cross section of society, and what legitimacy they once had has eroded rapidly over the last years.

It is true that the territorial reach and military strength of today's guerrilla groups as they enter into peace negotiations with the government are probably relatively greater than those of their early-twentieth-century Liberal counterparts. Certainly their capacity to sabotage the economy and discourage productive investment is beyond dispute. But if today's insurgents are stronger militarily than were the Liberal revolutionaries a century ago, they are much weaker politically and ideologically. And their prospects for winning the peace were they to lay down their arms appear doubtful, which may explain why the insurgents insist on waging war while negotiating peace, why they seek major reforms before agreeing to an armistice.

Nevertheless, the leftist insurgents must understand that, without widespread public support for any reforms won at the negotiating table, and without a strong political movement to ensure the implementation of such reforms in the democratic polity they say they support following peace, victory in the negotiations will prove Pyrrhic. The reforms they win may look good on paper, but like the Constitutional Reform of 1991 (see Chapter 3), in practice they will be limited or even reversed.

Unfortunately, as argued in Chapter 8, the insurgency itself has greatly undermined the possibility of creating such a political movement, at least in the short term. The guerrillas' use of tactics such as extortion, kidnapping, and terror brought forth a ruthless paramilitary right that, as noted previously, is now contending for control of some of the rural areas long dominated by the guerrillas. By pursuing a dual strategy of armed insurrection and democratic electoral politics, the left exposed thousands of dedicated grassroots leaders of civic organizations, labor unions, and alternative political parties such as the Unión Patriótica to assassination and intimidation by the right. Until the insurgents sue for peace and agree to disarm themselves or to integrate themselves into the armed forces, it is difficult to see how the paramilitary right can be dismantled. Without peace, it will be impossible to create an environment that favors the development of organizations and parties that can sustain and advance the democratization of Colombian society in the future.

Continuation of the armed insurgency, on the other hand, promises to make a bad situation worse. As noted above, it will most certainly bring increased intervention by the United States to shore up the Colombian government, ever greater militarization and polarization of Colombian society, and perhaps even the dissolution or dismemberment of the nation itself.

The future looks much brighter for all concerned if demobilization of the insurgency can be achieved through the negotiation of significant reforms. And the prospects for realizing and implementing such reforms are better than they may appear at first glance. This is true first, because one interpretation of the platform advocated by the insurgents since the start of the 1990s (see Part 4 of the Documents section) is that many of its goals may be met without the enactment of such radical reforms after all. That platform has been interpreted in recent pronouncements and gestures by the FARC as envisioning a society that resembles a kind of European-style social democracy more than it does a Soviet-style regime. Second, it is important to stress that the reforms realized in the Constitution of 1991 (see Chapter 3 and Part 1 of the Documents section) already constitute a significant democratization of Colombian political institutions. What continues to be lacking is a strong democratic movement and parties able to take advantage of this opening.

Third, the prospects for significant agrarian reform—the sine qua non of the FARC's historical struggle—would appear today to be much better than in the past. The nation is now overwhelmingly urban, which means that the scope of agricultural reform needs to be less extensive and therefore less central to both large landowners and workers than it would have had to have been a few decades ago. Moreover, in recent years there has emerged a broad multiclass consensus in favor of significant agrarian reform, such that even associations of large landowners have felt compelled to declare themselves in favor of reform. There are also significant existing and potential means to effect such reform. The expropriation of property bought with the illicit gains of drug trafficking is already under way. Another potential source that could be broadened to wider purpose is U.S. support for crop substitution by smallholders in areas of coca and poppy production. Cooperation between the FARC and the U.S. government on crop substitution is not an impossibility; under the aegis of FARC, and with ample U.S. funding, such a program could have considerable success. Programs for crop substitution and wider agrarian reform could also win support from the European Union.

A broad consensus also probably exists now within Colombia on the need to recapture more national control over petroleum policy, the central historical demand of the ELN (see the ELN's position in Part 4 of the Documents section). In this case, however, the market power of the multinational oil companies, and their control over investment decisions, may limit the effective reach of any reforms. Still, the importance attributed to national energy policy by the ELN, and its concrete proposals for advancing on this front, will resonate broadly within Colombia and could be the basis for meaningful reforms.

More generally, there is the vital question of whether the modification of neo-liberal economic policies advocated by the insurgents points in the direction of future worldwide trends. Or whether, on the contrary, as liberal apologists liked to put it a few years ago, the end of the Cold War signaled the end of history as we have known it, the unmitigated triumph of the liberal ideal. How the whole world moves on this larger question will determine in large part the fate of reforms in Colombia designed to foster the redistribution of wealth and power and curb the extremes of neo-liberal economic policies such as free trade and the privatization of public services. There is already widespread popular support in Colombia and many other nations for a reform of neo-liberal economic policy. And following the protests in Seattle in November and December 1999, there is even some cause for optimism on that score within the United States itself (see the material on U.S. labor in Part 6 of the Documents section).

On balance, I think it is reasonable to predict that, at a minimum, the extremes of doctrinaire liberal policy that accompanied the end of the Cold War will not be the order of the day in coming years. In fact, the eclipse of Communism on a world scale will undoubtedly favor the fortunes of democratic electoral reform politics in all capitalist countries. It is now harder to accuse reformers of being pawns in the totalitarian and expansionist designs of a worldwide Communist conspiracy.

For all these reasons, the prospects for achieving a lasting negotiated peace through significant reform in Colombia are better than may be generally appreciated. The greatest obstacle to initiating that process, as distinguished Colombian thinkers have eloquently argued for a long time now (see Chapter 1 and Part 2 of the Documents section), is the insurgency itself.

V

That said, there remains the question of the role of the United States in the Colombian conflict and the issue of how U.S. citizens can contribute to achieving peace. As indicated throughout this volume, the demand for narcotics in the United States and the government's policy of criminalizing their use have contributed in great measure to the escalation of violence in Colombia in recent years. Before the 1990s, as noted in the Preface to this volume, Colombian studies of the violence customarily focused on its internal and historical causes, rather than emphasizing the central role of the drug trade. Today, in contrast, the drug trade has escalated to the point that virtually no aspect of the crisis facing the nation is "drug free" (see the introduction to Part 7 of the Documents section).

Despite or because of ever more costly U.S. efforts to repress consumption, eradicate production, and interdict drug commerce, the magnitude of the drug trade continues to increase and its impact on Colombian society to escalate. From virtually every perspective, U.S. drug policy is a failure. In the United States, criminalization of narcotics has dramatically expanded the prison population, its primary targets being petty traffickers drawn disproportionately from the nonwhite underclass. In Colombia, it has brought powerful criminal organizations into direct confrontation with the State over the issue of extradition, corrupting the political process and leaving honest officials and innocent civilians at the mercy of mafia hit men and indiscriminate bombings. Eradication has inflicted incalculable damage on the Colombian ecosystem and the country's famed biodiversity while destroying the livelihood of thousands of small producers and driving them into the arms of the Marxist-led guerrillas whom U.S. policy also opposes. Yet despite the expenditure of billions of U.S. taxpayers' dollars on these programs and a massive effort to interdict the flow of drugs, this policy has reduced neither consumption nor production.

U.S. persistence in this failed policy of drug criminalization and repression seems difficult to comprehend. It is all the more surprising because, as drug policymakers are well aware, similar policies, employed with similar effect against alcohol during Prohibition, were eventually recognized as a failure and alternative methods were adopted to control its use (see the final piece in Part 7 of the Documents section). It is also recognized by many medical specialists that alcohol consumption is more, not less, destructive to most individual users and to society as a whole than the consumption of cocaine, Colombia's largest illegal drug export. A May 1998 *Harper's Magazine* Index tried to drive this last point home to readers by comparing the percentage of violent offenders in state prisons whose crime was committed under the influence of alcohol alone (21) with the percentage whose crime was committed under the influence of crack or cocaine alone (3).

One marvels at the kind of education and treatment programs at home, and crop-substitution programs abroad, that could be mounted with the U.S. government funds now expended on drug repression. Were narcotics legalized, controlled, and taxed just as alcohol and tobacco are, the resources available for such programs would be magnified. Revenue from a legalized drug trade could also go a long way toward strengthening the Colombian State, whose dispensation of justice and ability to provide education, health, and other social services, especially in remote rural areas, are notoriously weak, as several of the chapters in this volume make clear.

Were U.S. drug policy primarily concerned with drugs, one would think evidence and arguments such as these would have an effect and lead to fundamental change. Instead, what we get is more and more of the same. Unless one believes that U.S. policymakers are stupid or irrational—a view I do not share—the explanation for continuing and escalating the existing approach to drugs must lie elsewhere. A provocative case can be made that U.S. drug policy contributes effectively to the control of an ethnically distinct and economically deprived underclass at home and serves U.S. economic and security interests abroad.

Certainly, Colombia has been of great strategic importance to U.S. policymakers since the time of the canal treaty negotiations during the War of the Thousand Days. When the treaty negotiated between the two nations was rejected unanimously by the Colombian Senate in 1903, the United States backed the secession of Panama from Colombia. Then, following the building of the canal, the United States installed in Panama a complex of military bases to defend it and project U.S. military power throughout the region. The return of control of the canal to Panama and the abandonment of those bases at the turn of the twentieth century raises the strategic importance of Colombia to U.S. policy to a new high today. Colombia not only sits astride the two oceans next to Panama and close to the canal, but it also offers the best alternative route for a new, sea-level canal able to handle the supertankers and military ships that can no longer fit through the old one.

Petroleum must also be factored into the calculus of the U.S. economic and security concerns bearing on Colombia. As both U.S. consumption of oil and dependence on foreign suppliers have continued to grow, the government in Washington has sought to diversify its sources of supply and reduce its dependence on petroleum from the volatile Middle East. U.S. interests have long viewed Colombia as an important potential oil producer.

In fact, settlement of the Panama secession issue, including payment of a U.S. indemnity to Bogotá in the early 1920s, was predicated in part on the promise of increased investment in oil production by U.S. companies. Today, Colombia continues to figure as an important potential oil producer and U.S. supplier. And in the eyes of Washington policymakers, a stable, friendly Colombia is also important to the security of its neighbor Venezuela, the United States' primary New World supplier of petroleum.

For these and other reasons, U.S. drug policy is much more than it seems. And, given the larger issues it serves, it will not be easily changed. Nevertheless, legalization, control, and taxation of narcotics would ameliorate the domestic U.S. drug problem and greatly reduce the violence facing Colombia. For both reasons, changing the current policy should be a high priority for U.S. citizens. Until current drug policy is fundamentally changed, they can work to reduce its negative effects. They can oppose ever greater doses of military aid to Colombia (see the response to President Clinton's call for more aid in Part 5 of the Documents section) and lobby for a drug policy that places far more emphasis on crop substitution in Colombia and reduction of demand in the United States.

The other main avenue for effective action abroad against the continuing violence in Colombia is international human rights work (as advocated in Chapter 5 and elaborated in Part 3 of the Documents section). Historically, many defenders of human rights, both in Colombia and abroad, have seen the problem primarily as one of abuses by governments and their right-wing paramilitary allies. In dealing with the Colombian violence, many ignored or downplayed the human rights violations of leftist guerrillas. They did so despite the fact that for many years Colombian guerrillas have funded their activities in good measure through a fundamental violation of the human rights of their victims: kidnapping. These human rights organizations adopted what was in effect a pro-guerrilla political stance. And by making human rights protection a partisan affair, they not only discredited it in the eyes of many, but they also brought down the full fury of the violent right against human rights workers and organizations. But perhaps the most devastating effect of their selective defense of human rights was, ironically, to embolden and legitimate the paramilitaries who claim to protect people whose human rights have been violated by the guerrillas and who are not effectively protected by the State.

Today, fortunately, all this is changing, and human rights organizations are doing a better job of denouncing abuses from all quarters. This stance is not only evenhanded and honest, but it also best protects the integrity of the principle of the inviolability of basic human rights and the safety of those who work to make it a reality. And instead of encouraging the guerrillas who routinely violate human rights, it delegitimizes and weakens them, thereby making the possibility of serious negotiations more likely.

VI

Readers of the essays in this volume will have no illusions about the difficulties involved in reducing the current level of violence in Colombia. There is no doubt, however, that the single most important step in that direction is to end the guerrilla insurgency through a negotiated settlement based on meaningful social and economic reform. The vast majority of Colombians seem to understand this; and for some time, in increasing numbers and in all kinds of forums, they have been beseeching the armed contenders to accomplish just that (see Part 8 of the Documents section). At tremendous cost, forty years of armed struggle may have helped to place the question of fundamental reform on the table, but only peaceful political engagement by the majority of Colombians can make democratic reform an enduring reality.

Documents

PART 1 • ASPECTS OF THE CONSTITUTION OF 1991

As noted in Chapter 3, the Constitution of 1991 is a long and complicated document containing a panoply of reforms, many of them designed to protect basic human rights and democratize the Colombian political system. The few articles presented here are only a sampling of those reforms. Spanish readers interested in the Constitution as a whole, and commentary on each of its 380 articles (and 60 transitory articles), can consult Alfredo Manrique Reyes, *La Constitución de la Nueva Colombia: Con comenatarios y concordancias* (Bogotá, 1991).

Article 11. The right to life is inviolate. There will be no death penalty.

Article 12. No one will be forcefully disappeared, subjected to torture, or made to suffer cruel, inhumane, or degrading treatment or punishment.

Article 13. All people are born free and equal before the law, must receive the same protections and treatment from the authorities, and must enjoy the same rights, liberties, and opportunities with no discrimination for reasons of sex, race, national or family origin, language, religion, political or philosophical belief.

The State will see to it that equality is real and effective and will adopt measures to favor groups that are discriminated against or marginalized. . . .

Article 22. Peace is a right and a duty that must be complied with.

Article 86. Every person has the right to *acción de tutela* in order to demand in the courts . . . immediate protection of his or her fundamental constitutional rights whenever these are violated or threatened by action or lack thereof by any public authority.

Article 103. In exercising their sovereignty and right to participate in governance, the people have recourse to the following mechanisms: the vote, the plebiscite, the referendum, popular consultations, the town meeting, the legislative initiative, and the recall of public officials. . . .

Article 171. The Senate of the Republic will be composed of 100 members elected in national balloting.

Two additional senators will be elected in national balloting by indigenous communities.

Article 260. Citizens directly elect the President and Vice-President of the Republic, Senators, Representatives, Governors, Deputies, Mayors, City and District Council Members. . . .

PART 2 • COLOMBIAN INTELLECTUALS AND THE GUERRILLAS

THE LETTER OF THE INTELLECTUALS

In November 1992 a distinguished group of Colombian intellectuals (writers, artists, journalists, lawyers, and academics) published the following open letter addressed to the umbrella group (Coordinadora Guerrillera Simón Bolívar) of the Marxist-inspired guerrilla movements operating in the country. The intellectuals argued that armed struggle was no longer relevant and that in continuing the war, the revolutionaries were betraying their original ideals and bringing unmitigated disaster to the nation. Many of the signatories had originally sympathized with the guerrillas, believing that armed struggle, as the Cuban example seemed to show, was a viable path to socialism. The Nobel Prize-wining novelist, Gabriel García Márquez, to give one example, was a close friend of Fidel Castro and an active supporter of his regime in Cuba. Nicolás Buenaventura, for another, was a long-time member and activist in the Colombian Communist party. The publication of this document thus marked an important turning point in public opinion; henceforth, the guerrillas would be deprived of some of their most influential supporters. The document was published in the leading newspaper, *El Tiempo*, on November 22, 1992.

Santa Fé de Bogotá
November 20, 1992
Señores, Coordinadora Guerrillera Simón Bolívar

As convinced democrats, opposed to violence and to authoritarian solutions, we believe we have a moral right to question the legitimacy and efficacy of the actions you have been pursuing for several years now.

Given current conditions, we are against that form of struggle. We think that instead of leading to greater social justice, as might have been the case at the start, it is engendering all manner of extremism, the resurgence of reactionary forces, paramilitary depredations, merciless common crime, and the excesses of elements of the armed forces, which we condemn with equal energy.

We do not believe that you express the free will of the people. On the contrary, your actions have fostered a climate of political and ideological confusion that has turned Colombia into a battlefield where the most common form of freedom of expression is recourse to arms. Such a situation cannot lead us toward our common dream of a democratic, happy society.

Your war, understandable in the beginning, now goes against the tide of history. Kidnapping, coercion, forced contributions, which are today your most effective instruments, are all abominable violations of human rights.

Terrorism, which you yourselves always condemned as an illegitimate form of revolutionary struggle, is today a daily resource. Corruption, which you decried, has contaminated your own organizations through your dealings with drug traffickers. You ignore the drug traffickers' reactionary nature and the way they contribute to social decay. The uncounted, useless deaths on both sides of the struggle, the systematic attacks on our national wealth, the ecological disasters are all very costly and undeserved tributes exacted from a country that has already paid too much.

It is time for profound patriotic reflection, time for a radical rectification of years of mistakes, time for a serious search for new and novel forms of political creativity appropriate to the realities of the world today. Your war, gentlemen, lost its historical relevance some time ago. Recognizing that fact in good faith will also be a political victory.

Antonio Caballero, journalist
Gabriel García Márquez, writer
Nicolás Buenaventura, historian
Fernando Botero, artist
Eduardo Pizarro, sociologist
Apolinar Días Callejas, lawyer
Enrique Santos Calderón, journalist
Roberto Sáenz, professor
María Jimena Duzán, journalist
Hernando Corral, journalist
Socorro Ramírez, internationalist
Carlos Vicente de Roux, lawyer
Daniel Samper, journalist
Luis Alberto Restrepo, philosopher
Pilar Gaitán, political scientist
Salomón Kalmanovitz, economist
Alejandro Reyes, sociologist
Fernando Cano, journalist
Rubén Sánchez, political scientist
Juan Antonio Roda, artist
Nora Segura, sociologist
Hernando Valencia Villa, lawyer
Alvaro Guzmán, sociologist
Gonzalo Sánchez, historian
María Emma Wills, political scientist
Iván Orozco, lawyer
José Antonio Ocampo, economist
Jaime Garzón, comedian

María Teresa Garcés, ex-delegate,
Constitutional Convention
Hermes Tovar, historian
Myriam Bautista, journalist
Eduardo Lora, economist
Marison Cano, journalist
Doris Salcedo, sculptress
Elisabeth Ungar, political scientist
Elssy Bonilla, sociologist
Poly Martínez, journalist
Ricardo Camacho, theater director
Fernán González, historian/priest
Jorge Restrepo, journalist
Claudia Steiner, researcher
Santiago Pombo, editor
Mariana Serrano, political scientist
Javier Guerrero, historian
[More signatures follow]

The Guerrillas' Reply

Ten days after the publication of the intellectuals' letter the Coordinadora Guerrillera Simón Bolívar (CGSB) responded. The Coordinadora's letter was sent to major Colombian papers, but only the newspaper of the Colombian Communist party, *Voz*, published it in its entirety. The guerrilla leaders argued that armed insurrection was a path imposed on the Colombian people by an Establishment that historically had systematically terrorized and sought to eliminate all political opposition.

Mountains of Colombia
December 2, 1992
Señores Antonio Caballero, Gabriel García Márquez, Nicolás Buenaventura, Fernando Botero and the other signatories of the letter:

We send our greetings and thank you for your important observations on the insurgency in Colombia. We also want to share with you some reflections that we hope will be useful to you.

It is important to stress that the revolutionary guerrilla struggle in Colombia was born, developed, and continues to grow as a popular response to the permanent violence of the State, which opposes, through bloodshed and armed force, the existence of real opposition to the Establishment. Armed struggle has thus not been an end or an objective. It has simply been a means of resisting aggression and fighting for dignity and democracy.

The violence of the Colombian State against its opponents is as old as the Republic itself. The 63 civil wars we suffered through since the founding of the Republic are evidence of a culture of intolerance, imposed from the highest ranks of power. The powerful, furthermore, have developed assassination into a customary practice, which they use to annul different ideas about the management of the State. The attempts against the lives of the Liberator, Simón Bolívar, Marshal Antonio José de Sucre, Rafael Uribe Uribe, Jorge Eliécer Gaitán, Jaime Pardo Leal, Bernardo Jaramillo, Luis Carlos Galán, to cite only the most significant, fill the pages of our history with shame.

The truth is that long before the revolutionary guerrilla insurgency began, the practice of "dirty war," employed with virtual impunity, was widespread. *Pájaros*, paramilitaries, and State intelligence services are the principal protagonists in the long history of terror our fatherland has lived through. This is a history characterized at times by selective assassination, at others by massacres, and at all times by torture, disappearances, authoritarianism, and collective intimidation. As a consequence, many compatriots have had to choose exile as the only way to protect their physical and moral integrity.

It must be said that if certain practices and concepts have lost their historical relevance, they are, precisely, those relating to State terrorism. Terrorism by the State avails itself of the institutions of government to assassinate and systematically "disappear" the opposition. It thus makes despotism into the natural way of exercising power. In Colombia, to our misfortune, the Doctrine of National Security still holds sway, despite the march of history and the end of the Cold War. Under the guise of laws of the Republic, that Doctrine seeks to lend official sanction to a politics of hatred and endless retaliations.

The great problems of the nation revolve around this official intolerance, around the anti-people policies of economic and social development imposed by the International Monetary Fund, and around the incapacity and incompetence of the national administration itself. To place the burden of the long-term ills of our society on the shoulders of the CGSB is simply not serious analysis.

The CGSB remains committed to participating actively in the search for a political solution to the crisis. We are more than willing to participate. We regret the government's calls for "integral war." We call instead for "integral solutions" and a lasting peace. We call for peace accords that, without forcing a single Colombian to get on his or her knees, seek to fulfill the hope for democratic community and social justice. We call for a peace process that does not maim the dignity of our people, that leaves behind the fantasy of imposing a settlement. We think always of the future of Colombia and not in terms of individual or partisan interests.

The historical moment we are living through demands the active participation of everyone, particularly you. "Convinced democrats, opposed to violence and to authoritarian solutions," it is you who, from your newspapers, magazines, university chairs, and public forums, can contribute to moderating a climate charged with aggressiveness. The government must be persuaded to abandon its insolent and quarrelsome language, which hurts it more than it hurts those whom it seeks to disqualify. The government must be made to understand that press censorship, under whatever guise, only reveals the weakness of those who feel they are defenders of lost causes. These government practices serve only to intensify the polarization of our long-suffering fatherland.

The CGSB rejects and condemns drug trafficking. You must not let yourselves be deceived by a plan, put together by the U.S. Embassy, the Presidency of the Republic, State intelligence services, and a pair of Bogotá publications, that seeks to detract from our commitment to the most noble causes in Colombia. The phenomenon of the drug trade has social, economic, political, moral, and ethical dimensions that all of us must work to resolve. The starting point is the abandonment by the government of its hypocritical policies, which made all manner of concessions in order to expand its international reserves by more than six billion dollars and opened the door to huge investments of narco-dollars.

We who travel through this country daily, moving on foot, conversing with the people in the countryside and the cities, know what we represent for this great mass of Colombians. These people receive nothing from the State but aggression and promises, and are never consulted by the directors of official polls. We know about the great longing for peace that is seizing the nation. That is the peace we fight for, the peace that is our goal. But, as we said in Mexico, peace is much more than the absence of confrontation between the Government and the insurgency: it is democracy, it is sovereignty, it is social justice. Those concepts do not fit into the heads of those who designed the failed Strategy against Violence and that is what has impeded advancing in a serious way toward peace.

Following through on our understanding of the peace process, we put forth twelve proposals for constructing a strategy for peace. We did so so that we all could analyze them, so that between us all we could agree on the paths to make a New Colombia a reality. And we have indicated that we are ready to work on the construction of a Bolivarian movement, profoundly Latinamericanist and patriotic, and based on the most precious democratic traditions of our history. But the Government, in its profound arrogance, has closed off the possibility of political solutions. And it has erred in its strategy of seeking to detract from the value and merit of the revolutionaries' struggle. Being a revolutionary means abandoning all that we hold most dear: it means exchanging the daily routine of home for the uncertain fate of the battlefield, it means leaving behind personal resources and giving oneself wholly to the cause of all. It means, finally, ennobling politics because the personal whims and individual gain that are the hallmarks of politics these days are abandoned in favor of giving one's all to the ideal of a just and sovereign fatherland.

The government considers the present moment to be one of total war and it legislates by decree against popular movements, against industrialists, bankers, foreign companies, journalists, the media, popularly elected mayors and governors—all in the name of the strange conception it has of what a new country and national unity consists of. It has begun a virtual witch-hunt, with concentration camps included, as during the worst epochs of our country's history.

The CGSB believes, in contrast, that it is time to search for accords so that the civil population will not be affected by the confrontation, so that human rights are protected. We seek accords that guarantee the well-being of defenseless combatants who fall into the hands of their adversaries.

The CGSB looks with sympathy on the alternatives proposed by different groups around the country as ways of avoiding the escalation of the conflict into full-scale war. Especially important in this regard are those initiatives that propose national and international mediation as a way of guaranteeing that the rules of the game agreed upon are complied with, and that the agreements entered into are enforced. We also look with favor on those proposals that seek ways to involve the whole of society in the negotiating process.

The forms of struggle that the Colombian people have chosen to achieve a dignified future have not been freely elected. These forms have been imposed on them. The people have not been given an option. We must all work to create an environment that makes us a part of a situation in which the use of arms is only a bad memory from our troubled past.

Again, we appreciate your interest and your letter, and we hope you will continue in your peace endeavors. All of us, surely, will together be able to create the necessary conditions to close off the paths to war.

Sincerely,

Compatriots, Coordinadora Guerrillera Simón Bolívar

Manuel Marulanda V., Alfonso Cano, Raúl Reyes, Timoleón Jiménez, Iván Márquez, Manuel Pérez Martínez, Nicolás Martínez Bautista, Pablo Tejada, Francisco Galán, Milton Hernández, Francisco Caraballo, Diego Ruíz

A Response to the Guerrillas

On December 22, 1992, Gonzalo Sánchez, one of the authors of the intellectuals' original letter, wrote the following commentary on the guerrillas' response. Published in the left-liberal Bogotá daily *El Espectador*, his article sought to emphasize what he felt were positive aspects of the guerrillas' response, but he also elaborated on many of the intellectuals' original criticisms.

The differences between the intellectuals and the guerrillas outlined in this exchange continue to divide Colombians, particularly those on the left, to this day. Nevertheless, it is fair to say that in the years since the exchange, the guerrillas have lost much of the moral high ground and the support they once enjoyed among a broad sector of Colombians, especially professors and students at the nation's universities.

The reasons for the decline in support for the guerrillas outside the areas they actually control are many, and most are discussed in some detail in the essays in this book. Suffice it to say here that the guerrillas have lost much public support not so much because of what the intellectuals say about them, but because of what they do. Few Colombians condone kidnapping, for example, and many others are aghast at the economic and ecological impact of systematic destruction of the nation's oil pipelines. These, and other criticisms, are developed in Sánchez's commentary, which also includes an eloquent plea for a negotiated peace based on important reforms.

One must applaud the very fact that the Coordinadora Guerrillera has responded to the letter of the intellectuals and one must not fail to notice the tone adopted in their letter. In the first place, because their reply was not the boastful response, laced with bravura, that many predicted or feared. In the second place, because of the important fact that the reply contains political propositions, which is a relief, given the heated climate of war that preceded and surrounded it. It is a shame that the press has not made the reply widely known, since, in the present situation, it constitutes in reality a kind of opening to dialogue and debate, not so much with the intellectuals to whom the message was sent but with, especially, the whole of Colombian society.

An initial effort at coming to terms with the Coordinadora's reply might distinguish two sets of features. In the first set one could make an inventory of its positive aspects, which would primarily include the following points:

1. The commitment to search for a political solution to the crisis and the acceptance of national and international mediation to guarantee compliance with eventual accords.

2. Recognition of the need to adopt measures to humanize the war (meaning limits on acts of barbarism between the forces in combat), protect noncombatants, and respect human rights.

3. The emphasis on the instrumental character of armed struggle, expressed in a language that goes much further than many of the guerrillas' most exalted sympathizers would accept. "Armed struggle," the guerrillas affirm, "has simply been a means of resisting oppression and of fighting for democracy and dignity." That leaves open the possibility that in principle other means can be tried, not in combined but definitive form, to realize the same goals. All this, of course, on the condition that the State fulfill its own commitments. "We must all work to create," says the Coordinadora's document, "an environment that makes us participants in a situation in which the use of arms is only a bad memory from our troubled past."

These three points, taken separately, may not be new, but to find them reaffirmed in a text that puts them together and makes them interdependent gives them new meaning and significance. Moreover, and this is the point I wish to insist upon, the urgency of making these positions more fully and widely known derives not only from their intrinsic importance but also from the fact that they comprise a public commitment by the guerrillas, one on which society can call them to account at the appropriate moment. That is, one must take these points not only as a gesture, but also as a commitment that can be verified.

The second inventory that could be made concerns the silences and inconsistencies of the document.

There are revealing silences, especially, on three points. There is a silence about kidnapping, which may have begun as a simple operation of expropriation and financing, that is, of action against property, but has been converted deliberately into transgressions against the lives of hostages and defenseless victims.

There is silence regarding the attacks on oil pipelines, which, more than being operations of economic sabotage, are attacks on the environment, whose costs the whole society pays. More: these acts often constitute direct or indirect attacks on the lives of humble settlers, and their long-term effects may even be considered a form of deferred collective assassination of nearby population centers.

And there is silence on terrorism, a tactic that seemed to be the exclusive domain of the drug mafia and which ignores the fact that those who are besieged by terror are not so much the State but, as the journalist María Teresa Herrán has pointed out, "anonymous Colombians." As Lenin said, in texts that ceased to be read and practiced before they were buried by the Berlin Wall, terrorism is the recourse of "those who do not know how to link or have no possibility of linking revolutionary work with the labor movement into a whole. For those who have completely lost faith in this possibility, or have never had it, it is really difficult to find an outlet for their sense of indignation and their revolutionary fervor other than terror" (the citation is from Lenin's "What Is to Be Done?" available in any edition of his collected works).

Trotsky, for his part, in a 1909 text considers terror not only ineffective against the social system, but counterproductive. And he enunciates the following tendency: "The more *effective* terrorist acts are, the greater their impact; the more mass action is focused on them, the less interest the masses have in organizing and educating themselves." Terrorism is, in effect, a manifestation of spontaneity and impotence. It does not contribute to advancing the causes it invokes and it does not earn points at an eventual negotiating table.

These are all, of course, points that preoccupy those who are searching for a political solution to the conflict. It is possible to think that these silences reflect differences of opinion within the Coordinadora or a clear understanding that they are indeed indefensible, but in any case these practices are in flagrant contradiction to the invocations of respect for human rights and the need to humanize the war found in the document.

In summary, the optimism occasioned by the first inventory is diminished by the second: The revolutionary goals declared in the document are contradicted by practices disqualified by the whole of revolutionary tradition.

On the other hand, while the Coordinadora sketches an explication of the rise of narcotrafficking, it does not convincingly delimit its own relationship with that phenomenon. On this point, given the coincidence of guerrilla and narcoterrorist offensives, it is difficult to avoid the idea that there is a certain structural complicity between these two wars, both in their practices and their effects on the whole political system.

One perceives as well a clear aversion to acknowledging or weighing the implications of a military offensive at the moment when the fragile spaces opened up by the new Constitution are in an embryonic process of development. To tell the truth, there is a lot of posturing and little hard thinking on this issue on both sides.

Finally, the Coordinadora's document contains an extensive disquisition on the origins of armed conflict in the country, which the signatories of the letter of the intellectuals might, in general terms, share. But that should not be an argument to perpetuate this state of affairs, as in fact parts of the reply of the guerrilla chiefs, quoted above, recognize. If these things were put forward on other terrain, the points of convergence would multiply; many voices and pens would join in a struggle by other means against social inequality, against torture, against all forms of humiliation and degradation of human beings (including prisoners of war), against the primitive impulses of vengeance that are increasing, against the aberrant use of the judicial apparatus, such as paying for information, which can disguise a kind of "sicarianization" of justice.

What the nation, the whole society, can no longer tolerate are trials of strength between the State and the guerrillas before they return for the nth time to the negotiating table. The nation does not retract from one side in order to add to the other. The nation can absorb no more demonstrations of superiority by those at war. What the nation expects is that they put their cards on the negotiating table once more.

Gonzalo Sánchez G., Professor
Institute of Political Studies
National University of Colombia

A Letter from the ELN to "Progressive" Academics

The writers, artists, academics, and professionals referred to by Colombians (and Latin Americans in general) as intellectuals probably play a larger and more influential role in national political life than do their counterparts in the United States. The previous documents in this section reveal, for example, how interpretations of the nation's history, in particular, are often used to justify contemporary armed insurrection as well as opposition to it. Academics in Colombia continue to be considered important potential allies by elements of the guerrillas, as illustrated in the following undated letter sent to certain "progressive" university professors in mid-1999 by an "Urban Front" of the ELN. The letter discusses the issue of different and competing understandings of history and society, and notes some positive dimensions of academic investigation and debate. It insists, however, that the analysis developed by the ELN is based on ethics, revolutionary humanism, and "a scientific understanding of society," thus making it difficult to see how alternative interpretations, no matter how well documented or persuasively argued, could modify their own understanding.

The centrality of academics in the current violence in Colombia is also revealed in the growing incidence of assassination attempts against them. Academics in Medellín and other cities outside Bogotá have often been targets in the past. In late 1999 this kind of violence hit Bogotá when two university professors well known for their studies of Colombian history and violence, Darío Betancourt and Jesús Antonio Bejarano, were killed, and another, Eduardo Pizarro, a contributor to *Violence in Colombia* (1992), was seriously wounded. At this point, although theories abound and many in the academic community suspect the paramilitary right, no one knows for certain who was behind these acts.

Dear Professor:

Many are the changes that have occurred in the history of this century. Many ideas, points of view, and proposals have been put on the table in order to analyze and guide society. Nevertheless, the incessant movement of history, with its multitude of perspectives that apparently come from all the social sectors, are not yet sufficiently convincing in either concrete or argumentative terms to make us desist from our highest projects and ways of acting. The justification of the type of political and military action that we have been employing is based on a scientific understanding of society, an ethical stance, and the permanent search for a social organization based on a Revolutionary Humanism that enables us to identify the root causes and the particularities that impede men and women of this "nation" from achieving ever higher states of well-being and happiness.

The Army of National Liberation thus considers that intellectual work and research are of the greatest importance. The critical academy, questioning, proactive, alert to injustice, authoritarianism, repression, and exploitation, is for us of transcendental importance; it is a vital base for defining and carrying out both long- and short-range goals.

Consequently, we believe that there is a need to establish links with intellectuals like you who have adopted, in their own workplace, a critical, progressive, and autonomous position vis-à-vis the Establishment and the powers that control our fatherland, and who, at the same time, have demonstrated a constant concern over the issues that affect the popular classes.

Our hope in establishing a relationship with you is that you will accept published material from our Insurgent Organization so as to be fully informed, in the most up-to-date manner possible, of our thinking, theses, positions, and programs. We hope that the corrupt and fraudulent information put out on us by the media, government agencies, the army, the economic interest groups, and certain badly named "intellectuals" will not continue to make headway; it circulates freely because of the lack of knowledge about our project, practices, actions, methods, principles, and values.

We also want to tell you that the Army of National Liberation will always be open to anyone who wishes to undertake discussions of the different problems that weigh on our fatherland and point out how they might be overcome. The same invitation goes, of course, to those who wish to criticize our Organization. We are in the midst of proposing and effecting a structural change in our society that will place us on a path to build a just, popular, democratic, and fully revolutionary and fraternal Colombia.

We thank you in advance for your receptivity to this kind of relationship, which implies no commitment on your part, but does permit us to establish fruitful relations between two actors who find themselves close to each other, at least in the sense of their desire to do something from our different spheres of action in favor of a more just and egalitarian world.

Frente Urbano Oscar Fernando Serrano Rueda
Unión Camilista-Ejército de Liberación Nacional—UC-ELN

Part 3 • Human Rights

Human Rights Abuses: A 1999 Report

Human rights abuses have long been widespread in Colombia, but during the 1990s they reached unprecedented levels. Perpetrators included the armed forces, the paramilitaries, and the guerrillas. We know as much as we do about these abuses because of the courageous efforts of many Colombian human rights groups such as the Intercongregational Committee for Justice and Peace and the Colombian Commission of Jurists, and the concern of international organizations such as Amnesty International.

For a long time, however, as Luis Alberto Restrepo argues in Chapter 5, most human rights organizations inside Colombia and abroad focused their primary attention on the human rights abuses of the State. In Colombia, much attention centered on massacres of rural people by paramilitary forces, often with the collaboration of the military, who claimed their targets were guerrilla sympathizers. Meanwhile, many human rights organizations ignored or downplayed the human rights violations of the guerrillas. In recent years, however, this has begun to change. The following excerpt, from the 1999 *World Report* of Human Rights Watch (New York, 2000), provides a balanced account of the recent record of human rights abuses by all sides in the Colombian conflict and assesses efforts by the Bogotá government to protect human rights more effectively.

Paramilitary killings were stark in their savagery [during 1999]. In January, for example, paramilitaries reportedly dragged twenty-seven worshipers out of a church in Playón de Orozco, Magdalena, and then riddled their bodies with bullets. That same week, authorities registered over one hundred killings attributed to paramilitaries, who mutilated some of their victims and dumped the bodies into rivers to destroy the evidence.

The Working Group on Enforced or Involuntary Disappearances transmitted to the Colombian government fifty new cases of "disappearances" carried out in 1998. They occurred mainly in northwest Colombia and the department of Santander. Most of the abductions and detentions leading to "disappearances" were carried out by paramilitary groups. In a few cases, the army was allegedly responsible for the detentions.

The Human Rights Unit of the Attorney General's Office was among the most effective government institutions combating paramilitaries. In 1999 that office reported that 161 persons accused of involvement in paramilitary activities were arrested. Seventy-five members of the security forces were under arrest for alleged involvement in human rights crimes.

Success came at an increasingly high price, however. In 1998 and 1999 a dozen officials from the Technical Investigations Unit (Cuerpo Técnico de Investigaciones, CTI) of the Attorney General's Office were murdered or forced to resign because of threats related to their work on human rights. Prosecutors were forced to abandon their posts and seek refuge abroad because of threats, including those by military officers being investigated for paramilitary ties.

In February, seven CTI agents were briefly held by the Peasant Self-Defense Forces of Córdoba and Urabá (Autodefensas Campesinas de Córdoba y Urabá, ACCU), which claimed in a statement released to the press that the agents were carrying out a strategy "imposed by the subversives and now institutionalized as part of their overall strategy to seize power." The statement went on to threaten government investigators with death.

The government took some steps toward purging the military of suspected human rights abusers. On April 9, President Pastrana cashiered Gen. Rito Alejo del Río and Gen. Fernando Millán, who were both being prosecuted for alleged support for paramilitary groups. At this writing, the Attorney General's Office continues to pursue a case against Del Río for alleged support to paramilitaries who carried out dozens of massacres and selective killings in the Magdalena Medio and Urabá regions.

However, a similar case against Millán remained before a military tribunal. Given the long-standing practice of these tribunals, the case was likely to end in impunity. The Attorney General's Office and the Procuraduría, which investigates allegations against government employees, also found evidence implicating soldiers under Millán's direct command as well as police and agents of the Administrative Security Department (Departamento Administrativo de Seguridad, DAS) in a 1998 massacre in Barrancabermeja. The massacre had been carried out by paramilitaries who abducted and killed thirty-two people, apparently with the officers' help.

Separately, the Attorney General's Office suspended in May Gen. Jaime Humberto Uscátegui, commander of the Second Division, during an investigation for assisting a paramilitary massacre in the village of Onlineiripán, Meta, in 1997. This officer was also facing prosecution for the 1997 Puerto Elvira massacre and the 1998 San Carlos de Guaroa massacre. In October, General Uscátegui resigned his post. Uscátegui's arrest followed the March arrest of Lt. Col. Lino Sánchez Prado, who allegedly helped paramilitaries reach the village. At the time of the massacre, Sánchez led the Second Mobile Brigade.

Other security force personnel whom government investigators have tied to serious violations remained on active duty, including two sergeants who killed Senator Manuel Cepeda in 1994. The men, who worked for military intelligence, acted on orders from Ninth Brigade Gen. Rodolfo Herrera Luna, who died of a heart attack in 1996.

A military penal code reform, long supported by national and international human rights groups as a way to address impunity, fell short of demands to strengthen accountability, failing to clarify how cases involving military officers charged with human rights violations would be prosecuted. For example, article 3 of the code named only three crimes—genocide, torture, and forced disappearance—as human rights violations that must be heard by civilian courts. Left out was the most common violation attributed to Colombia's security forces, extrajudicial execution. In the code, the cited crimes were defined according to "conventions and treaties ratified by Colombia," a further complication. While Colombia had ratified the UN Convention against Torture, it had not even signed the OAS Convention against Forced Disappearances, making the use of these charges against security force officers open to legal manipulation. Although genocide was named as a crime, it has never occurred in Colombia. Another bill that would criminalize forced disappearances failed to receive adequate government support and was abandoned.

Despite the new code, already existing legislation, and court decisions mandating that human rights crimes be heard in civilian courts, the military continued to dispute and often win jurisdiction. Cases involving high-ranking officers, among them General Uscátegui, continued to be sent to military tribunals, where impunity was the likely result.

For its part, the Revolutionary Armed Forces of Colombia (Fuerzas Armadas Revolucionarias de Colombia, FARC) continued to flagrantly violate the laws of war. In February, FARC militants seized, then executed three Americans who had visited the U'wa indigenous group in northeastern Colombia. Apparently in order to mislead investigators, guerrillas took Terence Freitas, Ingrid Washinawatok, and Lahe'ena'e Gay into Venezuela, where they executed the three. After admitting its role, the FARC claimed that it would subject those responsible to trial, a development that Human Rights Watch protested since the guerrillas could not guarantee a fair trial.

Subsequently, the FARC announced that the guerrilla who, they claim, commanded the unit that carried out the executions might be punished. However, transcripts of FARC radio conversations allegedly recorded by the Colombian Army and released to the press suggested that the murders had not been carried out by low-ranking guerrillas, but had been ordered by Germán Briceño Suárez, a top FARC commander who used the alias "Grannobles" and remained at his post. In September, army troops claimed to have killed in combat two of the guerrillas believed responsible for the Americans' death.

The FARC appeared disinterested in peace, and suspended talks repeatedly into the latter part of the year. Meanwhile, in the area ceded to them by the government, the FARC carried out extrajudicial executions of at least eleven civilians whom they suspected of various crimes. Repeatedly in 1999, the FARC used gas cylinders as bombs, weapons that were impossible to aim properly and often caused civilian casualties.

The Army of National Liberation-Camilist Union (Unión Camilista-Ejército de Liberación Nacional, UC-ELN) also continued to commit serious laws of war violations. On October 18, 1998, just after midnight, militants bombed the pipeline of Oleoducto Central, S.A., near Machuca, Antioquia. According to official investigations, the resulting spilled oil and the gases took six minutes to descend a slope, cross the Pocuné River, and reach the population on the opposite bank. There, many residents depended on open flames for light and cooking. The mixture ignited, engulfing sixty-four dwellings and the sleeping families inside them. Seventy-three people, among them thirty-six children, ultimately perished. Some of the dead could be identified only through dental records since their bodies were completely burned. An additional sixty-four people were seriously wounded.

Weeks after the spill, the UC-ELN admitted its responsibility via a press interview with leader Nicolás Bautista, who claimed without providing evidence that the UC-ELN had investigated the case and "punished" those responsible. However, several months later, UC-ELN leader Antonio García claimed it was sufficient to simply "acknowledge" the error and insist that units be more careful.

In 1999 the group continued to bomb pipelines near civilian dwellings. In May the Attorney General's Office issued an arrest warrant for UC-ELN commander Luis Guillermo Roldán Posada as the alleged leader of the unit that carried out the Machuca attack.

In failed negotiations with the government in 1998, the UC-ELN made several pronouncements on the laws of war that served mainly to underscore how little the group respected them. On the subject of hostage taking, for instance, the UC-ELN committed itself to cease kidnapping civilians—already outlawed under any circumstances—only if its economic needs could be satisfied "by other means," and claimed that it would exempt the elderly, pregnant women, and children.

Within the year, however, the group violated even this meager pledge, sometimes in spectacular fashion. On April 12 the group abducted 41 passengers and crew members of an Avianca airliner, pioneering the tactic of the mass kidnapping of civilians in Colombia. A month later, the UC-ELN seized over 140 churchgoers from a Cali church. Pursued by the authorities, the UC-ELN released some 80 captives, but kept at least 2 children and hostages who, they hoped, would pay high ransoms. The bodyguard of a parishioner was shot and killed when he resisted abduction.

Months later, the UC-ELN apologized not for the Cali kidnapping itself, but for failing to wait until Mass was concluded to carry it out. In April, May, and June alone, police estimated that the UC-ELN increased its pace of kidnapping by 217 percent, having abducted 463 people by the end of the period.

One result of human rights and international humanitarian law violations continued to be mass displacement. According to the Displaced Person Support Group (Grupo de Apoyo a Desplazados, GAD), an alliance of human rights, religious, and aid organizations, an estimated 1.5 million Colombians had been displaced by political violence since 1985. In a 1999 report, the Consultancy for Human Rights and the Displaced (Consultoría para los Derechos Humanos y el Desplazamiento, CODHES), a group that studied forced displacement, found that displacement reached its highest level ever in 1998: an estimated 308,000 Colombians were forced to flee, an increase of 20 percent over the previous year. For every political killing in 1998, according to CODHES, an estimated 78 people fled.

Far from improving, forced displacement intensified in some regions in 1999, making Colombia the country with the third largest internally displaced population in the world, after Sudan and Angola. While the government mobilized to help thousands of Colombians left homeless by a devastating January earthquake in Armenia, Quindío, forcibly displaced families continued to live largely in the shadows, subsisting on their own meager resources.

An Account of a Kidnap Victim

Colombia has the highest incidence of kidnapping in the world. Many of the kidnappings are the work of leftist guerrillas who defend the practice as a means of waging war and who depend on ransom money as a primary source of income. The following testimony makes a powerful case that kidnapping violates the most elemental human rights. It is taken from a work by Colombian historian Herbert Braun. The voice of the victim is Braun's brother-in-law, Texas oilman Jake Gambini. Following months of captivity in 1988 in a remote guerrilla camp, and despairing of progress in seemingly interminable negotiations between the guerrillas and his family, Gambini began a hunger strike that eventually sped up the negotiations and led to his freedom. Following his liberation, Gambini returned to the United States. It was never established for certain which guerrilla group had held him captive.

Herbert Braun, who teaches Latin American history at the University of Virginia, is also the author of a major study of Jorge Eliécer Gaitán and the Violence in Bogotá that followed upon his death, *The Assassination of Gaitán: Public Life and Urban Violence in Colombia* (Madison, WI, 1985). In both of his studies of the Violence, Braun argues that Gaitán's assassination in 1948 virtually closed off the possibility that Colombian history might evolve in a less violent and more democratic fashion during the late twentieth century.

I urinated a few times on the first day. But the next morning I had to take a shit. I knew I couldn't just move about, go off in the shrubs or anything like that. They made a hole for me about a foot and a half wide, off to one side about forty feet or so.

It's a terrible feeling. You tried to pick your time when there wasn't that many people around or there wasn't a girl on guard. If you knew that the

From Herbert Braun, *Our Guerrillas, Our Sidewalks: A Journey into the Violence of Colombia* (Niwot: University Press of Colorado, 1994), 46–47, 60–61. Reprinted by permission of the University Press of Colorado.

guard would be a girl during the next four hours, you would try to see if you could go before it was her time to come on. You'd go with a man. It was a silly thing in a situation like that, but you still have certain . . .

Walking down there, with a guard behind you, you have a man who is standing guard over you. It's terrible. Just having this man there with a gun, it was the most demeaning thing of all. It made me feel angry that I was in a situation like that, that a situation like that existed. . . . It's a natural function. There shouldn't be any situation in this world where a man has to ask if he can go do a natural function. I think that is a basic right. But I had to wait for them to say okay. . . .

They kept telling me that they were a political group and that they were doing this for their movement. I said to myself, well, no matter what their political ideas are, no matter how they dress it up, it's still wrong to use this type of extortion to raise money.

I felt like my body was being used as a bargaining point. They've got you—you want him back, you've got to give us money. Whenever I thought about it this way, I felt very dirty. I felt violated. It's wrong. I mean, you're starting off on a rotten basis. These people who were ordered to get me, were they going to be running the country or parts of the country? I can't see how they'll ever be good for the country.

In some ways I might see that they have certain reasons. We all know the social injustices in Colombia. But I cannot condone a social group coming to power if they have used kidnapping as a means because I could never have faith in that group. . . .

They told me many times that they were sorry they got me. I felt like telling them, you all are talking about being just to everyone and about human rights, but what has happened to my human rights? If you take my human rights and justify it, you can take the rights of ten million people and justify it. Human rights are human rights.

PART 4 • PLATFORMS/NEGOTIATING POSITIONS OF THE ARMED CONTENDERS

THE GOVERNMENT

Since the 1980s, Colombian governments, with greater or lesser degrees of commitment, have endorsed the idea of negotiation with the guerrilla movements as a way to end the armed conflict. That policy, as detailed in Chapters 1 and 3, led to peace pacts with the M-19 and other smaller guerrilla groups in the early 1990s, and to the important political reforms of the Constitution of 1991.

Government efforts to effect a negotiated settlement with the two largest guerrilla groups, the FARC and the ELN, were stymied throughout the 1990s. At the end of the decade, however, as described in more detail below, serious negotiations began between the government and the FARC; and, by the start of the year 2000, negotiations with the ELN were also under way. These developments were made possible due to significant concessions made by the government, the most important of them a willingness to create demilitarized zones in areas of traditional guerrilla influence. Government military forces were to be withdrawn from these zones, and the zones were to become the sites of formal negotiations. Renewed government commitment to peace negotiations at the end of the 1990s not only reflected the growing power of the guerrillas. Within official circles there was also growing concern that the high levels of violence in the country were threatening the viability of the economy, and the integrity of society and the State itself.

The following document, disseminated in late 1999 by the government of Andrés Pastrana, suggests the complexity of the issues involved in the government's position and reveals the extent of the pressures, both international and domestic, facing the government at the start of the twenty-first century. Called Plan Colombia, it was part of the administration's efforts to explain its negotiating position vis-à-vis the guerrillas, demonstrate its commitment to an international "war on drugs," and secure large-scale infusions of foreign economic assistance to reactivate the economy and strengthen the State. Although the document stresses the need for a negotiated settlement with the guerrillas, it is silent on the question of the fundamental economic and social reforms historically demanded by the guerrilla groups as a condition for peace.

Plan Colombia: A Plan for Peace, Prosperity, and the Strengthening of the State

On the threshold of the twenty-first century, Colombia faces the challenge of consolidating the central responsibilities of the State. It must recover the confidence of its citizens and, as part of this process, reestablish the basic norms of social life.

It is the intent of this government to meet the central responsibilities of the State: the promotion of democracy, justice, and territorial integrity; the creation of conditions that foster employment, human rights, and human dignity; and the maintenance of public order.

The weaknesses of a State that is still in a process of consolidation have been made worse by the destabilizing impact of the drug trade. The progressive reforms of the early 1990s opened the doors to an era of greater opportunity for Colombians, but they were distorted by the pervasive influence [of drug trafficking] in both the economic and political spheres, a process that fostered violence and corruption. In recent times, the financial relationships between the various armed groups and the drug traffickers have worked to intensify the armed conflict, and that in turn has limited the capacity of the State to meet its most important responsibilities.

Restoring the State's capacity to meet its responsibilities depends on a process of social and community reconstruction. For this reason, peace is not a simple question of political will. On the contrary, peace must be constructed gradually. State institutions must be developed and strengthened in order to guarantee security and respect for the rights and freedoms of all citizens in all parts of the national territory.

A central part of this strategy is negotiation with the guerrillas, which seeks to bring an end to a conflict that has experienced profound change over the years. If this strategy is successful, it will facilitate the process of social construction. Moreover, a peace accord negotiated with the guerrillas on the basis of territorial integrity, democracy, and human rights will strengthen the state of law and the fight against drugs.

At the same time, peace also requires a strong and viable economy so citizens can improve their social and economic condition. A strong economy will contribute to an enduring reconciliation. The government has proposed an economic strategy, complemented by alternative forms of development, to achieve this goal; the strategy also offers incentives to reduce the cultivation of illegal crops. The idea is to stimulate new, alternative economic activities in agriculture that favor the environment and protect fragile ecosystems now threatened by the cultivation of illicit crops. The strategy focuses on the question of national and international demand and is based on the participation of the private sector, the State, and the beneficiaries of the program.

A central feature of the program is to create a collective vision shared by consuming and producing nations and all other nations involved in the chain of drug trafficking, a vision based on the principles of reciprocity and equality. An alliance based on this vision can facilitate a united response to the threat of narco-trafficking, which is one of the most lucrative activities in the world. Drug trafficking has not only fostered increased corruption in society and diminished confidence in legal commercial activities, but it also has fed the armed conflict. It represents an international source of financing for the different armed groups and has helped them augment their economic influence and territorial control. In Colombia and in other countries, with the elaboration and implementation of an integral strategy to combat the principal elements responsible for the growing of illegal crops, the fight against drug trafficking can achieve positive results that will benefit Colombia as well as the rest of the world.

Colombia has been working toward these objectives and has won notable victories in the fight against the drug cartels and narco-terrorism. Nevertheless, today Colombia confronts the worst economic crisis in its history. Unfortunately, the capacity of the government to resolve the problem is especially limited at a moment when violence in the country, intensified by narco-trafficking, is on the rise.

The Ten Strategies of Plan Colombia

1. An economic strategy that generates employment, strengthens the capacity of the State to collect taxes, and creates the economic strength to confront drug trafficking. The expansion of international commerce, accompanied by better access to foreign markets and free-trade agreements that attract foreign and domestic investment, are key factors in the modernization of our economic base and the generation of employment. Such a strategy is essential at a moment in which Colombia confronts its worst economic crisis in 70 years, with unemployment reaching up to 20 percent. The economic crisis in turn severely limits the capacity of the government to fight narco-trafficking and the violence it generates.

2. A fiscal and financial strategy based on severe austerity and adjustment measures in order to stimulate economic activity and recover the traditional prestige of Colombia in international financial markets.

3. A strategy of peace aimed at achieving negotiated peace agreements with the guerrillas that are based on the principles of territorial integrity, democracy, and human rights, and which also serve to strengthen the state of law and the fight against drug trafficking.

4. A strategy of national defense based on restructuring and modernizing the armed forces and the police so that by opposing organized crime and the armed groups and by protecting and promoting human rights they can reintroduce a state of law and provide security throughout the national territory.

5. A judicial and human rights strategy that reaffirms the state of law and ensures equal and impartial justice for all, and, at the same time, advances reforms under way in the armed forces and the police to ensure that they comply with their role in the defense of the rights and dignity of all.

6. A strategy against narcotics built on cooperation with all other countries involved in any or all of the components in the cycle of illicit drugs: production, distribution, commercialization, consumption, money laundering, provision of precursor chemicals or other inputs, and arms trafficking. In particular, the strategy should seek to impede the flow of the products of

the drug trade that feed the violence into the hands of the guerrilla and other armed organizations.

7. A strategy of alternative development that promotes farming and other profitable economic activities for peasants and their families. Alternative development also includes economically feasible activities designed to protect the environment by preserving tropical forests and bringing an end to the dangerous expansion of illegal plantings in the Amazon Basin and in national parks. These regions have immense bio-diversity and are of vital environmental importance to the international community. Within this framework, the strategy envisions productive projects that are sustainable and involve the participation of the cultivators. Such projects are to be developed in tandem with the necessary infrastructure. Of special importance are projects in regions that suffer high levels of conflict and low levels of State presence, limited social development, and severe environmental degradation, such as the Magdalena Medio, the southern Andean region, and the southeast.

8. A strategy of social participation aimed at fostering a sense of community. This strategy seeks to develop greater responsibility at the level of local government, a greater commitment by the community in efforts to combat corruption, and constant pressure on the guerrilla and other armed groups to eliminate kidnapping, violence, and the internal displacement of individuals and communities. This strategy also includes the collaboration of local entrepreneurs and labor groups with the goal of finding innovative and productive models in a more globalized economy, strengthening local farming communities, and reducing the risks of rural violence. Additionally, this strategy seeks formal and informal ways to encourage change in the cultural norms that favor violence. It also includes the development of mechanisms and educational programs to increase tolerance, community values, and participation in public affairs.

9. A strategy of human development that guarantees adequate health and education services for the most vulnerable groups in our society during the coming years. Of special importance are not only displaced persons and those affected by the violence, but also those sectors submerged in absolute poverty.

10. A strategy of international drug policy that affirms the principles of shared responsibility, integrated action, and balanced treatment in confronting the problem. Simultaneous action must be taken against each link in the chain of the drug trade. The costs involved in these actions and solutions should fall on all nations involved in the trade, and be apportioned on the basis of the economic capacity of each one. The role of the international

community is also vital to the success of the peace process, and that role should conform to the precepts of international law and be approved by the Colombian government.

The Peace Process

Colombia has experienced armed conflict for more than thirty-five years. The current government has begun a process of negotiation that seeks a peace accord with the guerrillas on the basis of territorial integrity, democracy, and human rights. If this strategy is successful, the rule of law and the fight against drug trafficking will be rapidly strengthened throughout the country.

The peace process is obviously one of the principal priorities of the government. President Pastrana has assumed personal leadership of the government's role in the process and shares that role with the High Commissioner for Peace, who is named directly by the president.

The Commissioner, who holds cabinet rank, works with leaders of society and the private sector who dedicate themselves, *pari passu*, to finding a solution to the conflict.

The demilitarized zone (*zona de distensión*) was created by law to guarantee the necessary security to move ahead in the negotiations with the guerrillas. This law allows the President to create such zones or suspend them, both actions being an expression of national sovereignty. The law only restricts the presence of the army and the police within such zones and suspends arrest orders; it does not restrict the activity of government functionaries elected at the local and regional levels.

The peace process is part of a strategic alliance against drug trafficking, corruption, and the violation of human rights. In order to make this process feasible and lasting, there is a need for complementary aid in the areas of security and defense. There is a need for a broad alliance that links the production and consumption of drugs—one that deals with the distribution and commercialization of drugs as well as the laundering of money and the traffic in arms. And there is a need for a development plan that generates employment and gives relief to the most needy.

Armed Conflict and Civil Society

In this conflict there are three protagonists. On the side of the guerrillas are the FARC and the ELN, whose respective roots can be found in the agrarian movement and the Cold War. On the other side are the self-defense groups outside the law, which seek an armed solution to the guerrilla conflict and greater political recognition for their organizations. Last, and in the middle of the crossfire, is the great majority of Colombians who often suffer at the hands of the armed contenders.

The guerrilla movement has its roots in the traditional antagonisms of the countryside and of Colombian politics. Both are fed in part by the ideological rhetoric of the capitalist-Communist confrontation. With the passing of the years, the guerrilla movement's struggle to broaden its territorial base and political and military influence has been financed by extortion and kidnapping and, more recently, by "taxes" levied on intermediaries in the drug trade.

In the last thirty years, Colombia has changed from a primarily rural economy to an urban one, and more than 70 percent of the population now lives in urban areas. According to recent polls, since the end of the Cold War, the formerly more ample support for the guerrillas has declined to 4 percent of the population. The guerrillas know that under these circumstances they cannot gain power through armed struggle. Yet in spite of the general rejection of their ideas and methods, the guerrillas continue to seek advantage through military means.

As a consequence, the peace process has been undertaken in a way that permits society in general to play a central role. A social consensus exists among representatives of society, economic interest groups, and even the armed groups that peace should be an immediate goal.

As a result, the participation of society as a whole is considered necessary in order to pressure the armed groups to find a peaceful solution to the armed conflict and respect human rights that are internationally recognized. The dynamic support of Colombian society is also essential for the development of ideas and proposals that propel the process forward. It also helps to guarantee the continuity of consensus that is required of a negotiated settlement with the participation of the international community.

The Present Situation

The process of peace has made real advances on several fronts. With respect to the FARC, a demilitarized zone was created to harbor negotiations and this has helped both sides formulate an agenda for discussion, a process completed by May 1999. Now that these conditions have been satisfactorily met, the phase of negotiations can begin.

With regard to the ELN, the government has authorized a group of important citizens to help negotiate the freedom of hostages and it has accepted the idea of beginning active talks to prepare a national convention immediately after their liberation.

The government continues to fight against the self-defense groups outside the law, but this fact does not mean that it is not disposed to finding alternative and peaceful ways to dismantle their infrastructure and operations.

During the peace process, the army and the police will necessarily continue to increase their capacities in order to maintain an effective presence in all of the territory of the nation and guarantee a peaceful resolution of the conflict.

Fundamentally, achieving peace rests on three pillars. First, it rests on the development of the agreements already achieved between the government and the principal guerrilla organizations (the FARC and the ELN) so that these organizations become clear-headed, legitimate agents in serious dialogues for peace. Second, it rests on the achievement of partial accords on the agenda of twelve points agreed upon between the government and the FARC that can ensure a permanent peace accord before the end of the present government's term in office. And third, and most important, peace rests on these accords actually being put into practice.

The International Community

The role of the international community is essential to the success of the peace process. Specifically, Colombia needs help in two areas, diplomatic and financial. The international community can act as intermediary, observer, or, at a later stage, as verifier of the fulfillment of any peace accord agreed upon. Additionally, it is very important that the international community repudiate by all means any and all terrorist actions and violations of international human rights law and that it exert pressure to push along the peace process.

In the field of bilateral relations, military and police collaboration is vital. Collective action by neighboring countries not only is less effective than bilateral action, but it may also serve as an impediment to the negotiating process. In this area, the coordination of military and police operations, improvement of border security, and help with equipment and technology are of the greatest benefit.

Regarding diplomatic action by neighboring countries, at this delicate point in the peace negotiations, the government of Colombia prefers bilateral dialogue and confidential consultations with the countries interested in the process. All international participation in the peace process should necessarily respect the norms of international law and be acceptable to the Colombian government. There must be strict observance of the principles of nonintervention in the internal affairs of the State, and this can only be achieved following consultations with the government of Colombia and with the support of the same.

The government of Colombia has established an Investment Fund for Peace as a channel for direct international financial assistance for the peace process. This fund will be used to support economic and social development projects in the areas most affected by the armed conflict.

Toward this end, a group of expert consultants has been formed with the help of the International Development Bank. The group's function will be to advise and monitor the use of these funds. These resources will be used to complement funds already assigned by the government of Colombia.

A successful peace process will also have a positive impact on the fight against drugs since the government will be able to expand its ability to enforce the law and put into practice alternative development programs in the areas most involved in the production of narcotics. Guerrilla activity and drug trafficking are problems that, although intertwined to some degree, have different origins and objectives. The guerrillas operate under a revolutionary political and military plan that requires a negotiated solution; none of this is applicable to the drug traffickers.

The FARC

Throughout the 1990s the negotiating position of the FARC, the largest guerrilla group in Colombia, has been based on twelve points enumerated in the following document, an "open letter" sent by the Coordinadora Guerrillera Simón Bolívar to Congress on January 25, 1992.

In 1998, following years of ineffectual on-and-off talks between the government and the FARC, newly elected President Andrés Pastrana began an intensive effort to start serious negotiations with the guerrillas. The government made a major concession to the FARC, declaring a huge area in southeastern Colombia a zone of disengagement, which was cleared of government forces and left under the control of the FARC. Finally, on October 24, 1999, in the context of national demonstrations in which millions of Colombians pleaded for peace, negotiations began that many people hope will produce a viable peace accord between the government and the most important guerrilla group.

Señores Congresistas:

An important achievement of the dialogue in Caracas has been the joint elaboration of a negotiating agenda that goes beyond the exclusively military matter of a cease-fire and deals with the elements that lie behind our national crisis.

Treating these themes cannot solely be undertaken by negotiators and specialists, but it is the responsibility of all who can contribute to clarifying the future of the nation: businessmen and workers, politicians and military personnel, church and lay people, students, artists, intellectuals, the government and the guerrillas, journalists, native peoples, and farmers—all of us have something to contribute to an agreement and peace.

For that reason we have proposed the convocation of three national meetings to gather together the opinions of Colombians on the great problems of our society. Toward this end it would be of enormous consequence to call together regional meetings of dialogue about peace. There, with the presence of government authorities, and political, social, civic, and community organizations, popular opinion could begin to be incorporated into the guidance of each region of the country.

Since we are about to renew our conversations, and Congress has begun its sessions, we call your attention to our themes, which were included in the Agenda of Caracas.

a. Socioeconomic Aspects

Substitution of economic liberalization for policies that stimulate, above all, national industry and agriculture by advancing credit, constructing infrastructure, importing modern technology, and creating markets. Making development and economic progress mean social well-being, respect for the rights of workers and employees, the opening of new sources of employment, and the fostering of cooperatives and small businesses.

Our incorporation into the international market should not be imposed through the shock treatments of the IMF and the World Bank, but rather as a consequence of national thinking that protects the vital sectors of economic production in the country. It is urgent that we renegotiate the national debt in order to impede the export of capital we need for our development.

b. Natural and Energy Resources

The natural resources of Colombia should be exploited, administered, and commercialized under patriotic criteria, taking advantage of our position of ownership. The benefits of mineral production—of petroleum, coal, gold, emeralds, platinum, nickel, copper, etc.—should be invested primarily in regional development under a national development plan.

It is necessary to review and modify existing contracts between the government and the multinational companies for exploitation of natural resources once [contract] terms are up so that ownership reverts immediately to the Colombian State and not to any private entity. We must build new refineries and develop the petrochemical industry so as to achieve self-sufficiency.

The National Energy Commission should be the planning agency for the energy policy of the country.

c. The Social Function of the State

Strengthening of the social function of the State by guaranteeing its administrative efficiency and protecting it from political abuse and by developing its capacity through highly efficient and productive agencies.

The State should guarantee the well-being of all Colombians through health, education, housing, transportation, culture, recreation, ecological balance, and public services.

d. Corruption

Administrative corruption is one of the main factors in the violence of our country. It is necessary to strengthen oversight mechanisms of the people, augment punishments for the corrupt, try public servants who enrich themselves illicitly, and return ill-gotten monies and goods to the State.

e. Armed Forces

The Colombian State must change its politics of total war against internal enemies. The application of the Doctrine of National Security and of Low Intensity Warfare, now that East-West conflict and the Cold War are over, sows hatred and tragedy in our fatherland.

We must demilitarize national life: reconstruct the armed forces under a democratic, nationalistic, and patriotic doctrine that represents the different currents of thought in the country; reduce expenditures and the numbers of people involved; dissolve the intelligence services; return the National Police to the control of the Ministry of Government; and cancel Colombian participation in international military treaties.

f. Paramilitaries

The paramilitary and self-defense groups must be dismantled. Those who inspired them, instructed them, financed them, and led them must be punished, as well as those responsible for assassinations and massacres. The armed forces must be cleansed of members involved in the "dirty war."

g. Human Rights

Restore and make effective human rights in Colombia, guaranteeing citizens life, dignity, respect, and the basic conditions for their development as human beings.

h. Impunity

Ending impunity requires complete revision of the Judicial branch of government, providing it with all possible elements to make justice speedy, effective, and impartial. There must be an end to the *fuero militar* [special military privileges, including military courts], a supreme form of pandering that has become the principal cause of impunity today.

i. Democracy

Colombia needs a democracy without pitfalls, one without antiterrorist laws that apply only to the opposition and nonconformists, one without privileges for the powerful members of the communications media, one without militarization of electoral campaigns, one with voter registration in the hands of an entity independent of the government.

It is urgent to bring liberty to the electoral process, make direct democracy greater and better by broadening the referendum, the plebiscite, the right of *tutela*, and the power of directly and popularly elected bodies. Above all, it is urgent to guarantee the lives of citizens and organizations who are in the opposition.

j. The Agrarian Issue

Land must be redistributed in areas where the large estate rules. Adequate roads and transport must be constructed, cheap credit for agriculture and cattle raising established, harvest insurance and the extension of inputs and modern technology made available to all who create wealth in our countryside. The sale of their products must also be guaranteed.

k. National Unity

National unity must be strengthened. The centralizing arrogance of governments and the lack of cooperation on social welfare and development plans have relegated the different regions of the country, as well as native peoples and ethnic minorities, to a marginal position, submerging them in injustice. To harmoniously reintegrate Colombia is a strategic priority in laying the foundations for peace.

l. Reparations for Those Affected by Violence

Those affected by violence must be indemnified. We must elaborate and put into practice a serious plan that commits the State, private companies, and the International Community to a healing, devoid of paternalism, of the deep wounds left by the confrontation.

We are certain that a Great National Accord on these themes will lay the foundation for reconciliation. Our proposal is in contrast to the conduct of those strategists of war who chose to enflame the conflict by attacking the Casa Verde [the Coordinadora's headquarters] on December 9, 1990, carrying the country toward the abyss and confirming once more the bankruptcy of official policy that seeks a military solution to the crisis.

Secretariat of the Central High Command
Coordinadora Guerrillera Simón Bolívar
Mountains of Colombia, January 25, 1992

The ELN

The ELN, whose complete name is the Unión Camilista-Ejército de Liberación Nacional, is the second largest of the Colombian guerrilla groups. The ELN is often called a "single-issue" faction because of its militant stance on the need to nationalize the petroleum industry and its strategy of winning that demand by blowing up oil pipelines and kidnapping and sometimes assassinating oil company officials and technicians. Over the years, however, the ELN has developed a comprehensive platform and negotiating stance. In general terms, it continues to endorse the twelve points outlined by the Coordinadora Guerrillera in 1992 and reproduced above. But its position has been elaborated and refined in a series of documents made public in subsequent years.

An effort to synthesize the ELN's position is contained in the pamphlet, "La paz sobre la mesa" (Bogotá, n.d.), prepared in 1999 by the Colombian Commission for National Conciliation, the Colombian Delegation of the International Red Cross, and the magazine *Cambio 16* (the pamphlet also provides policy statements for the FARC and the much smaller guerrilla organization, the EPL). Parts of that synthesis—those dealing with national sovereignty, drug trafficking, and petroleum policy—are reproduced here. Readers will note a more strident tone and radical content in some ELN positions compared to those of the Coordinadora/FARC.

National Sovereignty

We must put in place a patriotic sovereignty based on national self-determination and independence from the United States, other imperialists, and transnational companies. . . .

Neo-colonial relations, plunder by multinational companies, and the subordination of the Colombian oligarchy to the economic and political interests of their masters to the north have been the principal obstacles to our development.

For these reasons, we need to establish a new relationship with foreign capital and new conditions for investment by multinationals for the exploitation of natural resources. Foreign investment will be accepted as long as it transfers technology, leaves us with resources, and is linked to our priorities for economic and social development.

Relations with the IMF [International Monetary Fund] will also be put on a new footing. The foreign debt will be renegotiated, a moratorium will be declared, and a new framework for dealing with the international banks established. Treaties that harm the national interest will be eliminated; those dealing with international boundaries will be respected under the terms of international law.

Drug Trafficking

Our framework for dealing with this phenomenon includes establishing autonomous sovereign means for combating the business of narco-trafficking within our national territory. We need to push for an overall international accord that includes effective measures to control consumption and the mafias that process and commercialize narcotics in different territories. We will not permit the extradition of nationals.

We will reject any imposition or interference by the government of the United States and will demand reciprocal action for our national efforts.

In the substitution of drug cultivation and the eradication of the business, the need to find economic alternatives for small farmers will be kept foremost in mind. . . .

We will support education and means of recuperation for all addicts. . . .

True to the defense of human life and its integrity, the UC-ELN has historically followed a philosophy and acted in a way that reproaches and sets boundaries between all activity related to narcotics and the traffic in them; that conduct gives us the ethical and moral authority to put forth solutions and call for formulas that are agreed upon by all the nations of the world.

We have reaffirmed more than once that we have no link to, nor engage in any activity with, drug trafficking, either within or outside the country. . . .

This plague affects the whole of humanity, and consequently it is the responsibility of the whole international community to develop great plans to help and manage the substitution of cultivation, to stop the production and sale of precursor substances, to attend in a humane manner to those injured by the harmful effects of drug addiction, to educate so as to reduce consumption and protect youth and children.

Petroleum

We have proposed at different times the following: nationalization of the exploitation of natural resources; revision of joint contracts between the government and the companies; establishment of a strategic reserve of hydrocarbons; sovereignty in the determination of the price of our hydrocarbons in the world market; a tax of one dollar per barrel for the development of municipalities where oil fields exist; the establishment of a National Petroleum Council as the body representing national and popular sovereignty charged with analyzing petroleum issues and proposing formulas in the national interest.

Today [August 1996] we propose the following:

—Dialogue between USO [the petroleum workers' union], Ecopetrol [the national oil company], and insurgent forces with the goal of constructing a sovereign alternative to the management of hydrocarbons, which would be the basis for discussion of that issue in dialogue and negotiation aimed at finding a political solution to the conflict.

—Convocation of a National Energy Forum with participants from the oil, coal, and electricity sectors to devise a plan for the development of an energy sector that serves as the basis for building a strong, sovereign national economy and at the same time contributes to peace with social justice. In this forum the ELN will participate, advancing its own proposals.

—Discussion of the law governing hydrocarbons by communities, the labor and social movements, the academic sector, and the faculties of petroleum engineering so that the law can serve as an input into a peace accord among the State, the Insurgency, and society.

—Open dialogue between the Association of Petroleum Companies and the Insurgency with the goal of putting into place alternative forms of development in the areas and settlements surrounding the oil fields.

If the proposals advanced by us and by the oil workers are taken into account, we will begin to consider changes in our politics in defense of natural resources.

Paramilitary Groups

As detailed in Chapter 6, paramilitary groups, or self-defense groups as they prefer to call themselves, developed into a powerful armed force in Colombia during the 1990s. The document reproduced below, circulated in mid-1997 by the largest and most influential of these groups, the Autodefensas Unidas de Colombia (AUC), justifies the need for self-defense organizations and claims an equal place in any negotiations between the government and the guerrillas. Although the document is repetitive and its prose often convoluted, it gradually reveals the mindset, strategy, and tactics of a potent new actor in the conflict.

Since circulating this document, the AUC, under the leadership of Carlos Castaño, has developed increasingly sophisticated policy statements on all the subjects, from human rights to agrarian reform, addressed by the guerrilla groups in their own program statements. (Readers of Spanish can sample more recent policy declarations of the AUC in "La paz sobre la mesa," cited above in the ELN section.) In general, the AUC adopts a nationalist, procapitalist, but reformist stance on these questions. It is critical of the neo-liberal economic policies of recent governments, of the monopoly of the two traditional parties on political power, and, most of all, of the ineffectiveness of the State and of its failure to uphold the Constitution. Despite its rhetorical support for human rights, the AUC, like the guerrilla groups, often relies on force and terror to achieve its goals.

The Political and Military Nature of Our Movement

The Autodefensas Unidas de Colombia (AUC) is a civil defense organization in arms that has arisen as a consequence of the political, economic, and cultural contradictions of Colombian society. These contradictions have progressively worsened as a result of the failure of the State to fulfill clear constitutional provisions that require it to guarantee life, social order, and peace, the economic, cultural, and ecological patrimony of the nation, social and economic justice, free democratic participation, public security, and so on. The failure to guarantee these rights has led to the rise of armed groups whose existence is the sole responsibility of the State but whose violent acts are borne by the immense majority of defenseless Colombians living in the vast regions of the country where the government is unable to fulfill its constitutional obligations.

The Constituent Assembly placed in the hands of legitimate authority and the institutions that represent it the ineluctable duty to provide Colombians with political, economic, and social well-being under a framework that ensures a dignified, peaceful, cooperative, and just life. Nevertheless, the State has been remiss in fulfilling this constitutional duty, precipitating the angry and violent claims of different segments of society, which, in armed rebellion for several decades, have unleashed a cruel bloodbath leaving in its wake economic and moral ruin.

The longtime abandonment of the State in the economic, political, social and cultural fields is the backbone of the political discourse of the armed insurgency; similarly, the State's abandonment of guardianship over the lives, property, and liberty of its citizens has given rise to a political and military Movement of Self-Defense. The two armed movements share the same origin in terms of the objective causes of their coming into being. As a result, the Colombian State must use all its faculties to put into effect a vigorous set of reforms in order to remove the objective causes of the conflict. Doing so will, at the same time, delegitimate the expedient of armed struggle, both offensive and defensive. The institutional and physical presense of the State, guaranteeing social order, procuring justice, redistributing income, offering security to citizens, and so on, will effectively fill the space occupied by armed groups. Under such conditions, if the insurgency persists in its plan to take over the government of the nation, let it take on the military apparatus of the State, but not at the cost of the political, economic, social, and cultural laceration of the civil population, which is totally indifferent to the political aspirations of the guerrillas.

The process of reform, which we, like other sectors, call for urgently, should take place within the established institutional order, which is amply furnished with the instruments to accomplish reform by the Constitution of 1991. In Colombia, advancing a process of political, economic, social, and cultural reforms is not as complicated as it would be in other countries. Our presidential system has at its disposal a broad range of powers derived from its own authority and from the extraordinary powers Congress can grant under a declaration of internal disorder. If some projects, given their subject matter, require that Congress act, then the political will of those who participate in the debate, their peaceful intentions, and the clear interests of the nation will determine their fate. There is not a single item in the voluminous package of reformist proposals and demands placed before the national government by the various social forces that cannot be debated, approved, and executed by the State. To deliberately deny these constitutional and legal powers so as to mount an assault on power, leaving behind the democratic system, is to reveal that one's first, only, and supreme political goal is to install oneself violently in power. This seems to be the goal pursued by the subversive forces, not only because, up to now, they have used peace discussions as a means to strengthen themselves politically, economically, and militarily, without demonstrating a real will to solve the confict, but also because it has been proven that in the territories militarily occupied, dominated, and subjugated by the guerrillas, never have they promoted economic, social, or agrarian reforms that alleviate the misery that the violent occupation of these regions has brought with it.

The AUC considers that the principles of authority and political liberty, and those that define the formal and juridical structure of the State, are magisterially defined and guaranteed in the Constitution in force. That is why we emphatically demand that the State take the initiative and execute a number of profoundly social reforms so that the nation can recover peace, security, a tranquil rhythm of work, daily serenity, and the enjoyment of life. We seek a negotiated solution within a framework of justice and order that will serve as a definitive solution to this frightening bloodshed. We grieve for the dead at the hands of both sides, for the innocent victims who have been sacrificed, for the homes in ruins in town and countryside, for the displaced persons, for the orphans, for the dismembered, for the handicapped.

Under the guise of the reforms that the majority demands of the State, the armed insurgency assassinates, extorts, and kidnaps precisely those who are victims of the negligence of the State. The AUC rejects this. On top of the political and socioeconomic deterioration of the regions abandoned by the official Establishment is added the misfortune of violations of life, liberty, and property by the very people who raise the banner of political, economic, and social redemption. It is an undeniable sociological fact that, today in Colombia, the demand for protection of life and liberty is considered as important in zones of conflict as is the need to create political space, ideological tolerance, and socioeconomic change. It is from this perspective that the AUC, as a military-political organization, must orient its actions, both those that confront the military aggression of subversives as well as those that urgently demand of the State that it make a decision that cannot be delayed, that of transforming the places where violence reigns into fertile ground for development, peaceful coexistence, and security for citizens.

When over vast regions of national territory the State is unable to meet its constitutional duty to protect the lives and goods of its citizens, guerrilla activity develops and increases its local political control. This factor also pushes forward a process of civil resistance, and with it comes an escalation of violence as an expression of the contradictory interests at play. In short, the minimal presence of the guiding hand of the State allows conflicts to follow a violent path. Constitutionally, citizens delegate to the State that represents them the defense and security of their persons. But, if the State does not provide these attributes opportunely or efficiently, that delegated power must return once again to citizens who, in order to survive, have no other choice but to defend themselves.

The curse of violence, which eliminates defenseless people and humble homes, has, of course, complex causes, political as well as social, economic, cultural, and moral. But its growth, its unpunished escalation, is without doubt furthered by the inefficiency of the State as well as by certain communications media which, by taking sides in the conflict, bring on a war of disinformation that is as grave and pernicious as war itself. When dealing with the conflict, sectarian news and reports, perversely interpreted events, partial coverage, accounts that justify crimes or slant or leave out information all serve to cruelly polarize public opinion.

The way things are developing, the current conflict is threatening the survival of the existing democratic system. The guerrillas seek to take power in order to implant an authoritarian system. The challenge affects all of us who love democracy and know that keeping and preserving it depends on all of us defending its principles. In the first instance, it is the State represented by the government installed by majority vote that should actively and efficiently respond to this challenge, committing itself solidly to democracy's defense. The lack of political will to undertake the process of reform has played into the hands of the guerrillas and served to legitimate their drive for political power and the guidance of society that power entails. Faced with these circumstances, a third armed actor has inevitably arisen, not to oppose the political, socioeconomic, and cultural demands of the people, but in addition to them, to provide for itself a defense of life, liberty, and property. These were gravely menaced by a war in which one of the actors broke with its constitutional duty to serve as the guardian of the security, tranquility, and protection of citizens not involved in the conflict but innocent victims of it nonetheless. These are the conditions under which the self-defense movement arises. It arises in the bosom of the war that the

State itself sustains with the subversive movements. The State sustains the war because of its disinterest, its inefficiency, and its faintheartedness in removing the objective and subjective causes of the confrontation, because it is unable to isolate the conflict from the civilian population, and especially because of its prevaricating attitude of leaving the people exposed to the storm in the middle of the battlefield.

The AUC reiterates that opting for a military solution to the present conflict prolongs it, as long as the causes of the war itself are not contested. The three actors in the armed confrontation have fallen into a vicious circle that is fatal for national peace. The government, out of a lack of political will to use the resources at its disposal, neither proposes nor executes an efficient process of political, economic, social, and cultural reform to eliminate the conflict. The guerrillas, supposed carriers of a design to change an oppressive and unjust social, economic, and political order, depend on the horrors of violence, thus submitting the innocent to a bloodbath, prolonging the suffering of the people, and causing their economic and moral ruin. And the self-defense movement, which, while identifying with the struggle for social justice, militarily confronts the guerrillas in order to defend itself from the wave of kidnappings, extortions, massacres, and assassinations that the Colombian people have been victims of, abandoned to their own devices by the insolence of the State.

As long as a solution that directly eliminates the different causes of the conflict is not put forward and implemented, internal armed conflict will continue. Each of the armed actors will continue to justify its actions by reiterating the reasons that have motivated them throughout the war.

The AUC does not base its reason for being exclusively on the existence of the enemy it confronts in the field, but also on the grave lack of State action in fulfilling its duties and functions. In this sense, it is urgent that institutions channel their actions to address the political reasons that led to armed insurgency by the different actors in the conflict. We share the thesis that counterinsurgent efforts aimed at the physical extermination of adversaries are useless and sterile because they underestimate the political reasons that led to insurgency in the first place and constantly reinforce it on the battlefield. The sociopolitical component of armed self-defense, whose origin lies in the up-to-now insurmountable abandonment by the State (an abandonment that also nurtures the guerrillas), seeks to reorient our overall strategy away from armed conflict toward politics, demanding of the government positive, transformative policies that will demonstrate the sterility and uselessness of trying to win changes through violent insurrection, which is a strategy that has produced so many irreconcilable vindictive feelings, so much rancor, so much intemperance in society.

As we have said, the new constitutional order offers the correct mechanisms for achieving a negotiated political solution able to open the way to definitive peace. A solution based on mutual understanding will lead to frank dialogue about the demands facing the nation, about the model of society we long for, and so on. To achieve this end it is necessary to get beyond recurring memories of hatred and vengeance, to move beyond the anti-culture of sectarianism and intolerance, to learn to confront the positions of others in a climate respectful of both consensus and dissent. But this is impossible as long as guerrilla violence exists. Guerrilla violence intensifies the war and leads toward authoritarianism employed as an instrument in the political struggle to win adherents, to armed intimidation to finance the war and provide human resources for it, to political and ideological intolerance, to the destruction of productive infrastructure and public services, to threats, compulsion, and blackmail, to selective kidnapping, to summary executions, to mine fields, etc.

The extremely poor political balance sheet of the forty-year war of attrition waged by the guerrillas and the enormous loss of life that struggle has entailed demand of the leadership of both sides a civilized exit from the conflict. The country must be spared the costs of a war whose devastation and cruelty make the very intent of prolonging it an irresponsible historical act in the eyes of the fatherland. The dilemma facing the nation is clear and definitive. Either we advance toward PEACE through a negotiated settlement or Colombia will definitely fall into the abyss of a conflict of incalculable proportions.

The Civil Population and Human Rights

The present conflict, because of its very nature, lies outside the norms of International Law, which apply to conventional warfare. Nevertheless, the AUC considers that the norms of International Humanitarian Law, norms that describe the ethical and humanitarian conduct that contending forces should observe during the course of the war they fight, should be an inescapable obligation and should be applied with respect by both sides in the conflict.

The aforesaid principle is all the more valid if one admits, once and for all, that the civil population has played a decisive role in the development of the war. In the first place, this is a war that is not fought from fixed bases. It is a war of movement and as such it demands a very close relationship between military groups and the civil population. One could even say that all the inhabitants of a region dominated by one or another of the armed contenders are potentially combatants. This is true either because they are active sympathizers who, although they do not play a direct role in combat, nevertheless take on the vital responsibilities of transmitting orders and information, providing supplies of all kinds, infiltrating enemy positions, collecting funds, exercising local political functions, and so on, and who in addition are the link between the armed group and the general population. Or because they are passive sympathizers who take on the task of seeing nothing, hearing nothing, and, especially, of knowing nothing. The conduct of all these people is motivated by fear, psychological pressure, blackmail, convenience, or by inconfessable and never-declared sympathy. These last two reasons generally motivate civilian sympathizers involved in commerce who supply the goods (food, medicine, shoes, cleaning supplies, underwear, personal items, etc.) and who voluntarily contribute what we could call small change.

As one can see, active and passive sympathizers have an importance almost comparable to that of active combatants and all form part of the armed forces of the various actors in the war. Success in the conflict depends on the timely and symbiotic correlation of these two kinds of supporters. Those who pretend to fight a war only with active combatants and who lack the support of sympathizers in the civil population have lost even before they begin. In contrast, those who end up being the victors are those with as many or more sympathizers on their side than there are people who oppose them.

The surprise attack has been an especially valuable and successful tactic of the guerrillas during the present conflict. The statistics are replete with the very high number of violent takeovers of towns. The guerrillas plan the attack, hit with surprise, then submerge themselves in the populace pretending innocence. Theirs is an ability, carried out in practice, of coming together and disbanding rapidly, of having the option to make themselves highly visible during an assault and invisible once pursued.

The tactic of moving among the civil population as the fish does in water, as Mao Tse-tung advised, has allowed the guerrillas to pull off acts of war in the whole of national territory. This tactic means that the guerrillas fight everywhere but nowhere, they erupt where least expected and disappear camouflaged by the population, a fact that places at grave risk the lives of innocent people. This practice also allows the guerrillas to fragment the forces of the enemy, since it obliges him to be alert everywhere and above all to concentrate his forces efficiently on key areas, undermining his ability to control broad areas where the guerrillas are contending for power and magnifying his lack of presence in the extensive areas already occupied by subversive forces.

Obviously, it is a complicated matter for actors in the war to establish clear distinctions among active combatants, active sympathizers, passive sympathizers, auxiliaries, informants, suppliers, couriers, tax collectors, extortionists, transporters, advisers, commission agents who are benefactors, promoters, or disguised, etc., and the rest of the civil population. The very nature of this irregular war comes from the presence in it of the civil population. The war depends unfortunately on the civil population and the role it plays in the conflict.

Now that we have analyzed the inevitable participation of the civil population in the present war, the need for all actors to submit to the norms of international human rights laws appears even more important. In this sense it is necessary that we ratify our commitment to respect the rights of the noncombatant civil population, making the effort to rethink tactics and strategies of war with the reciprocal goal of isolating from combat the truly civil population. Equally important, the AUC proposes a discussion and approval of a joint code of military ethics with the guerrillas in which the following five aspects would be considered fundamental: (1) rights of combatants; (2) treatment of prisoners; (3) adjustment of and acceptance of the basic norms of international human rights law; (4) rights of the noncombatant civil population; (5) establishment of a tribunal charged with guaranteeing compliance.

Political and Ideological Considerations

1. Treatment of all forces that are involved in the present war as belligerents or legitimate combatants should be governed by an explicit declaration of, or at least pertinent actions showing, compliance with the laws and common practices of international humanitarian law.

2. We acknowledge the silent heroism, and the sense of responsibility and patriotic devotion, of the Armed Forces of the Republic. The casualties they have suffered in the service of maintaining public order and in carrying out their duties are cause for national grief. But we radically reject the idea that, under the shelter of political pretexts, military convenience, and the perverse disorientation of public opinion, the armed insurgency and its

satellites deny the self-determined nature of our armed movement. We have an autonomous command structure, our own geographic theaters of operation, our own political philosophy and ideology of struggle. We have the legitimacy to reestablish by our own means our rights that have been violated. It is our natural right to defend the lives, property, liberty, and peace of a citizenry that lacks efficient guardianship by a State that, although it is conscious of the lack of respect for law, does not reestablish it when it is violated. In a word, let no one deny the essentially political nature of our movement, which came about, as did the guerrilla movement, because of the GRAVE NEGLECT BY THE STATE of a people greatly in need and anxious for justice. And let no one deny the equally political nature of our struggle, which is outlined expressly in this document.

3. We will not compromise with the guerrillas and their satellites as long as they insist on the inhumane practice of kidnapping as a weapon of revolutionary struggle, trying in this way to give this atrocious crime a political character when in fact it is economic.

4. The AUC has always considered that there is an urgent need for great social transformations of benefit to the people. We recognize a certain identity and convergence between many of the demands of the State made by the guerrilla and self-defense groups as conditions for opening up the road to peace. But we reject in no uncertain terms the excesses of the ways used to achieve these ends, which are nevertheless altruistic and of great significance to the great majority of marginalized people in the country. From this perspective, the AUC declares itself respectful and tolerant of the ideological and political expressions of left and right that demand of the State social justice, institutional presence, security, economic justice, authority, etc.—in a word, PEACE.

5. Faith in the justice of the cause for which it fights gives the AUC—from its position of illegality—the understanding that its actions, under the exceptional conditions in which they take place, are *legitimate*. The ethical, political, and ideological dimensions of that faith in the justice of our cause are so great that they permit us to overcome all the inhibitions any person feels in the face of sacrifice or death itself. The justice of this cause is the defense of the interests of populations abandoned in the face of fratricidal violence caused by a war which one side has all the institutional and political means to moderate or stop, without diminishing the dignity of contending forces, or violating the nature and basic principles of the democratic State.

6. In developing the ideal expressed in the previous paragraph, the AUC, out of political conviction and as a result of unnegotiable doctrine, will

never serve foreign interests, interests that are removed from the essence of our fight or simply distant and aloof from the cause of those persons marginalized, excluded, or abandoned by the State.

Our Commitment to Peace

We were heartened by President Ernesto Samper Pizano's announcement asking for our presence at the negotiations that finally are to begin. Nevertheless, we believe that negotiations should be tripartite at a single table since the guerrillas have one set of differences with the government and the sector of the people we represent has another.

We believe our right to participate at the negotiating table is legitimate and we invite the guerrillas to allow that the sector of the people that they claim to represent be asked if they feel truly represented by them. We are ready to do the same with the great numbers of Colombian citizens who, we are convinced, feel represented by the AUC.

Mountains of Colombia, June 26, 1997
Autodefensas Unidas de Colombia (AUC)

Part 5 • U.S. Military Aid

In addition to the internal forces engaged in the Colombian conflict, there is the growing presence of an external actor, the U.S. government. Military aid to Bogotá, justified by Washington as part of the effort to reduce the flow of narcotics to the United States, has grown rapidly in recent years, reaching almost $300 million annually by 1999. That made Colombia the third-largest recipient of U.S. military aid in the world (after Israel and Egypt). In January 2000 the Clinton administration announced plans to dramatically increase the level of that aid to more than $1 billion for the next biennium, a level of support which, if approved, will significantly alter the balance of contending forces in Colombia.

U.S. military aid is a highly controversial issue, both within Colombia and the United States. Criticism centers on the efficiency of, and the motives behind, Washington's "war on drugs," on the human rights record of the Colombian military, and on the appropriateness, given the nature of the conflict and the state of current peace negotiations, of massive infusions of U.S. military aid. The following two documents illustrate a range of opinion on these issues within the United States. The first is President Clinton's statement, released on January 11, 2000, announcing the new level of aid for Colombia. The second is a press release issued on the same day by the Center for International Policy and the Latin America Working Group, a Washington-based coalition of some sixty human rights, religious, and other organizations opposed to increased military funding for Bogotá.

Statement by President Clinton

Office of the Press Secretary
(Grand Canyon, Arizona)
For Immediate Release
January 11, 2000

Today I am announcing an urgently needed, two-year funding package to assist Colombia in vital counterdrug efforts aimed at keeping illegal drugs off our shores. It will also help Colombia promote peace and prosperity and deepen its democracy. Building on our current efforts, over this year and the next our resulting support would total over $1.6 billion.

President Pastrana's inauguration in August 1998 brought to Colombia a new spirit of hope—for deeper democracy, for broader prosperity, for an end to that country's long civil conflict. But increased drug production and trafficking, coupled with a serious economic recession and sustained violence, have put that progress in peril.

President Pastrana has responded with a bold agenda—Plan Colombia. It provides a solid, multifaceted strategy that the United States should support with substantial assistance. We have a compelling national interest in reducing the flow of cocaine and heroin to our shores, and in promoting peace, democracy, and economic growth in Colombia and the region. Given the magnitude of the drug-trafficking problem and their current economic difficulties, neither the Government of Colombia nor its neighbors can carry the full burden alone.

In Fiscal Year 2000, much of our support will be focused on a one-time infusion of funds to help boost Colombia's interdiction and eradication capabilities, particularly in the south. The package will also include assistance for economic development, protection of human rights, and judicial reform.

Our bilateral aid to Colombia will be supplemented by multilateral agencies. The World Bank and the Inter-American Development Bank are considering hundreds of millions of dollars in loans for Colombia next year. The IMF has already pledged a $2.7 billion Extended Fund facility to help jump-start the economy. And we will also continue to encourage our allies to assist Colombia.

The obstacles to a better future for Colombia are substantial. We expect it will require years before the full benefits of Plan Colombia are felt. But I believe that with our support and that of other donors, Plan Colombia can soon accelerate Colombia's nascent economic recovery. Over the longer haul, we can expect to see more effective drug eradication and increased interdiction of illicit drug shipments.

Strengthening stability and democracy in Colombia, and fighting the drug trade there, is in our fundamental national interest. So, with President Pastrana and with our Congress, we must and we will intensify this vital work.

An Alternative Proposal

January 11, 2000

To: Press Contacts
From: Adam Isaacson, Center for International Policy
Lisa Haugaard, Latin America Working Group
Re: Colombia Aid Package

Today, the Clinton Administration will announce a two-year, $1.3 billion aid package for Colombia. The package, which will be introduced in Congress as a supplemental appropriation for 2000, is likely to include hundreds of millions of dollars in new assistance for Colombia's armed forces.

Colombia's military and police are already the world's third-largest recipients of U.S. assistance, with arms and training [funds] growing from about $65 million in 1996 to nearly $300 million in 1999. (For a detailed picture of current U.S. military and police aid to Colombia, visit www.ciponline.org/facts/co. htm.) Until 1999, U.S. support had primarily gone to the Colombian police; this changed with a number of military-aid initiatives such as the creation of a new counternarcotics battalion within the Colombian Army. Though purportedly for counternarcotics only, the proposed aid will greatly increase the U.S. financial commitment to Colombia's army, and will bring the United States still closer to involvement in Colombia's intractable conflict.

Fighting between the Colombian military, leftist guerrillas, and right-wing paramilitaries has escalated enormously since the mid-1990s, making the hemisphere's oldest conflict its bloodiest by far. The violence has forced about 1 million people from their homes in the past four years alone, creating a humanitarian crisis of global proportions. It is a conflict in which massacres and displacement are used as military tactics and civilian non-combatants account for at least two-thirds of the casualties.

Our organizations believe that the United States should help Colombia with substantial diplomatic and financial support. However, we are concerned about the military portion of the proposed aid package for the following reasons:

1. Its effect on Colombia's peace process. Colombia's president, Andrés Pastrana, has made the pursuit of a negotiated end to the conflict the centerpiece of his term in office so far. Though fraught with difficulty, talks with the FARC, Colombia's largest guerrilla group, have been proceeding for a year now, and the ELN guerrillas have also expressed an interest in negotiations.

The talks with the FARC are still in a fragile phase, and it is clear that both the guerrillas and the Colombian government are divided over whether to keep negotiating. In addition to escalating the conflict, infusing hundreds of millions of dollars in military aid risks weakening the process by radicalizing anti-peace elements on both sides.

Militarists in the FARC will see the aid as a reason to keep fighting, while the aid will give comfort to hard-liners in Colombia's ruling circles who already resist any further concessions.

Supporters of military aid sometimes argue that "gains on the battlefield will be reflected at the negotiating table." This ignores the nature of Colombia's "battlefield," in which civilian non-combatants are the main targets. If the United States introduces more weapons and trains more fighters to participate in this conflict, it risks intensifying the crossfire in which innocent civilians are already caught.

2. Its effect on human rights. Despite some positive steps taken by the Pastrana Administration to dismiss high-level officers involved in human rights abuses, concerns remain strong over the Colombian military's human rights record. Most center on the army's continuing connections to paramilitary violence. Paramilitaries were responsible for 78 percent of violations of human rights and international humanitarian law in 1999, according to the Colombian Commission of Jurists, a respected human rights group. Guerrillas were linked with 20 percent—including numerous horrendous cases of kidnapping of civilians—and state forces with 2 percent.

However, the percentage does not reflect state forces that routinely assisted paramilitary atrocities. "Cooperation between army units and paramilitaries remained commonplace," asserts Human Rights Watch's December 1999 report, "Colombia: Human Rights Developments" (available at www.hrw.org). "For instance, government investigators detailed direct collaboration between the Medellín-based Fourth Brigade and paramilitaries commanded by Carlos Castaño. Repeatedly, paramilitaries killed those suspected of supporting guerrillas, then delivered the corpses to the army. In a process known as 'legalization,' the army then claimed the dead as guerrillas killed in combat while paramilitaries received their pay in army weapons." The report went on to note: "The debate over percentages also leaves unaddressed continuing criminal activity by military intelligence, which government investigators linked to a string of high-profile killings and death threats, including the August murder of humorist Jaime Garzón." The report also notes the army's failure to control paramilitary violence: "Soldiers pursued guerrillas once an attack was reported. In contrast, although paramilitaries often announced plans to attack publicly and well in advance, authorities not only failed to act to stop killings, but rarely pursued paramilitary units even when they remained in the region after massacring noncombatants."

Policymakers insist that all new military aid will be dedicated to the war on drugs. The drug war and Colombia's real war overlap significantly, however, increasing the risk that the United States will again be drawn into the quagmire of another country's civil conflict.

Counter-drug and counter-guerrilla efforts in Colombia resemble each other in four important ways:

Location. Years of drug fumigation without providing economic alternatives have pushed Colombian coca-growers deeper into guerrilla-controlled territory. U.S.-aided units on counternarcotics missions will end up fighting the FARC in the guerrillas' own strongholds, placing Washington at the center of Colombia's war effort. The base of the new U.S.-created counternarcotics battalion in Putumayo, near the Ecuadorian border, lies within a 100-mile radius of some of the Colombian Army's most notorious recent defeats at the hands of the FARC.

Training. U.S. military trainers offer their Colombian counterparts training in skills that can be applied easily to counter-guerrilla operations. Small unit tactics, light infantry skills, ambush techniques, marksmanship and other skills are equally applicable for counterinsurgency situations.

Intelligence. In March 1999, the United States loosened its guidelines for sharing intelligence about guerrilla activity with Colombian military units. In drug-producing areas, guerrilla-related intelligence may now be shared even if it has no counternarcotics content.

Guerrilla involvement in drugs. Several FARC and ELN fronts earn profits by protecting the drug trade in areas they control. As a result, U.S.-supported units will inevitably become involved in the wider conflict even if pursuing a narrow anti-drug mission. At the same time, U.S. planners are not adequately taking into account paramilitary groups' own admitted involvement in the drug trade.

This is a continuation of a misguided policy. If the United States really has $1 billion to spend on the anti-drug effort in Colombia, it should be part of a long-term effort to eliminate the reasons why Colombians choose to cultivate drugs in the first place. These reasons—state neglect of rural areas, a nonexistent rule of law, a lack of economic infrastructure and opportunity—not only explain the flourishing drug trade; they also account in part for the proliferation of armed groups in Colombia's countryside.

President Pastrana has indicated a strong interest in bringing state services and the rule of law to rural Colombia. But U.S. assistance so far has been overwhelmingly military in nature. While military and police aid to Colombia totaled almost $300 million in 1999—plus $70 million for a crop-fumigation program—assistance for alternative development, judicial reform, and human rights added up to less than $7 million. While the upcoming aid package promises more economic assistance in the aggregate, it is likely to carry a similar imbalance in favor of military assistance. The United States' all-stick-and-no-carrot anti-drug strategy in Colombia not only has human rights implications—it is also not effective.

There are no easy answers in Colombia and there is no magic package. In our view, however, a positive Colombia package would center on the following:

1. Aid to strengthen Colombian government investigations into human rights violations and drug trafficking. While impunity for severe human rights abuses is the norm in Colombia, there are effective Colombian government institutions that could benefit from U.S. resources. The United States could expand existing judicial programs and fund technical training for judges, investigative techniques for police, and witness-protection programs.

2. Peace initiatives. The United States should fund civil society peace initiatives, which range from local community roundtables, consensus-building community development projects, local mediation programs and church-led programs of dialogue to anti-kidnapping campaigns.

3. Alternative development and other economic assistance. The United States should fund comprehensive alternative development programs for small coca and poppy growers to encourage them to switch to legal crops. Currently, the United States has allocated funding only for a small program for the poppy-growing area. The United States should make a sizeable multi-year commitment to fund programs for small coca growers in the areas where it is funding fumigation programs. The United States should provide other kinds of economic assistance as well, including for rural development in conflict areas.

4. Relief for the displaced. Colombian government and nongovernment programs are unable to address the needs of Colombia's enormous and growing displaced population. The United States should contribute substantially to emergency relief and especially long-term resettlement assistance for Colombia's displaced. The amount dedicated to date, $2 million, is far from adequate.

These programs must be accompanied by strong U.S. diplomatic support for a peace process in Colombia, along with efforts to encourage the Pastrana Administration to strengthen its human rights policy.

Finally, at the same time as the United States is considering a package of assistance to Colombia, it should consider expanded funding for U.S. drug treatment and prevention programs and programs for youth at risk in order to limit demand at home.

Part 6 • Labor

Labor leaders and activists have long been a primary target of violence in Colombia. International groups monitoring these abuses estimate that more than twenty-five hundred labor activists have been assassinated since 1987. Many union leaders have been accused by right-wing forces and government officials of ties to subversive groups and drug traffickers. Such accusations are especially aimed at leaders of the powerful left-wing unions in the strategic petroleum- and banana-export sectors. The selections below illustrate the gravity of the threats facing Colombian labor and the growing international pressure for the protection of labor rights in the country today.

A Lawyer Defends Jailed Petroleum Unionists

On February 27, 1988, a noted lawyer, Eduardo Umaña Mendoza, circulated a document in Colombia and abroad that denounced the repression of leaders of the Unión Sindical Obrera (USO), the oil workers' union. Reprinted below are the introduction to the document and its last two paragraphs. In the introductory material, Umaña denounces the widespread judicial abuses that have accompanied the efforts of the Colombian government to combat the guerrilla insurgency and crack down on the drug trade. In the penultimate paragraph he provides information on threats to his own life. The core of the document, not reproduced here, is a long, minutely detailed legal brief in which Umaña uses court documents from the proceedings against the oil workers to substantiate his general charges.

The son of Eduardo Umaña Luna, who coauthored the most influential book ever written on the Violence (*La Violencia en Colombia* [Bogotá, 1962]), Eduardo Umaña Mendoza was a long-time defender of political dissidents, trade unionists, and relatives of the "disappeared." On April 18, 1988, a little over six weeks after distributing the document excerpted here, Umaña Mendoza was assassinated by unidentified assailants in his office in Bogotá.

To the Workers of the World
Repression of the USO Workers
Faceless Justice without a Trace of Justice

It is my intention in this document to offer a view of the true character of Colombian justice, especially the system of regional justice, called "faceless justice," which has been in force for several years. "Faceless justice" was implemented for the investigation and judgment of crimes committed by drug traffickers and narco-terrorists. That notwithstanding, I am at present acting as defending counsel for leaders from unions such as that of the petroleum workers, the Unión Sindical Obrera (USO), who have been judged and imprisoned under the dark uncertainty of "faceless justice." This is because ways have been sought and motives unjustly invented to link narco-terrorism with activities that are exclusively related to unions.

I am at present the defending counsel in eighteen criminal lawsuits against top leaders of the USO. Three of them are currently in prison; others are provisionally paroled.

Let me try to characterize "faceless justice." Colombia is ruled by a formal democracy, but given the country's economic and political backwardness, which naturally has an influence on the judicial system, numerous guarantees stemming from democratic principles are proclaimed, but by no means practiced. This phenomenon is especially pronounced in "faceless justice."

In dealing with "faceless justice" in Colombia, two fundamental aspects must be borne in mind. The first is a juridical and bureaucratic structure with a clear inquisitorial bias because of its secret character, which offers no guarantees to an accused person. Consequently, the possibilities for defense are minimal. "Faceless justice" is an extreme violation of international treaties and accords including the Universal Declaration of Human Rights, the American Convention of Human Rights, the San José Pact, and so on. It violates, as will be shown below, the principles of due process, the right to defense, and the presumption of innocence.

In the second place, it must be made clear that "faceless justice" is not only a deformed juridical structure as compared with the universal principles of law, but also corresponds to a degraded, closed, corrupt, and reactionary political structure supported by public officials with the same characteristics. High-ranking officials of justice are a clear example. As a result, any expression of social discontent must be silenced by all means, judicial as well as extra-judicial.

The leaders of the petroleum workers' union (USO), who struggle for workers' rights, for national sovereignty, and for the defense of the nation's resources, have been the main victims of "faceless justice." Theirs is a clear case of political persecution. As a result, Pedro Chaparro, César Carrillo, and Alvaro Solano are imprisoned unjustly, and Fredy Pulecio was freed only with difficulty and his liberty is only provisional.

Let us look at some of the strategies most frequently used by the State in the criminal cases against the USO leaders. One must bear in mind that in Colombia criminal proceedings are fully written down and there is a record of all testimony and actions taken.

1. Interference by the executive power in criminal proceedings. As a first step, the government, using military petitions and intelligence reports, connects in a capricious and unfounded way the legal activity of defense of the workers' rights with crimes such as rebellion and terrorism. The intent is to stigmatize these labor leaders and raise charges against them before trial. Similarly, the Army prepares witnesses of low morality, pays them for their services, and lodges them in military installations; these people then confirm the accusations.

2. Irregular testimonies. As a result of the above, statements are often contradictory, a fact that renders them invalid before the law. Much testimony, because it is not spontaneous and is provided by people of very low morality, lacks coherence and concrete detail; much is obviously fallacious or contradictory. This notwithstanding, such accusations are the foundation upon which judicial officials pass rulings deciding on the imprisonment and subsequent condemnation of the accused persons, as was the case with the leaders of the USO.

3. Actions by high judicial officials that irrationally break with all judicial norms. When a judge acquits an accused person for lack of proof, instead of being freed, the person's case can be revised by a secret ("faceless") tribunal of high-ranking officials who can, at their discretion, revoke the decision of acquittal and condemn the accused.

4. Unjust treatment of defense lawyers and death threats against them. [Note: There follows a long section, not included here, that documents each of the points. The material on point 4 and the concluding paragraph of the document are reproduced below.]

On February 16, 1988, in the city of Bogotá, before the judicial officials involved in this investigation, I informed them about plans to assassinate me. I told them that early in February I received two different calls, both in the morning hours. In both, a masculine voice expressed concern over the imminence of my assassination by judicial officials involved in criminal investigations, members of military intelligence, and high-ranking security officials of Ecopetrol, the Colombian State petroleum corporation. The person informed me that the people responsible for the assassination plan have a direct connection with the investigations made in the criminal lawsuit against union leader César Carrillo and that the reasons for it were the denunciations and inquirics that I have made regarding the fabrications against Carrillo. Likewise, the person said that the authors of the plan considered me to be a danger because of the denunciations I have made against the State's security bodies and against Ecopetrol officials for their undue interference in criminal lawsuits.

"Faceless justice" sits at the center of this panorama of flagrant violation of civil and political rights, of denial of due process and the right to defense. What must be done now is to struggle for immediate change in order to right this situation. The most crucial change needed is the total derogation of "faceless justice," with all its trappings. Undue interference by government officials in the administration of justice must also be investigated. An appropriate climate for the defense during the procedural stage of criminal lawsuits must be established, and the allegations of defense lawyers and the claims of those defended must be duly taken into account. None of the above will be achieved without the definitive support of the International Community.

Eduardo Umaña Mendoza
February 27, 1988

The Killing of a Union Leader

On December 23, 1999, César Herrera Torreglosa, a leader of one of the important banana workers' unions, Sintrainagro, was assassinated in Ciénega, Magdalena. Violence against banana workers has a long history in Colombia and is intimately connected to major developments in national life. Ciénaga was the site of the infamous massacre of hundreds of banana workers and their families by the army during a major strike against United Fruit in 1928. The massacre contributed to the fall of the Conservative regime and the ascent to power of the Liberal party in 1930; helped launch the political career of Jorge Eliécer Gaitán, who investigated it before the Colombian Congress; and inspired the most powerful scene in *One Hundred Years of Solitude*, the world-famous novel of Nobel laureate Gabriel García Márquez.

At the time of his death, Herrera Torreglosa's union was engaged in contract negotiations with the banana employers' association, AGUARA, which includes transnational firms that have inherited the role United Fruit once played in the oldest of the Colombian banana zones. (The newest zone, in the region of Urabá, lies on the north coast some four hundred kilometers to the southwest of

Ciénaga; since the 1980s, as detailed in Chapters 1 and 9, Urabá has been the scene of some of the fiercest struggles between labor and capital and between guerrilla and paramilitary forces in Colombia.) The document below, a press release from the International Confederation of Free Trade Unions (ICFTU), was put on the Internet by the Colombian Labor Monitor (http://www.prairienet.org/clm), an important source for the country's labor news.

International Confederation of Free Trade Unions
Wednesday, 22 December 1999
Brussels, Belgium

The world's largest trade union body has expressed outrage at the killing of a senior leader in Colombia's trade union movement and vowed it "would not leave his assassination unpunished."

César Herrera Torreglosa, General Secretary of the Colombian agricultural workers' union Sintrainagro, was shot while entering the union's regional office in Ciénaga, capital of Magdalena province. His union represents workers in negotiations with the banana employers' organisation, AGUARA, which includes the multinational corporations Del Monte and Chiquita.

Herrera was also the leader of a coordinating body for Latin American banana workers. He had complained of repeated death threats prior to his murder on December 13, but authorities refused to include his union in a governmental protection scheme designed for threatened union activists.

"Our colleague's murder makes an utter mockery of the solemn undertaking signed by Colombia's government last month in Geneva to co-operate fully in bringing anti-union repression to a halt," ICFTU General Secretary Bill Jordan said in Brussels today. In November, Colombia's Labour Minister had signed an agreement with the country's trade unions calling on the Director-General of the International Labour Office (ILO), Juan Somavia, to dispatch an ILO "Direct Contacts Mission" to Colombia. This mission is now scheduled for the first half of February 2000. Its brief is to evaluate the situation and offer advice on how to curb the violence against trade unionists in the country.

"Herrera's brutal murder can only be seen as a slap in the face of the ILO mission, and undoubtedly brings us one step closer to the eventual appointment of a full-fledged Commission of Inquiry," Bill Jordan added. The agreement under which the Direct Contacts mission is sent to Colombia was seen as a last-ditch effort by Bogotá to avoid the appointment by the ILO's Governing Body of a formal Commission of Inquiry into violations of basic trade union rights, which have led to the assassination of over 2,500 trade union leaders and activists in the country since 1987.

Following the agreement, the ILO Governing Body is now committed to voting at its June 2000 session on the appointment of such a Commission. It would be the strongest-ever international legal investigation into Colombia's labour legislation and practice. The last ILO Commission of Inquiry, which examined Burma's systematic use of forced labour, led to the country's quasi-expulsion from the ILO, a UN Specialised Agency, in June 1999.

"By refusing Mr. Herrera special police protection in the face of repeated death threats, the Colombian Government has fully demonstrated, at best its incompetence, at worst its direct complicity in his assassination," the ICFTU's General Secretary also commented today. "I am shocked beyond belief that this was allowed to happen, especially so soon after Bogotá's signature of a formal international accord on this very issue. They must stop these killings from occurring, and they must do it now!" he added.

An ICFTU spokesperson said the organisation would now hold consultations with its Regional Inter-American Organisation (ICFTU-ORIT) and its other partners and examine practical measures aimed at stepping up its international campaign aimed at obtaining the appointment of the ILO Commission of Inquiry in June.

U.S. Labor and the Colombian Crisis

During the Cold War decades the leadership of the largest U.S. labor confederation, the American Federation of Labor-Congress of Industrial Organizations (AFL-CIO), uncritically supported the foreign policy of the U.S. government. Like the International Confederation of Free Trade Unions, in which it played a decisive role, the AFL-CIO opposed Communist-led and Communist-influenced labor organizations and generally supported the international capitalist agenda of the government of the United States. This began to change by the late 1980s, as U.S. labor began to realize that the expansion of U.S. manufacturing corporations abroad was steadily eliminating jobs and eroding the strength of industrial unions, and as the Soviet Union entered into crisis and the Cold War came to an end. During the 1990s the U.S. labor movement became increasingly critical of the neo-liberal economic agenda of successive Washington administrations and its leaders became more vocal supporters of workers' rights and democratic reform both at home and abroad.

These new commitments were dramatically revealed during the protests that disrupted the Ministerial Meeting of the World Trade Organization in Seattle in late November and early December 1999. In alliance with radical environmentalists and progressive church and community groups, unionists paralyzed the largest port of the most trade-dependent U.S. state, joined in demonstrations calling for cancellation of the Third World debt, and helped shut down the commercial core of the city in protest over free-trade policies that the demonstrators believed threaten the world environment and labor standards. It would be a mistake to overemphasize the radical implications of U.S. labor's current position, however; the leadership of the AFL-CIO remains beholden to the Democratic party, whose leaders continue to push the neo-liberal agenda at home and abroad.

In the following letter, addressed to the Secretary of State, the current president of the AFL-CIO, John Sweeney, expresses concern over violations of labor and human rights in Colombia. The letter provides a good overview of the current situation in Colombia and U.S. policy toward that nation from the perspective of a moderate labor leader.

September 15, 1999

The Honorable Madeleine K. Albright
Secretary of State
U.S. Department of State
Washington, D.C. 20520

Dear Madame Secretary:

I am writing to express my deep concern, which I know you share, regarding the continuing violations of worker rights and other human rights in Colombia. Colombia's trade unions have been the leading advocates for peace, human rights, and economic justice in a nation afflicted by internal violence and external economic pressures. But they have paid a high price for speaking out.

According to the International Confederation of Free Trade Unions (ICFTU), more than 90 trade unionists were murdered in 1998, mostly at the hands of paramilitary organizations with support from government security forces. Among the victims was Jorge Ortega, Vice-President of the Confederación Unitaria de Trabajadores (CUT) and one of many union leaders who have denounced both guerrilla and government violence and played key roles in efforts by civil society to achieve an effective and lasting peace. The violence has continued this year: on July 13, Humberto Herrera Gallego, President of the Sindicato de Trabajadores del Municipio de Puerto Rico, was killed; on August 1, the Human Rights Secretary of the CUT, Jesús Gonzáles, narrowly escaped an assassination attempt in which one of his bodyguards was killed; and on August 31, Domingo Tovar Arrieta, the Secretary of Organization of the CUT, was also the target of an assassination attempt in which a bodyguard was wounded.

As noted in the State Department's Human Rights Report, the International Labor Organization (ILO) has criticized the Colombian Government for failing, since November 1996, to provide it with information on a single case of detention, trial, and conviction of anyone responsible for the murder of trade unionists. Union members who strike or exercise other internationally recognized worker rights have been prosecuted in regional courts, where judges' and witnesses' identities are hidden and secret evidence can be admitted. The AFL-CIO has endorsed the position of the Workers' Party in the ILO in support of a Commission of Inquiry to Colombia this year, and I greatly appreciate the support that our government has given to this position.

While physical terror against unionists has drawn international condemnation, the Colombian government's program of economic deregulation, privatization, and flexibilization, fulfilling the prescription of the international financial institutions, has also undermined freedom of association and taken a severe toll on working families. The official unemployment rate now exceeds 20 percent, and mass dismissals and firings are widespread. Child labor is common in the cut-flower and coal-mining industries; studies indicate that there are 784,000 working children between the ages of 6 and 11. Despite the trade unions' support for the peace process, the Colombian government has been unwilling to involve labor in a substantive dialogue about social and economic reform.

Notwithstanding these threats to human and worker rights, Congress has sharply increased aid to the Colombian military for anti-narcotics efforts, while placing some limitations on aid to specific military units and training for individual officers implicated in human rights violations. The Director of the White House Drug Control Policy, General Barry McCaffrey, has now requested an additional $570 million in anti-narcotics aid, including sharing U.S. intelligence with the Colombian military with no restrictions on how such intelligence is used. Recent press reports indicate that the Administration is seriously considering a major increase in both military aid and IMF support for economic restructuring.

While I share the Administration's concerns about the conflict in Colombia and greatly appreciate the efforts that have been undertaken to reduce human rights violations by Colombian security forces, I believe that our government must be extremely wary of deepening military entanglement with a government whose anti-union record is so clear. At a minimum, existing conditions on disbursement of aid to the military should be retained and broadened to cover all military units, with additional supervision by U.S. Embassy personnel. Progress should be required on investigating the murders of union members and human rights activists and adjudicating those responsible, and on the dismantling of the regional courts. Additional assistance should be provided to strengthen the Colombian government's ability to investigate and prosecute human rights violations and to assist nongovernmental organizations engaged in peace, human rights, economic development, and humanitarian relief efforts. As is the case of all countries seeking aid for reconstruction, the financial institutions and government should seek full participation of trade unions and other civil society organizations.

I greatly appreciate your attention to these concerns, and I look forward to hearing from you.

Sincerely,

John J. Sweeney
President

Part 7 • Drugs

Readers of this volume have seen how central the drug trade is to the violent crisis facing Colombia today. Escalating demand for illegal narcotics, especially in the United States, and increasing production of coca leaves and poppies in Colombia have been accompanied by the growth of powerful, ruthlessly violent criminal organizations engaged in processing, transporting, and selling cocaine and heroin abroad. Using their enormous profits, drug traffickers have corrupted Colombian politics and at times declared war on the State itself. As detailed in Chapter 4, drug money has also helped destroy the vitality of the nation's economy. Drug money has led to the concentration of land ownership in areas of traditional agricultural production in northern and western Colombia, and to rapid destruction of tropical forests by coca-growing small holders on the agricultural frontier in the southern and eastern parts of the country. Drug profits contributed to the rise of the paramilitary right and have helped make the leftist guerrillas rich and increasingly well armed.

Under tremendous political and economic pressure from the United States, Bogotá's drug policy has been made to conform to Washington's priorities. The U.S. government has waged an escalating "war on drugs," emphasizing the reduction of production over that of demand, and repression of producers, traffickers, and users over efforts at crop substitution, education, and rehabilitation. Key to these efforts in Colombia are two controversial policies, extradition and eradication. The first has cost Colombia dearly as drug traffickers vulnerable to deportation to the United States have periodically unleashed bombing campaigns against the State and innocent civilians in attempts to force the repeal of extradition. The second relies on aerial spraying of the powerful herbicide glyphosate (known commercially as Roundup). Despite its widespread use—

and large-scale damage to the Colombian ecosystem—aerial spraying has not reduced the production of coca, which more than doubled between 1992 and 1998.

The abject failure of U.S. drug policy is widely recognized in Colombia today, and even political moderates, as the following two documents from the mainstream Liberal daily *El Tiempo* illustrate, are challenging its basic premises. The first is the lead editorial for October 8, 1999, while the second is a column by the respected journalist, Daniel Samper Pizano, published on November 10, 1999. [Translator's note: The quotations in this column have been retranslated into English from the Spanish in the text.]

Fumigation without Results

In the last four years the cultivation of illicit crops in Colombia has grown by more than 200 percent. That fact, revealed in a recently published report of the Transnational Institute, demands that we ask ourselves what has been the real effectiveness of the strategy of aerial spraying with glyphosate, which since 1994 has been applied with growing intensity over a great part of our national territory.

This controversial method of dispersing by air powerful herbicides on illegal plantings not only has not produced the expected reduction in the area cultivated. Rather, the cultivated area has multiplied in size, while the spraying has had devastating ecological effects on the fragile tropical jungle areas and the highland watersheds where coca and poppies, respectively, are grown. The coca-producing area in Colombia, which in 1992 was 40 thousand hectares, last year surpassed 100 thousand. That is more than half of what is cultivated in the whole Andean area. What is paradoxical is that, in the same time period, Bolivia and Peru—where historically coca was planted and where aerial fumigation is not used—have substantially reduced the area cultivated. That indicates that in those countries crop substitution and alternative development policies have produced better results. And it suggests that it is time to rethink the policies of eradication that we have been applying here.

The Colombian situation is particularly complex because the areas of drug cultivation are almost completely found in zones of guerrilla influence. That not only makes the task of eradication more difficult; it converts it into a factor favorable to the guerrillas and their recruiting efforts. The thousands of peasants and coca scrapers whose livelihood depend on this activity see as an enemy a State which, with the help of the United States,

This article originally appeared in Spanish as "Fumigación sin resultados," *El Tiempo*, October 8, 1999. It is published here by permission of *El Tiempo*.

arrives in armed helicopters bent on destroying their means of subsistence from the air. In the end they look on a guerrilla who protects their crops and fights against their eradication as an ally.

This is a self-destructive vicious circle. The more fumigation there is, the more cultivation. Those who cultivate the crop are pushed out of a given area only to reappear in another. Fleeing from fumigation, they go deeper and deeper into the jungle, expanding the agricultural frontier with devastating effects on the Amazonian ecosystem. More than a million liters of glyphosate have been dumped on the Colombian jungle and 1,200,000 hectares of forests have been destroyed by cultivators and fumigators. To the already-mentioned political, social, and ecological costs of this eradication strategy, one must add the millions of dollars invested and the dozens of planes and helicopters downed. Not to mention the human cost, and the police agents and soldiers who have lost their lives carrying out this controversial campaign.

Since the beginning in 1974 of the first fumigations with paraquat of marijuana plantings on the Sierra Nevada of Santa Marta—under the guidance and pressure of the United States—we have witnessed 25 years of chemical warfare against drugs and the result leaves much to be desired. Despite the sums invested, the hectares eradicated, the heroic efforts of the Antinarcotics Police, the results are dismaying, if not counterproductive.

It is time we completely rethink the strategy of fumigation of plantings as the central instrument of antinarcotics policy and pay more attention to its social and environmental dimensions. We are certain that the Colombian government understands this. But will Washington?

Chicago Once Again: Why Must We Repeat with Drugs the Disaster of Prohibition in the Twenties in the United States?

On January 16, 1920, the Volstead Law, a constitutional amendment that prohibited the manufacture, distribution, sale, and consumption of alcohol, went into effect in the United States. That night, bars and taverns were closed "forever"; distilleries became illegal factories; bottles were confiscated, and having a drink became a criminal offense. The United States opted to make sobriety an affair of State, and proclaimed itself the leader of a crusade. "Now we will take to the world the new doctrine that has shaken the foundations of our republic," said the politician William J[ennings] Bryan.

This article, by Daniel Samper Pizano, originally appeared in Spanish as "Otra vez Chicago," *El Tiempo*, November 10, 1999. It is published here by permission of *El Tiempo*.

Thirteen years later, the same voters who passed this transcendental reform approved its dismantling. In that short time, Prohibition had produced such devastating effects on society, justice, politics, customs, the prison system, and U.S. values that, once people understood that Prohibition threatened the very democratic stability of the nation, they decided to overturn it.

The repressive fight against alcohol fostered corruption, violence, and the mafia. Chicago revealed the extent of the putrefaction. Simple bodyguards such as Al Capone became powerful kingpins of organized crime. Honorable police chiefs rented themselves out to the mafia, and mayors such as William Dever put together sinister emporiums of corruption. In clandestine bars great fortunes were born, such as that of the Kennedys.

Justice fell apart. As the English author Sean Dennis Cashman wrote in his book *Prohibition*, "Prohibition stopped up the courts, impeded impartial justice, and undermined the application of the law." Jails were filled with citizens, few of whom were real criminals. In 1910 there were 32.4 people in jail for every 100,000 inhabitants; in 1926 the number had reached 41.8.

Violence exploded. Prohibitionists claimed before 1920 that alcohol stimulated delinquency. But a commission showed that, far from declining, crimes related to alcohol rose after Prohibition. Murders multiplied. Between 1920 and 1929, 135 criminals and 55 policemen had died as a direct result of the suppression of alcohol.

Bands of gangsters became a plague, as did contraband in rum and other liquor from neighboring countries. Between 1925 and 1928, illegal commerce from Canada grew 75 percent, and the production of Canadian alcohol doubled to supply clandestine consumption in the United States.

The worst thing about Prohibition is that it did not even reduce alcohol consumption. To the contrary, elevated to the status of forbidden fruit, drink became more attractive than before. The 0.97 gallons [consumed] per capita of 1919 fell to 0.73 in the first year; but from there on, consumption began to grow and in 1927 reached 1.14. Following Prohibition (1934), consumption per capita fell again to 0.97. (Today it is more than 2.5.)

Although cases of cirrhosis fell, alcohol of bad quality (the product of clandestine distilleries and imports lacking sanitary controls) left thousands of people blind, paralyzed, and sick. Between 1925 and 1929, adulterated liquor caused 4 deaths per million. In New York, in just four days in 1928, 34 died after drinking homemade whiskey.

The effects of Prohibition were so devastating by 1930 that future president Franklin D. Roosevelt came out against it. He said, "It has encouraged the consumption of powerful toxic substances, corruption, and hypocrisy, it has stimulated disrespect for law and order, and it has flooded the country with illegal liquor that pays no taxes." At the beginning of 1933, Prohibition was rescinded, and on April 7 bars and liquor stores reopened.

History Repeats Itself

It is unbelievable that the same policy that failed with alcohol seventy years ago could repeat itself with drugs. What interests or myopia lie behind the intention to impose as a good thing on poor countries a policy that proved so bad for the United States? Thomas Coffey, in *The Long Thirst*, writes: "The parallel between our present anti-narcotics politics and the prohibition of alcohol is too striking to ignore. . . . It is deplorable that methods that failed to suppress alcohol and that, on the contrary, encouraged its greater consumption, are employed now against narcotics." And he adds: "It is reasonable to ask if the agencies responsible for combating the drug trade are not being used instead to perpetuate it."

Two professors from Harvard, [James B.] Bakalar and [Lester] Grinspoon, affirm in *Drug Control in a Free Society* [(1998)]: "The prohibition of alcohol and that of marijuana today produce equal effects: costs of arrests and punishment, mockery of the law, organized criminal violence, police corruption, oppression, and the poisonous adulteration of the product."

The Colombian Extra-Cabinet Minister Jaime Ruiz has pointed out the failure of the repressive policy. The citations and reflections of a recent *El Tiempo* editorial back him up. Then, as now, the only way to solve the problem is "legalize, control, and educate."

It is time to begin a diplomatic campaign so that the International Community can understand this and support it.

Part 8 • A Call for Peace

The vast majority of Colombians want peace and for years have been expressing that desire through a variety of established organizations—political parties, unions, church and community organizations, even theater groups. Recently, new organizations whose sole purpose is to urge an end to the war have appeared, the largest and most influential of them being Colombia Libre. On October 24, 1999, Colombia Libre organized the largest peace demonstrations yet seen in that country; several million people took to the streets in Colombian cities and towns and many thousands more demonstrated in major cities around the world. The demonstrations were scheduled to coincide with the long-awaited opening of peace negotiations between the government of President Andrés

Pastrana and the FARC in La Uribe, Meta. Many on the left did not participate in these demonstrations, which were organized by Francisco Santos, scion of the traditional Liberal family that directs *El Tiempo*. Others applauded the idea but believed that the armed contenders would pay little heed to marchers in the streets. Be that as it may, the demonstrations were impressive for their size, the range of social groups that participated, and the commitment of those who attended.

The following document, a large paid advertisement that appeared in the newspaper *El Espectador* on October 10, 1999, is an example of the publicity that preceded the march. The text was accompanied by a gruesome photograph of a massacre.

Figures from last year
Dead: 6,000 people
Kidnapped: 1,700 people
Displaced: 450,000 people
Massacred: 1,750 people
Disappeared: 450 people
Municipios semi-destroyed: 30
Direct Costs: 3,000 trillion pesos
Civilians killed: more than half of the victims

Who gains from this absurd war?
You are paying for the cost of this war and you are the one who can stop it.
No more! Stand up for Peace.

First Nation-Wide March for Peace, October 24.

Appendix

A Comparative Statistical Note on Homicide Rates in Colombia

Andrés Villaveces

In this brief study, Andrés Villaveces breaks down statistics on homicide in Colombia and compares them to homicide rates in other countries in the Americas. The data confirm the extraordinarily high rates of homicide in Colombia in recent years. Villaveces then compares homicide rates in the United States and Colombia during the twentieth century, finding that both countries experienced two peaks of greatly increased homicide rates. In Colombia, only one of these may be drug related. In the United States, however, both coincide with efforts to prohibit the consumption of substances declared illegal: alcohol in the 1920s and early 1930s, and drugs such as cocaine in the 1980s and 1990s.

Andrés Villaveces holds a medical degree from the Universidad del Bosque in Bogotá and a master's degree in public health from Emory University. He is currently a doctoral candidate in the Program in Epidemiology in the School of Public Health at the University of Washington in Seattle. His dissertation analyzes the effects of alcohol policy on deaths resulting from motor-vehicle crashes in the United States in the late twentieth century.

The social burden due to violence has changed dramatically during the twentieth century, both within and among countries. Extremely high rates of violent episodes associated with war or social conflict have alternated with situations in which violence is a rare event, or vice versa. In the last decade, widespread violence has been characteristic of some places in virtually every region of the world, but in some regions the problem is especially severe. According to the classification of the global burden of disease published by Christopher Murray and Alan Lopez in 1996, two regions of the world stand out for carrying a substantial burden due to violence: Sub-Saharan Africa, and Latin America and the Caribbean.

In the years indicated in the table below, 12 countries in Latin America reported annual homicide rates greater than 10 per 100,000 people. During the 1990s, homicide was among the 5 top causes of death in 17 countries in the Americas; Colombia, Guatemala, and El Salvador reported the highest rates. Apart from political and drug-related violence, many other forms of violence have contributed to the high rates of homicide in the region. Domestic violence and child abuse are also part of the problem, but it is believed that these events are substantially underreported.

Crude Rates of Homicide (per 100,000 People) in Countries of the Americas

Country	*Last Available Year between 1988 and 1995*	*Last Available Year between 1994 and 1997*
Argentina	4.2	4.1
Brazil*	**17.8**	**23.5**
Canada	2.1	1.6
Colombia*†	**76.3**	**73.3**
Chile	3.0	3.1
Costa Rica	3.7	5.3
Cuba	7.3	6.6
Ecuador*	**12.6**	**12.3**
El Salvador*	**39.9**	**40.9**
United States*	**10.1**	8.2
Honduras	not available	not available
Guatemala*	**25.3**	2.2
Guyana	not available	**11.0**
Jamaica	1.8	1.3
Mexico*	**17.6**	**15.1**
Nicaragua	6.1	6.4
Panama	9.7	**12.7**
Paraguay	9.3	**11.6**
Peru	2.9	not available
Puerto Rico*	**23.2**	**22.4**
Dominican Republic	not available	**12.2**
Uruguay	4.3	4.4
Trinidad and Tobago*	8.0	**11.1**
Venezuela*	**11.2**	**13.5**
Average*	**14.7**	**14.7**

Source: Calculations based on basic indicators of health in Pan-American Health Organization, *Health Situation in the Americas* (Washington, DC, 1996, 1998).
*Rates higher than 10 per 100,000 people are considered high and are printed in bold.
†Country with the highest rates in the Americas.

Rates of homicide in Colombia have exceeded by far those of the other countries in the region. During this century, as shown in Figure 1, Colombia has experienced two periods of increased violence: between 1948 and 1966; and more recently, and with greater magnitude, from the mid-1980s until the early 1990s. During the last decade a steady decline has been observed in some parts of the country.

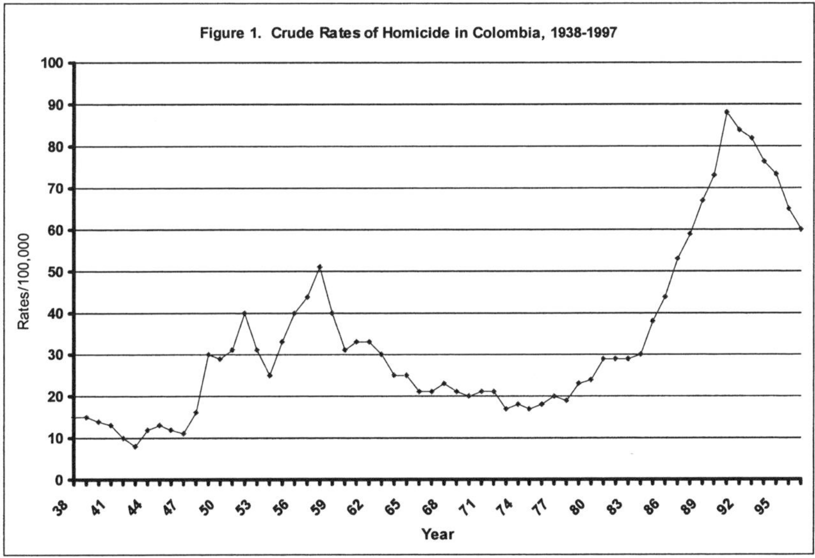

Sources: Víctor Cárdenas, *Tasas de homicidios en Colombia, 1938–1991* (Bogotá: Departamento Administrativo Nacional de Estadística, 1994), and Centro de Referencia Nacional sobre Violencia, *Reporte del comportamiento de las lesiones fatales y no fatales en Colombia* (Bogotá: Instituto Nacional de Medicina Legal y Ciencias Forenses, 1997).

Between 1983 and 1993 the annual rate of homicide in Colombia increased 366 percent, from 24 to 88 per 100,000. In 1997 there were 197,729 reported intentional injuries in Colombia. Of these, 87 percent (171,731) were nonfatal injuries. Of the 25,998 fatal injuries, 93 percent (24,306) were homicides and the rest suicides. Of the total number of fatal homicide incidents, 93 percent were committed by males. The ratio of male victims to female victims was 13:1. Among all the homicide victims, 64 percent were between 15 and 34 years old. The rate of homicide for males in 1997 was 229 per 100,000 people. For females it was 15 homicides per 100,000 people (Centro de Referencia Nacional sobre Violencia, 1995 and 1997). During 1997, the monthly average of homicides due to all causes was 2,026, or approximately 67 per day, or one every 3 hours. The highest rates of homicide were reported in the departments of Guaviare, Antioquia, Risaralda, Arauca, and Valle del Cauca. Inaccurate reporting of events in rural areas might underestimate the actual rates of homicide, especially in regions where active confrontations between regular and irregular forces are taking place.

Readers of this book may find it instructive to compare rates of homicide in the United States and Colombia during the twentieth century

(Figure 2). Two peaks in homicide rates have been observed in the United States: between 1919 and 1935, and from the mid-1970s to the beginning of the 1990s. As in Colombia, this later period has been greater in magnitude, although rates in Colombia were approximately 10 times higher than those reported for the United States.

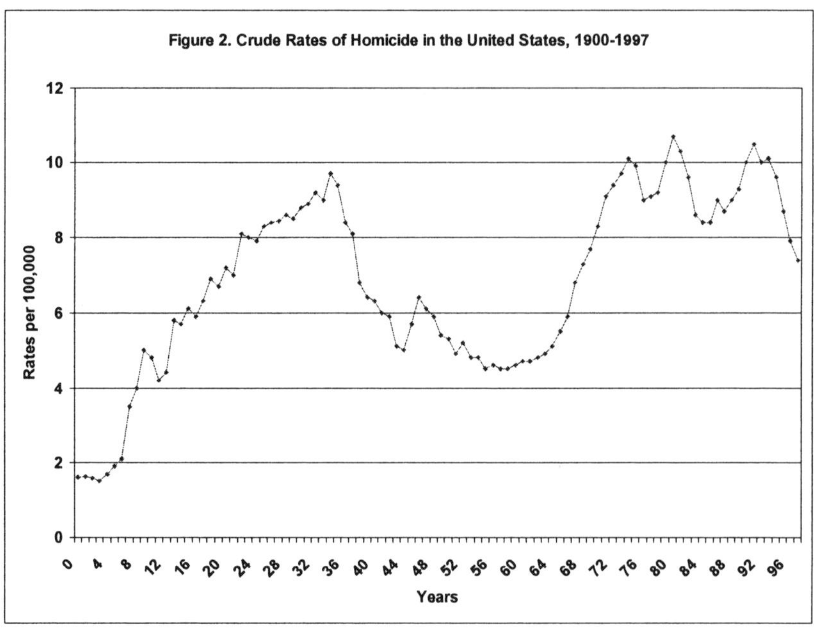

Source: National Center for Health Statistics, *Vital Statistics of the United States* (Washington, DC, 1997).

Although there are causal, temporal, and magnitude differences between the two countries, there are also some important similarities that may shed some light on the roots of the problem. The period of the Violence in Colombia was characterized mostly by a political confrontation between the Liberal and Conservative parties, but during the 1990s, confrontations among different armed actors seemed to be exacerbated by the drug trade. In the United States, the earlier period of increased homicides coincided with an era characterized by policies aimed at prohibiting alcohol consumption.

In the last two decades, a sharp increase followed by a steady decline in homicide rates both in Colombia and the United States has been observed. One hypothesis explains these changes mostly in terms of drug markets. During the growth stage of the illegal drug businesses, there is a period of competition for drug markets fueled by increased demand. The competition for these illegal markets manifests itself mostly in urban areas and through young populations who have easy access to firearms. The stabilization of such markets eventually leads to reductions in violent events (Blumstein et al., 2000). Reductions can also be achieved by policies aimed at reducing access to firearms (Villaveces et al., 2000). Additional factors may include economic policies that increase social inequality and demographic changes in the composition and distribution of the population. Migration to urban areas for economic reasons or because of political violence, and increases in the proportion of populations that engage in riskier conducts (such as adolescents and young adults), coupled with changes in their social attitudes, have also been associated with greater levels of violence.

During the 1990s, there has been an overall decline in homicide both in Colombia and the United States. In Colombia, this decline has been observed mostly in urban areas where most people now live. However, certain rural areas have experienced marked increases in homicide rates since 1995. The combination of structural violence (for example, the social inequality built into the system), reactive violence (including guerrilla insurrection), and institutional violence (such as that perpetrated by the State itself) continues to fuel the Colombian homicide rate.

References

Blumstein, Alfred, Frederick P. Rivara, and Richard Rosenfeld. "The Rise and Decline of Homicide—and Why." *Annual Review of Public Health* 21 (May 2000): 505–41.

Cárdenas, Víctor. *Tasas de homicidios en Colombia, 1938–1991*. Bogotá: Departpamento Administrativo Nacional de Estadística, 1994.

Centro de Referencia Nacional sobre Violencia. *Reporte del comportamiento de las lesiones fatales y no fatales en Colombia*. Bogotá: Instituto Nacional de Medicina Legal y Ciencias Forenses, 1995 and 1997.

Murray, Christopher J. L., and Alan D. Lopez. *Global Health Statistics*. Geneva: World Health Organization, 1996.

Pan-American Health Organization. *Health Situation in the Americas*. Washington, DC: Pan-American Health Organization, 1996 and 1998.

Villaveces, Andrés, Peter Cummings, Victoria E. Espitia, Thomas D. Koepsell, Barbara McKnight, and Arthur Kellermann. "Effect of a Ban on Carrying of Firearms in Two Colombian Cities." *Journal of the American Medical Association* 283, no. 9 (March 2000): 1205–9.

Glossary

acción de tutela

Legal provision in the Constitution of 1991 giving citizens recourse to the courts when they believe public officials have violated or failed to protect their constitutional rights.

ANUC

Asociación Nacional de Usuarios Campesinos (National Peasant Association). Organization of rural workers and smallholders promoted by the government of Carlos Lleras Restrepo in the late 1960s. It fostered radical agrarian mobilizations in the early 1970s, but declined rapidly thereafter as guerrilla groups and urban reformers attempted to capture its leadership and the government withdrew its support.

AUC

Autodefensas Unidas de Colombia (United Self-Defense Groups of Colombia). Formed in the late 1990s, and currently under the leadership of Carlos Castaño, this is the largest national organization of right-wing paramilitary groups in Colombia.

boleteo

Form of extortion. The term derives from the means—the short, anonymous, often handwritten notes, or *boletas*—used to convey threats and terms to victims, usually rural property owners. Widespread during the Violence, *boleteo* is once again common in many rural areas.

cacique

Local political boss. Taken from the Spanish word for Indian chief, *cacique* is used interchangeably with *gamonal*, or local strongman.

chulavitas

Conservative police involved in the repression of Liberals during the Violence. The name derives from Chulavita, the *municipio* in the department of Boyacá where many of them were recruited.

clientelism

Term used to describe a political system, like patronage in the United States, in which the extension of favors (spoils) by politicians (bosses) to their followers (clients) is more important than ideological or programmatic affinity in determining political loyalty.

CODHES

Consultoría para los Derechos Humanos y el Desplazamiento (Consultancy for Human Rights and the Displaced).

colonos

Land settlers. Term usually connotes those who clear land and turn it to agricultural use in frontier areas. If the land in question is part of the public domain, it can be adjudicated to the user as a freehold. *Colonos* may also be squatters on private land, often unused parts of the huge estates called *latifundios*.

Constitution of 1886

This centralist, pro-Church Constitution, significantly amended in 1910, 1936, and 1957, served as Colombia's basic law until replaced by the Constitution of 1991.

CONVIVIR

Cooperativas para la Vigilancia y la Seguridad Privada. Rural community self-defense associations, created by the government in 1993. Following much controversy and evidence that many were linked to paramilitary groups, they were officially abolished in 1999.

CUT

Confederación Unitaria de Trabajadores (Unitary Federation of Workers). Labor federation founded in the mid-1980s. It united Liberal-, Conservative-, and Communist-led unions as well as independent ones.

department

Administrative unit of Colombia, roughly equivalent to a state in the United States.

ELN

Ejército de Liberación Nacional (Army of National Liberation). Revolutionary guerrilla group founded in the early 1960s. Inspired by the

Cuban example, and drawing early recruits from among university students, it consolidated itself in the Magdalena Medio, especially around the oil enclave at Barrancabermeja, Santander. Championing the nationalization of the Colombian petroleum sector, since the 1980s the ELN has specialized in the sabotage of oil pipelines and the kidnapping of executives and technicians of foreign oil companies operating in Colombia. During the 1990s the group broadened both its geographical influence and its political platform.

EPL

Ejército Popular de Liberación (Popular Army of Liberation). Maoist-inspired guerrilla group founded in 1967 and linked initially to the pro-Chinese Communist party in Colombia, the Partido Comunista Marxista-Leninista (PCML). Never very large, it laid down its arms following negotiations with the government in 1991.

extraditables

Colombians who, because of their involvement in the illegal drug trade, are vulnerable to extradition to the United States. The term was initially associated with the infamous kingpin of the Medellín cartel, Pablo Escobar, who declared war on the State over the issue of extradition in the late 1980s. Escobar's bombing campaign against government officials and innocent civilians contributed to the decision to ban extradition in the Constitution of 1991. Extradition was later reinstated, in part because of U.S. pressure, and *extraditables* were probably responsible for a series of bombings in Bogotá and other places late in 1999.

FARC

Fuerzas Armadas Revolucionarias de Colombia (Revolutionary Armed Forces of Colombia). The largest and most powerful of the guerrilla groups in Colombia. Unlike the Marxist guerrilla groups formed in the 1960s under the inspiration of the Cuban Revolution, the FARC evolved in response to government offensives in the 1950s against Communist-led rural enclaves of smallholders in the departments of Cundinamarca and Tolima. By the 1990s, the FARC had dozens of armed "fronts" operating throughout the country, most of them in peripheral areas and including zones deeply involved in the cultivation, processing, and commercialization of coca. In 1999 the FARC entered into wide-ranging peace negotiations with the government.

Fiscalía

The Public Prosecutor's Office, the Colombian equivalent of the U.S. Attorney General's Office.

fuero militar

Special legal rights enjoyed by the military, including military court jurisdiction over crimes committed by military personnel.

gaitanista

A follower of Jorge Eliécer Gaitán, the immensely popular Liberal politician whose assassination on April 9, 1948, precipitated widespread destruction in Bogotá and fanned the violence in the countryside.

gremios

Sectoral economic interest groups (examples include associations of cattle ranchers, merchants, and industrialists) that exercise great influence over economic and social policy.

Guaviare

Region of recent settlement and coca production in eastern Colombia.

llanos

Plains of eastern Colombia. *Llaneros* (cowboys) from this cattle-raising region have played an important role in Colombian wars since the time of Independence. During the Violence, the largest and most radically reformist of the Liberal insurgent groups operated here. Today, an area of expanding agricultural settlement, widening social conflict, and guerrilla activity, it includes important zones of coca production and processing.

M-19

Movement of April 19. A revolutionary group formed in 1972 following the defeat of the populist candidate General Gustavo Rojas Pinilla in the presidential election of April 19, 1970. Many observers, not only M-19 partisans, suspect that Rojas received more votes than the National Front candidate, Misael Pastrana Borrero, who was declared the winner. An eclectic group of middle-class populist Conservatives and leftists, the M-19 evolved into one of the most powerful guerrilla groups in the country. It declined following a disastrous attack on the Palace of Justice in 1985; and in 1990, after protracted negotiations, it signed a peace agreement with the government of Virgilio Barco. In the elections of 1990, M-19's first presidential candidate, Carlos Pizarro, was assassinated; its second, Antonio Navarro Wolf, won a sizable share of the vote. Under Navarro's direction, ex-M-19 partisans played a major role in the framing of the Constitution of 1991, but since that date their political influence has waned.

Magdalena Medio

Central Magdalena River Valley, encompassing low-lying parts of the departments of Cundinamarca, Boyacá, and Santander to the east, and Tolima and Antioquia to the west. It borders on the emerald zone of western Boyacá, whose long-established organizations of contrabandists moved easily into the illegal drug trade, and includes the petroleum complex around Barrancabermeja, where militant leftist labor unions have existed since the 1920s. It is the scene of much recent agricultural development by smallholders and squatters as well as by large-scale commercial farmers and cattle ranchers. Since the 1980s the area has become a major theater of violence in which leftist guerrillas, the paramilitary right, the drug mafia, and the army are all involved.

municipio

Administrative unit of Colombia, roughly equivalent to a county in the United States. The name of a *municipio* refers both to its largest town, or county seat, and to the county as a whole.

National Front (Frente Nacional)

Bipartisan governmental arrangement (1958–1974) in which the two major political parties, the Conservatives and the Liberals, sought to end the Violence by agreeing to alternate control of the presidency and to divide governmental positions equally between them. Credited with effectively ending the Violence between Liberals and Conservatives, the Front was widely criticized by other parties as exclusionary and discriminatory and was cited by armed guerrilla groups as a justification for their rebellion against the State.

NGO

Nongovernmental organization. In Colombia many of these nonprofit private organizations are involved in human rights defense and social development.

pájaros

Literally, "birds." Hired killers active especially in southwest Colombia during the Violence of the 1950s. They often acted with the support of Conservative party and government officials.

pesca milagrosa

Literally, "miraculous fishing." A tactic, begun by some guerrilla groups in the late 1990s, of randomly kidnapping civilians on highways in order to extort ransoms.

Proceso 8000

The judicial process opened by government prosecutors to investigate the alleged flow of drug money into the political campaigns of Colombian politicians. Although it was occasioned by allegations against President Ernesto Samper, in actuality he was investigated by a congressional committee that ultimately found him innocent.

Procuraduría

Office of the Colombian government that investigates charges against public officials.

Quindío

Region encompassing primarily the present-day departments of Risaralda and Quindío and part of the department of Caldas in the central Andean range. The last to develop and the most productive of Colombia's major coffee-growing regions, it is also the one where small- and medium-sized family farms are most prevalent. Although among the areas hardest hit by the Violence, the region has proved resistant (although not immune) to leftist guerrilla activity in recent decades.

Quintín Lame

Guerrilla group formed by indigenous people in the department of Cauca in the mid-1980s. Its demobilization in 1991, following negotiations with the government, led to the important reforms pertaining to indigenous people in the Constitution of 1991.

Regeneration

The Nationalist Conservative regime (1886–ca.1900) that came into power in 1885 following the defeat in the civil war of doctrinaire Liberals who had controlled Colombian politics since 1863. The Nationalist

Conservative party evolved out of a coalition of Conservatives and the dissident Liberal faction led by Rafael Núñez. A centralist, pro-Church constitution was promulgated in 1886. Subsequent governments effectively excluded Liberals from power and pursued nationalist economic policies, most notably, issuance of unbacked paper money. Liberals revolted in 1899, starting the War of the Thousand Days, the greatest of Latin America's nineteenth-century civil wars.

sicario

Hired assassin. Originally, a teenage male recruited from the poor neighborhoods around Medellín and trained (in some cases by foreign, including U.S. and Israeli, mercenaries) in the use of weapons and explosives in schools financed by the drug mafia. Generally devoid of ideological convictions, the *sicario* sees the successful completion of his "job" as proving his manliness and professionalism. The suicidal nature of many *sicario* attacks often frustrates attempts to protect potential targets. Victims of *sicarios* range from presidential candidates to members of rival drug organizations, leftist party and union leaders, judicial officials, police officers, prominent figures in the media, and university professors. Victims also include ordinary citizens who might have angered a relative or an associate or simply been in the path of a stray bullet or within the destructive radius of a car bomb.

"Tirofijo"

"Sureshot," the nickname of Manuel Marulanda Vélez, the legendary leader of the FARC in arms against the government since 1949. In 1999, following a historic meeting between Marulanda and President Andrés Pastrana, the FARC entered into wide-ranging peace negotiations with the government.

tulela

See *acción de tutela.*

UP

Unión Patriótica (Patriotic Union). Leftist party, with close ties to the Communist party and the FARC, formed in 1985 to participate in electoral politics. Initially, it had significant electoral success, especially at the local level, but it was gradually decimated as hundreds of its activists, including its presidential candidates in 1986 and 1990, were murdered by right-wing forces.

Urabá

Major banana-producing region on the Atlantic Coast in northern Antioquia. Since the 1980s it has been the site of violent contention among powerful leftist unions, management-supported goon squads, rival leftist guerrilla groups, paramilitary organizations, and the army.

vacuna

"Vaccine," or immunization. Used to characterize payoffs to guerrilla groups in exchange for protection against violence, kidnapping, or other depradations.

Index

Latin American Silhouettes
Studies in History and Culture

William H. Beezley and Judith Ewell
Editors

Volumes Published

Silvia Marina Arrom and Servando Ortoll, eds., *Riots in the Cities: Popular Politics and the Urban Poor in Latin America, 1765–1910* (1996). Cloth ISBN 0-8420-2580-4 Paper ISBN 0-8420-2581-2

Roderic Ai Camp, ed., *Polling for Democracy: Public Opinion and Political Liberalization in Mexico* (1996). ISBN 0-8420-2583-9

Brian Loveman and Thomas M. Davies, Jr., eds., *The Politics of Antipolitics: The Military in Latin America*, 3d ed., revised and updated (1996). Cloth ISBN 0-8420-2609-6 Paper ISBN 0-8420-2611-8

Joseph S. Tulchin, Andrés Serbín, and Rafael Hernández, eds., *Cuba and the Caribbean: Regional Issues and Trends in the Post-Cold War Era* (1997). ISBN 0-8420-2652-5

Thomas W. Walker, ed., *Nicaragua without Illusions: Regime Transition and Structural Adjustment in the 1990s* (1997). Cloth ISBN 0-8420-2578-2 Paper ISBN 0-8420-2579-0

Dianne Walta Hart, *Undocumented in L.A.: An Immigrant's Story* (1997). Cloth ISBN 0-8420-2648-7 Paper ISBN 0-8420-2649-5

Jaime E. Rodríguez O. and Kathryn Vincent, eds., *Myths, Misdeeds, and Misunderstandings: The Roots of Conflict in U.S.-Mexican Relations* (1997). ISBN 0-8420-2662-2

Jaime E. Rodríguez O. and Kathryn Vincent, eds., *Common Border, Uncommon Paths: Race, Culture, and National Identity in U.S.-Mexican Relations* (1997). ISBN 0-8420-2673-8

William H. Beezley and Judith Ewell, eds., *The Human Tradition in Modern Latin America* (1997). Cloth ISBN 0-8420-2612-6 Paper ISBN 0-8420-2613-4

Donald F. Stevens, ed., *Based on a True Story: Latin American History at the Movies* (1997). Cloth ISBN 0-8420-2582-0 Paper ISBN 0-8420-2781-5

Jaime E. Rodríguez O., ed., *The Origins of Mexican National Politics, 1808–1847* (1997). Paper ISBN 0-8420-2723-8

Che Guevara, *Guerrilla Warfare*, with revised and updated introduction and case studies by Brian Loveman and Thomas M. Davies, Jr., 3d ed. (1997). Cloth ISBN 0-8420-2677-0 Paper ISBN 0-8420-2678-9

Adrian A. Bantjes, *As If Jesus Walked on Earth: Cardenismo, Sonora, and the Mexican Revolution* (1998; rev. ed., 2000). Cloth ISBN 0-8420-2653-3 Paper ISBN 0-8420-2751-3

Henry A. Dietz and Gil Shidlo, eds., *Urban Elections in Democratic Latin America* (1998). Cloth ISBN 0-8420-2627-4 Paper ISBN 0-8420-2628-2

A. Kim Clark, *The Redemptive Work: Railway and Nation in Ecuador, 1895–1930* (1998). Cloth ISBN 0-8420-2674-6 Paper ISBN 0-8420-5013-2

Joseph S. Tulchin, ed., with Allison M. Garland, *Argentina: The Challenges of Modernization* (1998). ISBN 0-8420-2721-1

Louis A. Pérez, Jr., ed., *Impressions of Cuba in the Nineteenth Century: The Travel Diary of Joseph J. Dimock* (1998). Cloth ISBN 0-8420-2657-6 Paper ISBN 0-8420-2658-4

June E. Hahner, ed., *Women through Women's Eyes: Latin American Women in Nineteenth-Century Travel Accounts* (1998). Cloth ISBN 0-8420-2633-9 Paper ISBN 0-8420-2634-7

James P. Brennan, ed., *Peronism and Argentina* (1998). ISBN 0-8420-2706-8

John Mason Hart, ed., *Border Crossings: Mexican and Mexican-American Workers*

(1998). Cloth ISBN 0-8420-2716-5
Paper ISBN 0-8420-2717-3

Brian Loveman, *For* la Patria: *Politics and the Armed Forces in Latin America* (1999). Cloth ISBN 0-8420-2772-6
Paper ISBN 0-8420-2773-4

Guy P. C. Thomson, with David G. LaFrance, *Patriotism, Politics, and Popular Liberalism in Nineteenth-Century Mexico: Juan Francisco Lucas and the Puebla Sierra* (1999). ISBN 0-8420-2683-5

Robert Woodmansee Herr, in collaboration with Richard Herr, *An American Family in the Mexican Revolution* (1999). ISBN 0-8420-2724-6

Juan Pedro Viqueira Albán, trans. Sonya Lipsett-Rivera and Sergio Rivera Ayala, *Propriety and Permissiveness in Bourbon Mexico* (1999).
Cloth ISBN 0-8420-2466-2
Paper ISBN 0-8420-2467-0

Stephen R. Niblo, *Mexico in the 1940s: Modernity, Politics, and Corruption* (1999).
Cloth ISBN 0-8420-2794-7
Paper (2001) ISBN 0-8420-2795-5

David E. Lorey, *The U.S.-Mexican Border in the Twentieth Century* (1999).
Cloth ISBN 0-8420-2755-6
Paper ISBN 0-8420-2756-4

Joanne Hershfield and David R. Maciel, eds., *Mexico's Cinema: A Century of Films and Filmmakers* (2000). Cloth ISBN 0-8420-2681-9 Paper ISBN 0-8420-2682-7

Peter V. N. Henderson, *In the Absence of Don Porfirio: Francisco León de la Barra and the Mexican Revolution* (2000). ISBN 0-8420-2774-2

Mark T. Gilderhus, *The Second Century: U.S.-Latin American Relations since 1889* (2000). Cloth ISBN 0-8420-2413-1
Paper ISBN 0-8420-2414-X

Catherine Moses, *Real Life in Castro's Cuba* (2000). Cloth ISBN 0-8420-2836-6
Paper ISBN 0-8420-2837-4

K. Lynn Stoner, ed./comp., with Luis Hipólito Serrano Pérez, *Cuban and Cuban-American Women: An Annotated Bibliography* (2000). ISBN 0-8420-2643-6

Thomas D. Schoonover, *The French in Central America: Culture and Commerce, 1820–1930* (2000). ISBN 0-8420-2792-0

Enrique C. Ochoa, *Feeding Mexico: The Political Uses of Food since 1910* (2000). ISBN 0-8420-2812-9

Thomas W. Walker and Ariel C. Armony, eds., *Repression, Resistance, and Democratic Transition in Central America* (2000). Cloth ISBN 0-8420-2766-1 Paper ISBN 0-8420-2768-8

William H. Beezley and David E. Lorey, eds., *¡Viva México! ¡Viva la Independencia! Celebrations of September 16* (2001).
Cloth ISBN 0-8420-2914-1
Paper ISBN 0-8420-2915-X

Jeffrey M. Pilcher, *Cantinflas and the Chaos of Mexican Modernity* (2001).
Cloth ISBN 0-8420-2769-6
Paper ISBN 0-8420-2771-8

Victor M. Uribe-Uran, ed., *State and Society in Spanish America during the Age of Revolution* (2001). Cloth ISBN 0-8420-2873-0 Paper ISBN 0-8420-2874-9

Andrew Grant Wood, *Revolution in the Street: Women, Workers, and Urban Protest in Veracruz, 1870–1927* (2001). ISBN 0-8420-2879-X

Charles Bergquist, Ricardo Peñaranda, and Gonzalo Sánchez G., eds., *Violence in Colombia, 1990–2000: Waging War and Negotiating Peace* (2001).
Cloth ISBN 0-8420-2869-2
Paper ISBN 0-8420-2870-6

William Schell, Jr., *Integral Outsiders: The American Colony in Mexico City, 1876–1911* (2001). ISBN 0-8420-2838-2

John Lynch, *Argentine Caudillo: Juan Manuel de Rosas* (2001).
Cloth ISBN 0-8420-2897-8
Paper ISBN 0-8420-2898-6

Samuel Basch, M.D., ed. and trans. Fred D. Ullman, *Recollections of Mexico: The Last Ten Months of Maximilian's Empire* (2001). ISBN 0-8420-2962-1

Sowell, David, *The Tale of Healer Miguel Perdomo Neira: Medicine, Ideologies, and Power in the Nineteenth-Century Andes* (2001).
Cloth ISBN 0-8420-2826-9
Paper ISBN 0-8420-2827-7